128901

Fascism, Aesthetics, and Culture

Fascism, Aesthetics, and Culture

EDITED BY

Richard J. Golsan

■

Published by

UNIVERSITY PRESS OF NEW ENGLAND

Hanover and London

UNIVERSITY PRESS OF NEW ENGLAND
Hanover, NH 03755
© 1992 by University Press of New England
All rights reserved
Printed in the United States of America 5 4 3 2 1
CIP data appear at the end of the book

Contents

Eight pages of illustrations follow page 26.

Acknowledgments

I wish to thank Alton D. Kelly, Steven Oberhelman, Christopher Flood, Luis Costa, Melanie Hawthorne, Kenneth Price, and Wulf Koepke for their advice and editorial expertise. I also wish to thank Janet Ray and Corina Terrazas for their help in preparing the manuscript. Finally, Jeanne West of UPNE has been most helpful, patient, and encouraging throughout the life of this project.

Earlier versions of the articles by Mary Jean Green, Janet Pérez, and Steven Ungar, and also Reed Dasenbrock's essay on Paul de Man originally appeared in a special issue of the *South Central Review*, "Fascist Aesthetics" (Vol. 6, no. 2 [Summer 1989]).

A grant from the College of Liberal Arts at Texas A & M University has helped make the publication of this book possible.

January 1992   R. J. G.

Introduction

In the preface to his study *French Fascism: The First Wave, 1924–1933,* the historian Robert Soucy characterizes fascism as "a movement which spawned Mussolini and Hitler, concentration camps and crematoriums, totalitarian thought-control and institutionalized sadism, the militarization of men and the depersonalization of women." Soucy concludes his assessment by stating that fascism was also responsible for "the banalization of art and the debasement of culture."[1]

Few would dispute the first part of Soucy's statement,[2] and many would share the view implicit in the second part, namely, that fascism and culture are fundamentally antithetical terms. This was certainly the position of those who opposed fascism in Europe during the heyday of the dictators,[3] and it remains a prevalent attitude in many quarters today. As Zeev Sternhell has argued, many on the Left and on the Right dismiss fascism as an "anomaly," an "aberration," that has no real substantive connection to the development of European culture.[4]

Under these circumstances, a collection of essays devoted to the relationship between fascism and culture and focusing primarily on questions of aesthetics might seem incongruous and unnecessary. Recent events, however, have made it difficult to assume that fascism and modern culture can be neatly divorced from each other. They also make it impossible to dismiss the relationship as insignificant or anachronistic on the grounds that fascism and its permutations are no longer a force to be reckoned with in the political sphere. Revelations concerning profascist involvements before and during World War II on the part of the distinguished critic Paul de Man and the philosopher Martin Heidegger have provoked scandals in the United States and Europe that continue to generate controversy. At issue is whether de Man's deconstruction and Heidegger's philosophy of Being were influenced by the past political commitments of the two men and if the work of those who have been shaped by their ideas has not been "contaminated" as well. If so, then significant currents in postwar thought must come to terms with an intellectual debt most would prefer not to acknowledge.

In politics, Europe has witnessed a resurgence of the extreme Right as a viable political force. Jean-Marie Le Pen and his Front National have had success at the polls in France in the past decade by promoting a xenophobic hostility toward Arabs and other immigrant groups. During the summer of 1991, with growing racial tensions, especially in the suburbs of French cities, Le Pen's popularity reached an all-time high. Although he has lost ground in the wake of German reunification, Franz Schonhuber, the founder of the Republican party and a former member of the SS, had been gaining political momentum by feeding German fears of foreign workers and encouraging Germans to overcome their guilt over the Nazi past. Since reunification, attacks by neo-Nazi groups against immigrants have been on the rise and have encountered little governmental resistance. In Austria, Kurt Waldheim's Nazi background did not prevent his election as president, and a well-heeled youth-oriented party of the extreme Right has recently made political headway. In Eastern Europe, neo-fascist groups have sprung up with the decline and disappearance of communism.

These events suggest that a reevaluation of fascism and its relation to culture is both timely and necessary, but they fail to provide the parameters of such an investigation or even hint at the complexity of the problem. The present volume proposes to furnish a framework for the discussion by focusing on fascism's impact on aesthetic practices during the interwar years and by examining its legacy in some of the artistic controversies and intellectual scandals of the postwar period. Issues raised in these essays include fascism's relation to both traditional and avant-garde literary forms, the impact of censorship on the works of individual artists, the role of public art in the fascist state, and the problem of collaboration with Nazi Germany during World War II. Especially in France, collaboration has been and continues to be fascism's most disturbing legacy.

Any treatment of fascism's relation to culture in general and artistic and intellectual life in particular must acknowledge a number of difficulties at the outset. Foremost is the problem of defining fascism itself. Zeev Sternhell states that "few contemporary political concepts are so fluid and so ill defined" (p. 2), and he goes on to note that like liberalism, socialism, and communism, it was a "universal category with regional and cultural variants" (p. 28). Italian fascism, for example, resembled nazism in a number of ways, but anti-Semitism was not an integral part of its ideology until the Nazi influence in Italy became predominant.

Similarly, in France, a number of Fascist groups were not particularly anti-Semitic. Robert Soucy asserts in *French Fascism: The First Wave* that the Fascist leagues including the Faisceau, the Jeunesse Patriotes, and the Croix de Feu "welcomed Jews into their ranks" (p. xviii).

The problem of defining fascism extends beyond simply locating and classifying its regional and cultural variants. Consensus has never been reached concerning the precise nature of fascist ideology or its intellectual origins. Sternhell notes that many are still unwilling to grant it the status of an ideology, dismissing it as "either entirely lacking in a system of ideas or as having rigged itself out, for partisan purposes, in the semblance of a doctrine that could not be taken seriously and that did not deserve even the minimum of consideration given the ideas of any other political movement" (p. 8).

Opinions differ widely, even among those who acknowledge the existence of a fascist ideology, as to precisely what that ideology comprises. In the French context, for example, historians disagree as to whether fascism was fundamentally leftist or rightist in its basic configuration. Sternhell argues that "the history of fascism can be described as a continuous attempt to revise Marxism and create a national form of socialism" (p. 20). Soucy, on the other hand, insists that on many of the most important issues, including "taxation, government spending, nationalization, property rights, class conflict, religion, education, and foreign policy, French fascism was overwhelmingly conservative" (p. xv).

Such conflicting opinions support the view that fascist ideology is contradictory in its very essence. In his essay in this volume, Jeffrey Schnapp speaks of tensions in Italian fascism between "revolutionary activism and institutional conservatism, between the celebration of heroic individualism and corporate conformity, between elitist and populist values, between cultural internationalism and nationalism, between antihistoricism and historicism." Similar contradictions are evident in other national versions of fascist ideology. In his essay on the painter Emil Nolde, Russell Berman notes that nazism "entailed both a flaunted irrational antimodernism and an aggressively forced modernization." French Fascist intellectuals, including Robert Brasillach and Pierre Drieu La Rochelle, among others, were drawn to fascism's antimodern primitivism as well as to its "modern" reliance on technology and propaganda.[5] Given these contradictions, it is no wonder that, as Jeffrey Schnapp points out, fascism "required an aesthetic overproduction, a surfeit of fascist signs, images, slogans, books, and buildings, in order to compensate for, fill in, and cover up its forever unstable ideological core."

The precise origins of fascist ideology are as debatable as its content. Unlike communism and socialism, with their common link to Marxism, fascism lacks a single source. As a result, historians and others have moved in opposite directions in pursuit of its beginnings. For example, in a series of articles recently published in the *New York Review of Books*, Isaiah Berlin has located a major source of fascism in the reactionary Catholic monarchist views of Joseph de Maistre.[6] Other historians and political theorists insist that its roots can be traced to the "activist" tradition in politics that began with the French Revolution, a tradition de Maistre abhorred.[7] In an article first published in 1933, at the time of Hitler's ascent to power, the novelist Robert Musil argued that what was so striking about the Nazi revolution in particular was the *absence* of any real, specific origins in German intellectual life:

I must go still further and identify myself even more with the intellectual—who today, with his humanistic scruples, already seems to belong to the past—by declaiming that the real reason he did not see what was coming was the peculiarly cryptic character of the intellectual underpinnings of the revolution. The French Revolution was preceded by famous writers; it was not the revolution that made them famous, and active discussion in the aristocracy and the bourgeoisie paved the way for new ideas. The year 1848 was the essence of intellect for those who wanted the revolution as well as those who didn't. Even Marxism produced a literature long before the Marxist revolution, which despite its one-sidedness contained much that compelled even grudging respect. *On the other hand it would be to misunderstand the sources of this third German Revolution* [after those of 1848 and 1918] *by looking for its sources in German intellectual life.* (My emphasis)[8]

As these differing views suggest, the debate over the intellectual origins of fascism is complicated not only by questions of historical perspective and context but by which redaction of fascism one is considering and what its most crucial features are in the view of the historian, political theorist, or witness attempting to analyze it.

Given the absence of a rigorous, comprehensive definition of fascist ideology as well as a generally accepted theory as to its origins, the elaboration of a "fascist aesthetic" becomes crucial. If an "aesthetic overproduction" is necessary to compensate for fascism's "unstable ideological core," then that overproduction must be expected to possess and provide a certain cohesiveness lacking in the ideology itself. The present essays reveal, however, that the definition of a fascist aesthetic both coherent and widely applicable is no easy task.

As Russell Berman points out, the initial problem is that "the political substance of a serious work of art is likely to be ambiguous." Only propaganda and crudely simplistic art are absolutely unequivocal in their political content. Be that as it may, there *are* major works of art that are fascist in their basic orientation, and the question remains how best to approach this orientation.

One approach is to link the work directly to the life of the artist and to show how the political commitments of that artist provide an appropriate context for interpreting the work. In his contribution to this volume, Robert Casillo demonstrates how Ezra Pound's Italian *Cantos* form an integral part of the poet's commitment to Mussolinian fascism. Sent to the dictator and published as inspirational pieces in a Fascist naval newspaper, the Italian *Cantos* sing the praises of Fascist heroes and rejoice in the murder of Allied soldiers.

The biographical approach, which works quite well in the case of a writer like Ezra Pound, is less applicable when one attempts to link the aesthetics of the painter Emil Nolde to fascism. Russell Berman points out in his essay that Nolde was a member of the Nazi party. He "had long espoused a virulent cultural nationalism, was 'exceptional in his racism,' and articulated notions of regional authenticity arguably homologous to the blood and soil tenets of German fascist aesthetics." Nevertheless, Nolde's work was condemned by the Nazis for its "cultural Bolshevism" and "corrupting liberalism." As Berman's article demonstrates, an examination of Nolde's fascist aesthetic must take into account an apparent disparity between his political commitments and his art as well as the gap between personal aesthetics and official public reception.

A more thematic approach entails isolating those particular features of the artist's thought or specific prejudices that are manifest in his work and that lead him to embrace a reactionary, fascistic ideology. In his essay on Gottfried Benn, Walter Strauss shows how Benn's "intellectualism," essential to his art, blinded him to the realities of the Nazi regime and made possible his initial *engagement.* In my own essay on Henry de Montherlant, I demonstrate how Montherlant's elitism, virulent antifeminism, and taste for violence, among other major themes in his prewar fiction, led him eventually to collaborate with the Nazis.

Such an approach is also not without pitfalls, as it is certainly possible for an artist to be misogynistic or antifeminist, for example, and be politically committed on the Left. In a recent essay, Susan Suleiman remarks on precisely these tendencies in André Malraux, a novelist whose politics were diametrically opposed to French fascist politics.⁹ It is also possible, as Rosemarie Scullion demonstrates in her essay on Louis-Ferdinand Céline, for a right-wing writer to be anti-Semitic without his anti-Semitism being informed by an absolute adherence to fascism and to nazism in particular.

Besides thematics, the possibility of a specific "fascist style" must be addressed. Here too there are obvious difficulties. Writers associated with fascism include both traditionalists and modernists, *précieux* and populists. In the French context, both extremes are evident. Despite his affinities with modern culture and with the cinema in particular, the *norma-lien* Robert Brasillach was, as Mary Jean Green remarks in her essay here, a traditional stylist who placed his novelistic account of "the development of European fascism within the structure of Corneille's tragedy, *Polyeucte.*" Céline, on the other hand, compared his writing to the movement of the modern subway and vaunted his popular origins and tastes.

This collection also demonstrates that no particular literary genre can be linked exclusively to a fascist aesthetics. Andrew Hewitt remarks on the Futurists' predilection for the manifesto, whereas in the French context, the novel is the preferred vehicle of expression, although Brasillach and Bardèche's *Histoire du cinéma* amply demonstrates that the critical study is an adequate vehicle for the elaboration of a comprehensive fascist aesthetic. Pound and Benn were, of course, great poets, and in Pound's case at least, the medium allowed not only for an apology for fascist ideals but for a fascist revision of history itself.

In his essay on Wyndham Lewis, Reed Dasenbrock argues that neither the biographical approach nor a close analysis of style or thematic content is adequate to determine what is fascist in Lewis's novels, in particular *The Revenge for Love.* Dasenbrock believes rather that it is these novels' "paranoid vision"—also exemplified in the Nazi's fear of the Jew and the fascist's fear of a nameless, insidious enemy sapping the nation's strength from within—that distinguishes them from the more generous or at least less conspiratorial vision of nonfascist fiction. Dasenbrock proceeds to claim that the same paranoid vision animates the fiction of other Modernists, like Céline (it is also in evidence in Montherlant's prewar journalism and his Occupation plays). He also argues that this same vision colors the postwar writings of novelists such as Norman Mailer and Thomas Pynchon. If Dasenbrock's assessment is accurate, then fascism's impact on aesthetics extends well beyond the fall of the dictators and indirectly affects major works by artists whose politics are squarely on the Left.

The problem of defining a fascist aesthetic assumes another dimension if one moves beyond questions pertaining exclusively to the work of art itself or the ideology, vision, or prejudices of the artist who created it. The work of art is also a "public" object, and its reception is crucial. In an essay titled "Modernism, Fascism, and the Institution of Literature," Russell Berman argues that what makes a work of art fascist is precisely its intended impact on the reader:

Fascist Modernism ascribed to the work of art the role of imitating a reactionary revolution. If the fascist political movements intended to overcome the alleged chaos of liberal capitalism by returning to the ideological vision of a primitive stability and homogeneity, the fascist work of art appropriated this regenerative goal for itself. No longer an autonomous object of beauty to be contemplated by a passive recipient, it was designed to transform the status of the recipient in order to reunite him or her with the primal order of race and the permanence of unquestionable values.[10]

Berman's claim for a "fascist modernism" is applicable, of course, not only to individual works by individual artists (Berman cites as examples Wagner's operas, the poetry of Pound and Eliot, and the novels of Hamsun and Lawrence) but to larger, state-sponsored projects involving large numbers of contributing participants. The example of such a project that comes immediately to mind is Leni Riefenstahl's classic film, *Triumph of the Will*, whose fascist aesthetics have been brilliantly analyzed by Susan Sontag.[11] A larger and more intriguing example is the 1932 Exhibition of the Fascist Revolution, discussed here by Jeffrey Schnapp. Involving the participation of avant-garde artists, architects, and academics, as well as functionaries from the Fascist National party, the exhibition narrated the history of Italian fascism through "a kaleidoscopic fusion of Rationalist inspired architectural schemes, a Futurist-inspired aesthetics of collage and photomontage, and an emergent mythico-heroic architectural classicism." In tracing fascism's history, the exhibition was intended to transform Italian culture. Its "regenerative" impact was evident in the enormous number of visitors who came to see it. For many, these visits were nothing less than pilgrimages, and the spectators became part of the show, enhancing the spectacle itself. They became, in effect, part of the work of art, "mass ornaments" forming the "human architecture" so typical of the vast extravaganzas of the fascist regimes.[12]

If the 1932 Exhibition of the Fascist Revolution ultimately blurs the distinction between artist and recipient as well as between individual aesthetics and state-sponsored propaganda, it also exemplifies the fundamental heterogeneity of fascist aesthetic production. The tensions in fascist ideology between "revolutionary activism and institutional conservatism" are answered in the joining of avant-garde and traditional aesthetic forms. Under these circumstances, fascist modernism loses its specificity and is disseminated all the more easily in subsequent aesthetic practices and traditions.

It is perhaps for this reason that "postmodern culture" is occasionally convulsed by scandals in which the fascist pasts of influential artists or thinkers are dramatically revealed or shown to be more extensive or important to their work than is commonly assumed. Heidegger and de Man are not the only figures to be mentioned in this context; the list also includes the critic and novelist Maurice Blanchot and Ezra Pound.[13] The issue at stake is less the details of these political commitments than the possibility that the enormous influence of these figures has helped to create a "postfascist culture," an intellectual and artistic environment in which the insidious presence of fascism shapes us more than we realize. As Steven Ungar states in his essay on Heidegger, this is "one of our big cultural nightmares."

A number of considerations have prompted the choice of essays in this collection, and a word on these considerations and the logic of its organization is in order.

Although only a few fascist dictatorships came to power in Europe between the wars, fascism's impact on European artistic and intellectual life was widespread, even in those countries whose governments were markedly antifascist. The essays in this collection were selected to demonstrate this diversity in an effort to elucidate the complex interrelationships that obtain between national traditions, fascist prerogatives, and individual aesthetics. The inclusion of essays on German, Italian, and Spanish artists on the one hand and French and British artists on the other make it possible for distinctions as well as parallels to be established between official, public art and more private, "oppositional" aesthetics. In the dictatorships, especially Germany and Spain, censorship and official tastes played a restrictive role not in evidence elsewhere. At the same time, most fascist art from the dictatorships and the democracies shared a number of thematic concerns, including extreme nationalism, elitism, a taste for violence, and a pronounced antifeminism.

Needless to say, not all national literatures, art forms, or artists influenced by fascism are represented here because of limitations of space. The present essays do address, however, a wide range of aesthetic objects and concerns and employ a variety of critical approaches in assessing precisely how fascism informed the work under consideration. Moreover, the works studied are for the most part major artistic or critical achievements or, in the case of the Spanish novels treated by Janet Pérez, for example, representative works of important literary movements. They are, so to speak, "canonical texts" of fascist modernism.

It may at first seem surprising that more essays in this volume deal with French artistic and intellectual life than with the national culture of any other country. France, after all, was never ruled by a fascist dictatorship on the order of Nazi Germany or Fascist Italy, and during the interwar years it frequently was governed by moderately leftist governments, the most notable being Léon Blum's Front Populaire during the mid-1930s. One might think, therefore, that France would not be a particularly good spawning ground for fascist art or for the study of fascist culture and ideology. Zeev Sternhell argues, however, that both assumptions are false. Insisting on "the remarkably high standard of French fascist literature and thought," he continues: "Apart from Gentile, nowhere else in Europe was there a body of ideological writings of comparable quality" (pp. 6–7).[14] Sternhell also contends that "fascist ideology came into being [in France] a good twenty years before similar ideologies appeared elsewhere in Europe, particularly Italy" (p. 26).

The richness and potential of French fascism during its heyday must certainly be a factor in its disturbing "afterlife" in France during the postwar period. Although the majority of the French intelligentsia is on the Left, neofascist intellectuals have not been completely marginalized and still manage to make themselves heard, sometimes in a spectacular fashion. The publication of Robert Faurisson's *Mémoire en Défense-contre ceux qui m'accusent de fasifier l'histoire: La question des chambres à gaz* in 1980, in which the author labeled the Holocaust an "enormous hoax," created a storm of controversy and resulted in legal charges being brought against Faurisson. In May–June, 1981, Faurisson stood trial in the Palais de Justice in Paris on the charges of slander, willful distortion of history, and incitement to racial hatred.[15] At the time of the publication of his book, Faurisson was lecturer in French literature at the University of Lyons II.

Faurisson is certainly not the only academic or intellectual in contemporary France to hold extreme right-wing or fascist views, nor is the intellectual forum the only arena in which these views are occasionally expressed. In the spring of 1990, the French public was shocked by the desecration of Jewish cemeteries at Carpentras, Clichy-Sous-Bois, and elsewhere. Despite all efforts at eradication, a virulent anti-Semitism still persists in France.

The continuing presence of a neofascist intelligentsia and a vicious anti-Semitism are not the only signs of fascism's disturbing legacy in France. The specter of the Occupation and collaboration with the Nazis still haunts the French national memory, producing scandals in the courts and in public life. The trial of Klaus Barbie and the upcoming trial of René Bousquet, former head of Vichy police, continue to challenge the Gaullist myth (fostered by intellectuals such as Jean-Paul Sartre)[16] that only a few marginal individuals collaborated with the Nazis. Documentaries such as Marcel Ophuls's *Le chagrin et la pitié*, in which the full extent of French complicity with the Nazis is exposed, have proved so disturbing that they have on occasion been censored. In her essay here, Lynn Higgins notes that Ophuls's film, released in 1968, was not allowed on French television until 1981.

The Occupation and collaboration in particular have also provided the inspiration and subject matter for a number of the most important literary and cinematic works produced in France in the postwar period. Writers such as Marguerite Duras, Michel Tournier, and Patrick Modiano, as well as filmmakers such as Louis Malle and François Truffaut, examine the Occupation not only as an event crucial in shaping contemporary French sensibilities but as an experience that challenges the notion that collaboration, and through it fascism itself, are always "other." [17]

The essays by Steven Ungar and Lynn Higgins in this collection deal with these two sides of fascism's legacy in France. The scandal surrounding the publication of Victor Farías's *Heidegger et le nazisme* in 1987 raised a number of issues concerning intellectual debts to the German philosopher and the institution of philosophy in France, which Ungar discusses in his essay. In her contribution, Lynn Higgins examines a certain "aesthetics of collaboration" and discusses the public controversies attendant on the appearance of works that treat such an aesthetics.

The essays in this collection are organized chiefly according to national cultures or the national origin of the artist being considered. In most instances, they are also placed in roughly chronological order. This arrangement is intended to allow the reader to witness as much as possible the diversity of fascism's impact on a particular national culture as well as the development of the relationship through time. For example, the two essays concerning Italy reveal both the avant-garde as well as the conservative, institutionalized dimension of fascist aesthetics. In the French context, the discussion of fascism's relation to culture embraces not only the prewar aestheticism of a Brasillach or a Montherlant but postwar explorations of the Occupation and collaboration and the intellectual legacy of figures such as Martin Heidegger.

Any such organization has its limitations. Ezra Pound and Wyndham Lewis are placed next to each other to form an "Anglo-American" context, although Pound, an expatriate living in Italy during his involvement with fascism, could just as easily be studied alongside Marinetti and the Exhibition of the Fascist Revolution. Likewise, Andrew Hewitt's study of Marinetti and futurism could be placed next to those essays dealing with more recent topics because the politics of futurism cannot be divorced from current debates on the nature of the avant-garde. Reed Dasenbrock's essay on Paul de Man, which concludes the volume, could initiate it because de Man's wartime writings concern not only current critical debates but also classic works of fascist modernism. In short, as these essays clearly reveal, fascism's links to aesthetics and culture should interest us not simply in a regional or historical context. They should concern us here and now as well.

Fascism, Aesthetics, and Culture

JEFFREY T. SCHNAPP

Epic Demonstrations
Fascist Modernity and the 1932 Exhibition of the Fascist Revolution

We mustn't remain solely contemplatives. We mustn't simply exploit our cultural heritage.
We must create a new heritage to place alongside that of antiquity. We must create
a new art, an art of our times: a Fascist art.[1]

Delivered by Mussolini before the Academy of Fine Arts in Perugia, these words called upon Fascist writers, artists, and architects to forge a new fascist culture and to renew the cultural debates of the movement's early years. The timing of Mussolini's invitation was significant. Having overcome the crisis brought upon it by the Matteotti assassination, the Fascist state had consolidated its hold on power by weakening or eliminating the most resistant democratic institutions. The result was renewed confidence but also a deepening sense of anxiety about how to ensure that fascism would be more than a passing phenomenon. If the Fascist revolution was to become irreversible, it was felt, more would have to change than simply the structure of Italy's political institutions. Beyond the achievement of consensus, the revolution would have to leave its imprint on the Italian national psyche, to penetrate the Italian subconscious and mold a genuinely "Fascist" political subject. This it could hope to accomplish only be extending fascism's reach into new areas such as education, culture, the family, youth organizations, and life outside the workplace.

A key link in this so-called fascistization process was the domain of culture. Mussolini's pilgrimage to Perugia was preceded by a series of cultural-political initiatives beginning with the 1925 Congress on Fascist Culture, called by the philosopher and one-time minister of public instruction, Giovanni Gentile. This congress brought together some 250 leading intellectuals, including Bottai, Soffici, Marinetti, Pirandello, and Venturi. It resulted in the publication of a "Manifesto of Fascist Intellectuals," which challenged the opposition's claim that culture and the fascist cudgel were antinomies. A sharp rejoinder—originally entitled "A Response from Italian Writers, Professors, and Journalists" but later rechristened the "Manifesto of the Anti-Fascist Intellectuals"—soon followed, authored by two prominent members of the opposition, Giovanni Amendola and Benedetto Croce. The ensuing furor, rather than slowing the regime's efforts at cultural self-legitimation, accelerated them. It led to more ambitious and far-reaching measures, among others the establishment, in late 1925, of an Istituto Nazionale di Cultura Fascista (INCF) under the directorship of Gentile, the creation of the Royal Academy (decreed on 7 January 1926), the foundation in April 1926 of the Opera Nazionale Balilla (which placed the Fascist youth groups under a single umbrella), and state sponsorship of the *Enciclopedia Italiana* project, directed (once again) by Gentile.

If such initiatives created the institutional framework for the propagation of fascist "culture," they did little to address the question of precisely what such a culture might consist in. In his Perugia speech, Mussolini's response had been characteristically gnomic, calling for a fascist culture that is "traditionalist and at the same time modern, that looks to the past and at the same time to the future." The task of fleshing out this skeleton of paradoxes—to whatever extent such a fleshing out might be either possible or desirable—was left to ideologues and artists (as was his usual practice, the Duce would reserve for himself the role of arbiter and judge). It is they who would have to infer just how radically an authentic fascist culture ought to embrace modernity and innovation at the expense of tradition and, conversely, to what degree fascist culture ought to inscribe itself within a specifically Italian historical narrative. At stake, beyond the prospect of state patronage, was the deeper matter of fascism's identity. Did the triumph of fascism entail a decisive break with Italy's past or, instead, the recovery of a lost origin (for instance, of the glory of Imperial Rome)? Or, as Mussolini had implied, did it mark both a rupture and a return, at once the reassumption of a historical legacy and the transcendence of that very legacy?

Divergent answers would battle it out during the next decade and a half, both in the daily newspapers and in such reviews as *Novecento, Quadrante, Il Selvaggio, Casabella-Costruzioni, Quadrivio,* and *Primato,* but to little avail. Perhaps the most emblematic of these polemics was that which occupied the pages of the regime's most open ideological forum, *Critica Fascista,* between October 1926 and February 1927.[2] Inspired by Giuseppe Bottai, then undersecretary of the Ministry of Corporations, the debate proposed a wide spectrum of responses to the question of what is fascist culture. From the radical Modernist redaction of fascism proposed by Marinetti and Bragaglia to the synthetic mythic redaction of *novecentisti* such as Bontempelli and Soffici to a diversity of conservative, nationalist, or radical populist positions advocated by the likes of Pavolini and Malaparte, the *Critica Fascista* debate opens up a window onto fascism's core. And what it reveals are further paradoxes. Even within the confines of a single contribution, one finds recurring tensions between themes of revolutionary activism and institutional conservatism, between the celebration of heroic individualism and corporate conformity, between elitist and populist values, between cultural internationalism and nationalism, between antihistoricism and historicism. While these contradictions are seen as resolvable—and indeed, as always, already resolved in the figure of the Duce—the debate, considered as a whole, suggests the opposite, namely, that these tensions are "fundamental" in the strictest sense. They represent nothing less than the structural undergirding of fascist ideology: the taut but hollow frame over which a canvas must be stretched in order for the illusion of fullness to spring forth.

This preface concludes with a painting metaphor to highlight one deeper reason why aesthetic production and the patronage of culture were central concerns of the Italian Fascist state. Unlike communism, its enemy twin, fascism could not settle the question of its identity via recourse to the utopias of science and/or theory (no matter how resolutely it sometimes strove to do so). Rather, fascism required an aesthetic *overproduction*—a surfeit of fascist signs, images, slogans, books, and buildings—to compensate for, fill in, and cover up its forever unstable ideological core. So art and the new mass media were for fascism more than simple instruments to be manipulated for purposes of propaganda and crowd control. Nor did fascism simply "aestheticize" politics, as Walter Benjamin's suggestive formula would have it. Rather, putting forward the first Modern(ist) politics of spectacle, it placed the conventional polarities of Marxist and Liberal theory under constant pressure, confusing superstructure with structure, private with public, the state with civil society. Fascism may thus be said to have ushered in a new dispensation in which all oppositions between aesthetics and politics are swept up into a new image politics.

Neither monolithic nor homogeneous, fascism's aesthetic overproduction relied on the ability of images to sustain contradiction and to make of paradox a productive principle. Hence, the rhetorical figure that (perhaps inevitably) lurks at the core of every analysis of the fascist phenomenon: oxymoron. Formulas like "conservative revolution" or "reactionary modernism" suggest a genealogical link to the Western lyrical tradition, a tradition whose hallmark, at least since Francis Petrarch, has been the oxymoron. Indeed, once probed, the genealogical ties between fascism and lyricism prove remarkably strong. Like the Petrarchan sub-

ject's tempestuous passions, the violence of fascism's inner conflict—
whether on the level of the individual subject or of the collective—is such
that it requires the controlling, sublimating presence of the most rigid of
forms, forms no less smooth and mechanical, no less impersonal and
regular than the Petrarchan sestina and sonnet. (Technology and the
iconography and materials of the machine age are fascism's analogy to
the sestina and sonnet.) Fascist artifacts are therefore distinguished by an
uneasy coexistence of impulses that, echoing the Petrarchan "icy fire,"
may be designated as "hot" and "cold." By "hot" I mean to describe an
impulse that affiliates fascist artifacts with a moment of violent rupture,
rapture, and desublimation, opening the door to new forms of selfhood
and unleashing chaotic elemental forces. By "cold" I mean to designate
instead a simultaneous call to sober formalism: a drive to stylize, strip of
ornament, objectify, and distance. In the lavish and constant acts of self-
(re)presentation by means of which Italian fascism defined itself during
its second decade, these two impulses were forced together to tell the
story of the movement itself, of its roots, and of its future aspirations.
And in the gap between the prose of Italian history and fascism's lyrical
icy fire, there arose the distinctive form of modernism embodied in "ex-
hibition-events" such as the 1932 Exhibition of the Fascist Revolution.

> That which opened in Rome is not simply the exhibition but something greater; it is the
> demonstration of the Fascist Revolution. And here I employ the verb 'to demonstrate' in
> its literal and figurative, its mathematical and physical meanings. The show makes
> the Revolution plain, palpable, and intelligible, while at the same time providing
> proof, a definitive proof of the experiment's success by means of figures and calculations
> (italics in original).[3]

If there were a single work that could be said to crystallize all of the
tensions noted above, it would surely be the Exhibition of the Fascist
Revolution (or Mostra della Rivoluzione Fascista), the multimedia "museum in motion" with which the Fascist regime celebrated the ten-year
anniversary of the March on Rome. Held at the Palazzo delle Esposizioni
in the heart of modern Rome, the exhibition opened on October 29,
1932, and closed exactly two years later. Its success was such that, declared "permanent" by Mussolini in October 1933, it gave rise to subsequent avatars in 1937 and 1942. A collaborative enterprise involving
avant-garde artists, architects, academics, and functionaries from the
Fascist National party (PNF), the exhibition narrated the history of fascism from 1914 through 1922, not according to the conventional methods of museum display but rather via a kaleidoscopic fusion of Rationalist architectural schemes, a Futurist-inspired aesthetics of collage and
photomontage, and an emergent mythico-heroic architectural classicism.

As stated above by Margherita Sarfatti, the prominent Mussolini biographer, the exhibition was to be more than a mere assemblage of historical documents; it aspired to be "history in action," lived history presented not at a comfortable contemplative remove but rather palpable and direct, history mythically embodied in allegorico-symbolic terms.[4]

But no less than an epitome of fascist modernism, the exhibition was also a sociocultural event of considerable proportions. Over the biennium that it was open to the public—always from morning until 11 P.M. every day, including Sundays, Easter, and Christmas—a total of 3,854,927 visitors attended it, which is to say, roughly, one in eleven Italians or more than five thousand visitors on an average day.[5] Attendance was boosted by means of the coordinated efforts of the PNF, the state railway system, the youth organizations, and the Fascist labor unions. Yet efforts to promote and organize group visits proved unnecessary in many cases. A majority of the visitors came of their own volition, motivated by political conviction or by curiosity more than by discounts on railway tickets. Moreover, the exhibition gave rise to sometimes orchestrated but often spontaneous outpourings of public sentiment reflected in the daily newspapers, archival records, and private memoirs and letters. Veterans' organizations vied for the privilege of serving in the exhibition's honor guard. Commemorative books and poems were composed. In short, the transformed palazzo rapidly evolved into a kind of Saint Peter's of fascism: a site of pilgrimage for Fascists from throughout Italy and Europe, a shrine in which the revolutionary values of fascism were revived and commemorated (but ultimately distanced and entombed).

This essay provides a comprehensive account and interpretation of the 1932 Mostra and of its sociocultural dimensions. The exhibition's story is not an easy one to recount because the historical record consists of large quantities of sometimes incomplete records housed at the central state archive in Rome (including some closed to public view until after the year 2000) as well as in scattered private holdings.[6] Yet it is a story well worth telling, for the 1932 exhibition represents fascism's first sustained effort at a self-interpretation in the mirror of twentieth-century Italian history and this at a crucial juncture when the regime's revolutionary and anarchist components were being eroded by a growing institutional conservatism. At the very apex of its fortunes, enjoying substantial domestic and international support, Mussolini's regime celebrated that which was new and radical in fascism's revolution at the very moment that many revolutionaries were increasingly finding themselves abandoned, increasingly haunted by the revolution's unfulfilled promises. The paradox turns out to be integral to the logic of the 1932 exhibition. A monument to the movement's violent origins, it ends up burying the very thing it claims to resurrect.

I. The Idea

The idea for a tenth-anniversary celebration of the March on Rome may be traced back to the Milanese Istituto Fascista di Cultura (IFCM) and to its president, Dino Alfieri, later minister of popular culture (1936–1939). Sometime in early 1928, Alfieri and his entourage had begun to plan an exhibit in Milan, entitled the Mostra del Fascismo to commemorate the foundation in March 1919 of the first *fasci di combattimento* on their ten-year anniversary. At the beginning of March in that same year, a formal proposal was submitted to Mussolini, who approved it on March 23, appointing a supervisory committee made up of the Duce himself, Alfieri, the Quadrumviri (De Bono, De Vecchi, Balbo, and Bianchi), the general and administrative secretaries of the PNF (Turati and Marinelli), Arnaldo Mussolini (director of the "official" newspaper of the regime, *Il Popolo d'Italia*), the mayor of Milan, and the secretary of the Milanese Federazione Fascista. Developed by Alfieri with the then director of IFCM Leo Pollini and two aides, Antonio Monti (the historian/director of the Museo del Risorgimento at the Castello Sforzesco) and Commander Bertarelli, this proposal set forth detailed plans for an exhibition to be subdivided into five chronological units:

1. The period of interventionism and neutralism (1914–1915).
2. The war (on land, at sea, and in the air; the Italian role in the Allied victory; the battle of Vittorio Veneto [1915–1918]).
3. The dawn of fascism and its "struggle to save the nation" (1918–1922).
4. The March on Rome (1922).
5. The "regeneration of Italy accomplished by Fascism" (1922–1929).[7]

The narrative sequence was to reach its climax in the rooms devoted to the March on Rome, an event Alfieri did not hesitate to describe as "the synthesis and resolution of an epos, a new historical beginning."[8] The exhibition's overall subject would be twofold: on the one hand, it would present the historical development of the Fascist movement qua mass movement (hence a greater emphasis on period relics and a lesser one on the charismatic function of the Duce); on the other hand, it would exalt the actual accomplishments of the regime between the March on Rome and 1929. Each historical unit was to be represented via a mix of objects, documents, and photographs belonging to the era's protagonists. To this end, the IFCM began to organize an ambitious gathering and sorting operation.[9] In mid-October 1928, the organizing committee sent out a memorandum to all federal secretaries of the PNF urgently requesting their assistance. Accompanied by copies of the preliminary proposal and of a pamphlet entitled *Cosa sarà la Mostra del Fascismo*, the directive granted priority to the following two classes of materials:

1. Badges, medals, pins, and Bolshevik symbols recalling the strikes in the public sector, the occupation of factories, the FIOM (Federation of Metal Employees and Workers), and more broadly, Soviet propaganda in the form of postcards, stamps, allegorical scenes, portraits, and the like.
2. Photographs, drawings, sketches, and postcards representing offenses to the flag, religion, and wounded veterans; interior scenes relating to the occupation of factories and fields; the military organization of the Fascio; the strikes of July and August; the occupation of the government ministries and chambers of commerce; the Congress of Naples; the March on Rome.[10]

Once supplied to the IFCM, such materials were to be selected as a function of their historical importance, visual impact, and appropriateness to the show's narrative.

From the very start, however, the organizing committee recognized that if the 1929 exhibition was to faithfully translate the revolutionary spirit of the early *fasci,* it would not be sufficient simply to amass a profusion of period documents. It would be necessary to visually supplement and enhance all documentary materials and to reduce them to so synthetic a statement that "a single gaze will be sufficient to grasp the entire phenomenon."[11] The exhibition's task, according to Alfieri, could be nothing less than to

bring alive before the eyes of the visitor and to suggest fifteen years in the history of the Italian people, perhaps the Nation's most dramatic and decisive since Roman times, to evoke the reawakening after centuries of torpor . . . [that accompanied] the outbreak of the European war via the interventionist movement, that revealed to the Country its vigorous health, its new youthful audacity, its determination to redeem the Nation once and for all by means of sacrifice and struggle, to unite the Fatherland but, most important of all, to forge a single race, long divided by differing traditions, by historical circumstance, by barriers created and reinforced by foreigners, century after century.[12]

Although I have been able to gather only scattered evidence as to how the 1929 exhibition would actually have implemented this objective, preliminary plans suggest that Alfieri's narrative of national reawakening was to have been presented by means of a montage-based approach, combining the use of graphics, photographs, signage, maps, and statistical tables with actual objects. That such a modernist ideology of design should have prevailed over more traditional display practices is hardly surprising given the international acclaim garnered by recent Soviet exhibitions such as El Lissitzky's kinetic pavilion at the Cologne International Pressa Exhibition (1928). Indeed, it is hard to imagine that the latter's success, amply documented in the Italian press and supplemented by the presence of a substantial body of Russian constructivist works at the Venice Biennale of 1928 and at the 1929 Soviet exhibition in Zurich, did not fuel fascism's drive to stake out its own claim on cultural-political modernity in the form of rival "revolutionary" exhibitions. If proof were needed of this contention, one might note the special weight accorded to Bolshevik and Soviet artifacts in Alfieri's above-cited memorandum; such artifacts were to be assembled perhaps not only to document the historical events of the postwar period but also to highlight the triumph of Mussolini's revolution over its Soviet competition.

The 1929 Fascist exhibition was to have opened its doors on March 23 at Milan's Castello Sforzesco, one day before the inauguration of the Zurich Russische Ausstellung.[13] Its success would have been ensured by abundant publicity within the Fascist media and party apparatus, by the granting of railway discounts to exhibition visitors, and by means of the printing and nationwide distribution of posters, postcards, and multilingual guidebooks. But the exhibition never took place. By late November 1928, the PNF directorate had launched (with Mussolini's backing) a successful drive to persuade the organizers to transfer the exhibit from Milan to Rome in the pursuit of a "grander consecration and greater success."[14] There were, however, deeper motivations behind the change of venue. In the late 1920s, Turati was engaged in reshaping the Fascist party and centralizing its operations. This was also the case in the cultural arena, where local institutions like the IFCM increasingly found themselves placed under the supervision of Gentile's national institute (INCF), as well as being criticized for their "lack of discipline" and for the redundancy or insufficiently fascist character of their activities.[15] Milan presented a special challenge to Roman centralism. As the crucible in which the early *fasci* were forged and the homeland of the most radical "Fascists of the early hour," it stood for a violent, anarchic era in the movement's history, which the regime was now struggling to subdue and absorb into a neo-Roman iconography of institutional continuity built around the cult of *il Duce*. Accordingly, it seemed essential to the PNF that a celebration of fascism's Milanese origins carry the message that, in the Fascist era, all roads lead straight to Rome and to the leadership of Mussolini.[16]

Whatever the precise motivations, the move led to a renaming—the exhibition was retitled the Mostra *Nazionale Storica* del Fascismo— and to a series of postponements. Although the earliest PNF press release had spoken of "not even a minimal delay," it was announced in January that the accompanying agricultural exhibitions would be delayed until 1932. The schedule for March 1929 *was* overly busy. Opening day would have coincided with the inauguration of the Italian Academy, with a national plebiscite on the regime, and with a number of other regional fairs and national exhibitions (including that of the colonies, which eventually opened in late September 1931). A first postponement, to April 21, was announced soon thereafter and was followed by another, sine die, because the "noble and spontaneous" offerings of the population had "demonstrated that the Exhibition would take on a greater scope than the organizers had originally foreseen, and would require the selection of an appropriate extremely spacious locale."[17] The end result was the exhibition's absorption in the regime's plans for the year 1932: the ten-year anniversary of Mussolini's March on Rome. Instead of celebrating fascism's ties to Milanese anarchosocialism, instead of recalling the movement's violent and uncertain origins, the Roman version of Alfieri's exhibition would thus commemorate an event that identified the nation's fate with fascism's movement from the periphery to the center, from street power to state power. The symbolism would resonate all the more powerfully because fascism's March was itself a reenactment of two foundational moments in Italian history: Caesar's crossing of the Rubicon and the march of Garibaldi's Mille.

Whether in conception, in design, or in its immediate political consequences, the unrealized 1929 exhibition would prove of decisive importance to the cultural history of the period. First, a practical effect: it contributed to the elevation of Dino Alfieri from the role of regional Fascist deputy to that of undersecretary of corporations, a position Alfieri would hold from 1929 until 1932, when he assumed the directorship not only of the 1932 Mostra but also of numerous other Fascist cultural organizations. To some degree this may have amounted to a rehabilitation. As founder of the Milanese group of the Italian Nationalist Association, Alfieri had struggled against fusion with the PNF in the wake of the March on Rome and, despite a subsequent about-face on the issue, was viewed with skepticism by some *sansepolcristi*. Alfieri's promotion would also prove consequential in the longer run, inasmuch as he would soon become one of Galeazzo Ciano's closest allies. Named Ciano's successor in

1936 to the Ministry of Press and Propaganda (renamed the Ministry of Popular Culture in 1937), Alfieri would eventually move on to become ambassador to Germany in the decisive years of World War II, attempting without success to promote Italy's early exit from the war.

A second important attribute of the 1929 exhibition was that, however modest its scale, it prefigured the narrative scheme (as well as certain key design concepts) that the 1932 Mostra would adopt. Instead of simply commemorating fascism's origins in the mirror of the regime's year-by-year achievements, it constructed a collectivist epos, an allegory of the Italian nation's emergence out of the chaos and fragmentation into the utopia of (fascist) form. Of the exhibition's five narrative units, fully four are devoted to the crescendo of revolutionary ferment (on both the Right and the Left) that led to the Fascist seizure of power. The latter event, in turn, is portrayed as an apocalyptic hinge event, as the passageway to a bold new industrial kingdom in which the traditional constraints of space and time are overcome; hence, the shift in the exhibition's concluding narrative unit from diachronicity to synchronicity. The "regeneration of Italy accomplished by Fascism" is presented less as a historical process than as an eternal instant in which the accent is on youth and mobility, national communications and transportation, colonial expansion and institutional innovation. The 1932 exhibition would preserve this epic structure, adding only one crucial element: an epic protagonist and giver of form able to embody the national collective—*il Duce*.

A third but no less characteristic aspect of the 1929 Mostra del Fascismo was the organizers' intent to make coordinated use of state and party resources to ensure popular participation. Artifacts would be collected nationwide, discounted railway tickets would encourage visits from even the remotest regions, and exhibition posters were to have been ubiquitous. Alfieri and his cohorts, that is, did not conceive of the exhibition as an event addressed to the traditional patronage classes or to nostalgic Fascist veterans. Rather, they wished to stage a spectacle for—and even, to a degree, by—the Italian masses. It was this "public" that, like the other cultural initiatives of the late 1920s and early 1930s, the fascist exhibitions would strive to interpellate, to organize, and to mobilize.

II. The Realization of the 1932 Exhibition

Make it new, ultramodern and audacious therefore, free from melancholic echoes of the decorative styles of the past.[18]

Sometime in early 1931 the PNF directorate requested that Alfieri, now undersecretary of corporations, reformulate the original IFCM plan for a 1932 Mostra del Fascismo to be held in Rome at the Palazzo delle Esposizioni between 28 October 1932 and 21 April 1933, as per the Duce's instructions.[19] In a confidential memorandum discussed and approved at Palazzo Venezia on 14 July and later made public, Alfieri envisaged, once again, not "a mere historical re-evocation" but an "immediately comprehensible and perceptible" representation of fascism's achievements; "not an 'exposition' or 'show' in the conventional sense, but rather a survey of activities and forces, a balance-sheet of the first ten years in power out of which implicitly arises the future plan."[20] If this quotation echoes the design concept found in plans for 1929, it also suggests a reorientation toward the post-1922 era. The new drift is reflected in two key proposals: first, that the accomplishments of the regime in four domains—the state, the labor world, the armed forces, and the spirit—be granted special prominence; and second, that the entire exhibition, including the portrayal of the four areas just noted, be devoted to the celebration of a figure almost absent from the 1929 plan—"the pulse of a higher, animating, shaping will must be felt: the will of the Chief, in whom all of the mysterious forces of the race seemingly converge." This Mussolinian turn has a powerful impact on the exhibition's historiography. The pre-1922 history of fascism would still be represented "synthetically" but now with the accent on *il Duce*'s emergence as leader during the "heroic period that stretches between March 23, 1919 and October 28, 1922." As for the prehistory of fascism, it is to be reduced to "a sort of introduction."[21] The battle for Italy's intervention in World War I, for instance, would be illustrated by recalling only its "most genuine and synthetic expression": the foundation of the newspaper *Il Popolo d'Italia* by Mussolini.[22]

Despite the Mussolinian emphasis in Alfieri's revised proposal, the fundamental concept remained much the same. The exhibition was to be divided into two distinct units: a "historical" section recapitulating the period from 1914 through the March on Rome in chronological sequence and a "propaganda" section displaying the realizations of the regime between 1922 and 1932 in synchronic fashion. A sequence of rooms devoted to Mussolini, to the banners of the *fasci*, and to fascism's martyrs would serve as a symbolic hinge between these sections (the latter two had already been prefigured in preliminary plans for 1929). Moreover, Alfieri continued to envision the Mostra not as an isolated event but rather as fully woven into a dense fabric of mass meetings, congresses, parades, demonstrations, and other media events commemorating the seizure of power. Both government ministries and the entire party apparatus, from the grass-roots level up to the top PNF brass, were explicitly designated as participants and contributors. They were to assist in the gathering of materials; to mobilize the combined resources of the ministries, the media, the state tourism authority, and the national transportation system; to aid in reducing the costs of construction, maintenance, and diffusion. And to this rhetoric of mobilization corresponds an aesthetics of immediacy. Documents were to be selected "qualitatively." Yet because even the most evocative documents cannot speak with adequate force, they were to be enhanced by means of the "liveliest and most convincing signs, signs in which the artist's genius translates and expresses even the most arid subject matter," graphic emblems that "spontaneously burst forth with the power of Fascism's achievements." [23] Contemporary artists and architects would, in other words, be called upon to elaborate a formal and pictorial language capable of embodying the revolutionary rupture achieved by fascism: signs of a breakthrough into modernity against overwhelming material and historical odds, signs of an ultramodern, audacious reality, free from melancholy. [24]

By mid-1931 a commission of leading artists, architects, and sculptors—mostly younger members of the futurist, Novecento, Strapaese, and rationalist movements with proven fascist credentials—had been formed and placed under the supervision of Cipriano Efisio Oppo, a prominent war veteran, artist, and art critic. In the meantime a new gathering and sorting operation was being established, closely modeled after its Milanese predecessor though grander in scope. To the earlier assemblage of historical documents from local PNF party headquarters and private citizens now was added the task of locating and producing contemporary materials to illustrate "*all* of the regime's works and accomplishments during the past decade, even minor ones, in order that the collection be exhaustive in every domain and area of activity." [25] The result was a work load of monumental proportions. By mid-October 1932, more than seventeen thousand period documents and fifteen hundred photo reproductions had made their way to a warehouse on Rome's Via Cernaia. There and at the Mostra's headquarters on Via Nazionale a team of ten "historians"—a mix of museum curators, academic historians, and party ideologues—carried out sorting operations under the guidance of Luigi Freddi, a former journalist and secretary of the international *fasci,* to whom the exhibit's overall historical scheme had been entrusted. [26] Once they arrived at Via Cernaia, materials were evaluated for their visual impact and historical import. If selected for inclusion, they were assigned to a particular room in the exhibition hall, the precise design of which was the joint responsibility of a "historian" and one or two artists. [27] The burden of giving the exhibition a coherent overall shape rested mostly on Alfieri's shoulders, although the Duce was in regular contact with the organizers and did not hesitate to define himself as the ultimate architect.[28]

Budget restrictions, the volume of documents to be processed, the complex chain of command, and the resultant difficulties in coordination soon gave rise to enormous strains. Tensions were aggravated by the fact that because of a major exhibition marking the fiftieth anniversary of Garibaldi's death, the Palazzo delle Esposizioni would be unavailable until 5 August 1932. Before that date, preparations would be restricted to the Mostra's headquarters and warehouses. This meant squeezing all construction work into a feverish three-month period and employing the services of 520 daytime and 230 nighttime construction workers, as well as those of fifteen separate building contractors.[29] As would be the case with so many of the Fascist regime's grand enterprises, the accelerated nature of the schedule was both a symbol and a matter of pride. The exhibition catalog would thus provide detailed accounts of the organization and quantifications of the exact number of hours worked, exalting the enormity of the obstacles overcome through fascist discipline. To this it would add a technical description of the precise woods, metals, stones, and composite materials employed in construction, the surface area they covered, and their weight. But perhaps most significant of all, the technical description extended even to the building's engineering, reaching its conclusion in a precise account of the new electrical and air conditioning systems.[30] The symbolism here is clear enough: the Palazzo delle Esposizioni, already identified by association with the Garibaldian revolution, was to become a symbol of Mussolini's new Italy. Its nineteenth-century beaux-arts interiors and exterior, redolent with melancholic echoes of past grandeur, were not simply to be disguised. Rather, they were to be overcome, thrust forward, suddenly and almost miraculously, into the fascist century via a construction process that placed in relief the advent of heroic new temporality. What once seemed unthinkable was now, if not probable, then entirely possible.[31]

Such was the public facade the organizers strove to put forward. But from the very outset, conflicts seem to have arisen between members of the PNF directorate and the exhibition management, as well as among representatives of party associations and government ministries. The most droll of these involved Freddi, who over the coming years would be regularly denounced by his colleagues for laziness and incompetence, for maintaining a Russian mistress in a luxury hotel, and for gambling excesses. From April 1932 onward, having been passed over for a top administrative job, Freddi launched a series of demands for raises, complaining that he had "slaved like a dog," created ex nihilo the exhibition's historical narrative, and cost less than the other "historians" while contributing the lion's share of inspiration, ideas, taste, advice, and passion. By the latter half of 1932, his carping had become shrill; with typical hyperbole he would write to Alfieri: "Why do you treat me like this? Am I demolishing the Regime or contaminating humanity? I have a strong urge to cut and run. I see that it's all useless."[32] Despite such threats, Freddi continued in the employ of the exhibition for another year or two.

Much more serious was the dispute that pitted Alfieri against Giovanni Marinelli, the administrative secretary and treasurer of the PNF. Many times in the course of, first, the organization and, later, the administration of the Mostra, Alfieri would find himself obliged to call upon Mussolini to intervene in financial matters. Already, in November 1931, less than a month after the directorate had approved the exhibition's budget, Marinelli's office was restricting access to PNF funds. The problem reached a head in mid-1932 when, with construction about to commence, Alfieri and his collaborators were forced to seek an audience with *il Duce* in order to overcome the administrative secretary's "obstructionist attitude." The meeting caused an outburst on the part of Marinelli, and in a follow-up memo dated 8 July, Alfieri would clarify that

to my many worries concerning the difficulty of getting work out of the "historians" and artists, and to the time strictures, was added that of gaining access to necessary funds without running up against the legitimate and proverbial hindrances created by Comrade Marinelli. And I therefore entreated Your Excellency that, whenever the occasion arises, you might put in a good word in order to prompt him to loosen up the purse strings.[33]

For his part, Marinelli continued to resist. A letter in mid-September complains that "this constant nibbling away with additions and modifications represents a veritable financial disaster, all to the benefit of speculators!"[34] Nor would disputes over contractors' fees and costs of plans abate, even after the exhibition's consecration as a popular and financial success.

The existence of budgetary conflicts does not imply that the resources made available for the 1932 Mostra were either inadequate or meager. On the contrary, in a period of acute economic hardship, a period when nearly one million Italian workers were unemployed and when Italy's industrial production had declined by 27.3 percent over three years, the PNF directorate had not hesitated to allocate 2.25 million lire of party funds—the rough equivalent of 900,000 current U.S. dollars—for what amounts to little more than a lavish self-celebration.[35] While it is true that the original plan foresaw an eventual return of 2 million lire, leaving only a deficit of 250,000 lire (or roughly $100,000), actual costs were as much as four times higher because, among other things, the labor of PNF personnel and ministry employees was excluded from the budget.[36] To get a sense of just how extravagant was the regime's desire for this sort of aesthetic potlatch, one need only consider the 620,000 lire (or approximately $248,000) devoted to transforming the interior and exterior of the Palazzo delle Esposizioni. These were one-time expenditures that, once the intended six-month duration of the exhibition had elapsed, would prove irrecoverable. Add to this figure expenditures for the other events scheduled in and around the anniversary of the March on Rome—shows concerning farm tools, cereal production, land reclamation and internal colonization; cultural, juridical, and scientific congresses; rallies of Fascist veterans and university youth; the construction of Via del Impero—and the evidence becomes overwhelming. The need to define and figure fascism publicly, to grant it intellectual and cultural legitimacy at home and abroad, and the need to mobilize and rally the Italian masses, to renew symbolically the Fascist revolution while rerooting it in contemporary state institutions, were seen as far more essential to the future of the regime, far more effective from the standpoints of social and political utility, than investing those same millions in programs for revitalizing the national economy.

III. Shaping a Public

After personnel and building expenses, one of the largest entries in the preliminary budget for the 1932 exhibition was that covering publicity costs. A total of 300,000 lire, or some $120,000, was allocated for purposes of printing and distributing posters and billboards and of ensuring newspaper and film coverage. The organizers' objective was nothing less than the exhibition's ubiquity within the nation's borders.[37] The event's success was predicated on the participation of the Italian masses, and to this end 100,000 full-size posters (designed by Sironi, Paolucci, and Testi) were printed, as well as 200,000 postcards (mostly by Carpanetti and Guerrini), and 1,330,000 *cartelli,* or advertising posters (Fig. 1).[38] Even if one omits from this list the printing of unauthorized postcards and approximately 250,000 exhibition catalogs, one still reaches the staggering total of 1,630,000 printed items, or roughly one for every twenty-three inhabitants of the Italian peninsula.[39]

The use of advertising posters is especially telling as regards the organizers' ambitions. Of the total printing run of 1.33 million, 1 million were for placement at public sites in cities and towns. Of the remaining 330,000, fully 180,000 (54.5%) were designated for display on trains, 20,000 (6%) for airplanes and ships, 35,000 (10.6%) for intercity buses,

65,000 (19.7%) for means of urban transport (buses, trams, local trains), and 30,000 for collective taxis (9.1%). The emphasis on public transit as a means of diffusion is significant for two related reasons. First, it specifically designates the mass public as the exhibition's addressee, appropriating a marketing technique from the private sector to political ends. Second, it identifies the exhibition itself with themes of modernization and mass mobility, themes at the very heart of the regime's domestic policy agenda. The national train system, locus of well over half of the public transit advertisements, had become an emblem of national paralysis in the pre-1922 period. Notoriously inefficient and costly, it was also an ideal target for strikes, being the hotbed of some of Italy's best organized Socialist labor unions. So from the start, Mussolini's regime had striven not just to discipline the railway unions and to make "the trains run on time" but also to modernize and centralize the train system, transforming it into a living symbol of the new Italy: an electrified and tightly interconnected industrial nation founded on the values of efficiency, speed, and technical innovation.[40] In this spirit, the ten-year anniversary of the March on Rome was accompanied by a press campaign, by renewed efforts to promote electrification, and by initiatives to increase ridership.[41]

Among the latter was a program designed to encourage excursions to the Roman Mostra. Group visits—usually organized by schools, employee groups, or Fascist organizations like the Balilla—were promoted via tariff reductions of up to 70 percent (extended to, among others, tourists and foreign honeymooners). A special booth was opened at the Rome train station to accommodate requests for information. Last but not least, the exhibition catalog was to undergo a "vast diffusion" through the national train system: "in all railway bookstores, on all carts inside train stations, the volume [should be] permanently on exhibit, possibly in numerous copies."[42] Already a sign of fascist modernity, the train was to become the royal road to the Roman capital during the banner year 1932. And its image and the image of the transmogrified Palazzo delle Esposizioni were meant to meld in the collective imagination.

The train system was not the sole device by means of which Alfieri's committee attempted to promote direct participation by the masses. As a complement to their use of print technologies, photography, cinema, and the radio were all employed to ensure the entire nation's involvement, even if only at a distance. The palazzo's dramatic new facade and its interior contents were all scrupulously photographed and reproduced in contemporary magazines and newspapers such as *Casabella, Emporium, La Rivista Illustrata del Popolo d'Italia, Corriere Padano, Corriere della Sera,* and *Capitolium.* Contests were held for the best essay and non-documentary screenplay concerning the exhibition, and sometime in mid-1933 the noted filmmaker Alessandro Blasetti, director of the experimental film *Sole* (1929), was consulted about the production of a Mostra documentary.[43] The result was the most ambitious propaganda film ever undertaken by the Istituto Luce: a full-length documentary titled *Il Decennale* that, by order of the then minister of education, Francesco Ercole, was shown in all elementary and middle schools.[44]

IV. The Event and Its Reception

This is no Exhibition. It's an act of faith.[45]

This exposition-demonstration is like a cathedral where the walls talk. For the first time in the modern era, a contemporary event is drawn into the fiery atmosphere of religious affirmations and manifestations.[46]

The Mostra opened its doors to the general public on 30 October to much fanfare and front-page coverage. Construction work had been completed a few days earlier, and a provisional guidebook by Alfieri and Freddi was printed in lieu of the official catalog, whose production had been delayed due to the hectic preparations. A solemn opening ceremony was held on 29 October, presided over by Mussolini himself, and included among its 23,784 invited guests the Fascist Grand Council; the PNF directorate; top officials from the government ministries, the legislature, the military, and the justice system; members of the royal family; all of the surviving *sansepolcristi*; journalists from throughout Italy; and, perhaps most revealing of all, the entire membership of the Italian Academy, including Enrico Fermi, Filippo Tommaso Marinetti, Luigi Pirandello, Massimo Bontempelli, Ugo Ojetti, and Marcello Piacentini (Fig. 2).

Once open to the public, the exhibition immediately became a site for the elaboration of rituals. An "honor guard" was constituted by the *squadristi* and with it a daily ceremony for the changing of the guard. Fascist organizations were soon vying for the privilege of serving as "guardians of the Fascist Revolution." Within two years, the honor guard's ranks would swell to a total of 11,442 individuals and would include such groups as teachers' and workers' associations, the Balilla, the Fascist war veterans, various military and police units, the GUF (or Fascist university youth), and the *avanguardisti*. To such coordinated efforts corresponded an early influx of visitors arriving in small groups. (So as to ensure a controlled flow, Alfieri and the PNF secretary Starace had set an initial limit of two hundred visitors per delegation.) Encouraged by railway discounts and by reduced admission fees—the standard ticket cost only two lire (or 80 cents)—schoolchildren from all over Italy and particularly members of the Balilla, journeyed to Rome to see the "epic of the Italian nation" with their own eyes. Equally frequent visitors were groups, often numbering in the thousands during the later years, organized by entities like the Opera Nazionale Dopolavoro and by local chapters of the PNF. (Archival records reveal, for instance, that there were more than five thousand organized visits from the city of Bologna in the first year alone.) High-level officials, including Admiral Ellis of the U.S. Navy, top Chinese and Japanese brass, Sir Anthony Eden, the Nazi leaders Goebbels and Goering, and countless others, were also paraded through the transformed Palazzo delle Esposizioni as one of the formalities of their state visits.

Yet even at the start, the presence of such organized and coordinated visits can only begin to account for the enormous success of the 1932 Mostra. Originally intended for no more than five hundred thousand spectators, originally planned to last only six months, the exhibition quickly exceeded even the wildest ambitions of the organizers. By the end of March 1933, the figure of seven hundred thousand visitors had already been attained, and rather than slipping, the pace of admissions began to accelerate as Alfieri loosened the restrictions on group visits and launched a new press campaign.[47] No less significantly, the largest proportion of attendees was made up not of organized Fascist groups but of ordinary citizens. Among the latter were many tourists and foreign delegations. Admission records for the period between 19 November 1933 and 27 October 1934 are especially detailed and register the presence of groups (sometimes political but more often not) from Germany, Switzerland, France, Portugal, Bulgaria, Holland, the Americas, England, Belgium, Spain, Lithuania, and many other countries.[48] Moreover, they indicate an increasing representation of religious organizations, including large delegations from Azione Cattolica and schoolchildren from Hebrew schools. A dramatic case in point occurred during the Easter holidays of the Holy Year 1934, when some twelve thousand to thirteen thousand visitors a day, many Salesian priests and nuns, flooded the exhibit.

The consequence of this tremendous influx was that, contrary to Marinelli's fears (or perhaps thanks to his thrifty habits), the exhibition soon evolved into the ancestor of today's moneymaking "blockbuster" museum shows. The closing date was twice postponed, and by late October 1934 total admissions were closing in on the four million mark. This appears to have generated a huge and unintended profit: Between 29 October 1932 and 22 November 1933 alone, archival records show a net gain of at least 5.6 million lire (or something in the range of $2.24 million in current U.S. dollars); and even if one subtracts from this figure additional overhead and personnel costs, the profit must have remained considerable.[49] By mid-January 1933, Alfieri could write with confidence to

Starace: "I maintain my conviction that by the closing of the Exhibition, foreseen for April 21st, not only will all expenses have been covered, but *a notable financial gain will have been obtained*" (my italics).[50] Telling in this regard is the fact that, despite all of the organizers' efforts to encourage mass attendance, half of the requests for discount tickets, whether from Fascists or non-Fascists, appear to have been rejected.[51]

Thus far this chapter has emphasized three main points: first, the organizers' efforts to render the 1932 Mostra an effective mass spectacle; second, their attempt to situate it within an evocative politico-ideological framework; and third, their bid to mobilize and shape the Mostra's audience in accord with the regime's political objectives. All three points fall within the broad parameters of what may be described as "consensus studies," best exemplified in groundbreaking works such as Philip V. Cannistraro's *La fabbrica del consenso* and Victoria de Grazia's *The Culture of Consent*, of how the Fascist regime ensured and administered the consent of the Italian populace via its instrumentalization of the realms of media, art, culture, and intellectual inquiry.[52] Consensus studies have proved remarkably fruitful in advancing the study of fascist cultural politics beyond the once standard clichés, but they prove less nimble in addressing one of the implications of my third line of analysis, namely, that the mass response to the 1932 Mostra was fundamentally "excessive" with respect to the organizers' plans. No matter how thoroughgoing were the attempts to stage a *certain* spectacle, to summon and shape a *certain* audience, and to control the transaction joining audience to spectacle, the fact remains that the resulting event provoked a response quantitively and qualitatively *well in excess* of the organizer's aims. In other words, an explanation is needed for why the Mostra's audience not only felt interpellated, not only heard and gave heed to the organizers' "call," but also expanded upon and reinvented this call, transforming it into its own calling. I would venture to say that it is this principle of excess, exemplified by the move from mere consent to participatory enthusiasm, that poses the greatest interpretive and methodological challenge to contemporary studies of fascism and especially of fascism's cultural-political dimensions. In the case of the 1932 Mostra, the challenge requires a twofold approach: first, an investigation of the reception of the spectacle as elucidated by period documents, and second, by way of a conclusion, an analysis that attends to the aesthetic/formal complexities and specificity of the spectacle in question.

As regards the purely quantitative aspects of the 1932 exhibition's success, little more need be said. In the year following the opening ceremonies, some six thousand-plus visitors a day streamed through the portals of the Palazzo delle Esposizioni, roughly a quarter of them belonging to organized groups. Whether solitary or in groups, many of these visitors did indeed arrive in Rome by means of the national rail system as the organizers had intended. But it is perhaps those who did not do so who provide the best point of departure for an inquiry into the qualitative dimensions of the event's reception. Beginning in early 1933, scattered press accounts began to appear concerning "patriotic pilgrimages" by visitors to the exhibition. On 26 February 1933, in an article on group visits, the *Corriere della Sera,* for instance, noted "the visit of a young Paduan Fascist Renzo Aviani, who traveled by foot from Padua to Rome. Departing from his hometown on the third day of the current month, he reached Rome on the 22nd, after a journey in seventeen stages. Aviani passed through Rovigo, Ferrara, Bologna, Florence, Siena, Chiusi, Orvieto, and Orte, everywhere receiving a fraternal welcome from his comrades."[53] Although never coordinated or promoted (so far as I am aware), such pilgrimages were becoming routine by mid-1933. Between 19 November 1933 and 27 November 1934, I count forty-nine arrivals by bicycle from such faraway locations as Paris, Brasow (Rumania), Innsbruck, Palermo, Messina, Venice, and Turin. Among these, two are worth singling out: the arrival from Brescia on 25 February of a one-legged war veteran and that from Reggio Emilia on 10 August of a mother with her two children. Journeys by foot, like that of Renzo Aviani, were even more preponderant: 129 in total for the same period, many from places as distant as Berlin, Budapest, Madrid, Zurich, Amsterdam, Milan, Trieste, Udine, Cosenza, and Taormina. These included the arrival of two blind men who had walked all the way from Cismon del Grappa in the Dolomitic Alps.[54]

That this phenomenon demands to be examined against a religious backdrop is self-evident. The Roman destination, the enormous distances covered, and the arduousness of the means of locomotion all relate the "patriotic pilgrimage" to its sacred counterpart: the pilgrimage of faith that many Salesians had also embarked upon during the Holy Year 1934. Like his or her Catholic double, the patriot-pilgrim too is participating in a kind of sacrament. To take on the onerous journey is to make of oneself a ritual offering, a sacrifice, in this case not in imitation of Christ but of the Fascist "martyrs" recollected in the exhibition's *sacrarium.* As for the exhibition hall itself, the act of pilgrimage clearly designates it as a sacred shrine, a place of worship granting access to some kind of vertical, transcendental realm or apocalyptic kingdom where history's losses are recuperable. Transpositions of this sort between the secular and sacred domains are ubiquitous in the personal testimonies left behind by Mostra visitors. A letter by the Florentine Fascist Renato Taiuti is typical in this regard, recalling the "legion of ineffable emotions" kindled by the exhibit and the way that it "exalted and inflamed the spirit of countless visitors." The letter continues by pleading with Mussolini that he declare the exhibit permanent so that it may become the memorial chapel for "that Holy Revolution that You willed" and serve as "an eternal example, warning and incitement." [55] Another letter describes the exhibition as "the Sacrarium of our Epic," "a basilica," "our Altar of the Revolution" and "the reliquary of our battle" visited by "pilgrims of love and faith." If made permanent, the Mostra would become, in the words of the same letter writer, "our Temple open at all hours, guarded over by Black Shirts and always receptive like an asylum of fiery passion." [56] No less characteristically, another emphasizes the awe aroused by the exhibit's representation of the theme of sacrifice: "where the history of Italy and of the war epic sustained by the Italian people is recounted, our Fascist Martyrs could hardly have found a more dignified place, a more glorious exaltation of Their sacrifice." [57] A contemporary newspaper article describes how the Mostra generated its own "apostles," who preached the fascist word and led the faithful back to their temple. [58] Last but not least, every account notes the churchlike silence that prevailed despite the crowds: "as soon as one crosses over into the atrium, the first sensation is silence"; "they enter as if they were entering a church." [59]

For all that these testimonies and behavior patterns are informed by Roman Catholic conceptions of piety, it would be a mistake to view them either as fundamentally otherworldly in their orientation or as inherently conservative. The Fascist pilgrim may well be reenacting a Christian pilgrimage to Peter's Holy See, but his is a pilgrimage with a difference. Since the early nineteenth century the Roman itinerary had been undergoing a distinctively secular, anticlerical, and revolutionary revision within Italian history, a revision codified in the writings of Mazzini, Carducci, and others but "updated" and "completed" by Mussolini's 1922 Train Ride to Rome. The destination of the Mostra's visitors is thus neither the "first" Rome of the Caesars nor the "second" Rome of the popes but the Mazzinian Third Rome: a this-worldly apocalyptic city, a city that is "holy" and "universal" inasmuch as it stands for the fulfillment of Italy's "sacred" destiny as a nation via the fascist revolution.

Viewed from this perspective, the secularized rhetoric of the sacred encountered in so many contemporary accounts of the 1932 exhibition comes into clearer focus. It does not indicate a mere relapse into prior deeply rooted cultural patterns but rather serves as a kind of hinge between two contradictory but not irreconcilable modes of reception. On the one hand, it accommodates a backward-looking "nostalgic" or "monumentalist" mode of reception, one in which the imitation and commemoration of the fascist revolution's past in and around the Mostra gives rise to an experience of historical continuity, community, and order. On the other hand, it accommodates a forward-looking "modernistic" mode of reception that experiences the Mostra as an event of rupture on the political level, erasure on the historical level, and disorientation and/or rapture on the level of the individual subject. Whereas the former mode prevails in spectators' descriptions of their overall experience of the exhibition (particularly as they try to situate it within a broad socio-historic context), the latter takes precedence in their accounts of the show's aesthetic impact. In her essay "Mothers of Martyrs," for instance, the poetess Ada Negri interrupts her nostalgic musings on the sufferings of Fascist mothers with passages like the following:

The first four rooms: the war, from the massacre of Sarajevo to Vittorio Veneto. How vertiginous! Grandeurs and horrors figured or realized with a representational audacity I never dreamed of: the gigantic statue lives and bears witness alongside the printed and written document, displaying an archive's stamp; paintings, caricatures, photographs, are peers with the historical dates and names recalling the heroic battles. Seeming already a legend, the history of those years leaps out at our eyes synchronically and thrusts us into a vortex. There is no defending oneself against its violent assault.[60]

The writer's sense of a proper distance between present and past is violated by the confusion of fictions with facts, the mixing of the gigantic with the small, the blending of visual images with dates and names. Her mourning and monumentalization of Mother Italy's losses, therefore, can no longer proceed in an orderly fashion. Assaulted, thrust into the center of war's vortex, she is no longer far enough removed from the scene of history to be able to "look back" in remembrance. History has shed its diachronicity to become an immediate and rapturous enfolding legend.

Metaphors of assault, informational overload, shock, and memory loss recur constantly. Margherita Sarfatti speaks of the exhibition hall's walls "screaming out in the most ardent fashion . . . the historical message with which they are laden."[61] Louis Gillet, national curator of the French museums, writing in the *Revue des Deux Mondes*, theorizes the dreamlike effect in terms of contemporary media technologies: "The whole forms a strange ensemble: a series of episodes, of reconstructions and autonomous scenes, assembled with all the cuts, welds, ellipses and emphases of a film specialist . . . in short, it is all very Futurist, of an adroit and unfettered Futurism in which everything is calculated according to a unique ballistics so as to machine-gun the spectator, to increase the power to shock."[62] Although Gillet's allusion to the cinematic analogy is unusually insightful, the terms of his analysis resonate throughout less erudite "modernist" responses to the Mostra as well. One interesting case in point is that of a Neapolitan poetaster named Giuseppe Molteni, whose "Lyrical Impressions" are reproduced in Appendix 1. Much like Gillet and Negri, Molteni identifies the Mostra's disruptive effect on viewers with the practice of an anti-illusionist aesthetic, closely related to futurism.[63] In the course of Molteni's doggerel text, "illusionism" comes to be associated not only with the decorative styles of the past but also with nostalgic myths ("the good old days") and dreamy solutions ("cure-alls"). The artists of the Mostra destroy all such "cool" illusionistic constructions, elaborating in their place a crude, "hot," and vigorously hypermimetic model of representation, the aesthetic counterpart to fascism's politics of activism and antiparliamentarianism. Such an art is "modern" because it employs the new expressive means and motifs embodied by the soaring wings of an airplane. It is "revolutionary" because it is a violent art that seizes, subdues, and conquers "at first sight." Yet Molteni's conflation of modernity with violent revolt does not preclude a return to the values of monumentality affiliated with the cult of ancient Rome. On the contrary, Molteni's poem as a whole and its final tercet in particular betray a monumental conception of art as well as politics. In fact, despite their title, these verses provide nothing at all like lyrical *impressions*; rather, they form a solid column atop whose crown rises up the allegorized figure of a reborn Imperial Rome.

If in Molteni's poem one perceives the oscillation already alluded to between monumentalist and antimonumentalist modes of response, a much more characteristic example may be found in Negri's description of the silence observed by visitors:

The men and women walking with me in an uninterrupted line all bear the same astonished and reverent expression, the same strange pallor. No one speaks. It is the Exhibition that speaks, in a language composed of one hundred different languages, and yet precise, cutting, piercing, universal. The artists who have given it spirit—the best of young Italy—seem to have touched here the limits of a new art, heaving into the creative furnace even the most disparate, crude elements of life and heroic death.[64]

The reverential demeanor of the viewer-pilgrims, their orderly procession, their silence, all clearly signal receptivity. Into this receptive setting, connected with the "monumentalist" response outlined above, the Mostra erupts with its violent multimedia cacophony, speaking one hundred tongues, slashing and piercing, mixing the disparate with the crude, death with life. This formal, cognitive, and taxonomical violence, intimately associated with Romantic notions of the sublime, produces astonishment and even "a strange pallor" on the viewers' faces. But significantly, it does not foreclose the potential for a return to order. The viewers may have been shocked and visually "machine-gunned," but a number of key terms affiliated with the secularized sacred—terms such as "spirit," "universal," and "heroic"—suggest that there exists a bridge between modernist chaos and monumental order, between the immediate sensate impact of the show and a vast objective (and constructive) historical process. Within the pictorial logic of the Mostra, this "bridge," as will now be seen, is figured by three interrelated signs: the X, the fasces, and the face of *il Duce*. All three pervade the exhibition as a whole. Constantly repeated, paired off, altered in scale, and transmuted into one another, they are compacted into symbols both of historical continuity and of fascism's mythic/utopian rupture.

V. Fascist Monumentality and Mourning

One exits stupefied: is this still Italy? Is this the land of smiles, sun and beauty? These somber tints, this lugubrious Pantheon, this Dies Irae that is also a Ça ira, seem to belong under another sky, or to a foreign race. A powerful impact on the public. Thus Fascism impresses upon souls the cult of sacrifice and the legend of its martyrs.[65]

The 1932 Mostra's trajectory has now been retraced from its prehistory through various stages of planning and development to its successful realization. Its social, cultural, and ideological repercussions have been surveyed both from the standpoint of the intentions of the regime and organizers and from that of spectator-participants. What remains to be examined is the artifact at the center of these developments: its structure, its formal and aesthetic properties, and the cultural-historical memories that it invents, elicits, and/or suppresses.[66] Turning from the Mostra's context to the event itself, one question emerges as paramount: how is it that this artifact, the collaborative creation of twenty architects and artists belonging to rival Modernist movements, can sustain and shape the diversity of responses, pressures, and demands already discussed?

The exhibition was built around a narrative scheme that, as shown earlier, was first formulated by Dino Alfieri and his collaborators at IFCM in 1928. Although mostly identical to its predecessor, the 1932 version of the scheme was reshaped by the new imperatives of centralism and by the growing cult of *il Duce*. It may also have been influenced by the design of a contemporary work of PNF historiography: Giorgio Alberto Chiurco's four-volume *Storia della rivoluzione fascista*, published in 1929.[67] Like Chiurco's history, the 1932 Mostra's historical component begins with an extremely condensed survey of the events leading from the outbreak of World War I to the founding of the first *fasci di combattimento* in 1919, all of which takes up only four rooms. This is followed, as in Chiurco, by an exhaustive presentation of the period between 1919 and 1922, the so-called heroic phase of the fascist movement, occupying a total of eleven rooms. Here the crescendo of events leading from the labor strikes of the postwar era through the seizure of Fiume to the March on Rome is portrayed as an epic struggle between the advocates of national paralysis and of progress, between Bolshevists and Fascists. Strictly speaking, the full sweep of the Mostra's historical narrative is contained within these fifteen rooms. The chronological sequence, however, is extended and enhanced by the inclusion of four additional large rooms whose contents are "historical" yet whose order is nonchronological: a Hall of Honor (containing the Duce's first Milanese office), the Gallery of the Fasci (displaying banners of individual Fascist groups), the "Mussolini room" (including the dictator's second Milanese office), and a Sacrarium dedicated to memory of the "martyrs" of the fascist revolution. This complex of nineteen "historical" rooms (plus several administrative offices) takes up the entire ground floor of the Palazzo delle Esposizioni and represents the heart and soul of the exhibition. As for the building's second floor, it consists in an ahistorical appendix dedicated to the regime's plans and realizations. It comprises only five rooms and represents but a partial fulfillment of Alfieri's original plan to document fascism's accomplishments in the domains of the state, the labor world, the armed forces, and the spirit. Since these four areas were to be fully represented in a future "Exhibition of Realizations," the 1932 Mostra offers but a foretaste. It limits itself to one room representing the activities of Fascist organizations abroad, a library containing some five thousand works concerned with fascism, and three small rooms dedicated to the regime's achievements in the fields of labor, agriculture, transportation, industry, and commerce.[68]

Such a general description of the exhibition's structure only begins to hint at the acuity with which the organizers developed their plan. By exploiting the symbolic potential of the palazzo's layout and by making an asset of the stylistic/ideological divergences between Mostra artists, they strove to mold the visitor's itinerary through the building into a unified and artfully constructed whole. Through the careful modulation of spaces, visual effects, lighting, and sounds, they transformed the narrative of fascism's triumph into an allegory of the (national) will to form, an allegory in which the emotions of awe and terror associated with the revolutionary violence of fascism-as-movement are transmuted into feelings of order and solemn elation associated with fascism-as-regime. It is this itinerary that will now be retraced from its point of origin out on the sidewalk of one of the busiest and noisiest streets of modern Rome.

Approaching the Mostra from either end of Via Nazionale the visitor would first have been struck by the Palazzo delle Esposizioni's new streamlined Moderne black, red, and silver facade (Fig. 3). With its four twenty-five-meter tall tin-plate fasces and its twin six-meter X's, this fiercely contemporary "face" would have been almost as recognizable as that of *il Duce*; hundreds of thousands of postcards, photographs, and posters had transformed it into the hallmark of the ten-year anniversary of the March on Rome. Yet no less than recognition, the new facade would surely have produced a sense of shock. (One visitor speaks of it as a "terrorist composition," so thoroughly "Bolshevist" in spirit that "with a change in emblems the piece would bring applause in Moscow.")[69] In the place of the neoclassical beaux-arts facade that had graced Via Nazionale for half a century, a facade last identified with the commemoration of Garibaldi's death, the visitor beheld instead signs of erasure: two X's atop red boxes with an immense black box at the center, all fronted by four freestanding cylinders evoking an industrial iconography of smokestacks, pop-riveted conduits, and iron ships.

If this Modernist front suppresses the references to traditional building types found in the beaux-arts original, characteristically, it does not evade historical meanings altogether. History is permitted to enter, as it were, "through the back door," through oblique or indirect allusion, and conventional color symbolism is omnipresent. The black fasces of the facade, for example, echo the columns of the original Roman colonnade. No longer performing a supporting role, these Fascist "columns" stride out in front of the building as if they were monumental soldiers leading classical architecture, as revived in the Umbertine Palazzo, into the industrial age (Fig. 4). They are the Fascist avant-garde, the cutting edge of the revolution. The symbolism is enhanced by the fact that the new (architectural) order is personified by the ancient Roman symbol of the state's absolute authority over life and limb. Later appropriated in the French Revolution and the Risorgimento, the Fascist symbol is modernized and updated in the new facade so as to imply that fascism's heritage encompasses the revolutions of both antiquity and modernity. The giant red and black X's on either side of the facade further elaborate this program. They too are Roman, signifying the Roman numeral 10: a sign both of the ten-year anniversary being celebrated and of the revolutionary calendar inaugurated by the March on Rome (1922 = the year 0). No less important, the X's also affiliate the fascist revolution with Christian sacrifice—the X of Christ's cross—and Modernist negation, the X as sign of crisis. The X is the sign of a new dispensation, of a new founding blood sacrifice, of a national fresh start.

Having taken in the facade and reflected upon its iconographic valences, the visitor would have climbed a dozen or so stairs. He would then have stood face to face with the broad (38-meter) lintel stretching

1. Posters for 1932 Mostra.

2. Opening ceremonies, 29 October 1932. *Courtesy of Archivio Centrale della Stato, Rome.*

3. Side view of facade.

4. Vertical view of facade.

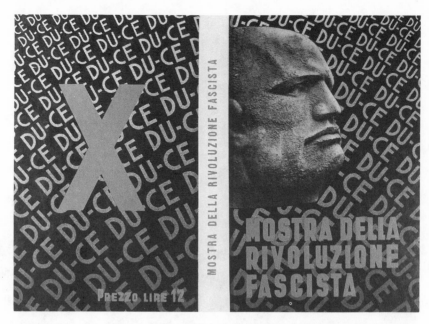

5. Cover of the guidebook by Alfieri and Freddi.

6. Room A.

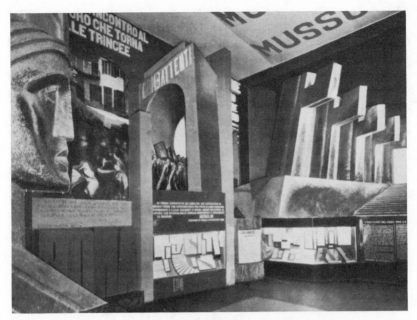

7. Room E.

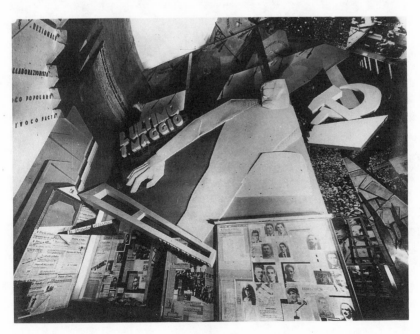

8. Room O.

9. Room R.

10. Room S.

11. Room U (general view).

12. Room U (detail).

across the entrance, pierced and held up by the towering fasces. Framed beneath the lintel he would have encountered the exhibition Honor Guard (usually *squadristi*); supported above it, the blood-red inscription MOSTRA DELLA RIVOLUZIONE FASCISTA in large (1.6 meters tall) three-dimensional Roman letters—letters stripped of ornamental serifs, sober, geometrical, and bold. Passing in between the guards and the two central fasces while still ascending further stairs, the visitor would have entered a fourteen-meter-tall arcade, a shimmering metallic hybrid combining elements from Roman triumphal archways and cathedral entryways.[70] At the end of the arcade glowed the Mostra's doorway: a forbidding triple X jutting out over a severe rectangular corridor and grill. Here the visitor would finally have left the hubbub of the street behind and entered the exhibit proper, moving down a tall corridor flanked by large display racks filled with exhibition guidebooks, their black covers profiling Mussolini's head and a large red X against a sea of cries of "Du-ce" (the cheers of a Fascist mob) (Fig. 5). The corridor reached its end in a wall framed by large metallic fasces on which the Fascist oath was imprinted in large black capitals. Reaching this wall, the visitor would have turned right and begun a counterclockwise rotation through the fifteen historical rooms of the exhibition (rooms A through Q) that have already been discussed.[71] The visitor's trajectory would, in effect, have taken him or her around the entire periphery of the building, yet never permitting a glimpse into the four halls (R–U) that made up the central axis.

These fifteen rooms were even more radical and thoroughgoing in their implementation of avant-garde design principles, at least to the extent that, unlike the facade, they refused to accommodate even oblique forms of historical allusion. Every one of them not only masked the beaux-arts structure concealed beneath (erasing in the process all decorative and historicist elements) but also transformed and destabilized the original layout. The palazzo's orderly sequence of rectangular floor plans thus gave way to an unpredictable progression of asymmetrical rooms with irregular spatial relations and proportions. Dummy walls broke off right-angled corners; partial walls jutted out aggressively at odd angles; sculptural volumes and reliefs pushed forward or backward off sloping planes; ceilings dropped, slanted, or rose up; floors became illusionistic. This constant alteration of the spatial configuration of individual rooms produced a sense of perpetual movement and instability. The effect was deepened on the presentational level by constant shifts in scale and by a blurring of the distinction between documents and contexts, art and architecture. For the visitor, it would no longer be possible to tell what was framing what. Documents were compressed within the bodies of anthropomorphic giants; photographs, minute and enormous, were superimposed on top of one another; figures, facts, symbols, and dates marched without distinction across walls and ceilings; three-dimensional objects (daggers, an anchor, a bridge, a bell, flags) appeared now inside, now outside display cases (Fig. 6). The documents, in turn, obeyed the same law of infinite variation. Intimately private objects, such as letters, family photos, and articles of clothing, occupied the same plane of reality as official documents (newspapers, memos, edicts, and posters); some documents were isolated and individualized; others were massed in geometrical configurations (Fig. 7). The overall result was a sense of agitation, compression, and disorientation. Bombarded with visual/verbal/documentary information, the visitor would thus have experienced the events of 1914 through 1922 in strict chronological sequence, but the immediate impact would have been less diachronic and analytical than synchronic and sensate. Thirteen of the fifteen total rooms, that is, probably would have "read" almost as well if they were traversed out of sequence. They presented variations on a single theme: that of *masses* (both spatial and human) *in constant movement*, unstable masses swirling about in a hot vortex that denied the spectator any reflective distance or sense of historical process (Fig. 8). Order (in the form of competing taxonomical and display schemes) surfaced here and there but only locally. Partial exceptions were the last two rooms (P and Q), dedicated to the hinge event in the Mostra's narrative: the March on Rome. Designed by the Novecentista painter Mario Sironi, these cool and solemn rooms foreshadow what looms just around the corner: a monumental architecture identified with fascism's passage from movement to regime. To enter them was, in the words of Ada Negri, like "climbing up out of the catacombs into the open air and sun."[72]

Finishing this counterclockwise rotation around the periphery of the palazzo, the visitor zigzags into the Hall of Honor (room R), having completed his or her "detour" through fascism's early history and rejoined the central axis along which the building was first entered. The move from periphery to center is accompanied by an aesthetic shift prepared in rooms P and Q. Here the "hot" Modernist chaos of the strictly historical rooms yields to the "cool" and orderly streamlined Moderne that will prevail in rooms R through U. Unlike their fifteen predecessors, the four rooms in question are linked together by a straight corridor, similar to the central aisle of a cathedral. Spacious and symmetrical, almost sepulchral in their sobriety and heroic in their scale, these rooms constitute themselves as a kind of spiritual hub and hermeneutic key, bringing order to and organizing the vortex of historical rooms. Their overarching theme is the sacred bond between the leader and his followers; hence, their alternation between the staging of Mussolini as epic protagonist (rooms R and T) and the commemoration of the Fascist collective, whether the individual *fasci* (room S) or the martyrs of the revolution (room U).[73] Accordingly, they do not extend the diachronic sequence of rooms A through Q but rather recapitulate and reinscribe it within a ritual order.

Coming into the first of these four rooms, the Hall of Honor, also designed by Sironi, the visitor would immediately have been struck by the shift in mass and scale back to the proportions of the entryway and facade (Fig. 9). Upon entering, he or she would encounter two massive rectangular columns holding a large X aloft. Opposite this X on the facing wall there would have loomed the figure of Mussolini above the title DUX, flanked by the limit dates 1919 and 1922 and by the mottos ORDER AUTHORITY JUSTICE and BELIEVE OBEY FIGHT inscribed on intruding blocks. A reconstruction of Mussolini's first editorial office was placed below the slogans. As in the succeeding room, also by Sironi, the walls, ceiling, and floors were studded with hyperstylized figures: dates, X's, flags, muskets, stars, fasces, the words ITALIA, DUCE, and DUX. Sometimes presented in bas-relief, sometimes in inlays or *intaglio,* these signs functioned much like hieroglyphs, reinforcing the visitor's sense that he or she was advancing toward the inner chamber of some sort of latter-day Assyrian temple.

The air of mystery and solemnity extended into the Gallery of the Fasci, a vertical corridor lined by five massive pairs of buttresses interspersed with the banners of the original Fascist organizations (Fig. 10). Moving down the corridor, the visitor would have felt a growing sense of expectation: the sequence of dates appearing on wedgelike projections extending into the room suggested a chronological crescendo, while the DUCE and fasces on, respectively, the ceiling and wall hint at an impending disclosure. The hallway ended in a rectangular portal crowned by a five-meter sculpture representing the Fatherland triumphant. Passing through the portal, the visitor reached the "Mussolini Room" (room T)—a kind of antechamber to room U, the exhibition's climax and sanctum sanctorum. Designed by Leo Longanesi, the journalist and painter, room T provided a minute documentation of Mussolini's biography and works, just as the Garibaldian exhibition did in the case of Garibaldi. It was restrained in tone and conventional in its display methods, as befit the hagiographic intent. Images and relics of *il Duce* (including a reconstruction of his second Milanese office) here summoned up the visage of a figure who permeated the Mostra from start to finish. Like the recurrent X's and fasces with which it was juxtaposed, Mussolini's image underwent a multiplicity of elaborations in the course of the exhibition. Sometimes it was presented whole, sometimes fractured; sometimes humanized, sometimes abstracted. More often than not, it was cast in the image of the facade: bullet-like and streamlined, monumental and modern. This figurative ubiquity of Mussolini called attention to the crucial function performed by the Fascist leader within the narrative and imagistic economy of the show. Mussolini unified; he provided the glue. His was the "face"—the *volto*—that brought singularity and identity to an otherwise chaotic and multifaceted revolution.[74]

Having completed the long detour through fascism's history and traversed the three central halls, the visitor finally reached the Sacrarium of the Martyrs (room U) (Fig. 11). This large cylindrical space, over thirteen meters in diameter and seven meters in height, was designed by the Rationalist architect Libera and the theater designer Valente (creator of the famous Carri di Tespi). It was universally acknowledged as the centerpiece, if not the masterpiece, of the 1932 exhibition and soon became the focal point of patriotic pilgrimages. That this room should be designated with the Latin term *sacrarium* suggests that it was a place for the keeping of holy ancient things, a secret recess or inner sanctuary; and such is indeed the case. Dark and mysterious, it mixed, modernized, and transfigured ritual signs from Roman antiquity and Christendom.

Upon entering the circular chamber, the visitor would have been startled by the irruption of song. Wafting faintly down through the ventilation system, amid the darkness, a recorded chorus continuously sounded the lyrics of "Giovinezza," a hymn adopted by fascism from the Arditi—assault troops instrumental in the violent early era of the movement. "Giovinezza"'s theme is the passage from adolescence into young adulthood, from the innocent diversions of youth to the pursuit of honor, sacrifice, and death on the battlefield. The latter complex of sacrificial themes governed the overall conception of the room. Barely visible, black banners bearing the names of the revolution's "martyrs" shimmered beneath and beyond the outer periphery of the cylinder's base. Above them rose six circular back-lit tiers aglow with the word PRESENTE! repeated one thousand times (as if to infer that those "present" are in some sense identical to Garibaldi's Mille). A riveted metallic cross towered above a blood-red metal pedestal at the center of the circles. Inscribed with the phrase PER LA PATRIA IMMORTALE! (or "for the immortal fatherland"), this last of the exhibition's X's—evidently, an abstract double of Mussolini—is engaged in a visual dialogue with the chorus of singing/signing "voices" (Fig. 12). Their interplay simulates a Fascist rally, with its ritual exchanges of slogans and crowd responses. But this is a rally of a different sort: a rally of the living dead, a rally taking place in some indeterminate secular otherworld, "immortal" yet of this world, where history's victims are forever present to each other.

Within this cylinder, the visitor's itinerary reached its terminus. (The upstairs rooms proved little more than addenda.) In a virtual exorcism of the disorder out of which the movement itself had emerged, the final room presented a vision of absolute order and symmetry: "here the heroic symphony comes to its conclusion in a final chord that seems to echo paradise."[75] Gone were the agitation and labyrinthine asymmetries of the historical rooms. Gone were the lesser irregularities of the monumental central rooms. Here the tone was sober and funereal. The patriotic cross— a figure of history and sacrifice—was inscribed within the circle—a figure of eternal plenitude—in what amounts to a "normalization" of the epic drama of the first fifteen rooms. Reformed and reshaped into a perfect circle, the revolutionary vortex no longer threatened to intrude into the space occupied by the viewer. The dead affirmed their presence as a collective, but their voices were faint, even mute. The threat of contagion has passed. The legend became at once enveloping and remote.

As the Fascist regime's first comprehensive effort to represent itself in the mirror of history, the 1932 Mostra is caught up in a web of paradoxes. The exhibition's goal was to commemorate and renew the fascist revolution within the setting of the decennial celebrations. It was therefore meant not as a memorial of the permanent or static sort but rather as a provisional and evanescent rallying point: a *living* monument capable of serving as the focal point for mass happenings that would mobilize the Italian nation as a whole, from the highest government offices to the factory floor. To this end, the exhibition set out to be revolutionary: new, ultramodern, audacious, free from the melancholy and mourning that usually accompany the remembrance of things past. Instead of simply embalming the movement's origins, it strove to reactivate and embody them, first, through the transformation of the Palazzo delle Esposizioni into an epitome of fascist modernism and, second, through the use of a panoply of modern representational techniques, materials, and media. By these and other means the organizers and artists hoped to present fascism's "heroic era" with such shocking intensity and immediacy that it would almost literally be brought back to life. Denied any critical and/or reflective distance, the visitor would succumb to the images' contagion. He or she would partake of sensations and emotions just like those that accompanied the actual events. No sense of loss or discontinuity would divide the past from the present.

But discontinuity there was. Ten years after the March on Rome, the Fascist regime had long abandoned its sense of provisionality. It was committed to building up and consolidating a monumental state, a dictatorship built around the cult of Mussolini. It is therefore hardly surprising that the Mostra's attempt to bring fascism's origins "back to life" should, in the end, entail a burial of them. Renewed and recreated, these origins are also distanced and framed within the Mostra's overarching drive toward monumentality and order. They are engulfed and introjected, ultimately displaced and erased in the very act of consecration. For Mussolini's state to triumph it was essential that the black of fascism still conjure up all of the accursedness and heroic nihilism evoked by early slogans such as "Me ne frego!" ("I don't give a damn!") and "Vivere pericolosamente!" ("Live dangerously!"). But it was also essential that fascism's black become the color of mourning. The revolution is dead. Vive la révolution!

So what had begun as a Modernist anti-museum, a "museum in motion," an evanescent happening to be followed by others of its kind, soon evolved into a permanent structure. The exhibition's closing was twice postponed and would eventually become unthinkable. Declared permanent by Mussolini in October 1933, it shut down one year later, only to reopen in September 1937, at the Museum of Modern Art in Valle Giulia, in the context of a joint celebration of the fascist empire and the two-thousand-year anniversary of the birth of Augustus Caesar. This second version remained on display at this location until 1942, after which its place was taken by a third and final version. Only in 1943, as the Allies advanced and the Fascist government retreated to Salò, did the Mostra definitively close. Its library, which by that time included nearly seventeen thousand documents, was abandoned in place. The rest of the exhibition was packed in crates and shipped to the lapidary museum of Salò, where it would await the arrival, two years later, of the victorious enemy forces.

Even though they still contained many fragments of the 1932 original, the Mostre of 1937 and 1942 served more as archives and mausoleums than as rallying points. Instead of epic demonstrations, they stressed didactic presentations. The role of the library was expanded accordingly, as was the use of conventional devices such as busts, maps, tables, diagrams, and lists. Moreover, the sparsely decorated walls increasingly bore lengthy quotations from Cato, Cicero, Augustus, Machiavelli, Guicciardini, and Vico alongside the usual ones from Mussolini. Fascist *romanitas* had triumphed over fascist modernism.

For a diversity of reasons, the response of visitors was absenteeism. In late 1940 the Mostra's director could write that the event had been denied "that daily participation in the political life of the capital that was achieved on Via Nazionale, leading gradually to a total absenteeism on the part of visitors, whose daily attendance now barely averages eight to ten persons." [76] Like the regime that stood behind it, the exhibition had lost its power to rally the Italian masses to the fascist cause. The earlier summons to revolution had been replaced by a call to regimentation as Italy prepared to enter a new world war.

Appendix: Documents from the 1932 Exhibition of the Fascist Revolution

Note: the following text was a spontaneous submission sent to Marinelli by Giuseppe A. Molteni, a theater critic, novelist, and (it appears) a midlevel executive at the Compagnia Napoletana del Gas. It is reproduced from ACS: PNF–Carteggio del Direttorio, b. 272 ("Offerte Varie").

The Exhibition of the Fascist Revolution

Lyrical Impressions

Not one of those exhibitions
that's illusionistic
about the good old days
and is too restrained,
but an ardent vision
of great Italic passion
in all of its potency
rendered ultra-evident
by the bold expressive means
and by the new conventions
of an art at once robust
and bewitching,
that captures and conquers
at first sight!
It's revolutionary
this crude and varied art
without fetters and chains!
It sweeps across the vast fields
of our azure skies
—beauty unveiled!—
with aeroplane wings
and descends into the gaping
furrows of the trenches,
not with the cure-alls
of every old style
but with the virile means
of the Fascist dagger!
None can resist it!
Down with the passè manners
of the pallid masses
of gutless artists!
Different and prouder
is this art's face!
It has something of Mars
and of Rome even more
—the city it's named for!—
from Rome victorious
on its feet and glorious
imperial and imperious!!!

La Mostra della Rivoluzione Fascista

Impressioni liriche

Non un'esposizione
di quelle "ad illusione"
del buon tempo passato
e troppo compassato,
ma un'ardente visione
della grande passione
italica possente,
resa più che evidente
dai gran mezzi espressivi
e dai nuovi motivi
d'un'arte insiem gagliarda
e maliarda
che afferra e che conquista
a prima vista!
È rivoluzionaria
quest'arte rude e varia
senza pastoie e inciampi!
Spazia nei vasti campi
del nostro azzurro cielo
—bellezza senza velo!—
con ali d'aeroplani
e scende negl'immani
solchi delle trincee,
non con le panacee
di tutto il vecchio stile
ma col mezzo virile
del pugnale fascista!
Non è chi vi resista!
Giù le antiche maniere
delle pallide schiere
d'artisti senza nerbo!
Diverso e più superbo
è il volto di quest'arte!
Ha qualcosa da Marte
e molto più di Roma
—e da quella si noma!—
di Roma vittoriosa
in piedi e gloriosa
imperiale e imperiosa!!!

Artists, Architects, and Historians
(Key to Floor Plans)

FACADE   *Architects*: Mario de Renzi and Adalberto Libera

First Floor

ROOM A   *Title*: "From the European Conflagration to the Foundation of *Il popolo d'Italia* (1914)"
Artist: Esodo Pratelli
Historian: Luigi Freddi

ROOM B   *Title*: "From the Gathering of the Fasci d'Azione Rivoluzionaria to Italy's Intervention in the European Conflict (1915)"
Artist: Esodo Pratelli
Historian: Luigi Freddi

ROOM C   *Title*: "The Italian War (1915–1918)"
Artist: Achille Funi
Historian: Antonio Monti

ROOM D   *Title*: "The Italian Victory (1918)"
Artist: Achille Funi
Historian: Antonio Monti

ROOM E   *Title*: "From Victory to the Foundation of the Fasci di Combattimento (1918–1919)"
Artist: Arnaldo Carpanetti
Historian: Giovanni Capodivacca

ROOMS F & G   *Title*: "The Year 1919"
Artist: Marcello Nizzoli
Historian: Dante Dini

ROOMS H & I   *Title*: "The Year 1920"
Artist: Amerigo Bartoli and Mino Maccari
Historian: Gigi Maino

ROOMS L & M   *Title*: "Fiume and Dalmatia"
Artist: Giovanni Marchig
Historian: Riccardo Gigante

ROOM N   *Title*: "The Year 1921"
Artists: Guido Mauri and Esodo Pratelli
Historian: Alessandro Melchiori

ROOM O   *Title*: "The Year 1922 up until the Events of October"
Artist: Giuseppe Terragni
Historian: Arrigo Arrigotti

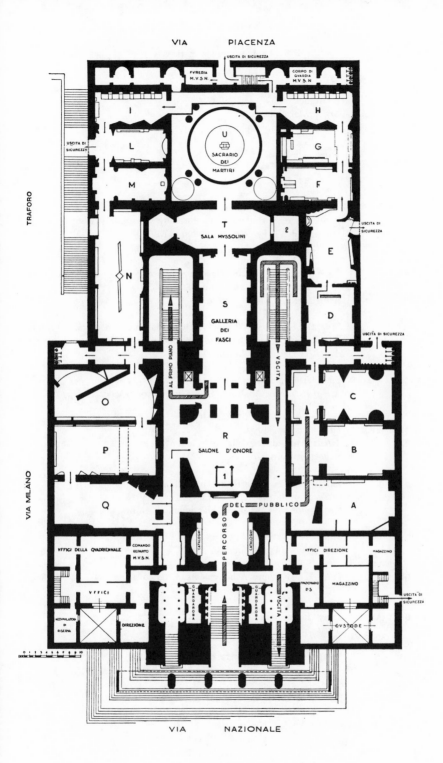

First Floor

ROOM P   *Title*: "The Naples Gathering and the Preliminaries of the March on
              Rome"
              Artist: Mario Sironi
              Historian: Francesco Sacco

ROOM Q   *Title*: "The March on Rome"
              Artist: Mario Sironi
              Historian: Francesco Sacco

ROOM R   *Title*: "The 'Hall of Honor' Dedicated to the Person, Ideal and Works of
              the Duce" (includes the office used by Mussolini between 1914 and
              1920 on Via Paolo da Cannobio in Milan)
              Artist: Mario Sironi

ROOM S   *Title*: "The 'Gallery of the Fasci' Symbolically Glorifying the Actions of
              the Fasci between 1919 and 1922"
              Artist/Historian: Mario Sironi

ROOM T   *Title*: "The Mussolini Room" (includes the Duce's memorabilia and the
              office used by him between 1920 and 1922 on Via Lovanio in Milan)
              Artist/Historian: Leo Longanesi

ROOM U   *Title*: "The Sacrarium of the Martyrs"
              Artist/Architects: Adalberto Libera and Antonio Valente

Second Floor

ROOM 1 (E)   *Title*: "Fascism abroad"
              Artists: Morbiducci, della Torre, and Mancini
              Historian: Piero Parini

ROOM 2 (D)   *Title*: "The Fascit Spirit—Fascist Bibliography"
              Artists: Antonio Barrera and Enrico Paolucci
              Bibliographers: Cornelio di Marzio and A. G. Bragaglia

ROOM 3 (C)   *Title*: "The National Activities of the Fascist Regime"
              Artist: Enrico Prampolini

ROOM 4 (B)   *Title*: "The Regime's Achievements in Agriculture and Transportation"
              Artist: Gerardo Dottori

ROOM 5 (A)   *Title*: "Labor under Fascism"
              Artist: Antonio Santagata

SERVICES   *Designers*: Antonio Barrera and Enrico Paolucci

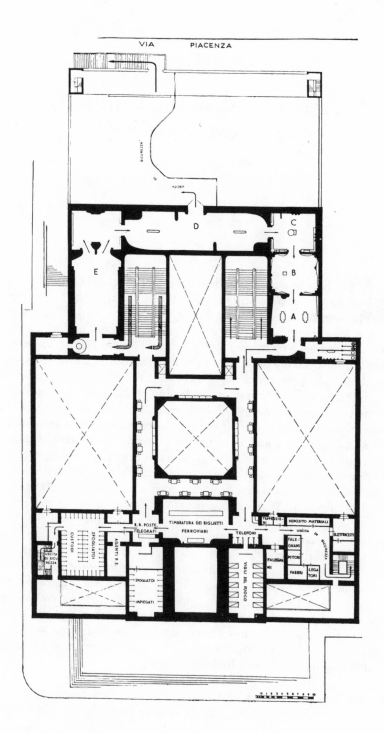

Second Floor

ANDREW HEWITT

Fascist Modernism, Futurism, and "Post-modernity"

T he idea of a fascist modernism has been a long time in the making, its emergence both facilitated and hampered by the development of a systematic theory of the avant-garde. The possibility of at least thinking a fascist modernism was opened up (or reopened, since the idea was, of course, first articulated by the Fascist Modernists themselves) by a crisis of the avant-garde in the 1960s, a crisis that questioned both the position of the artist within the relations of production and the historical function of aesthetically "progressive" art in general.[1] On the one hand, the distaste of high modernism for the dictates of the marketplace had revealed itself to be disingenuous because modern artworks had begun to command immense prices on the open market. As a result, the postwar avant-garde had already begun to explore the possibilities of a precommodified art, an art that faced squarely the inevitability of its own exchange function, thematizing the process of commodification itself. Such artistic productions, however, threatened to become purely affirmative by sublating the commodity into the value sphere of the aesthetic. At the same time, this exploration of the aesthetic of *bricolage*—the re- and deconstruction of the everyday—was also taken as an indication of the exhaustion of the modernist aesthetic imperative of innovation. What remained for the theory of the avant-garde to theorize was the anachronism implicit in any "progressive" model of modernity predicated upon continuous and constant innovation and the possibility that such a modernity—both aesthetically and socially—would, in any case, be complicitous with the revolutionizing and commodifying demands of capitalist rationalization.

This was a crisis both of aesthetics and of politics—a crisis, in fact, of their apparent dissociation. The most crucial and consequence-laden expression of the *Theory of the Avant-Garde* of Poggioli, for example—a theory that was to be but the first of a new wave of thinking about the avant-garde—was the recognition that "the hypothesis (really only an analogy or symbol) that aesthetic radicalism and social radicalism, revolutionaries in art and revolutionaries in politics, are allied, which empirically seems valid, is theoretically and historically erroneous."[2] The critical conflation of political and aesthetic "progressiveness" was at an end. It was now possible to think of an artist as politically "reactionary" and at the same time aesthetically "progressive," or vice-versa. Theoretically, at least, fascist modernism became thinkable.

"Empirically," however—to insist on Poggioli's own usage—fascist modernism still did not seem to exist. All that Poggioli articulates in the passage cited above is a theoretical possibility that he seeks to foreclose at the level of the empirical, where the collaboration of political and aesthetic revolutionaries "seems valid." Poggioli simply attempts to replicate at the level of theory a dissociation of aesthetics and politics that a critique of fascist modernism must confront. This maneuver was to stall serious consideration of fascist modernism for well over a decade. Notably, the one example Poggioli offers of the collaboration of political reactionaries and aesthetic revolutionaries is the relation between Italian futurism and Mussolini's Fascists, but his failure to draw any substantial conclusions from this collaboration results in a double strategy of exclusion, which can subsequently be traced from Poggioli's work through to such studies as Bürger's infinitely more rigorous *Theory of the Avant-Garde*.[3] "From the start," Poggioli assures us, "Italian futurism was also nationalism, as was all the culture of the young generation in that epoch; the fascism of the epigones of that movement was mere opportunism" (p. 95). In other words, futurism was not fascistic but merely opportunistic. The "proof" adduced by Poggioli to support this fact serves to indicate quite clearly the ideological reasons for the critical maintenance—albeit merely "empirical" now—of the separation of fascism from modernism. For if Italian futurism was opportunistically fascist, Poggioli points out, "[t]he same thing happened in the ultimate phase of Russian futurism, which at its beginning was subversive and radical in politics, on the extreme left as the Italian movement was on the extreme right"(pp. 95–96). Futurism cannot be truly fascistic, for it is at one and the same time—in the USSR—also communist!

It should be stated at the outset that Poggioli is quite simply wrong about Italian futurism, which is radically and fundamentally fascistic. It was fascistic before Mussolini had even appropriated the term, fascistic after Mussolini had ceased to be a Fascist, fascistic to the end, in Marinetti's final reconciliation with Mussolini.[4] For the moment, however, I would like to explore the ideological strategem that grounds the exclusion of futurism from theories of the avant-garde, rather than the political basis of futurism itself. The key to Poggioli's theory is a conflation of Italian and Russian futurisms as a means of proving the political opportunism of art once it begins to take an interest in politics. This conflation, however, far from legitimating an exclusion of political analysis from the assessment of the historical avant-garde, is itself politically loaded, for Poggioli both equates and differentiates communism and fascism. He distinguishes "the extreme left" from "the extreme right" and yet insists that the process to be observed is, in essence, "[t]he same thing." Poggioli's *Theory of the Avant-Garde* both springs from and seeks to legitimate a conflation of fascism and communism; it is the result of a cold war theory of totalitarianism that even today serves to frame the prevailing canon of modernism.[5]

Poggioli's own political agenda becomes explicit in his championing of a "climate where political liberty triumphs" (p. 95) as the only arena (free of both oppression and of oppressive patronage) in which avant-garde art can flourish. What his work is really about is "the rapport between avant-gardism and the capitalist bourgeoisie" (p. 94). By apparently excluding political consideration and then privileging the aesthetic of the avant-garde, Poggioli engages in an aesthetic relegitimation of capitalism itself. Whereas we may be familiar with the aesthetico-political conflation of fascism and communism from modernist rejections of both Nazi monumentalism and socialist realism, that same conflation is being practiced here *within* the canon of modernism itself.

Or is it? For the second strategy of dissociation practiced by Poggioli—and replicated by Bürger—is the exclusion of futurism from the modernist canon. Futurism is characterized by Poggioli as "vulgar experimentalism, formless and imitative" (p. 137), as "an external and vulgar modernity, more of matter than of spirit, a modernism considered only as a snobbist variant of romantic 'local color'" (p. 220), and as the prime example of "the dross of that ridiculous and cheapened modernism which afflicted Western culture just before and after the First World War" (p. 220). In the face of fascist modernism, theory reverts to a form of self-contradictory "kettle-logic": fascist modernism does not exist because it was not "really" (but only opportunistically) fascistic; and anyway, even though it *was* fascist, it was never truly modern, merely vulgar, ridiculous, and cheapened.

Although Bürger is less explicit and vitriolic in his exclusion of futurism, he excludes nevertheless. This time, however, the exclusion is necessitated by different political concerns; for whereas Poggioli sought to relegitimate a depoliticized formalistic canon of modernism, it is *against* precisely this canon that Bürger wishes to reestablish the claims of a politically oriented avant-garde exemplified by Brecht. Taking as his theoretical paradigm the avant-garde's attempt to reintegrate art and life after their uncoupling in the ideology of aestheticism—and seeing in this reintegration the possibility, at least, of a "progressive" aesthetic—Bürger can but be embarrassed by Marinetti, the Futuro-Fascist who claims that he too—in a diametrically opposed fashion for which Bürger cannot satisfactorily account—seeks to render life itself a work of art.

The development of a theory of fascist modernism seems only to have overcome these ideological and theoretical resistances by the time of Jameson's work on Wyndham Lewis.[6] Nevertheless, within Jameson's broader project there persists a residual disinclination to pursue the critique of the modernist canon as far as one might. Thus, for example, in *The Prison House of Language*, he still argues that "[t]hat familiar split between avant-garde art and left-wing politics was not a universal, but merely a local anglo-American phenomenon."[7] Technically, Jameson is on firm ground as long as he limits himself to observations on the Left's failure to recruit avant-garde artists. One can but sense, however, a desire to delimit any critique of modernism and to project onto the continent the possibility of a redemptive modernist project. Marinetti and the Futurists would mark the frustration of any such desire; for, once one begins to look at the active collaboration of avant-garde artists and the Right (rather than the absence of any such collaboration—within the Anglo-American tradition—with the Left), it becomes more and more difficult to limit one's critical perspective to the "local, anglo-American" arena. Fascist modernism must be theorized at the level of active collaboration between artists and politicians, and there is no clearer example of this collaboration than the relationship of the Futurists to Italian fascism.

Primarily, I will be addressing the ideological continuum that made it possible for the Futurists to work alongside the Fascists in the early years. I would also contend, however, that despite the vicissitudes of Marinetti's personal relationship to Italian fascism—and to Mussolini in particular—the difference between the aesthetic tastes of fascism as a movement and as a regime are less pronounced in Italy than in Germany.[8] The plurality of aesthetic possibilities within the Third Reich was never really sustained to the degree that it was in Italy.[9] It seems fair to surmise that Mussolini's own aesthetic tastes tended toward the avant-garde. As early as 1914, in a letter to Paolo Buzzi, he assumes that "Boccioni will have told you—if he has ever spoken of me—that all my sympathies—in the realm of art also—are with the innovators and demolishers: with the 'futurists'."[10] As an early indication of the sympathies uniting futurism and Italian fascism, this letter provides an interesting starting point for the consideration of fascist modernism. Mussolini's statement reads as the acknowledgment of a debt: *his* sympathies are with the Futurist, rather than the reverse. More important, however, the vital *anche* in

Mussolini's formulation (i.e., "in the realm of art *also* [emphasis mine]) suggests that his affinity to futurism is not primarily aesthetic. Mussolini sees the *futuristi* as innovators and demolishers in both the political and the aesthetic realm. It is important to stress Mussolini's early perception of the political valency of futurism in order to combat the critical tendency that attempts to recuperate early futurism by depoliticizing it. The division of futurism into an "early" or "heroic" first period and a derivative, politicized late period has served, since the early 1960s, as one more way of avoiding any confrontation with the phenomenon of fascist modernism. In this case, the dissociation of aesthetic from political progress has led to a radical dissociation of aesthetics and politics in general; each is mapped out neatly and chronologically in the narrative of the decline of "heroic" futurism.[11]

At this point, it is perhaps important to clarify this destructive aesthetic for which Mussolini is expressing sympathy. Just what was futurism propounding in those early years that allows us to assign it paradigmatic avant-garde status? First, it is important to stress the futurist attack on the very *institution* of the aesthetic, on the museum, and on the auratic solemnity of postromantic art.[12] The celebration of the machine, of speed and productivity, in the *Founding Manifesto*, for example, expresses a profound rethinking of the possibility of historical narratives of progress. On the one hand, there are—in the hopelessly antiquated celebration of the automobile—remnants of a modernist celebration of progress, but this celebration has been radicalized to the point of self-destruction. In futurism we seem to reach that point wherein the ideology of progress itself has been rendered anachronistic, surpassed by progress itself. What Marinetti insists on is the *self*-destructive impetus of capitalism, forced as it is to revolutionize constantly its own productive mechanisms. It can no longer be a question of being *for* or *against* capitalism—and in this sense Marinetti counts himself "beyond" communism—for to champion capitalism in its pure form is to envisage the chaos of its self-destruction.

What Marinetti rejects more clearly than anything else is the view of government as a series of checks and balances and of the market as an imperturbable balancing act. The rejection of an *aesthetics* of harmony goes hand in hand with a rejection of *political* conciliation. Marinetti and the Futurists also celebrate the revolutionary possibilities of the masses of the new urban centers, masses who are never characterized as a proletariat and whose revolutionary capacity is essentially *aesthetic*, grounded in their very physical presence rather than in a deferred utopian moment. Thus, when Poggioli disparagingly claims that the Futurists are not futurists at all but mere "presentists," he is, in a sense, quite correct.

But this is a presence—a physical presence, a violent aesthetic shock—that shatters the self-substantiating plenitude of any presence understood in the philosophical sense. It is an ephemeral presence, insisting upon history as a process of displacement and negation rather than of ultimate redemption. Thus, whereas Bürger insists on the category of "institutional criticism" as the basis of any avant-garde movement (a critique, that is, of the very institution of the aesthetic, rather than a purely "system-immanent" critique of one preceding artistic movement), what we have in the *Founding Manifesto of Futurism* is a critique that refuses the closure of the institutional, that purposefully engages in futile and marginal internecine disputes with other aesthetic movements, that recognizes the importance to the institution of art itself of the concept of totality and *presence* that any institutional criticism presupposes. This, in a nutshell, might be said to constitute the ideological and aesthetic nexus that so appealed to Mussolini in the early years.

If Mussolini's letter—and his collaboration with the Futurists in favor of Italian intervention in World War I—provide historical grounds for questioning the critical depoliticization of early futurism, this wholesale division of aesthetics and politics clearly raises theoretical problems also. As Luciano De Maria has argued,

We must remember that from the beginning Futurism wished to assert itself not only as one among the many literary schools, but as a movement possessing a global ideology embracing the various spheres of human experience, from art to clothing, from morality to politics. That which had been more or less implicit in the romantic tradition up until Symbolism is here—in Futurism—made explicit, encoded more or less organically, but always profoundly marked. Thus, in this sense Futurism can consider itself the first authentic avant-garde "movement."[13]

In other words, it is precisely *because* the political can no longer be extricated from the aesthetic—precisely, in other words, *because* Marinetti displays from the very outset a fascistic tendency toward the aestheticization of politics—that futurism must count as the first avant-garde movement. It is not longer a question of avant-garde *or* fascism, no longer a question of the accidental or opportunistic collaboration of one Avant-Gardiste and one Fascist demagogue—it is a question of the fundamental fascistic potentiality of the avant-garde itself. Fascist modernism is not just a branch of modernism, not a quirk nor an exception; it is instead—theoretically if not empirically—*the* single most pressing issue for theories of the avant-garde, for it raises also the question of the possibility of a postmodern avant-garde.

If this is the case—if fascist modernism is truly central to any understanding of broader questions of modernism; if fascist modernism does, in fact, stake out a certain liminal territory between modernism and the avant-garde—how has it been possible to suppress the role of futurism in the cultural history of this century? The motivation is clear enough: in light of the atrocities of fascism and nazism, culture per se acquires a redemptive and affirmative value. Fascism does not simply compromise the Right but seems somehow to stigmatize the entire discourse of politics and to motivate—by way of reaction—a postwar return to the aesthetics of autonomy. Theoretically, however, our desire to marginalize futurism can be explicated with reference to a body of work much more sensitive to the interplay of aesthetics and politics—work, in fact, in which futurism was of central paradigmatic importance—the analysis of fascism sketched out by Walter Benjamin.

It is in the epilogue to "The Work of Art in the Age of Mechanical Reproduction" that Benjamin first foregrounds Marinetti and the Futurists in order to develop his theory of fascism.[14] Quoting extensively from one of Marinetti's more bellicose manifestos, Benjamin concludes:

"*Fiat ars, pereat mundus*," says Fascism, and, as Marinetti admits, expects war to supply the artistic gratification of a sense of perception that has been changed by technology. This is evidently the consummation of *l'art pour l'art*. Mankind, which, in Homer's time was an object of contemplation for the Olympian gods, now is one for itself. Its self-alienation has reached such a degree that it can experience its own destruction as an aesthetic pleasure of the first order. This is the situation of politics which Fascism is rendering aesthetic; Communism responds by politicizing art. (p. 242)

In this famous passage, Benjamin summarizes the main elements of his analysis of fascism as the "aestheticization of political life." The genealogy he traces is both aesthetic and political (or economic). Politically, Benjamin argues that Marinetti articulates more clearly than any critic of fascism the dependence of capitalism on a war economy. Obliged, on the one hand, to revolutionize the *forces* of production and to resist, on the other, the revolutionary potential of the social *relations* of production, capitalism attempts to externalize the destructive forces of technology. Social order is maintained at the cost of national destruction. In turn, it is a decadent aesthetic, an aesthetic of *l'art pour l'art*, which is capable of refunctioning this process of externalized destruction as a form of aesthetic, contemplative distance and consequently of enjoying destruction itself as an aesthetic event.

Paradoxically, then, the "aestheticization of politics," which seems to entail a confusion of discourses, actually functions on the basis of one of the most radical reaffirmations of the *autonomy* of the aesthetic—*l'art pour l'art*. Thus, when Benjamin recommends "politicizing art," he is arguing not simply that fascism somehow confuses aesthetics and politics but rather that maintaining a traditional discursive differentiation between the two is itself potentially fascistic. The problem, it would seem, is one of totalization and fragmentation. By externalizing the socially destructive (or "progressive") powers of the new productive forces, capitalism (in its transition into fascism) at once hypostatizes a totality,—the protected socius—and creates an economically necessitated excess or supplement—war—that negates the putative self-sufficiency of that totality. In the same way, the disinterested and contemplative stance of *l'art pour l'art* at once objectifies and totalizes the world as an aesthetic phenomenon and yet fragments that totality by locating the contemplative subject outside that to which, supposedly, there is no outside—namely, the world as totalized aesthetic artifact.

It remains to be seen to what extent Benjamin's analysis holds true for futurism. First, it should be pointed out that Benjamin's concentration on the warlike rhetoric of Marinetti invalidates from the very outset one model of aestheticization that seems to have enjoyed a certain critical success in the analysis of fascism. Aestheticization does not simply mean the false reconciliation of social contradictions at the level of the aesthetic; it is not enough simply to invoke an aesthetics and a politics of the *schöner Schein*. Harmony and reconciliation are not being offered—in the case of Marinetti—as a social facade, imposing a false aesthetic unity on an unruly political situation. If a model of harmony and social cohesion is being produced, it is produced only by the invocation of its opposite, by an aesthetic of aggression, opposition, and disunity. In other words, it is no longer a question of a falsely totalized and harmonious aesthetic experience being offered to the increasingly fragmented subject. On the contrary, an experience of contradiction, antagonism, and fragmentation is being offered to an increasingly totalized and systematized subject. Aestheticization—at least in the case of Marinetti—is not the illusion of a solution; it is the illusion of a problem, the illusion of a possible liberating contradiction in a society that already has consigned such contradictions to the liminal and supplementary arenas of war and aesthetic experience.

Benjamin's citing of decadent precedents for Marinetti's brand of fascism suggests a second model of aestheticization, which the broader context of his argument should lead us to resist. According to this line of interpretation, aestheticization would consist in a straightforward displacement of one set of values by another. Instead of judging political decisions in terms of their efficacy, their ethical value, or their justice, an aestheticized politics—or so the argument would run—makes such judgments on the basis of their beauty. To argue along these lines is to tie both futurism and fascism more closely than is necessary to a certain aesthetic brand of nineteenth-century anarchism. For Marinetti at least—and this may, in fact, be what finally distinguishes Fascist Modernists from a more doctrinaire or nazified form of fascism—it can never be a question of simply replacing one value system with another. Or rather, it cannot be a question of simply replacing one *fetish* of systematicity—justice, for example—with another (such as beauty). Simply to redefine the central organizing value of a discursive system is to leave intact the discursive economy of the system itself, to ignore the fundamental systemic issue in the name of one more totalizing value. That "aestheticization" and "politicization" can so neatly and rhetorically be opposed would serve as evidence—for Marinetti—of their complicity in the subjugation of the play of discourse to its putative object, of signification to the referent, of economy to the commodity, of production to representation. It is precisely this fixation that futurism strives to resist. To assert any value system is to retotalize, to impose a false harmony on the political discourse itself, a discourse that, as we have seen above, Marinetti insists must function only antagonistically and oppositionally.

Benjamin is correct, then, in insisting on the centrality of war to the futuro-fascistic aesthetic, but this is a war at the level of discourse as well, a war that cannot so readily be subsumed under another discourse of the political or the economic. It is interesting that Benjamin should cite as his example of futurism's complicity with fascism a work of Marinetti's from the period of the Ethiopian war, for it is precisely around the question of imperialism that one might best begin to understand both the links uniting Marinetti and Mussolini and the differences that separate them. Marinetti's own brand of nationalism first became apparent before World War I and was developed in response to two very different political impulses.[15] The two ideological strains behind Marinetti's "nationalism" continued to assert themselves throughout his career and are central to any understanding not only of his politics but also of his conception of an avant-garde aesthetic. On the one hand—clearly visible from the very beginning—there is a sympathy with the claims of Italian irredentism and a demand for the restitution of Italy in its entirety. On the other hand—and generally conflated with with the first, irredentist strain under the generalizing category of "nationalism"—there is an enthusiasm for the nascent Italian imperialism first displayed in Marinetti's response to the Libyan adventure. Far from being simple manifestations of a single overarching value system, these two forms of nationalism tendentially oppose and conflict with each other, making impossible any ideological closure around the figure of the Nation. It was this ambiguity in Marinetti's nationalism that was subsequently to estrange him from the regime of Mussolini.

For Marinetti, both irredentism and imperialism were aesthetically legitimated; each represented a certain response to the revolutionizing claims of the avant-garde. The logic of irredentism is one of closure and plenitude; it brings into play a redemptive metaphysics of presence, celebrated as the restitution of Italy as a territorial and popular unit. The legitimation for the return of the Austro-Italian territories was drawn from a logic of totality and completion: that which has been separated from itself must be reunited and made complete. (A similar logic would clearly legitimate German expansionism in Europe in the early stages, although in the case of Germany this ideology was radicalized and biologized through the racial notion of *Volk*.) The aesthetic of irredentism is, essentially, an aesthetic of harmony, a non-avant-garde aesthetic projecting Italy as a unified and autonomous work of art.

Imperialism, meanwhile, draws upon a quite different logic. First and foremost, it clearly displays contempt for traditional notions of autonomy and national "closure" in its quite literal transgression of the borders of the invaded country. To view imperialism solely as the negation of the autonomy of the Other, however, is to ignore the implications of imperialist transgression for the integrity and self-identity of the aggressive power. The transgression of borders is a transgression not only of the line that defines the Other but also, potentially, of the line that defines the Self. Marinetti's exhortations for an attack on Libya or an attack on Ethiopia at the same time urged toward an attack on the integrity of Italy itself. Politically reactionary, this imperialistic strain of nationalism nevertheless corresponds more profoundly to Marinetti's avant-garde project, for he took imperialism to be predicated on a logic of dissemination and self-destruction that questions the very logic of national self-identity that seems, superficially, to impel it.

Clearly, Marinetti's interpretation of the imperialist project is somewhat willful, to say the least. Nevertheless, he obliges us to reexamine the terms within which any attack upon aggressive, imperialist nationalism tendentially legitimates an alternative nationalism grounded in "irredentist" notions of national plenitude and self-presence. It is Marinetti's willful interpretation of imperialism as a political expression of the avant-garde spirit that would ultimately bring him into conflict with Mussolini. As early as 1911, Marinetti was agitating for an *Italian* empire. In the "Manifesto a Tripoli italiana" he demands:

1. All freedoms must be granted to the individual and to the people, except for the freedom to be a coward.

2. Let it be proclaimed that the word ITALY must predominate over the word FREEDOM.

3. Let us cancel out our fastidious memory of the greatness of Rome with an Italian grandeur one hundred times more splendid.[16]

One can already sense the admixture of irredentist and imperialist strains of nationalism—a nationalism of plenitude and a nationalism of transgression. The prevalence of "Italy," for example, over "Freedom," serves to mark the territorial closure of Marinetti's nationalism at this point. However, the question of restitution and self-presence has been displaced, in this instance, from the spatial to the temporal plane. Spatially, Italy predominates, but temporally and historically, there is a rejection of the historical precedent of Rome. Marinetti is playing off the contradictions of Italian nationalism in terms of confrontation of time and space, geography and history.

Mussolini's nationalism, meanwhile, sought to assimilate geopolitical ambitions and historical precedent. In contradistinction to the antihistorical pronouncements of Marinetti, Mussolini's imperialism was unabashed in its evocation of the splendor that was Rome. Thus, within the imperialistic nationalism of Italian fascism, plenitude and redemption are no longer figured *spatially* but rather *temporally* and *historically*: what is restored is no longer the territorial unity of Italy but the historical continuum from Rome to Italy. In other words, the displacement of geopolitical considerations onto the historical plane involves an idealist reconstruction of history as a process of fulfillment, as a movement toward completion that takes as its telos a movement *beyond* the linearity of historical time into the *presence* of historical redemption. It is precisely this ontologization of a historical imperative that Marinetti resisted. Thus, in his polemic with Mussolini, he insisted: "Yes! Yes! We must march on and not fall short of our sacred ambitions. Let us urge on Italian youth (already prepared and eager both in muscle and in spirit) to the conquest of an Italian Empire. It shall and must be Italian, for a Roman Empire would be a mere restoration, a plagiarism" (*FF*, 243). The terms of Marinetti's opposition are interesting: what for Mussolini is a return to the historical origin (Rome) is for Marinetti a *plagiarism*. What comes to the fore, then, in Marinetti's resistance to Mussolini's fascistic appropriation of imperialist rhetoric is quite strikingly *not* a movement *beyond* Mussolini, not an avant-garde insistence on transgression, but rather a retreat, a *regression*, to the very terminology of modernism that is elsewhere rejected. Retreating from the level of an institutional criticism, in which all aesthetic forms potentially shed their historical necessity and become equally (in)valid—in which Barock,

Gothic, and Modern, for example, lose their function as historical loca-
tors and become mere stylistic possibilities within what Bürger terms the
"simultaneity of the radically disparate"—Marinetti resorted to an ultimately *modernist* insistence on originality and innovation in his attack
on imperialist plagiarism. To reject the grounding of the new Italian empire on historical precedents, Marinetti was obliged to resort to the modernist imperative of innovation, thereby relegitimating a historicity of
progress and linearity. Thus, as we observed earlier, Marinetti moved
beyond the historical purview of modernism precisely by *refusing* to
move into the spatiality of a metaphysics of presence.

One can trace this ambiguity vis-à-vis modernity at every level of Marinetti's aesthetic. Most fundamentally, perhaps, it informs his very conception of the body. Just as the politics of nationalism is split along the
fault line of plenitude and transgression, so Marinetti's politics of the
body strains between an ideal of discipline and an ideal of liberation.
Indeed, it is the body that serves as the most consistent political figure
for Marinetti. "Italian democracy," he declared, "is for us a body which
must be liberated" (*FF*, 126). This bodily liberation, however, is not
simply (or not even) a liberation *of* the body but also a liberation *from*
it. Once again, Marinetti developed his political considerations in two
seemingly opposed directions here. On the one hand—in the tactilist
manifestos—he advocated a move beyond a fixated genital sensuality toward an erotic potentialization of the entire body (politic). Second, however, and more troublingly, he also sketched out a project for the *destruction* of the body. This apparent opposition resolved itself, as we shall see,
much in the same way that the ambiguities vis-à-vis capitalism were resolved. Self-destruction is not the opposite but rather the fulfillment of
liberation. One need only examine the manifestos on the art of performance and declamation to observe how consistently Marinetti's writings
moved toward the virtual effacement of the body, which is perpetually
contorted, deconstructed, and refunctioned as a signifying machine. Alternatively—and this is the characteristic alternative with which Marinetti himself played constantly—one might argue that the body itself is
actually *foregrounded* in these writings by virtue of its function as a signifying and performative entity. The body—as that which represents,
rather than that which is represented—resists any teleological orientation
of signification toward its referent, resists the role of representation as
mere *plagio*.

The most evocative and chilling invocation of the *destruction* of the
body, however—as the telos of liberation—occurs in a passage from a
manifesto entitled "The Birth of a Futurist Aesthetic." What is particu-

larly troubling about this text, which forms a part of Marinetti's celebration of War, the World's Only Hygiene, is the affinity it seems to suggest to a broader fascistic ideology that transcends the limits of Italian fascism. In short, this narrative of the destruction of bodies might mislead us to a hasty equation of futurism and a nazified form of fascism. The passage reads as follows:

The plainest, the most violent of Futurist symbols comes to us from the Far East. In Japan they carry on the strangest of trades: the sale of coal made from human bones. All their powderworks are engaged in producing a new explosive substance, more lethal than any yet known. This terrible new mixture has as its principal element coal made from human bones with the property of violently absorbing gases and liquids. For this reason countless Japanese merchants are thoroughly exploring the corpse-stuffed Manchurian battlefields. In great excitement they make huge excavations, and enormous piles of skeletons multiply in every direction on those broad bellicose horizons. One hundred *tsin* (7 kilograms) of bones brings in 92 *kopeks*. (*SW*, 82)

At the very least, we are obliged to raise the question of the status of this description in the light of the genocidal form subsequently taken by fascism in Nazi Germany. Is there, perhaps, something in the *aesthetic* ideology of fascism—exemplified here in futurism—that transcends geopolitical distinctions and provides a coherence to the phenomenon of fascism that its various historical forms would seem to belie?

Certainly, Marinetti himself was no anti-Semite,[17] and his celebration of the burning of bodies, framed though it is by a eugenic invocation of war as hygiene, lacks the racial specificity of Nazi rhetoric. To get to the root of Marinetti's celebration of the burning body, one must instead view it in the context of the celebration of flux and exchange that runs through his entire oeuvre. The scenario of the burning of bones and the subsequent commodification of the body articulates at one and the same time Marinetti's relationship to capitalism and, potentially, fascism's relationship to modernity. For Marinetti, the process of commodification *was* flux, and his writing demands that we reassess the caricature of commodification as stasis and reification, to see instead the vital forces that drive and impel exchange. In the same way that the commodity is only a fetish of capitalism, which must itself be understood as a *system* of exchange, so the body (and, elsewhere, the psychologized subject in general) is simply a fetish of the vital and productive/destructive forces that pass through it. The body represents and gives form to those forces and yet traduces in that representation by imposing the stasis of embodiment. The static (bodily) reification of life forces is swept aside by a *new*, explosive commodity (even more powerful in death than in life). Commodities and bodies were, for Marinetti, but the by-products and momentary re-presentations of a vital system of exchange to which they might otherwise have been assumed to be central. The Japanese businessmen reject the stasis that is the body by burning it, exchanging it, and thereby reinvigorating it.

The relationship of this quintessential futurist gesture to the genocidal anti-Semitism of Nazism is complex and can be traced only by way of a consideration of Nazi figuration of capitalism. It is through nazism's identification of the Jew with the deleterious effects of capitalism that a connection of sorts is reestablished to the "economic" concerns foregrounded in Marinetti's presentation of the Manchurian war. For Marinetti, the burning of the body reintegrated that body into the vitality of exchange itself. In burning the body, the businessman was not burning something identified with capital; rather, he was redeploying the dynamic of an exchange economy by *refusing* the fetishization of the body either as a static representation or as the finitude of exchange. In other words, the commodification of the body does not consist in its fixation and objectification but rather in the destruction of any such fetish before the all-consuming economy of exchange. The body is not the ultimate commodity, precisely because no commodity *can* foreclose the logic of exchange itself.

Nazism's construction of the Jew as the embodiment of capitalism makes clear, I think, the distinctions that must be drawn between fascism in its nazified form and the futuro-fascism of Marinetti. Ideologically at least (if not in practice), nazism attacked capitalism's subjection of all value to the law of exchange; anti-Semitism and spurious anticapitalism necessarily coincide here. Futurism, meanwhile, celebrates precisely the process of exchange that nazism sought to foreclose. By confronting this passage from Marinetti with the anti-Semitic ideology and practice of nazism, one begins to uncover the paradoxes of the Nazi closure. That which has been burned (capital/the body) can itself still be exchanged and capitalized by the Japanese Futurist. In destroying the embodiment of the commodity, one creates yet another commodity, instigates yet another exchange. The vitality of exchange, as Marinetti makes clear, transcends even the moment of death, for these bodies serve as gunpowder to create more dead bodies, to serve in turn as gunpowder, to . . . ad infinitum. That which for the Nazi was the *Final* Solution was for Marinetti proof that no such finality is possible. Death is not the end point of commodification but its very modality; commodification is that murderous process that leaves no static, self-identical entity in its wake. In seeking to "murder" capital, the Nazi only became even more embroiled in the murderous logic of commodification itself.

The double bind of Nazi logic is replicated at the level of representation. The Jew represented not only the process of commodification and relativity of all values but also a broader logic of abstraction that involved, for example, abstraction in the arts—*Zivilisation* as opposed to *Kultur*. But in destroying this abstraction in the name of embodied values, the Nazi necessarily attacked a *body*, which represented that abstraction. The destruction of the representation of the abstract entails the destruction of *bodies* and thereby replicates the very process of abstraction itself. In terms of the opposition of abstraction and embodiment, nazism paradoxically attempted to destroy the abstract by destroying a body. Moreover, the Jew, as the *embodiment* of the *abstract*, was himself a scandal within the representational system that stigmatized him. In an ideological opposition of abstract and concrete, body and idea, that which bodied forth the idea (the Jew) necessarily deconstructed the supposed opposition. In burning the body, then, the Nazi did not simply rid himself of the negative term of an ideological opposition; he burned the contradictions of his own ideological system, the embodied abstract. The Jew had to die, not only because he *was* abstraction but also because he was *not*. The material trace of the body had to be sacrificed in order to identify the Jew completely with abstraction and immateriality; and yet once that body was disposed of, one had necessarily capitulated before the power of pure, disembodied abstraction. The opposition of abstraction and materiality itself became purely abstract.

It is, of course, somewhat disturbing to discuss something as "real" as the atrocities of nazism in terms of representation, and yet the historical aestheticization of politics makes it well-nigh impossible to discuss fascism in any other terms. The question one inevitably faces in dealing with fascism as an aestheticization of politics is the pertinence of the categories of the political and the aesthetic themselves: if, indeed, politics has been aestheticized, how is one to disentangle the aesthetic from the political in such a way as to define the process of aestheticization? It has been argued that the manifesto art of Marinetti serves as one exemplary instance of the scrambling of discursive codes, fusing the hyperbole of a polemic with the symbolism of an aestheticist tradition, insisting on the truth value of rationale discourse from within the protected, autonomous space of the aesthetic.[18] In this sense, at least, Marinetti does seem to exemplify the reconciliation of art and life that Bürger has used to define the avant-garde.

It is surprising, then, to find that in a thinker as radical as Marinetti, traditional discursive parameters are actually reaffirmed and reconstituted rather than demolished. The distinction between aesthetics and politics is *not* simply erased. Thus, in one of the manifestos most crucial to the development of the futurist aesthetic, "Destruction of Syntax—Imagination without Strings—Words in Freedom" of 1913, he writes: "My Technical Manifesto of Futurist Literature (11 May 1912), in which I invented *essential and synthetic lyricism, imagination without strings* and *words in freedom* deals exclusively with poetic inspiration. Philosophy, the exact sciences, politics, journalism, education, business, however much they seek synthetic forms of expression, will still need to use syntax and punctuation. I am obliged, for that matter, to use them myself in order to make myself clear to you" (*FM*, 95–96). Far from inaugurating a radical break with existing categories of theory and practice, the futurist manifesto sees itself as constrained to operate within those categories, to elaborate its grammatology from within a given syntax in order to destroy that syntax. The first casualty of the division of *synthetic* and *nonsynthetic* forms of expression, of course, is the poetic text of Marinetti, the text that effects the division. The recourse to a traditional syntactical arrangement in a manifesto that attacks that arrangement should not, however, be taken as a simple falling away from the radical demands of the manifesto itself as an exhortation. Marinetti seeks to undermine the formal criteria of his own utterance, as if to build into his own statement the inevitable process of anachronism, which he elsewhere celebrates as the dynamic of cultural systems. In a passage that ostensibly resigns itself to a division of discourse—one language for poetry, another for everyday affairs—that resignation is undercut by the use of a traditional syntax that denies the poetic status of the work itself. The manifesto—as an expository text and at the same time the archetypical futurist genre—serves to question the divisibility of the aesthetic and the political even at those moments when it provides for their dissociation.

It is not only the aesthetic that is reaffirmed and subverted in one and the same gesture. Marinetti insisted on a very similar division of discourses along traditional lines in his launching of futurism as a full-scale political movement. In the "Manifesto of the Italian Futurist Party," he launched futurism into the political sphere in the following terms:

The futurist political party which we are founding today and which we will organize after the war, will be clearly distinct from the futurist artistic movement. The latter will continue its work of rejuvenating and reinforcing the genius of Italy. The futurist artistic movement, the Avant Garde of the Italian artistic sensibility, is necessarily always in advance of the sensibility of the people. . . . The futurist political party, on the other hand, intuits the needs of the present and interprets exactly the consciousness of the entire race in its revolutionary hygienic development. All Italians will be able to belong to the futurist political party—men and women of every class and age—even if they reject certain literary and aesthetic concepts. (*SW*, 134–35)

Marinetti's articulation of the role of the political within the futurist project is interesting for the way in which it seems to carve up the futurist interventions into traditional categories of the political and the aesthetic. However, despite the attempts to divide futurism into an early "heroic," depoliticized period and a later political bastardization, the relationship of aesthetics to politics is not simply one of supersession, here. Politics does not replace aesthetics; the two coexist but do not necessarily coincide. The real degeneration of the radical futurist project consists less in the betrayal of an early, heroic aesthetic by a subsequent politics than in the apparent possibility of dividing up the two projects at all. The aesthetic serves now as an avant-garde to the political, its futurism a beacon to the presentism of the political party. There seems, at least in Marinetti's formulation, to be something intrinsically "presentist" in the pragmatics of the political, something that stands in the way of a completely futurist aestheticization of politics. The discursive distinction is being figured in specifically *temporal* terms.

If, as Poggioli argues, "the futurist moment is more or less present in all the avant-gardes" (p. 69), then the lack of collaboration between aesthetically and politically "progressive" groups—within or beyond Jameson's "anglo-American" context—should not come as any surprise. For what futurism seems to be saying about futurism (i.e., what the specific movement seems to be saying about the broader phenomenon) is that it is, in some sense, inimical to the political in any traditional sense. The dichotomy of Left and Right will therefore necessarily be deconstructed by any futurist politics, but this deconstruction of political oppositions has, paradoxically, traditionally served as the ideological underpinning of quite specifically rightist political formations. Marinetti urged upon us the recognition that the dissociation of aesthetics and politics need not necessarily lead—as it does, for example, in Poggioli's *Theory of the Avant-Garde*—to a resurrection of the aesthetics of autonomy. The most explicit in his articulation of the division of art and politics, Marinetti was at the same time the most forceful and effective in his linking of the two. The question of the aestheticization of politics might, therefore, be thought—in accordance with the terms of the futurist political manifesto—as a clash of futurity and presentism. In like terms, fascist modernism marks a crisis point within modernity itself, a crisis brought on not by the collapse of the modernist project but by the aporias of its own success. For once the imperative of innovation—the logic of modernity—has established itself, the temporal coordinates of modernity itself begin to collapse. The future becomes, as Poggioli implies, little more than the future of the present or, indeed, the future *in* the present: the future is always already encoded, according to a logic of innovation and negation, within the present of modernism.

Fascist modernism, in turn, responded to this threat of modernism's totalization and self-sublation: it inaugurated what has subsequently become the debate on postmodernism; for fascist modernism faced the challenge of a move "beyond" the modern that would not automatically reinscribe itself into the transgressive logic of modernism. The most vulgar—and indeed, the most "modern"—move beyond modernity would be the move beyond the "beyond" of modernity. This move ultimately, if inadvertently, results in a classicizing insistence upon transcendent, transhistorical values and aesthetic essence and might be exemplified in the bureaucratized kitsch of official Nazi art. In this case, the temporality of modernism is simply inverted: the imperative of innovation is replaced by a logic of restitution. All such art must necessarily be "anachronistic" because it continues to work within a temporal model of cultural development, which has simply been refunctioned as a process of return or a redemption. The temporal logic within which anachronism is thinkable has not been radically refuted.

The fascist modernism of Marinetti, however, acknowledged the complicity of the "postmodern beyond" of modernism with the transgressive logic of modernism itself, the implication of the "post" of "postmodernity" in the temporal ideology it sought to dislodge. In fact, Marinetti moved "beyond" modernism only by refusing to do so, by invoking and inhabiting modernism itself as one of those aesthetic possibilities made possible within the avant-garde "simultaneity of the radically disparate." To use Bürger's terms, institutional criticism becomes possible only by and through the system-immanent critique of the modernist gesture. What this means is that Marinetti operated at times within the modernist logic of negation and innovation and at times against it. Or rather, by working within it, by refusing to negate and rejuvenate it, he *necessarily* worked against it.

Perhaps this, finally, explains why we must repress the cultural impulse represented by futurism—because it is politically volatile and unpredictable; because, for example, Marinetti could invoke the modernist charge of plagiarism against the pretensions of fascist imperialism, but at one and the same time he could also invoke modernist notions of transgression to legitimate and aestheticize his own imperialistic project. It is in vain that criticism resists that aestheticization of politics that it has long sought to isolate in fascism, in vain that Benjamin proposes a politicization of aesthetics. From the perspective of a postmodern, postfascist critique, aesthetics and politics have already lost their taxonomic force. Criticism cannot contain but only escalate the aestheticization of politics in its vain theorization of fascist modernism. With fascist modernism we fear not the object of critique but its reemergence within the critical subject.

German Primitivism/Primitive Germany
The Case of Emil Nolde

Early in the summer of 1937, the most prominent Nazi painter, Adolf Ziegler, led the operation that removed all representatives of so-called degenerate art from the public museums of Germany. Many of the works were soon shown again in the Exhibition of Degenerate Art that opened in Munich, and they were later destroyed, sold (both domestically and abroad), or, most cynically, confiscated by Nazi leaders for their private collections. As was typical of the bureaucratic confusion that characterized the National Socialist dictatorship, there appears to have been no precise administrative guideline as to which works or which artists were to be judged contraband (one result of which was to augment the insecurity of the public, which, never sure of the legal limits, was pressured into a posture of vigilant self-censorship). Yet, according to one count,

sixteen thousand works of art—paintings, sculptures, drawings, and prints—by nearly 1400 different artists were gathered up [including] more than a hundred works by the sculptor Lehmbruck; between two and three hundred examples each of Dix, Grosz, and Corinth; between three and four hundred by Hofer, Pechstein, Barlach, Feininger, and Otto Mueller; more than four hundred Kokoschkas, five hundred Beckmanns, six hundred Schmidt-Rottluffs and Kirchners, seven hundred Heckels, and more than a thousand Noldes.[1]

Theda Shapiro numbers the confiscated works by Nolde at 1,052, making him presumably the artist most strongly persecuted, at least in this numerical sense, by the cultural policies of the fascist state.[2]

This sort of introduction to the case of Emil Nolde appears to set the stage for a heroic narrative of the modern artist martyred by the political dictatorship that denounced his work as degenerate as early as 1933 and, in 1941, issued an official prohibition on his engaging in any further painting. It is perhaps interesting to note that an East German encyclopedia, eager to highlight the antifascist pedigree of any major cultural figures, underscores this aspect of Nolde's biography, without, however, mentioning the other side of the story: his membership since the 1920s, long before it had become opportune, in the Nazi party (or rather, its corollary in Denmark to which his residency in northern Schleswig had been ceded under the terms of the Versailles Treaty).³ So the plot thickens, and the anticipated story of the beleaguered Modernist, glowing with the glory of aesthetic autonomy but hounded by the stooges of totalitarian evil, just will not do because there are villains of sorts on both sides of this barricade. The same Nolde whom the Nazis lumped together with other artists allegedly representing a putative "cultural bolshevism," corrupting liberalism, and a Jewish art market had himself long espoused a virulent cultural nationalism, was "exceptional in his racism," and articulated notions of regional authenticity arguably homologous to the "blood and soil" tenets of German fascist aesthetics (Shapiro, 114). Protesting the inclusion of his works in the Exhibition of Degenerate Art, Nolde wrote to the minister of propaganda, Joseph Goebbels, with the patriotic plea that "my art is German, strong, austere and sincere" (Shapiro, 212).

None of this historical information, of course, amounts to conclusive evidence for a judgment on Nolde's oeuvre or for a determination of the substance of a fascist aesthetic. One would certainly not want to proceed by accepting the Nazi position and then simply reversing it—that is, by arguing that because the Nazis opposed Nolde, his work *ergo* displays an anti-Nazi substance. One would thereby not only surrender any autonomous critical capacity but also would end up with unacceptable results in the cases of figures appropriated by the Fascist regime; the celebration of Dürer, Goethe, or Shakespeare tells us nothing about the aesthetic character of the works. Consider also the case of the author Oskar Maria Graf, whose writings, presumably because of their peasant coloration, were not consigned to the flames of the book burnings in May 1933 but who, on the basis of his own leftist sympathies, issued a public protest of his exclusion. Similarly, Nolde's protest that his works were included in the Munich exhibit has the status of any artist's self-judgment: it may have historical or biographical interest, but it is by no means binding for a serious aesthetic-theoretical consideration. In short, the Nazi condemnations exculpate Nolde as little as do his entreaties condemn him.

Similar caution is called for in the face of claims found in the larger, highly politicized aesthetic discussion of the 1930s. One could point to Georg Lukacs, arguing during his most socialist-realist period that expressionism represented an artistic corollary to fascism, a judgment the Communist obviously meant to be a denunciation.⁴ On the other hand, a minority position within the German Fascist camp briefly tried to claim expressionism positively as the genuine art form of the Nazi revolution (Lehmann-Haupt, 73). Yet these claims and counterclaims by no means cancel each other out. It would be very wrong to conclude that the plethora of incompatible political judgments on the same set of aesthetic objects, and on Nolde's work in particular, indicates that the relationship of politics to art is ultimately arbitrary and that art therefore basically stands outside of politics. For one is still faced with the magnetic attraction this art exercised on the political imagination, as well as the frequently volatile political character of the self-understanding of early twentieth-century artists and writers. To understand this connection—the attraction, repulsion, and resonance between Nolde's expressionism and German fascism—one must first renounce any simple solution, forgo the security of tendentious judgments, and presume that the political substance of a serious work of art is likely to be ambiguous and multivalent. With this methodological caveat in mind—particularly crucial given the sensationalism of the topic—one can turn to the specific construction of the artistic practice.

For the sake of this argument, I want to focus on Nolde's primitivism rather than on some other, perhaps equally constitutive element, such as his personal reclusiveness, his predilection for religious topics, or his use of color. For both the distance from and proximity to the fascist discourse on art are particularly prominent with regard to the issue of primitivism, a term that refers simultaneously to his exoticist interest in artifacts displayed in ethnographic museums, his cultural critique of modern civilization, and the ramifications of his journey to the South Seas in 1913–1914 on a mission sponsored by the imperial German colonial ministry. Most obviously, it was the integration of stylistic features apparently borrowed from encounters with non-European cultures that set him at odds with a fascist aesthetic compulsively concerned with European supremacy and racial purity. Writing in the *Völkische Beobachter* on 7 July 1933, the chief ideologue, Alfred Rosenberg, insisted that a "definitive ideal of beauty has ruled the artists of nordic origin. This powerful and natural ideal is nowhere more beautiful than in Hellas, but it prevails as well in Palma Vecchio, Giorgione and Botticelli, who painted decidedly Gretchen-like figures. This ideal appears in Holbein as it does in the image of Gudrun and Goethe's Dorothea. It rules the face of Pericles and the Rider of Bamberg." Against the background of this Western tradition, Rosenberg turned to Nolde (and to Karl Barlach); he at first conceded that "both artists undoubtedly display an explicit talent, a seascape by Nolde in the Kronprinzenpalais, for example, is strong and weighty. "Yet," he continued, "next to it are a few attempts at portraits: negroid, impious, raw, and lacking any genuine inner power."[5]

That Rosenberg was willing to put forward a minimally nuanced judgment is indicative of the fact that the internal fascist debate on expressionism had not yet been resolved. Therefore, Nolde, the regionalist painter of the maritime German North was treated as acceptable, but the Modernist Nolde, who, like other Expressionists as well as the Cubists—think of Picasso's *Demoiselles d'Avignon*—integrated a non-European iconography into his portraiture, was condemned. He stood beyond the pale of a racial aesthetic uniting Greek antiquity, the German Middle Ages, and the Italian Renaissance. His primitivism evidently amounted to a proscribed aesthetic miscegenation. It is paradoxical but not wholly unexpected that one can find Nolde himself elsewhere effectively concurring with a similar cultural racism, although tempered by more relativism than Rosenberg might have allowed:

In the long run, no race may be better or worse than another—all are equal before God—but they are different, very different, in their stage of development, their life, their customs, form, smell, and color, in all their internal characteristics, and it is not at all the intent of nature that they should mix. . . . Some people, and especially those who are already mixed, have a burning wish that everything—people, art, cultures—be mixed, whereby the human community of the earth would end up consisting of mixtures, bastards, and mulattoes. Of people with impure faces and negative characteristics. Some places in the tropics are frightening examples of complete race-mixing. The sweetness of sin is unconscientious. There is a striving for self-corruption.[6]

If this first version of primitivism entails direct appropriations of iconographic elements from non-European settings, a practice that both Rosenberg and Nolde programmatically condemn (even though Rosenberg accuses Nolde of engaging in it), a second, more sophisticated version evaluates the primitive positively as a more powerful and authentic vehicle of expressive representation. Now it is Nolde himself who is cast as the primitive, the prototype of a young, German art counterposed to an increasingly established and tame impressionism of French, which is to say excessively civilized, provenance. Commenting on his break with the Berlin Secession in 1910 when his *Pfingsten* was rejected, one of his strongest proponents, Max Sauerlandt contrasted Nolde's style with that of Max Slevogt: "While Slevogt's color plays the role of a means for an individualizing characterization and has become a vehicle for an illusionist depiction of reality in the idealizing sense of an impressionistic naturalism, Nolde's color has grown into a pure form of expression for emotional values, a 'hieroglyphics of sentiment.'"[7] The terms of Sauerlandt's prose set Slevogt as the paradigm of a post-Renaissance—and in this sense "modern"—metaphysics of a means/ends rationality, the subjectivity of bourgeois individuality, illusionist aesthetics, and the determinist materialism of an external, sensory perception. In contrast, Nolde is posed as both postmodern and more original; he goes beyond the logic of bourgeois culture by retrieving the archaic expressivity of a nonsubjective language of hieroglyphs.

This substantive primitivism transcends the obsolete representational aesthetics of the nineteenth century by returning to an origin of emotion, instinct, and power. Moreover, it is this constitutive primitivism that both precedes and explains Nolde's interest in Oceanic art:

The by no means ironic modern artist took these exotic grotesques, the artful masks of the South Seas, so seriously and was so profoundly moved by them because of the mystical power of sentiment that led to a stylistic heightening of expression far beyond any banal depiction of reality. He found here an essential stylistic element of his own art in a most naive and penetrating version. Like the anonymous carvers of the South Seas, he recognized that the mimic expression of the gesture or the facial features, when most intense, has something purely grotesque and is internally related to the rigor of a mask. (Sauerlandt, 80)

Consequently, Nolde's relation to the non-European material is by no means a matter of borrowing or "mixing," which—Sauerlandt was writing in 1933—might be denounced within the terms of fascist racism. On the contrary, Nolde, presented as the radical alternative to French cultural hegemony and the terms of liberal-bourgeois culture, discovers or rediscovers the terms of his own aesthetic in the antimimetic art of the islanders. Perhaps Sauerlandt was tilting his argument in order to make Nolde palatable to the new rulers; in any case, primitivism here ceases to be a geographical import inimical to European identity and instead turns out to be congruent with the German nationalist rejection of the impressionist canon, the fascist critique of civilization, and the Nietzschean call for a new barbarism.

An additional third dimension of Nolde's primitivism might be considered a combination of the other two, the encounter with the non-European world as a central component in the demolition of the terms of nineteenth-century liberalism. Yet where the Nazis denounced a putative influence of Oceanic or African art in racial terms, what is at stake now is the legacy of colonialism. European expansionism was always an internally contradictory project; although it drew its legitimation from an ideology of a civilizing mission, narratives of progress, and a "white man's burden" imagined to be a vehicle of benign improvement, the real experience of the colonizers vis-à-vis the overt or covert resistance of the colonized populations entailed practices of violence, domination, and inhumanity antithetical to the sometimes sanguine intentions and illusions with which they had set out. Whatever colonialism's impact may have been on its victims, the process of victimizing also transformed the colonists, rendering increasingly implausible the terms of bourgeois liberalism. In other words, in the wake of colonial violence, the ideals inherited from the Enlightenment and the French Revolution grew more and more intangible; thus, Hannah Arendt could argue that the brutality of the colonial administrations served as a proving ground for the inhumanity of the totalitarian regimes—fascism as colonialism come home.

The nexus of colonial politics and primitivist aesthetics is further complicated by a two-stage process of mediation. Modern artists, Cubists and Expressionists alike, first discovered works of non-European art in the metropolitan centers, especially, if not exclusively, in the various ethnographic museums that had been founded during the final third of the nineteenth century. Colonial artifacts were displayed as specimens of anthropological interest, and one can trace how painters like Nolde struggled to transform them from objects of scientific scrutiny into sources of artistic innovation. When Nolde asks, "Why are Indian, Chinese, and Javanese art still classified under science and anthropology?" a certain solidarity with the colonized cultures is evident, insofar as he ascribed to them an otherwise denied capacity for genuine aesthetic representation. Yet this anticolonial gesture turned out to be part of a dubious political agenda, a revaluation of the primitive as an alternative to a European civilization allegedly too rational, egalitarian, and feminized: "In the original, primitive state, it is not women and children who have a playful, ornamental desire but rather strong, manly men" (Nolde, *Jahre*, 177, 181). Here and elsewhere, Nolde defends the primitive art of the colonies as a vehicle with which to carry out an agenda of antiliberalism to rediscover the primitive in Europe, where "manly men," rather than women or, presumably, effeminate Impressionists, ought to be celebrated as the genuine creators of art.

Yet the anthropological collections themselves were not only displays, scientific or artistic; they were also institutions firmly rooted in the larger process of colonial expansionism, with all of the violence that entailed. Therefore, the artistic appropriation of primitive art, even if framed by an anticolonial and antiprogressivist gesture, was presumably implicated in some way in the colonial practices of domination. In Nolde's case, that complicity can be traced through a second stage in the reception of non-European artistic forms. After the initial encounter with ethnographic material, around the beginning of the second decade of the century (when he completed his paintings with the most explicitly exotic topics), he subsequently undertook a journey through Russia and the Far East to the German Pacific colonies. That the journey was sponsored by the colonial ministry as part of an effort to research the cause of the declining birthrate in the colonies—understood as an economic threat to the viability of the colonies—only makes more emphatic the connection between the politics of expansionism and primitivist aesthetics.

Facing colonialism, Nolde is horrified by its brutality (even though he patriotically reserves the strongest criticism for Germany's colonial competitors). Yet he also accepts colonialism and its destruction of the indigenous cultures as an inevitable fate, thereby subverting the possibility of an effective anticolonial critique: "'The law of the strong,' is a natural law, just like for animals and plants—this is the only comfort, if it is comfort at all, for us humans with our societies to protect animals, our humanist doctrines and our Christian faith of love."[8] The reality of colonialism is proof enough that humanism and all of the other illusions of the European nineteenth-century are pointless. Thus armed with an oppositional stance that declares itself helpless, the melancholy colonist easily slips into his preordained role: "Each of us was given a 'boy.' Young brown natives, Tulie and Matam, were ours" (Nolde, *Welt*, 58).

For all of Nolde's counterposing of primitive authenticity to civilizational veneer, for all of his explicit attacks on colonial practices, he participates in them with no apparent discomfort—not only in his prose or his behavior as a traveler but in the construction of the scene of painting itself. "When painting the natives became difficult, we showed the picture of the Kaiser of Germany and said, 'This big fellow Kaiser wants to see what you look like and that's why you are being painted.'" (Nolde, *Welt*, 106). Other strategies were available too: "I had my watercolors and painted; some of them soon noticed; others, frankly, did not. Near me lay my revolver with the safety off, and behind me stood my wife, covering my back with hers, also cocked. I have never worked in such a tense situation, but everything before my eyes was so beautiful, so splendid. As [we reembarked and] the ship once more started across the flat sea, the pages went from hand to hand and gave us so much joy" (Shapiro, 100).

As Nolde grew into the role of the colonist, his primitivist expressionism revealed itself to be an aestheticization of colonialism, transfiguring domination into a source of pleasure and an aesthetic justification of exploitation. Painting was implicated in what Renato Rosaldo has called imperialist nostalgia; Nolde prided himself on his contributions to the expedition while simultaneously regretting its results.[9] In the end, his solidarity with the victims of colonialism was displaced by a stronger solidarity with the agents of colonialism, even at the price of moving close to the sort of scientific rationality he had condemned in the ethnographic museums:

During my childhood years I had heard and read about Stanley and Livingstone, and I was later very interested in the adventurous polar journey of Fridtjof Nansen and the expeditions of his friend Knud Rasmussen too. I believed to have also contributed to genuine research with my many works, perhaps just a little when compared with the great scientific travellers, but something special and almost opposite. My vision had been "artistic" and alive, not "scientific" and photographic, like so much before. And such primitive types [Urtypen], as in my drawings of the natives of New Guinea, probably no longer exist. In our economically active, but modern civilizing age, everything original and essential disappears, never to return. Where are enclaves of primitive soil being preserved, with their people, their animals, their plants in an untouched primitive state, for the benefit of anthropology in the coming centuries or millennia? Few have the farsight to think of the human community [Gemeinschaft], nearly everyone thinks only about one's little, proper "me." (Nolde, Welt, 145)

Evidence like this pushes us toward a rather hypotactic argument: Nolde's painting derives centrally from a complex discourse of primitivism, which is a function of colonialism, which in turn is a crucial stage in the prehistory of fascism. Indeed, one might reorder the linkage more polemically by suggesting that the cultural ramifications of colonialism were transformed through the aesthetic practices of some wings of European modernism and thereby made available to the fascist hegemonies in the wake of World War I. Yet even if one were able to prove conclusively the individual claims within the larger concatenation, and despite the seductively compelling character of the full argument, it remains more suggestive than convincing because of its generalizing abstraction and because of the many counterexamples, where primitivism is located on trajectories toward nonfascist or antifascist positions (e.g., Carl Einstein's interest in African art or, for that matter, Picasso as the painter of Guernica). If colonialism was the necessary precondition or, better, the context of primitivism, primitivism contained too many multivalent potentials to be regarded as a self-evident term in a fascist aesthetic. If Nolde's primitivism fades into his fascism, it evidently has to do with the specific character of his primitivism, and a closer look is in order. For unless that specificity is clarified, the whole inquiry could be disqualified by the objection that Nolde's political affiliation remained thoroughly external to his artistic achievements.

Reexamining the last quoted statement, in which Nolde puts himself in a line with Stanley and Livingstone, one cannot help but be struck by the tension between Nolde's insistence on the difference between his own "artistic" and other "scientific" undertakings and, paradoxically, his inability to name that artistic difference. On the contrary, art, like science, is engaged in a project of preservation and collection, driven perhaps by a heroic resistance to the march of progress (which Nolde accepts as inevitable); but it remains a collection of objects that appear to have no validity except that they are otherwise disappearing, and that imminence of disappearing is probably the definition of the primitive. Because of a catastrophic historical vision—modernization will soon eradicate all authenticity—Nolde imagined himself at the penultimate moment, and the ensuing urgency forced him to rescue the material through depiction of the *Urtypen*. Thus, for all of Nolde's expressed contempt for the illusionist fictions of impressionism and naturalism, his painting always remained figurative. His reception of primitive art never led to the formal abstraction of the Cubists, nor did his expressionism take the decidedly allegorical turn characteristic of Beckmann. The primitive material remained primarily a matter of topicality: figurative representation of primitive objects.

Yet the objects are, after all, always primitive archetypes, never individuated subjects. Note how his professed admiration for the scientific and artistic project of collection finally flips over into a mysticism of community, counterposed to the egoism of individuality. Nolde's project seems stretched between the objects of collection and transcendent values, between reification and religion, with no intermediate dimension of formal rationality, secular sociability, or subjective practice. The islanders of his portraits are trapped in an ethnographic present where no change is possible. They are profoundly expressive but never active or nuanced, and, one is tempted to argue, the same erasure of history, the same proscription on innovation—formal or thematic—characterizes his paintings of noncolonial topics as well. This structure explains the power and the ambiguous politics of his oeuvre. The simultaneity of radical objectification, the compulsive preservation of the figure, and the overarching religiosity reproduces the amplification of commodity fetishism into the aesthetics of fascism: the meaningless world of sensory data forced, as it were, into meaning by a charismatic prophecy. Yet even if that prophecy remains unmediated and therefore becomes terroristic, the promise of redemption can still draw on utopian values; hence, the expressive beauty of the renditions.

The point, then, is not at all to suggest that Nolde's paintings ought to be treated as tendentious vehicles of a fascist message; Nolde may have believed that was the case in his letter to Goebbels, but he was evidently wrong. The whole question of fascist aesthetics has to be posed in a more interesting way. To be sure, there were other cases of crude propaganda, and the border between propaganda and serious aesthetic works may at times be blurred; but for Nolde's work, what is at stake is not the intentional meaning but a structural homology between his expressionist paradigm and the cultural ideological character of German fascism.

In *La peinture française (1905–1914) et "l'art negre,"* Jean Laude cogently presents the by-now standard account of a basic difference between the French and German reception of primitive art. For the Parisian Cubists, so the argument goes, African masks suggested new solutions to aesthetic problems and contributed to a rationalization of form within the emergence of modern art; for the German Expressionists, on the other hand, non-European material was of interest as a topic marked as authentic, religious, and redemptive, documentation of a cultural alternative to a desiccated modernity. Overstated in this fashion, the dichotomy ignores a good deal: expressive values in cubism, formal innovation within expressionism, and counterexamples within each camp. The account depends, moreover, on familiar clichés regarding French rationality and German irrationalism.[10]

Nevertheless, for some of the German Expressionists, and perhaps most emphatically for Nolde, the association of primitivism and irrationalism did hold, as described by Carl Einstein:

Geographical exoticism may have depended a bit on the expansive imperialism of the prewar era, but it also entailed a protest against excessive sophistication, derisively pointing out its opponent's alexandrianism. The more the biological basis, the breadth of human existence, expanded, the more important did the primitive become, who had preserved forgotten links and stages of human behavior. For the European yearning for past times and distant places, the primitive cultures became the frequently abused means to expand history backwards. This tendency also grew out of the struggle against the rational enlightenment; reason was regarded as only a final tip, resting on the predominant forces of dream, instinct, and emotion; among the primitives one could still find mythical cultures, the hierarchy of the instincts oppressed in Europe, the tyranny of dream and ecstatic ritual.[11]

Einstein himself tended toward an account much closer to that of the Cubists, that is, a rational appropriation of the innovative aesthetic models evident in African and Oceanic art. Still, his characterization of the expressionist stance is not only a critical caricature. On the contrary, it foregrounds the internally contradictory character of Noldean primitivism: simultaneously an emancipatory search for a greater range of experience and a regressive flight from the Enlightenment, leading to a desire for "hierarchy" and "tyranny."

These two components in a expressionist primitivism—the dynamic expansion of expressivity and a search for a static order—indicate how, in Nolde's particular case, modern aesthetics could take a right turn and end up with considerable fascist sympathy. For National Socialism could be misunderstood as a path out of stultifying modernity and back to an authentic culture of genuine experience; that is, the search for a primitive alternative to modern culture that had led Nolde to New Guinea might have appeared to come to a conclusion when Germany was redefined as

the locus of the better primitives, and Nolde was clearly eager to participate in that illusion. It was, moreover, an illusion that had a long history
and considerable currency; one finds it in the young Paul de Man's readings of Ernst Jünger (representing mythical Germany versus a rational
and psychological France), just as it remains the structuring aspect in
Laude's differentiation between expressionism and cubism.[12] In the latter
case, ironically, the attack on expressionist irrationalism, clearly made
with the best of political intentions, falls into the trap of adopting the
cardinal point of the right-wing agenda: Germany as the bulwark of the
antienlightenment and the counterrevolution.

To make this simple equation on the political level (Germany as the
locus of irrationalism) or on the aesthetic level (German expressionism
as mystical, regressive, or irrational) is a grave error that obscures the
complexities of the real situations. For early-twentieth-century Germany
was a modern society, just as German expressionism was part and parcel
of modern European art. The point is not German irrationality, political
or aesthetic, but rather that the ideological assertion of this German
specificity was (and apparently remains) a crucial component of the German and European cultural and political discourse.

Irrationality as a refusal of knowledge or an intentional restriction of
cognitive capacity is necessarily regressive and a retreat from the best of
the Enlightenment legacy, the admonition to use one's mind: *aude sapere*.
In this sense, fascism was indeed irrational, for example, in its restrictive
policy on aesthetic experience, which is itself a form of knowledge. Yet
the critique of reason that is driven by a genuine discontent with characteristics of modern society—alienated labor, the loss of community, the
domination of nature—can hardly be denounced as fascist. On the contrary, that agenda is central to an enlightenment that can scrutinize itself
critically, a self-reflective enlightenment. The internal contradictions of
fascism included the ideological mobilization of these discontents and
their simultaneous repression, insofar as fascist policy entailed both a
flaunted irrational antimodernism and an aggressively forced modernization. Nolde found himself trapped in this dialectic: the German primitivist enamored of the illusion of a primitive Germany. That fascist
Germany was not a return to primitive origins indicates the false consciousness inherent in his political solution. If his artistic solution, historically, was not untouched by that political context, it has a more important ramification as well. For the authenticity of his works depends
on an expressive value and experiential authenticity, categories that shed
a critical light on the modern world and goals that remain the sine qua
non of an emancipated society.

W A L T E R   A .   S T R A U S S

Gottfried Benn

A Double Life in Uninhabitable Regions

A poet's anti-Semitism, a poet's eugenics, may therefore connect him not only with the
debased pragmatism of men he ought to despise, but with a crude primitivism
of the sort he would never regard as relevant to his own more refined progress.
—Frank Kermode, *The Sense of an Ending*

O ne of the central questions that gives unity to the present volume might be phrased: Is there—can there be—a fascist aesthetic? This question revolves around a problem: Since we think, rightly, that the word *fascist* refers to a political orientation embodied in a specific sovereign state, must we understand the question as referring to a specific doctrine sponsored or imposed by the state, or can we take the liberty—since aesthetics tends to originate in the temperament or conviction of the individual (regardless of groups or movements or state policy)—of speaking of an aesthetic that is the characteristic creative mark of an individual or a group, acting more or less independently? The problem is quite knotty because we tend to speak of these two aspects of the arts (the individual side and the official side) in somewhat loose semantic terms. For this reason, it might be best at the outset to clarify the present author's perspective on the problem.

It *is* possible to speak of a fascist aesthetic. A better (but more cumbersome) term would be an aesthetic oriented toward an irrational and generally elitist and usually racist ideology, which tends to seduce certain types of mind that are drawn to intellectualized formulations of irrational impulses or phenomena, invariably occurring in situations of historical disorientation, threats of major social and political reorientations that drive Fascist aesthetes and ideologues in the direction of political and artistically reactionary positions. Nevertheless, such reactionary positions often have all of the earmarks of revolutionary objectives because they always gravitate toward affirmations of the "primal" or the "primitive" in human experience. We have known such individuals in the Western world since the outbreak of the French Revolution (their patron saint is Jean-Jacques Rousseau and in some cases his funhouse-mirror parody, the Marquis de Sade); and we have seen a certain type of dandy, or aesthete—with increasing frequency since the 1840s, notably in the form of the *décadent*—as the bourgeoisie triumphed more and more decisively in England, France, and Germany: from Baudelaire to d'Annunzio, from Fichte to T. S. Eliot, to mention only a few of the substantial list of names. Quite obviously, there are also significant differences among them, and it would be preposterous to put them all in the same compartment. Since art and aesthetics arise out of individual needs and preoccupations, the history of the arts may be described as a series of variants on previous models of art, which are in this way modified by historical and political circumstances and elaborated in an ambience of freedom (total or limited). Nevertheless, it is possible—particularly in the case of certain thinkers, poets, and prose artists of the period from approximately 1885 to 1914—to state a number of general characteristics that are "pregnant" with fascism because they are likely to be used in the interests of a fascist regime as soon as it comes to power. These criteria are the following:

1. A belief (better: a mystique) centered on the destiny of the nation or the race. In Germany, the trademark of this creed always involves the romantic notion of the *Volk* and may easily become extended to the Nordic race, or the white race, or the Aryans.
2. Closely allied with this is the cult of leadership and the discipline and submission demanded of and for the *Volk* to bring about an ideal or utopian community of superior spiritual and physical beings.
3. This whole cultic irrationality glorifies sacrifice and heroism; underneath it there throbs an eroticism or ecstasy that is darkly connected with death and the will-to-death, even though officially and publicly the rhetoric and techniques of eugenics and of future vitality are always exalted.

All of these, or a combination of most of these, constitute the core of fascist aesthetic ideology. This is what many analysts and ideologues have described as the transformation of politics into aesthetics: the insistence on embellishing these irrational and ultraromantic notions with such key terms as beauty, strength, discipline, nobility, pride, sovereignty. In this respect fascist doctrine and rhetoric differ cardinally from the totalitarian aesthetics of the political left, which tends to stress the straightforward "utility" of the arts for the purposes of the state. But in actuality, the aesthetics of all totalitarianism have this in common: they are strictly propagandistic, dogmatic, and utilitarian; and in our time they are not easily distinguishable because they quickly become bureaucratized by individuals having no real culture but merely a petit-bourgeois mentality concerning the *uses* of the arts (i.e., there is no real difference here between Hitler, Goebbels, Goering, Stalin, Zhdanov, and Mussolini). Thus, the totalitarian doctrines of art quickly seek and find the lowest common denominator: monumental and chauvinistic art and music and architecture, lower-middle-class "realism," melodrama in the service of propaganda—in brief: kitsch.[1] Thus, the misbegotten individual notions of aesthetics—even of fascist aesthetics—are quickly converted into art for the masses and manipulated as state doctrine.

Yet this means that the one major area in which fascist art can and does reach the masses is the cinema, which lends itself superbly to propaganda because it is mass-produced and therefore can be utilized to indoctrinate the multitude directly. The main example that must be cited here is the work of Leni Riefenstahl, especially *The Triumph of the Will* (1935) and possibly *Olympia* (1937), genuine works of art by virtue of their visual power; *Triumph of the Will* communicates perfectly, in the shape of a contrived documentary, the hypnosis—hysteria—ecstasy of the Nazi party congress of 1934, in the interest of ensnaring the mind and emotions of the viewer by means of a super-Wagnerian staged cult-spectacle. It can easily be seen that these Nazi-sponsored works by a superb creative intelligence working in the medium of the cinema exemplify most of the criteria set forth above as the distinguishing traits of a fascist aesthetic.[2]

A totalitarian regime always manifests its inherent Manichaeanism in matters of restrictions placed on the arts: there is a kind of art that is either forbidden or, if it exists in the museums or libraries or concert halls, is suppressed or hidden away or else outright destroyed; its historical existence is, so to speak, negated. In its place some suitable version of pseudo-art, or kitsch, is enthroned. The Nazis carried this to insane extremes; *entartete Kunst*—degenerate art—was the term proposed by Goebbels, and the Nazis, in typical fashion, carried this atrocious farce to the point of organizing an exhibit of "degenerate art" in Munich during the summer of 1937, with appropriate descriptive panels and placards ridiculing and slandering the works and the artists (mainly Expressionists and Cubists).[3]

Because of the extreme tension between the official requirements imposed on the arts and the individual sensibility, it is impossible to separate the artist's biography and his (mis)fortunes from the public arena in which he is not only visible but under scrutiny, even surveillance. Those artists who were expelled (i.e., Jews and anti-Nazis) continued to work in exile; others chose to stay, either out of approval of the regime or for the sake of sheer opportunism; still others misread the signs and found themselves before long personae non gratae. The last group, with some justification, were later to designate this situation as "inner exile"; or if they read the signs more or less correctly, as Ernst Jünger did, they withdrew into solitude and into various forms of escapism that might enable them to look upon the Nazis (preferably from a distance) with elitist contempt. Most of them lapsed into silence or near-silence, finding ways to evade or to protect themselves against continued attacks (which would have resulted in expulsion or worse). Yet the author with whom this essay is concerned, Gottfried Benn, presents a particularly curious and exasperating case because he failed to see the vulgarity and brutality of the National Socialists while endorsing the new regime, only to fall into disgrace very quickly because of his expressionistic affiliations. Benn illustrates only too well the dilemma of the historically detached and "unpolitical" artist in a setting of political hooliganism. It may be instructive (and ultimately mystifying) to consider why such a lucid mind as Benn's fell victim to a colossal political misjudgment.

II. *Kunst und Macht*: The Lyre and the Sword

In the essay "Lebensweg eines Intellektualisten" (The Way of an Intellectualist [1934]),[4] we find the following paragraph, in which Benn is discussing the crisis of Western civilization:

The botanists throw light on our situation in a truly new way by means of a very remarkable discovery: artificially bred plants are tougher, more vital, more resistant against damage, in other words: more capable of heredity than natural ones; breeding, injection of knowledge, insertion of the spirit [*Geist*] into the natural process consolidates the hereditary substance, strengthens the species, creates something biologically positive—no question of decline, enfeeblement, degeneration, all those moral concepts which the bourgeois associate with the word breeding [*Züchtung*]; but on the contrary: interruption of degeneration, sustenance of things that otherwise would be doomed to extinction. This is obviously the expression of a universal law, which is drawing nearer to us, and this age which speaks of blood and soil will become an age of eugenics, of form and of heightened spirit, an intellectualistic age, that is to say, something specifically European, probably important from an anthropological point of view within the scope of our knowledge. Condensation of vitality, the ascent of the West might be just around the corner, and the people [*Volk*] will assume the kind of leadership which offers the clearest account of this law. (IV, 58–59)

The entire paragraph can be used as a study in misorientation and finally as a showpiece of Germanic irrational idealism. The key concept with which Benn's argument begins lies in the favorite and heavily loaded words *Zucht* and *Züchtung*, which one may begin by translating as "breeding" and "discipline"; but it really ends up by meaning "eugenics."[5] Here the language parallels that of the Nazi party ideologues, such as Alfred Rosenberg and Joseph Goebbels (and of course Hitler himself), on the purification of the race (for Benn it is more frequently a question of the Caucasian race rather than the "Aryan" fabrications of the party). All of this is fortified by notions of mutation and reinforced by the intervention of the intellect, and the vision that emerges from such fantasies as "blood and soil" finally envisages the reversal of degeneration. In effect, it claims to be an anthropological revolution pointing toward a new *volkisch* utopia of form, style, and spirit: the ascent of the West and the new vitalism are within reach, to refute Spengler's dire predictions.

Benn is not being dishonest here; he is as blind as only an "intellectualist" can be when it comes to political hoodlums endowed with a gift for organization and for rhetoric (and supported by a large arsenal of firearms and a still vaster arsenal of violence). What kind of intellectualist is this, anyway? Here is Benn's own definition: "Intellectualism means simply: to think, and there is nothing that obliges thinking to halt before anything, with the one proviso inherent in thought itself and which has to do with those who are weak thinkers. Intellectualism means: finding no other way out of the world except to turn the world into concepts, to cleanse the world and oneself by means of concepts" (IV, 57). Benn's intellectualism is thus exclusively a matter of abstractions. There is nothing intellectually wrong with that, but there is implicit in it a moral defect because intellectualism is not related nor accountable to anything outside itself: it is *pure* thought. In Benn's case, this purified abstractionism is paralleled by a conviction that poetry ought to be equally uncontaminated: it must be and must remain a formalistic art.

Thus, we run headlong into the question of expressionism. Since 1912 Benn had acknowledged himself to be a member of the expressionist movement (which he tended to regard as a German variant of all of the modernist (i.e., antinaturalistic) tendencies in all of the arts); and in 1933 he was under the naive impression that expressionism might become the official artistic doctrine of the Third Reich. He failed to see that his vision of *Rasse und Kunst* and *Kunst und Macht* (race and art, art and power) was already pregnant (perhaps unintentionally) with what was to be translated and utilized by the Nazis in the form of racism and propaganda and violence; the Nazi regime *appeared* to tolerate the Expressionists at the beginning but lost no time in condemning them as degenerate.[6]

Anyone who was familiar with the artistic and stylistic rebellion known as expressionism would have had to be a bit uneasy about joining a set of political gangsters. Benn's poetry was hardly the kind of patriotic exhilaration they were looking for. His finest early poems speak of decay and ugliness, frequently in clinical terms; or else they escape—in the fashion of Baudelaire—to distant climates. Here is a poem written in the late 1920s that at first glance may look like the kind of critique of the Western world welcomed by the Nazis, but on closer scrutiny it turns out to be a rejection of life itself in favor of the artifice of form. It is not one of Benn's most important poems, but it illustrates excellently the weariness and morbidity of the early works and the insistence on transcendence through art:

> Life—what a vulgar delusion
> Dream fit for striplings and slaves,
> But you, of a family that's ancient,
> Of a race at the end of its days,
>
> What can you have in view?
> Yet one more surge of elation,
> A moment's exchange of station
> Between the world and you?
>
> Still looking for woman and man?
> Had you not all preparation
> Faith and its slow separation
> And dissolution then?
>
> Form alone is faith and is deed.
> Only what hands first mold,
> Taken then from hands that enfold:
> Statues salvage the seed.
>
> (Trans. Robert M. Browning, PEP, 213)[7]

The poem is full of disdain and anguish. If life is a base form of madness, if it is a dream for the immature and the lowly, if nothing is to be expected from it other than the certainty of final destruction, and if the only genuine activity is the creation of forms, which transforms sensuous experience into the only seed-harvest there can be—if all of this is really so, then no regime concerned with renewal and conquest—fascist or nonfascist—is likely to be impressed by these sentiments, not to mention the earlier grim poems by Benn that sing of the human body's disintegration and the rottenness of the flesh and the deceptiveness of "reality." For some reason, this astute clinician, this disciple of lucidity (who also carried within him a heavy accumulation of irrationality) did not see the light in 1933 and 1934, or else he chose to be blind. Attacks against Benn the poet came very quickly from less gifted and more opportunistic writers within the Nazi orbit, and by 1936, on his fiftieth birthday and on the occasion of the publication of his collected poems, he ran into severe difficulties. By 1938 he was officially silenced by the cultural despots of the Third Reich (IV, 103–4); by that time he had already withdrawn from public sight to serve as an army medical officer, and any poetry that he wrote between 1936 and 1945 was either privately published (only 20 poems) or kept in the drawer until the end of the war.

It is, in a way, a sad but also grotesque story of foolishness and blindness on Benn's part. The degree of misdirection is clearly in evidence in

Benn's wrongheaded attempt to defend expressionism as a creed in an article published on 5 November 1933. This is also one of the low points in Benn's misreading of the future of Germany. I want to quote the entire first paragraph of the essay to show the aesthetic mist that Benn's enthusiasm manages to generate:

The degree of interest manifested by the leadership of the new Germany on the subject of the arts is extraordinary. Their leading minds are concerned with the question whether Barlach and Nolde should be counted among the foremost German painters, whether there can be and must be such a thing as a heroic literature to serve as surveillants and regulators of theater playbills and concert programs, so as to bring to the virtually daily attention of a public the fact that art is a first-priority concern of the State. The enormous biological instinct for racial fulfillment, which governs the entire movement, does not prevent the State from losing sight of this one idea, despite the whirlpool of internal and external politics, of social and pedagogical problems, which beset it. This instinct senses that here is the center of gravity of the whole historical movement: art in Germany, art not as achievement, but as a fundamental fact of metaphysical Being, which determines the future, so as to *be* the German Reich, and more: the white race, its Nordic component; *that* is Germany's gift, its voice, its appeal to the declining and endangered Western culture; and for us it is a new sign for that which Europe until today has not been able to see or does not wish to see: how strenuously this movement has assumed duties, accepted responsibility, met the challenge of immense spiritual struggles, struggles which it is fighting for the whole continent, in whose center it is located. (I, 240)

One is tempted to ask, "How is it possible for the greatest lyric talent of the time writing in the German language to be so self-deluded?" When one considers that, after all, this poet had produced a sizable quantity of poetry of the first order, remarkable for its mastery of the language, full of brilliant verbal and syntactical formulations—a genuine poetic voice, harsh, angry, negative but precise and uncompromising, a poet to be measured against his illustrious precursors Hofmannsthal, George, Trakl, and Rilke; when one considers all of those factors, how can one avoid shaking one's head in disbelief or even shaking one's fist in rage? All of the clichés of the New Order are there: leadership, spirit, heroism, biological instinct, racial fulfillment, white race, Nordic, spiritual struggles, center of universality (and a slight hint of martyrdom). And yet the essay is also a plea (here Benn surely protests too much!) that expressionism, which has been the new international wave in art (and thus includes cubism, futurism, atonality) should serve as the German spearhead of at least the white race: "Spirit and deed, transcendental realism of heroic nihilism—these marks of the individualistic tragic era cannot be eradicated completely, but as a whole they can be embedded more within a happy fortune; the individual can become more closed, less Faustian, than commonly understood. Amalgamation of the architecture of the South and the lyricism of the Northern mists . . ." (I, 255). The union of the aesthetic of North and South: Greece, Italy, France, and Germany fused into one great synthesis—one can see that Benn's vision is not at all narrowly Germanic but that the Third Reich was to provide the fusion. But imagine a Reichsminister or a Gauleiter reading this!

Troubles for Benn were not slow to arrive. Here too we find another mixture of the ridiculous and the brutal. A lesser poet, bearing the somewhat memorable name of Borries von Munchhausen, accused Benn of being a Jew because, according to him, Benn was a Jewish name occurring regularly in Jewish names (such as, for example, Moses ben Maimon, Rabbi ben Ezra, etc.). Benn then felt compelled to defend himself on racial grounds, to prove his Aryan pedigree; he felt he had to prove that he came of good Lutheran stock on his father's side and of good French stock (*reine romanische Rasse,* "pure Roman stock," [IV, 24]) on his mother's side. There was another attack, from a different quarter, namely, the National Socialist League of Physicians (*Ärztebund*) claiming that his mother's maiden name, Jequier, was nothing more than the good Jewish name Jacob. This whole apologia of Benn's would be ludicrous if it weren't also pathetic, and it is necessary in this context to note that there is no evidence of any anti-Semitism on Benn's part. Benn had, as one might surmise, many friends among the Expressionists who were Jewish; for him the question of the New Germany bore some relation to the white race and to Europe but not to theories of Aryanism. It also must be said, in all honesty, that Benn did not carry his concerns beyond the point of friendship with his Jewish friends; he did not seem to care particularly about the virulent racism of the Nazis. Like many other well-intentioned but naive German artists, such as Furtwängler, Benn merely tried to help his friends. But as an "unpolitical" (which really in Germany meant "supra-political") artist, he felt that the new regime was either rational enough or sufficiently interested in the arts to make his attitude valid and significant.

The real challenge to Benn came from Klaus Mann, the son of Thomas Mann and author of the revealing but somewhat untrustworthy roman à clef *Mephisto* (1937). Klaus Mann had emigrated immediately after Hitler's accession to power; the letter he wrote from southern France as early as 9 May 1933 (quoted by Benn in his revealing autobiographical essay "Doppelleben" [A Double Life] of 1949 [IV, 69–172]) berates Benn for being the *only* German author who did not resign from the Prussian Academy of the Arts, for remaining loyal to the regime. "It seems to be nowadays an almost unconditional law that too great a sympathy with the irrational leads to a political reactionary position if you don't remain devilishly vigilant" (IV, 76). Benn replied to the letter *publicly* over the radio two weeks later, and the text was published in the *Deutsche Allgemeine Zeitung* on the 25 May 1933. Benn angrily retorted, "There you sit in your spas and rebuke us for collaborating with the renovation of a State" (IV, 243). He defended himself strenuously against the charges of barbarity and then flew off into one of his favorite anthropological fantasies: "it is a question of the emergence of a new biological type; history is mutating, and a people wishes to discipline (*züchten*) itself" and "what is at stake is not at all a form of government [!], but a new vision of the birth of man, perhaps it's an ancient vision, perhaps it is the last grandiose conception of the white race, probably it is one of the most grandiose realizations of the World Spirit itself" (IV, 243). Finally, he insists that "*I do not belong to the Party, nor do I have any connection with its leaders, nor am I expecting a new set of friends.* It is my fanatical purity, of which your letter speaks so admiringly, my purity of thought and feeling, which impels me to make this declaration" (IV, 247). The claim of "fanatical purity" when applied to the collaboration with the Nazis sounds sordid today; however, Benn's insistence that he was not acting from opportunism is surely correct.

But there is another, somewhat comic sequel to all of this. Klaus Mann wrote his *Mephisto* in 1937 and sent it to Benn "with a charming and melancholy dedication" (IV, 88). The novel contains a thumbnail sketch of Benn, whom Mann chose to call Benjamin [!] Pelz, "whose obscure rhapsodic verse had delighted to the point of ecstasy a generation of young people who were now for the most part outlaws," who was the vice-president of the above-mentioned Academy of the Arts, and who had become an outright arriviste. The portrait is frankly malicious; Benn was gracious enough to speak of "poetic license" on the part of Klaus Mann. Actually, Mann has Pelz utter monstrosities like this: "Our beloved Fuhrer is dragging us toward the shades of darkness and everlasting nothingness. How can we poets, we who have a special affinity for darkness and the lower depths, not admire him? It is absolutely no exaggeration to call our Fuhrer godlike. He is the god of the Underworld . . . etc."[8] This is patently unfair[9] to Benn and has the effect in *Mephisto* of turning Pelz/ Benn into a sort of comic-strip maniac. Benn does not comment on this but simply defends himself against the charges of opportunism. Then he concludes, rather lamely: "I am convinced that many of those who at that time remained behind and continued to carry on their work, acted that way because they hoped to be able to safeguard the places for those who had emigrated, in order to give them back to them after their return" (IV, 89). How is one to reconcile this with the disdainful statements about the emigrants who sit around in the foreign spas, and is it really possible to make such a claim seriously about the Jewish [10] or other non-Aryan or political exiles unless Benn assumed that the Nazi regime would collapse soon? This is certainly not the last of the many contradictions in Benn's thought and writings with which we shall be concerned.

Benn's "fanatical purity" was soon to be violated. In 1936 the official newspaper of the S.S., *Das Schwarze Korps*, brutally attacked him in the vilest language, so common to Nazi hate sheets (particularly *Der Stürmer*); the diatribes and insults continued through November of that year. Benn had to remove five poems from his *Ausgewählte Gedichte* (*Selected Poems*) of 1936 for a new expurgated edition. A glimmer of the truth can be detected in a letter written on 11 May 1936:

What is the real meaning of this attack in its brutal, in its truly inexplicable intensity? It can only mean: this is *art*, and if this is what art is and the German public may regard it as art, then it is not the sort of art which we want to propagate or presumably "breed" here, the Nordic, victorious kind, which is still to come. There must be some kind of impetus from the Rosenberg quarter behind all this, similar to the attacks on Barlach, Hindemith, etc.[11]

In a way, it was the end of Benn's involvement in the Nazi "renewal," and the silencing of Benn only made matters official. At this point, Benn might have had the choice of voluntary exile and continuation of his poetic activity; but since he was also a practicing physician, he chose silence. This silence took the most aristocratic form (as Benn put it) of "inner" exile": the medical corps of the German army. The other half of Benn's "double life" begins here.

III. *Artistik*

In 1937, just before he was blacklisted as a writer, he had written, in the short prose work "Weinhaus Wolf":

It is quite obvious—all the great minds among the white nations have felt only one inner task, namely the creative camouflaging of their nihilism. This fundamental tendency, interwoven with the most varied trends of the ages . . . was the basic element in all their works. . . . On every page, in every chapter, in every stroke of the pencil or brush they approach it with ambiguous questioning, with turns of the most exquisitely groping, equivocal character. Not for an instant are they unaware of the essential nature of their own inner creative substance. It is the abyss, the void, the unsolvable, the cold, the inhuman element. (III, 146–47; PEP, 49)

After his return to poetry in the remaining decade of his life, the question of Benn's nihilism and his formalism becomes even more prominent than before, and it is necessary here to include a brief discussion of the topic. One might say that one man's nihilism can easily become the same man's National Socialism and finally his own version of entropy. Above all, Benn's nihilism is riddled from the very start by contradictions.

The term *nihilism*, like the term *decadence*, lacks clear definition; it probably is not satisfactorily definable. Think of Turgenev and Dostoevsky, on the one hand, or of Nietzsche and the Dadaists or of Benn and Beckett: Could one establish any common denominator other than the fact that, historically speaking, the word has been in restricted general use for a hundred years and has been more frequently used since the end of World War II? Does it mean (a) the conviction that there is, metaphysically speaking, no intelligible reality at all, (b) that some kind of belief in the ultimate nothingness is the authentic basis of modern consciousness, or (c) that the term designates something lost or no longer believed in—an absence? Benn usually refers to nihilism as the condition of the modern world since the collapse of "humanistic" values after the end of the eighteenth century—after Goethe—and reaching its apex in Nietzsche, followed by a long and in some ways productive aftermath in the twentieth century, especially in the various rebellions against "realism" in *all* modern art.[12] But if this nihilism is based on an absence of values (or an unwillingness to accept the mainly bourgeois, mainly democratic values), is it really possible then to rally to the National Socialists or to any other political movement (Benn had refused to endorse the pro-Communist tendencies of many of his Expressionist friends) in the expectation of a total renewal of Western man? When Benn talks of "discipline" or "eugenics" and "Volk" between 1933 and 1934, he is conveniently putting his nihilism on the back burner, only to move it forward again after being disgraced and disgruntled from 1936 to 1946. One can take as an example his remarks on 7 April 1934 celebrating his illustrious predecessor, Stefan George, in many respects Benn's true poetic model, alienated from the modern world with the same disdainful and icy passion. Benn asks in this *hommage* what it is that enables the "human" (*das Menschliche*) to overcome the demonic.

How does the human vanquish the daemonic, not man seen as absolute but contemporary man, historical man, who no longer lives in the age of monotheistic conjurations, but in the post-Nietzschean age, no longer in the age of pacifistic restraints and individualistic ecstasies of refinement, but in the age of storms of steel and imperial horizons. The answer is the following: Western contemporary man conquers the daemonic by means of form, his daemonism is form, his magic is technical construction, his universal glacial doctrine[13] says: creation is the need for form, man is a cry for expression, the State is the first step in that direction, art is the second step, other steps do not exist. (I, 472–73)

Once more, what is missing in this aesthetic argument is the clarification of what the demonic really is (presumably the modern world of decadence), why this demonism is recognizable as nihilistic (rather than as evil or destructive), and how form and nothing but form, without relation to matter, without *context*, can overcome it. There seems to be no question of even a relationship to ideas or a confrontation with ideas. First, the state, then art-as-form. Form thus becomes the triumph of spirit over nihilism (which is now seen as an interregnum) in the new order of discipline and eugenics.

And then comes a final, lyrical, and often beautiful expression of the late negativism of Benn's final poems, after the new "storms of steel" (Ernst Jünger's phrase) had engulfed Germany and finally been dispelled by alien storms of steel. Perhaps these late poems, despite or because of their technical excellence, ring less true than Benn's earlier poems, which were full of anger and despair concerning the human condition and therefore, it could be argued, not altogether withdrawn from human events. By 1946, Benn's flight from history is total (and therefore inexcusable); what has now restored the nihilism is a deepened pessimism and a painful melancholia, which once more touches us—in spite of ourselves, it must be admitted. Benn's unwillingness to come to grips with *his own* historical experience makes much of his later work ring hollow; the flight from the genuine atrocities he saw (but refused to witness) virtually necessitate an aggravated emphasis in his work on art for art's sake, or *Artistik*, and on an intransigent formalism. If form, or style, is "superior" to truth (as he claimed), where does this leave either form or truth? After all, is it not the complex interrelation of form and style to truth (or at least the quest for truth) that matters in the arts? A corollary of this is a kind of aesthetic narcissism, which intensifies the isolation and the sadness of the poet. Consider the following poem of 1950:

Morality of the Artist

Only in words may you show yourself
those that are clearly placed within forms;
whoever is thus beset by torments
must be silent concerning his humanity.

You must consume yourself alone—
make sure no one sees it,
and do not let anyone complain
of what happens to you so secretly.

You bear your own sins,
you bear your own blood,
you may only proclaim to yourself
upon whom your mortality rests.[14]

This anguished silence is at the opposite pole from Nietzsche, whom Benn regarded as the patron saint of nihilism. But Nietzsche at least confronted nihilism, as he understood it, with all of his formidable arsenal of thought and words (for example, his quarrel with the "nihilistic" Wagner, which was also a struggle with the nihilistic components within himself). It is as though Benn had taken for his motto a dictum of Nietzsche that was more of a starting point than a fixed position or conclusion for Nietzsche: "We have art in order not to die of reality." For Nietzsche this statement never suggested a retreat into *l'art pour l'art* but a dialectical battle between reality and art, fought on Apollonian–Dionysian ground with the weapons of critical, psychological, and ethical polemics. In that sense, Nietzsche was a witness of his time, albeit a biased and tormented one, who lived on the knife edge between sanity and madness, because that was the only way.

IV. A Valediction Forbidding Mourning

"Wir alle leben etwas anderes, als wir sind" (We all live something different from what we are; II, 212). This quotation from Benn's novella *Der Ptolemaer* (The Ptolemean, 1947) sounds like a Sartrean formulation of *mauvaise foi*, but as a matter of fact it describes not only artists like Gottfried Benn but all who choose, or are compelled to choose, "inner exile." Benn makes an interesting counterpoise to Heidegger, who remained blind and unwilling (unable?) to brush the scales from his eyes. So Benn, after 1937, felt obliged to retreat into the *Heimat* of his own pessimism—not to the *Volk* and its regeneration, as he had erroneously envisaged four years earlier—and to console himself with formalism and "absolute" poetry. But as Michael Hamburger, referring to Benn's expressed desire to be remembered for only the few perfectly wrought poems that a poet is able to create, observed correctly, "he has written the six or eight consummate poems which he believes to be all a contemporary poet can achieve; and more often than not, even his failures have the fascination of uninhabitable regions." [15]

According to one commentator, Benn "had no political instincts, no political passions, and compared to Brecht he appears naive, uninformed, and out of touch" (PEP, xxvi). Still, when Benn was once more free to recover his poetic voice and his artistic authority after 1948, he gave us an exquisite poetic capitulation, impressively articulated in the last two sections of "Epilog 1949":

IV

There is a garden which I see sometimes,
east of the Oder, where the plains are wide,

a ditch, a bridge, and I stand
by lilac bushes, blue, and ready for bliss.

There is a boy, for whom I sometimes grieve
who by the pond entered the reeds and the waves,
not yet flowed the stream, before which I now shudder,
which first had a name like happiness, and then forgetfulness.

There is a saying I've often remembered,
which says it all, since it offers you no promise—
I have woven it also into this book,
it was on a gravestone: "tu sais"—you know.

V

The many things which, deeply sealed,
you carry through your life, within youself, alone,
and never revealed, even in conversation,
nor permitted to enter either letters or glances,

those silent things, good ones and bad ones,
things suffered, within which you move,
those you can resolve only in that sphere
in which you die and, ending, are resurrected.[16]

The mood is a poignant nostalgia for youth, for home: the setting is a garden, a childhood paradise, recalled before the stream of life brought along bitterness, suffering, and inner resignation; and Benn here voices the only conclusion possible in the terms of his narrow and unhistorical moral/aesthetic situation: death and resurrection (one assumes: through inwardness, through art), this painfully won wisdom: "'tu sais'—you know."[17] Such is the testament of a man who buried his knowledge deeply within himself and who therefore remains the poet of burning glaciers sealed with the depths of his ego. "Kann keine Trauer sein" is the title of one of his last poems: No mourning possible. No mourning, no sentimentality, only melancholy and *tristesse*.

Yet we must return once more to the question that we posed at the beginning: "Can there be a fascist aesthetic?" In a sense, yes—on an official plane only; in a sense, no—if no individual freedom of expression is permitted. Totalitarianism takes no risks in the arts and is threatened by criticism and humor: by the individual sensibility. A genuine artist, one who follows out his inner law and sensibility, will only end up by withdrawing, or in silence; that is to say, by disappearing as a creative being.

REED WAY DASENBROCK

Wyndham Lewis's Fascist Imagination and the Fiction of Paranoia

To discuss the literature of fascism or to ask whether a work of literature is fascist is already to be engaged in a problematic—because interdisciplinary—endeavor; for of course, fascism did not present itself as a literary movement but as a movement within society and politics. Though no single definition of fascism is universally accepted, nonetheless fascism has a specificity and a concreteness for a historian, as a movement that began in Italy in the period immediately after 1918 and convulsed Europe until 1945, that it obviously does not have for a literary critic. Fascism made things happen, made many terrible things happen, and for a historian it can be identified with those events relatively straightforwardly. For an intellectual historian or a student of political philosophy, fascism is perhaps more nebulous than for the historian; but nonetheless, fascist ideology is a well-defined object of study even if the relation between fascist ideology and fascist practice is not invariant.

Much less precision obtains in the study of fascist literature. What does it mean to be a Fascist writer? Is it enough to be a Fascist and to be a writer or must a demonstrable relation exist between one's fascism and one's writing? Even less precision obtains when considering writers from countries that were never ruled or dominated by fascism because they never had to make the hard choices forced on writers from Fascist or occupied countries. It is well known that many of the century's important English-language writers, including W. B. Yeats, T. S. Eliot, D. H. Lawrence, Wyndham Lewis, and Ezra Pound, were sympathetic to fascist movements at points in their careers. But does this make their work fascist in tendency? Debate has raged over this in the case of all of these writers, and one of the reasons we have not been able to reach closure in this debate is that its terms have been largely borrowed from other disciplines, from frames of intellectual reference other than the study of literature.

The contours of the discussion about any of these writers' involvement with fascism tends to begin with history and biography. What did the writer do, if anything, in the sphere of practical politics? And at what point and in what context did he express profascist sympathies? How did his personal history overlap with the public history of fascism? (One can safely use the masculine pronoun here since profascist sympathies are found exclusively among male Modernists.) There are writers for whom the overlap is so considerable that such an approach seems to resolve the question. For example, Ezra Pound's broadcasts on Rome Radio in favor of the Axis throughout World War II clearly tied his own life and career to the fascist cause. Yet a writer such as T. S. Eliot, less prone to public statements and more circumspect when he did make them, doesn't seem as amenable to a biographical-historical focus on what was said and done when and where. Nor is such an approach equally workable at all points: there is much more consensus about Pound's commitment to fascism from 1938 to 1945 than there is for the post-1945 period, when his connection to public events was necessarily less close. It is apparent, to move to another controversial figure, that the German philosopher Martin Heidegger supported the Nazi regime publicly during the Nazi conquest of power, for he served as rector of Freiburg University from 1933 to 1934 and made a number of pro-Nazi statements at that point. But he didn't remain rector for very long, so how is one to interpret the retreat from public pro-Nazi activity after 1934 and the long silence after 1945? Here a focus on public events seems less useful, as we are asking about private attitudes and beliefs.

Where the methods of the historian and biographer fall short, we tend to turn to ideas, to the study of political ideology. If Heidegger didn't publicly comment on nazism after 1945 but his ideas seem largely congruent with nazism, then we may conclude that his distance from official nazism cannot or should not be read ironically. Although studies of the politics of Anglo-American modernism long seemed to rest content with the biographical and historical,[1] they have recently begun to take this ideological turn. The advantage of this shift seems clear: the study of a writer's ideology can take a step back from the welter of conflicting detail found in any biography to look for the pattern of ideas behind the biographical and historical details. Robert Casillo, for example, claims in his recent study of Pound that he has found "the deep structure of the Poundian worldview."[2] Given his belief in such a deep structure, he can argue for a continuity in attitudes and beliefs between the active Fascist Pound of the 1930s and the 1940s and the less politically active but—in

Casillo's presentation—equally Fascist Pound of the 1950s and 1960s. Thus, where biography and an external connection with public history fail us, the impulse has been to turn to ideology, to see a writer's life and work as embodying a consistent and presumably knowable ideology.

Now, the study of the history and ideology of fascism is absolutely indispensable for anyone interested in the study of Fascist writers and the question of fascist literature. But an approach to fascism in literature based strictly on approaches from other disciplines will come up short, I think. Moreover, there is no reason that literary critics should be simply importers in this intellectual economy. Fascism had a style, an aesthetic, a repertoire of imaginative themes, as well as an ideology and a history; and this aesthetic style was of considerable importance for fascism, as Walter Benjamin expressed in his famous remark that "the logical result of Fascism is the introduction of aesthetics into political life."[3] So we need to move beyond an approach based exclusively on questions of political history and ideology. If we are to call a piece of writing fascist, it should betray a fascist imagination as well as fascist ideology and a role in the public history of fascism.

What I hope to show in the essay that follows is how these three kinds of investigations, the historical/biographical, the ideological/philosophical, and the imaginative/thematic, can complement each other in the investigation of fascism in literature.[4] My example is Wyndham Lewis's novel, *The Revenge for Love*, and I will argue that a description of *The Revenge for Love* based on the externals of historical context and ideology misses perhaps what is most distinctively fascist about Lewis's novel. But I want to close by asking a different question. What have we said when we have called a work of literature fascist? Sartre said long ago that "nobody can suppose for a moment that it is possible to write a good novel in praise of anti-Semitism,"[5] and this belief that a great work of art could not be written in defense of evil ideas has controlled much of the discussion of the politics of Anglo-American modernism. Defenders of Pound, Lewis, and others have sought to separate the work from the politics, arguing in effect that because it was great art it could not be in defense of evil ideas. Critics of this approach have reversed the argument but accepted the dichotomy, arguing that it was not great art because it was in defense of evil ideas. But only a philosopher such as Sartre would approach literature so relentlessly in terms of its ideas, its intellectual content. An approach to fascist literature based on how it works rather than on what propositions it argues for seems to me to redraw the picture slightly but significantly. And I want to close by sketching what that new picture looks like.

Wyndham Lewis's novel *The Revenge of Love* was published in May

1937, ten months after the outbreak of the Spanish civil war.[6] The plot of the novel involves gunrunning into Spain, and the first and the last of the novel's seven parts are set in Spain and on the French–Spanish border. Lewis is not generally a widely studied writer, despite the praise of his work by Yeats, Pound, Eliot, and other influential friends and allies; but *The Revenge for Love* remains one of Lewis's most widely read and most widely available novels, the only novel by Lewis available in Britain and the United States continuously since its reprinting in both countries in 1952. And the reason the novel has had so much attention paid to it, at least relative to Lewis's other works, is simple—its Spanish setting. The Spanish civil war was, of course, a central event for a whole generation of artists and intellectuals in France, Britain, and the United States as well as, of course, in Spain itself. Many writers were in Spain and wrote about it. Auden's "Spain," Malraux's *L'Espoir*, Orwell's *Homage to Catalonia*, and Hemingway's *For Whom the Bell Tolls* are only the most famous of these works; memoirs, biographies, and studies of the foreigners involved in the Spanish civil war continued to be produced a full half-century after the end of the conflict. If, as has been estimated, one book has been written about every one hundred Puritans resident in New England in 1650, making them the most intensely studied society ever, I would guess foreigners involved in the Spanish civil war would run a very close second.

This is the context in which *The Revenge for Love* has had a broader currency than Lewis's other works, but there are a number of ironies attendant upon this—for *The Revenge for Love* is not a Spanish civil war novel at all. The novel was written in 1934 and 1935 and was sent to the publishers in January 1936, well before the outbreak of the civil war in July, and it was only because of a prolonged dispute with the publisher over the "obscenity" of the novel's language that publication was held up until 1937. So though Lewis clearly did intend the novel to refer to a concrete sociopolitical reality, the Spain of the Lerroux governments from 1933 to 1935, that reality was irretrievably transformed by the time the novel was published. The novel was immediately read and has continued to be read as if Lewis intended to write about the Spain of the civil war. The cover blurbs of both the American and British paperback editions of the novel refer to it straightforwardly as a Spanish civil war novel, and it continues to be discussed in the context of the civil war.[7]

So there is an easy way to fit Lewis's novel into history, but such a fitting involves rewriting the novel, ignoring what is distinctively Lewisian about the novel: that he would write a political novel about Spain and finish it before the civil war. This is in miniature the fate of all attempts to read the relation of Lewis to fascism in biographical and historical terms. The relationship is always complex, never univocal. A novel published in 1937 deeply critical of Communist involvement in Spain—such as *The Revenge for Love* is and was at the time—is inevitably taken as profascist, pro-Franco; but its completion before the outbreak of hostilities makes any such reading an anachronistic imposition of meaning. Likewise, in 1931, Lewis published *Hitler*, a collection of journalistic pieces on Hitler and the Nazi movement written in 1930 on a visit to Germany. The publication of this book is one of the facts helping to position Lewis as "that lonely old volcano of the right," as Auden called him in the 1930s.[8] Both Right and Left read Lewis as endorsing Hitler in such a book; Ezra Pound, in particular, kept praising Lewis for his early "discovery" of Hitler. But a reading of *Hitler* shows how far Lewis from being a supporter of nazism in the way Pound was of Italian fascism. What it shows him to be is an utterly inept interpreter of German politics: Hitler's anti-Semitism is described as something endemic in the German character but nothing out of the ordinary; his warmongering is also read ironically, and Hitler is called "a man of peace." As Fredric Jameson has pointed out, "This is very different from the hero-worshipping tones with which Pound salutes Mussolini's 'genius.'"[9] In the most perceptive discussion of the book, Jameson has put his finger on what was wrong in the reception of *Hitler*: "Most discussions of the book (which is generally passed over in embarrassed silence) have centered on the false problem of whether, on the strength of this misguided assessment of Hitler before he came to power, Lewis is to be thought of as a fascist or fascist sympathizer" (*Fables*, 183). I'm not sure that this is a false problem, but it is the wrong question to ask of a book such as *Hitler* because it assumes a consistency of historical stance not found in such a book. Lewis wasn't endorsing (or criticizing) Hitler or Nazism; he was trying to do something else, so one cannot drag an endorsement (or critique) out of him.

Jameson has his finger on the problem here, but his solution creates a new problem in turn. After arguing that Lewis's opinion of Hitler—the connection of biography with history—is not the key issue, Jameson argues that "what is essential from our point of view is that *Hitler* is informed by *all* the ideological positions which will remain constant to the very end of Lewis' life: those fundamental themes do not change, even if his view of Hitler did" (*Fables*, 183). And this is precisely the turn from history to political thought, from historiography to the study of ideology, that we have already traced. If inconsistency is found at the level of practical engagement with political life, then consistency is sought at the more abstract level of ideology. Jameson easily finds that consistency in what he elsewhere, in *Fables of Aggression*, calls Lewis's "implacable lifelong opposition to Marxism" (p. 18). Discussing *Hitler*, he sees the key as

Lewis's identification with fascism as an opposite to communism: "The figural value of fascism as a reaction is determined by the more central position of Communism, against which the anticapitalist posture of protofascism (of which Lewis approved) must always be understood" (*Fables*, 184). And though Jameson is usually identified with a more sophisticated post-Althusserian notion of ideology and though he explicitly distinguishes his concept of ideology from "a labelling operation" (p. 12), what he means by ideology here is nothing more than the old-fashioned notion of ideology as a conscious political perspective, and what he is engaged in is precisely "a labelling operation." But there is a serious problem with this attempt to find in Lewis's opposition to communism an ideological consistency underneath the bewildering variety of his concrete political stands. Jameson attempts to define Lewis's ideological position primarily by reference to Lewis's works of fiction, which means that he ignores Lewis's own attempt to clarify his ideological position in numerous works of nonfiction. The key text here is undoubtedly Lewis's massive work published in 1926, *The Art of Being Ruled*, a book that Jameson cites only once in passing, even getting the date of publication incorrect. Any attempt to define the center of Lewis's political ideology as a proto-fascist rejection of communism makes little sense of this complex book.

If Lewis is implacably opposed to anything in *The Art of Being Ruled*, it is the contemporary liberal society in which he lives, not a socialist alternative. In fact, Lewis consistently praises the Soviet Union in *The Art of Being Ruled* as providing a challenge to the bourgeois order and at one point states that "in the abstract I believe the Sovietic system to be the best." [10] The reason for this preference is important if unusual: he did not consider the Soviet Union or the communist system to be more democratic or more egalitarian. He had none of the illusions about communism that persisted so long among Western intellectuals. His preference was because he felt that the Russian dictators were more honest about their dictatorial position. They didn't hide behind the pretense of "serving the people" in the way contemporary Western politicians did; instead, they exercised their power in a straightforward way. This is the context in which Lewis praised Leninist Russia as a superior alternative to the liberal democracies of the West. But Leninist Russia was not the only alternative he endorsed for this reason; just a few sentences below the one I have quoted, Lewis declares that "for anglo-saxon countries as they are constituted today some modified form of fascism would probably be best" (pp. 320–21), and the chapter in which these two passages are contained is called "Fascism as an Alternative."

Jameson ignores this chapter—as he ignores the entire book—but other critics anxious to find a consistently fascist ideology in Lewis's work have seized upon these few sentences of this chapter as the key to Lewis's political position in *The Art of Being Ruled.*[11] But how can they be the key when they are contradicted by so much else in the book? Only someone who had decided in advance what Lewis's ideology must be would find this chapter the real point of a four-hundred-page book; on the other hand, it must be taken into account, for to ignore these passages would also be to decide in advance what Lewis's position must be.

How do we explain such ideological inconsistencies in a work dedicated to political theory? Again, by paying careful attention to how the book works as well as what it says. Jameson was correct in suggesting that no position on Hitler was to be found in *Hitler*; Lewis didn't seem to have a concrete political position in writing the book. But Jameson's search of an ideological position is vulnerable to the same critique: Lewis isn't advancing a consistent ideological position in his works, and the reason for this is given in the title of the book. *The Art of Being Ruled* is about being ruled, not ruling. Lewis is not attempting to design an ideal society or even to improve this one; what he is attempting to do is provide us with a survival guide, an art of being ruled, for the modern liberal democracies he criticizes so severely. What this means is that Lewis is developing in *The Art of Being Ruled* not a consistent ideology but a complex critique of ideology.[12]

What is most surprising about *The Art of Being Ruled*, if one approaches it thinking Lewis is a Fascist ideologue, is that much of *The Art of Being Ruled* is a detailed exposition of socialism. Large sections are also devoted to accounts of how feminism and the increasing prominence of homosexuality are changing contemporary society. Lewis does not necessarily endorse any of these movements, but he does not overtly attack them either, and all of these are given much more space than fascism. Lewis never spells out the logic organizing his massive study, but there is one. Thus, there is a consistency to *The Art of Being Ruled* even if that consistency does not lead to a consistent political perspective. In Lewis's presentation, contemporary society was increasingly defined by the presence of a number of different "wars": most obviously, the nation wars of the recently concluded Great War but also what Lewis called the "class-war," the "sex-war," and the "age-war." Society was increasingly being differentiated and divided on generational lines as well as class and gender lines, and identity in modern society was increasingly conferred on people according to where they stood in terms of these various wars. These wars have increasingly mesmerized our perceptions, according to Lewis, until we think that a great deal is at stake in these wars and we buy into the ideologies sustaining them. What occupies Lewis's attention in *The Art of Being Ruled* are these ideologies: socialism is the ideology of the class-war, feminism (and, in a sense, homosexuality) provide the sex-war with its ideological support, and the age-war is sustained by the cult of the child and other phenomena Lewis analyzes in *The Art of Being Ruled*. Lewis does not wish to attack (or endorse) any of these ideologies as much as wants us to stop and ask why it is that these wars or social conflicts have become so intense at this point in our history. For Lewis's deepest suspicion was that something is behind these wars. These conflicts are essentially bogus, to use one of Lewis's favorite Americanisms. What is going on behind the scenes is a fundamental centralization of power, making us, even though we are convinced of our complete freedom, more homogenized and controlled than ever before. The modern world is a kind of puppet show, and we are naive children thinking the puppets are real, ignoring the puppet masters pulling the strings, pulling our strings. The four wars and their concomitant ideologies are designed to make us not notice the fundamental changes and the fundamental concentration of power going on behind the scenes.

Thus, we misread Lewis if we take his endorsement of Leninist Russia and Fascist Italy as an endorsement of the ideology of communism and fascism. We would, in any case, be faced with the problem of which one he really endorsed, given the differences between the two ideological systems. We would have to create an ideological consistency where none existed. But Lewis isn't endorsing the ideology of either society; what he is endorsing is their attitudes toward ideology, what he saw as their franker admission that power, not ideology, was their concern. What he likes is the willingness of the puppet masters in Russia and Italy to reveal themselves, to admit that they are rulers.

So Lewis had no intention of advancing a fixed point of view, a fixed ideological position, in *The Art of Being Ruled*. Jameson is surely incorrect to declare an opposition to Marxism as this unwobbling pivot, and his search for such a pivot seems further from his own declared Marxist perspective than Lewis's own view is. What Lewis wants to do instead is to create a theater in which his readers come to be suspicious of all ideologies and to question all fixed points of view. He wants us not to think the puppets are real and are fighting over something important but to ask who is the puppet master and how is he trying to dupe us through the show. Lewis is, of course, the puppet master of his world, so he would be being inconsistent and untrue to what he hopes to accomplish if he were to deliver a fixed position and set ideology in the world of his text. *The Art of Being Ruled* is a kind of training course in becoming a suspicious member of the ruled class: Lewis wants his readers never to take anything at face value, and this includes what he gives us.

Lewis created exactly the same kind of theater in his novels. The themes of Lewis's fiction had been caught up in this play of illusion and reality from the beginning: His first novel, *Mrs. Dukes' Million*, a "potboiler" he wrote at the beginning of his career (though not published until 1977), is a novel about an "actor's gang" controlled by a mysterious Persian, Raza Khan. The gang swindles a poor woman out of an inherited fortune she is unaware of by impersonating her and staging a gigantic masquerade. But the chief actors then betray Raza Khan and escape from him through more disguises and masquerades. Acting, disguises, false appearances, conspiracies—these are the material out of which Lewis constituted many of his plots. Readers of Lewis have concerned themselves more with the intellectual frameworks of his fiction than with this plot machinery, but this emphasis has been largely misplaced. For Lewis wrote intellectual fiction in the sense that his novels are full of ideas, but he is not advancing a set of ideas in any of his novels as much as examining what happens as those ideas go into action in the laboratory of real life. Even where one finds an echo of the nonfiction works in the fiction, as one often does, that is no particular warrant for seeing this as Lewis's "real" perspective, given that the notion of a fixed perspective is one of the things Lewis wants to challenge. It is not that an ideology is being advanced by Lewis in his novels, as much as that the relation between life and ideology is being interrogated. And that is why Jameson has to misread the fiction and ignore the nonfiction in order to come up with the fixed ideological position he sees Lewis as advocating.

Everything that has been discussed for the past several pages could be the prelude to a grand clearing of Lewis of the common charge that he was a Fascist sympathizer. For if a consistent support of fascist political regimes cannot be discerned, as Jameson points out, and if a consistently fascist ideology cannot be discerned either, despite Jameson's attempt to discern one, then can any connection be drawn between Lewis and fascism at all? Derrida, in his attempt to defend his friend Paul de Man from the charge of supporting fascism, analogously stresses de Man's "heterogeneity," the difficulty of coming up with a consistent position from his wartime journalism.[13] But though Lewis is, I think, the only one of the Anglo-American Modernists whose engagement with fascism has been over, not underestimated, that is not the line of argument I am engaged in here. What I would like to suggest is that Lewis's deepest engagement with fascism is on the level of imagination and plot (the kinds of stories he tells), not on the level of ideology or practical politics (what he abstractly or concretely advocates).

What is crucial here is the plot machinery, the way Lewis constructs his narratives, and it is *The Revenge for Love* that reveals the political implications of this way of writing most clearly. The original title for *The Revenge for Love* was "False Bottoms," changed only at the insistence of the publisher, who also demanded considerable changes in the language of the novel. But Lewis had far more on his mind than sexual innuendo in titling his novel "False Bottoms." The world on display in the novel is full of false bottoms of various kinds. The plot turns on a Communist conspiracy to run guns across the border into Spain. The masterminds of the gunrunning had previously organized a racket involving art forgery in London, and one of the funniest scenes in the novel is one in which the not very skilled painter Victor Stamp puts his foot through a fake Van Gogh self-portrait (bandaged ear and all) that he gives up on. Despite this, the gunrunners Abershaw and O'Hara recruit Stamp for their gun-running scheme. Wishing to distract the attention of the Spanish away from themselves, they had earlier perfected the faking of Stamp's signature, and then they forge various documents implicating Stamp as the real mastermind of the conspiracy. Passing these on to the Spanish authorities, they send Victor across the border in a car full of fake recesses. Thinking the car full of guns, Victor kills a member of the Guardia Civil in an attempt to escape arrest. Then he discovers that the false compartments were themselves false: he was carrying nothing but bricks. The conspiracy had a false bottom to it, just as the car did; and the false bottoms have tragic consequences, as the novel ends with Victor and his wife Margot dead and his fellow hoodwinked conspirator, Percy Hardcaster, back in a Spanish jail.

Thus, the politics of the play of illusion and reality with which *The Art of Being Ruled* is concerned are also central to *The Revenge for Love*. The novel's title might be how not to be ruled, and Victor Stamp's passive acceptance of surfaces, his willingness to go along with Abershaw and O'Hara and not ask too many questions, dooms him. He is altogether too willing to be ruled. If surfaces are appearances, if apparent reality has false bottoms concealed within it, then one had best try to discover those false bottoms instead of taking things at face value. It helps to know if one is running guns or bricks across a border, and this is essentially—if more abstractly—Lewis's point in *The Art of Being Ruled* as well.

But how does one do this? How do the ruled ever find out what the rulers are up to if the rulers are so systematically misleading and never say what they are up to? How could Victor Stamp have avoided his fate? Lewis's answer—at least, in *The Revenge for Love*—is not terribly hopeful. For there are two characters who see something of the machinery of deception that destroys Victor, and they offer two different paths to knowledge. The first is Percy Hardcaster, the Communist agitator who is the novel's protagonist. The reason he knows that the world is a sham, full of false appearances manufactured behind the scenes, is that he is one of the manufacturers. One way out of the position of being ruled is to aspire to rule. This is, in short, the program prescribed for the working classes by socialism, and Percy, as a member of the working class who has become a professional Communist, embodies this. The novel begins with Percy in prison in Spain for his political activities, but the political prisoners in jail, Percy included, are not powerless even though they are in jail. The first false bottom in the novel, in fact, is in Percy's lunch hamper, in which Percy's friends outside the jail smuggle in newspapers and information.

And just as Lewis's critique of ideology resembles the Marxist critique, so too does Percy's understanding of reality resemble Lewis's. (Percy is in fact Wyndham Lewis's first name, a name he disliked, so there is simultaneously an identification and a rejection in his choice of this name for his protagonist.) Percy has a fundamentally conspiratorial understanding of power and a sense that victory goes to whoever controls the appearance of reality, so upon his return to England, he blithely tells what he knows are complete lies about his mistreatment in Spain, lies whose importance he dismisses as atrocity propaganda. He also willingly joins in the gunrunning scheme, though he is not informed about the part of the scheme implicating Victor as the chief gunrunner. Thus, Percy represents one obvious option for the ruled: the road to power, the path of joining the rulers in their plots and cabals.

The other character who sees some of what destroys Victor is Victor's wife, Margot. Margot, though in many ways a weak character like Victor, nonetheless has a good eye for the places where appearance and reality don't quite fit together. It is she who discovers that Abershaw and O'Hara have learned to forge Victor's signature perfectly, and it is she who keeps wondering why they would do this. She mistrusts where Victor trusts, and she is also the one who discovers that the place Victor was supposed to deliver his "guns" was surrounded by police. If Percy represents the option for the ruled to try to become rulers, Margot represents the option for the ruled to try to be more perceptive members of the ruled class. Though her preferred reading is Ruskin and Virginia Woolf, she is the one character in the novel who seems to have absorbed Lewis's point, in *The Art of Being Ruled*, about the necessity of remaining vigilant about the machinations of the ruler.

Unfortunately, neither approach works, and both characters are destroyed just as surely as Victor is. Percy's mistake was being partway in but not the whole way: he knew some of the conspiracy but not all. And this is, of course, the problem with the pursuit of power, particularly conspiratorial power. Conspirators may also be conspired against, and there is no way to know who might be conspiring against you. Percy should have learned this lesson in the Spanish prison in Part 1, for the "false bottom" containing information about the time of his escape reached Percy only after it had been discovered by the prison warder. He countered Percy's conspiracy with one of his own. He waited outside the prison until Percy had escaped and then calmly killed the other prison guard, who was helping Percy escape, and shot Percy's leg off. But Percy never learns this elemental fact about conspiracy, and he is duped at the end by Abershaw and O'Hara just as he was in the beginning by the prison warder. Percy has thought of himself as a puppet master creating reality and has never understood that others may, in the same spirit, be trying to fool and manipulate him. It is therefore perfectly appropriate that Percy would end the novel where he began, in a Spanish prison.

Percy may get what he deserves, but Margot clearly doesn't. She and Victor escape the trap set for him only to die in the Pyrennees trying to cross the border back to safety in France. And the lesson contained in her death is just as important: it is not enough to unmask power and be aware of its operation. Power's coerciveness is not lessened for those who are aware of it, even though power always—and here Lewis comes close to Gramsci—works hard to disguise its own operation.

Each of these characters shows how Lewis has revised the vision of *The Art of Being Ruled* in a significant respect. If, for Lewis in 1926, both fascism and communism were systems of government superior to liberal democracy because of their comparative lack of dishonesty, by the time of *The Revenge for Love*, Lewis felt that communism had become at least as systematically dishonest as liberal democracy. Here Lewis is again prescient, as his imaginative prewar portrayal of Percy Hardcaster disseminating atrocity propaganda anticipates the criticisms made by Orwell and others about the deliberate inaccuracy of communist propaganda about the civil war.[14] But there is no corresponding revision of what he had said in 1926 about fascism, surely revealed by this point to be as systematically dishonest as communism and for many of the same reasons. Does Lewis's reallocation of communism from the ranks of the truth-tellers to those of the dishonest leave fascism standing alone as the preferred alternative? There is no explicit support in *The Revenge for Love* for such a reading, and it does depend upon assuming a consistency between *The Art of Being Ruled* and *The Revenge for Love* on every point where there is not an explicit inconsistency. Yet the question remains: has Lewis turned here into an ideologue, a defender of one position at least by virtue of attacking every other?

To ask this is to ask Lewis to situate—as we might say today—his own writing. He claims to know that there is more than meets the eye; he is the one aware of the puppet masters pulling strings. And this, in the world of *The Revenge for Love*, puts him in the position of Margot, who joins no conspiracies but can sense their presence in a way others cannot. The ineffectiveness of Margot's insight makes us question the effectiveness of Lewis's. What's the point of pointing out the puppet master if he still goes on pulling the strings? What is the political effect of political writing that, in effect, offers a critique of all political action?

This is precisely where *The Revenge for Love* intersects most closely with the imaginative themes of fascism. Lewis's work, from *The Art of Being Ruled* to *The Revenge for Love*, is both a critique of ideology and a critique of any political action based on ideology. Because, like the Marxist critique of ideology, Lewis could see the flaws of other ideological understandings of reality, and because, unlike the Marxists, Lewis had no "true ideology" or "science" of politics to supplant the others, Lewis was left in the position of Margot, perceptive about political events but unable to engage in any action to change those events. This brings him close to the Fascists' contempt for the ordinary political process and their desire to go beyond those ordinary forms and work through extra-parliamentary means. Fascism succeeded in those countries where a substantial percentage of the population had something like Lewis's disgust for the flaws in democratic machinery, and one of the keys to fascism's success was its ability to present itself not just as an alternative to liberal politics but as an alternative to politics itself. In *The Art of Being Ruled* and *The Revenge for Love*, Lewis accepts the political landscape as all there is but presents no hope for working within it, and this is close to an endorsement of—or at least offers support for—the extrapolitical politics of fascism.[15]

The reason for Lewis's critique of ordinary politics also brings him close to fascism. Ordinary politics didn't matter because the real decisions were being made elsewhere. Political life was a gigantic false bottom. Lewis's entire body of work can be said to be a fiction of paranoia, a fiction in which suspicions about other people's motives and even about their authentic existence is both encouraged and generally confirmed. And clearly a comparable paranoia is central to the fascist worldview, to the fascist way of imagining the world, particularly to its Nazi variant. The fascist vision of the world runs something like this: "We the nation are fundamentally sound, fundamentally to be trusted, but our strength is sapped, our institutions are corrupted by the secret machinations of others." Italian fascism received a tremendous boost from the Italian perception that the other allies had formed an anti-Italian cabal at Versailles; nazism drew on similar and more intense postwar German perceptions.

And of course, anti-Semitism is always a paranoid structure in precisely this sense, presenting the problems of the whole as caused by a secret, scheming, conspiratorial few. Lewis is not at all anti-Semitic at any point, but his vision of the modern world as controlled by secret forces is one readily echoed in anti-Semitic thinking and writing.

A handy reference point here is Louis-Ferdinand Céline. There are some obvious and enormous differences between Lewis and Céline. None of the ambiguities that have concerned us here in Lewis's case are evident in Céline's case, given his clear anti-Semitism and his collaboration with the Germans during the war.[16] Yet despite these differences, Lewis's obsession with deceiving surfaces and false bottoms is remarkably parallel to Céline's. Céline shares what I have called Lewis's paranoid aesthetic, both the sense that others are out to get him and the ability to use this as the basis of original, fascinating, powerful, and yet politically repellent fiction.

But does this comparison to Céline establish once and for all Lewis's essential fascism? If a writer's aesthetic is congruent with fascism in this way, is this the level on which literary fascism can be conclusively established? Even here there are no easy answers, as one can see by examining where this current of paranoid fiction goes after the work of Lewis and Céline. There are a number of American writers who continue in Lewis's and Céline's vein after 1945, and not coincidentally, their point of origin and central intellectual reference remains World War II. The key works here are Norman Mailer's *The Naked and the Dead* and Thomas Pynchon's *Gravity's Rainbow*, though lesser works such as Joseph Heller's *Catch-22* can be mentioned as well.[17]

Both Mailer's and Pynchon's novels are thematically close to Lewis's work, though the mode of narration of Mailer's fairly conventional war novel is further from Lewis in style than Pynchon's work is. But readers of *The Art of Being Ruled* will recognize that they are in familiar territory in the conversations between General Cummings and Lieutenant Hearn that carry much of the thematic burden of *The Naked and the Dead*. The general presents the war against fascism as a heaven-sent opportunity, not to destroy fascism but to build on its concept. As he says to the idealistic leftist lieutenant, "You're misreading history if you see this war as a revolution. It's a power concentration."[18] The fullest statement of this comes much later in the novel:

Historically the purpose of this war is to translate America's potential into kinetic energy. The concept of fascism, far sounder than communism if you think of it, for it's grounded firmly in men's actual natures, merely started in the wrong country. . . . But the dream, the concept was sound enough. . . . America is going to absorb that dream, it's in the business of doing it now. When you've created power, materials, armies, they don't wither of their own accord. . . . For the past century the entire historical process has been working toward greater and greater consolidation of power. Physical power for this century, an extension of our universe, and a political power, a political organization to make it possible. (*The Naked and the Dead*, 253–54)

And here Lewis' "reflex of seeking other orders behind the visible, also known as paranoia,"[19] is clearly entering in. Although Hearn's idealistic notion of the war is the one Mailer wants to embrace, and General Cummings represents everything that is wrong with American involvement in the war, Cummings by virtue of his superior power sends Hearn off on a patrol on which he is killed. Mailer seems no more optimistic about escaping the modern powerhouse than Wyndham Lewis was, and he is advancing a comparably paranoid vision, but the more important point here is that this is being advanced from a political perspective that one has to call both leftist and antifascist.

This is also obviously true of Pynchon's *Gravity's Rainbow*. Far more explicit about its own procedures and aesthetic than Lewis ever is, the novel contains extensive meditations on what Pynchon calls "creative paranoia" (p. 638) and on why paranoia is an appropriate belief system in or response to the modern world. The reason this is so is again congruent with Lewis's and Mailer's stress on the consolidation of power: for Pynchon, World War II was a kind of technical exercise in which all sides perfected both the organizational techniques and the technologies of control. It is almost irrelevant in Pynchon's vision that fascism was defeated, for the power grids he fears and warns against include the winners as well as the losers in the war. Pynchon thus closely echoes Mailer's vision of the war, with thirty-five more postwar years to confirm his diagnosis. Now, a full reading of these novels would take us well beyond the limits of this argument, and I find neither novelist nearly as inventive or compelling as Lewis or Céline. But my point here is that these novels, working in a Lewisian and Célinian vein, are deeply political works, and they have made left-wing, libertarian work out of what we have identified as a fascist aesthetic mode.

Where does that leave any attempt to place Lewis in relation to fascism? Lewis himself knew that others had trouble locating him politically, and he took a certain delight in this, defining his politics once as "partly communist and partly fascist, with a distinct streak of monarchism in my marxism, but at bottom anarchist with a healthy passion for order."[20] And elsewhere he took equal delight in anticipating a future Marxist appropriation of his work: "I know that at some future date I shall have my niche in the Bolshevist pantheon, as a great enemy of the middle-class idea. Keats said: 'I shall be among the English poets after my death.' I say: 'I shall be among the bolshie prophets.'"[21] And what

Lewis is paying attention to here is not just the complexity and heterogeneity of his own ideas but the way in which a complex dynamic of
assimilation and transformation constitutes the history of ideas and of
art. The categories within which we try to map the fascist period tend to
take for granted certain oppositions, primarily between the right and the
left, as is these were naturally constituted oppositions. But, just to take
some obvious examples, if Hegel is of the Right, how then was Marx able
to use his work in a "left-Hegelian" direction? Right and Left are metaphors, after all, and we fail to understand the dynamic of the 1914–1945
period if we regard them as fixed and mutually exclusive entities. Benito
Mussolini, Oswald Mosley, Hendrik de Man—these are only a few figures important in the history of fascism who led left-wing socialist movements earlier in their careers. Zeev Sternhell has caught this aspect of the
period well in his title *Neither Left nor Right*,[22] though for many of these
figures, it might be put "both left and right," or "anything but the
middle." We make no sense of the complex political evolution of a figure
like Wyndham Lewis if we pin on him the single label of Fascist, nor do
we make better sense if we refuse to admit the accuracy of that label at
important moments in his career.

Yet I don't think the final word on a work of art is to evaluate its
propositions according to our judgment of them. By that standard, the
work of the Modernist Fascists stands condemned because of its involvement with fascism. But for political theory I go to political theorists, not
to novelists and poets. What writers can give—and what the Modernist
Fascists do give—is not a set of propositions as much as an experience of
what it might be like to accept those propositions and, more important,
those beliefs, those feelings, those attitudes. If one wants to recover the
experience of Europe from 1914 to 1945, then one cannot go just to
"politically correct" writers, whoever they may be. Céline's works give
us an incomparably richer experience and understanding of the horror of
nazism than Mann's *Doctor Faustus* ever can. This is not to say that only
Fascists could write perceptively about fascism. James Joyce's *Ulysses*,
the greatest political novel of the century, anticipated and diagnosed nazism years in advance of the historical phenomenon, and the humanist and
left-wing credentials of Joyce's masterpiece are beyond question. What
we need is an approach to the politics of the Modernist writers that is
not exclusively concerned with identifying the heroes and villains of the
story. We need to be more concerned with how these works of literature
give us what literature can give us—an exploration of concrete situations,
beliefs, and attitudes—and less concerned with how literature reflects
other, more analytic and propositional forms of linguistic expression. I
am afraid that, despite Sartre, it is perfectly obvious that it is possible to

write a good novel in praise of anti-Semitism. And at a time when literary criticism, at least in the English-speaking world, is becoming more and more political in the sense of being relentlessly judgmental about the attitudes and propositions embodied in literary works, this fact raises some very important questions. If we read only what we see as sharing our values, as embodying "correct perspectives" on issues of race, class, and gender, then we are going to close ourselves off to much of the enduring expression of the world's cultures, including most of what has created the cultural perspective from which we confidently criticize those now alien texts. Fascist literature raises this problem in a particularly urgent form, and that is one reason a consideration of fascist literature seems so important at the present time.

ROBERT CASILLO

Fascists of the Final Hour
· Pound's Italian *Cantos*

Written in Italian and published in an obscure Italian newspaper in 1945, Ezra Pound's Cantos 72 and 73 were excluded or rather suppressed from the standard edition of *The Cantos* until 1987. The reason is not hard to explain. In 1940, Pound intended to complete *The Cantos* in accordance with their long-projected and loosely defined Dantescan schema. After Canto 71, the last of the Adams *Cantos*, he envisioned a final section centered not in heaven but in the earthly paradise of an Italian fascist utopia. Instead, Pound was swept up by World War II, and his literary production consisted mainly of Axis propaganda delivered over Rome Radio. On 25 July 1943 Mussolini was dismissed by the Fascist Grand Council with the backing of King Victor Emmanuel III and Marshall Badoglio, who on 8 September capitulated to the invading Allies. On 10 September, as the Nazis took over Rome, Pound left the city for his daughter's home in the Tyrol, eventually returning to his home in Rapallo. By late September the Germans had rescued Mussolini and installed him in a neofascist puppet "republic" based at Salò on Lake Garda. There Mussolini summoned faithful Fascists to renew Blackshirt solidarity while attempting to muster recruits. Pound was impressed by the Salò Republic's quasi-socialistic pronouncements but feared that mistrust and bickering among loyal Fascists and the return of subversive "plutocratic" and "pro-Semitic" elements would undermine the new regime. Convinced that it needed an "inspired" intelligentsia, he continued to write radio propaganda, issued a fascist manifesto, and produced banners inscribed with exhortatory slogans from Confucius and Cavalcanti.[1]

Then, in December 1944, moved by the death of his friend Filippo Tommaso Marinetti and outraged by the supposed destruction of the Tempio Malatestiano, Pound resumed work on *The Cantos*. He put aside the paradisal section and turned to immediate concerns. Early in 1945 he sent copies of Cantos 72 and 73 to Mussolini. Bearing the title "Presenza," lines 9–35 of Canto 72 appeared in the 15 January issue of *Marina Repubblicana*, a Salò naval newspaper. Canto 73 appeared in its entirety in the same paper on 1 February 1945, under the title "Cavalcanti: Corrispondenza Repubblicana." Their publication seems to have been assisted by Pound's good friend Admiral Ubaldo degli Uberti.[2] Apart from piety and lament, these cantos were inspired by the propagandist aim of rallying the Italians. This motive explains their comparatively easy intelligibility, especially the second, a sort of folktale. Their sometimes buoyant optimism stems from the fact that their composition coincided with the resurgence of fascist hopes during the winter of 1944, when the Allies bogged down in the Battle of the Appenines. These cantos, the chief poetic effort during the entire war, celebrate the Axis uprising of that winter, when five or six German armored divisions and the whole of Mussolini's neofascist forces (including the infamously brutal Black Brigades) met with some success against the Allies and partisans.[3]

Signaling what Hugh Kenner describes as a seismic shift or "fault line" in the structure of Pound's epic,[4] the Italian *Cantos* mark the permanent interruption of Pound's paradisal hopes by World War II while pointing in theme and form toward the Pisan *Cantos*, where the politically emarginated Pound draws inward and contemplates the collapse of fascism. That the Italian *Cantos* have been largely ignored is best explained by the fact that their disturbing politics cast long shadows backward and forward over the rest of the poem.[5] They need to be better understood in the personal and historical context from which they emerged and which determines their rhetorical and ideological aims. They also need to be seen in their integral relation to Pound's other writings, especially *The Cantos*, as they demonstrate the inseparability of Pound's poetry from his fascist ideology. (An English translation of the Italian *Cantos*, is provided at the end of this essay.)

II

Reiterating many of Pound's familiar themes, the opening of Canto 72 reminds us that World War II is a struggle between Jewish usury, concealing itself behind the facade of liberal democracy and standing for all forms of repression and sadism, and the Axis, which represents peace, justice, economic abundance, and erotic vitality: "That one may begin recalling the shit war / Facts of the case will arise. In the beginning, God / The great aesthete, having created heaven and earth, / After the volcanic sunset, having painted / The rocks with lichens in the Japa-

nese manner, / Shat the great usurer Satan-Geryon, prototype / of Churchill's bosses." Massimo Bacigalupo describes this deity as the object of
Pound's admiration, as a fellow aesthete who, like Pound, imitates Japanese art but who regrettably leaves humanity adrift in usurious excre-
ment.[6] Actually, this is Pound's representation of his conception of the
Jewish god as evil. Pound was no ninetyish aesthete; he neither admired
aesthetes nor thought of himself as one, nor could he have admired an
aesthete god. Mauberley's chief failing is aestheticism, and in Canto 40,
Mussolini's virtue is in grasping what aesthetes ignore. Being an aesthete,
this god is (like Jehovah) remote and passive, molding (or rather excret-
ing) reality *ab extra* rather than with the passionate participation of
Pound's craftsman-carver. The volcanic sunset evokes Hell, Jehovah's fire
and brimstone, and impending darkness, to which Pound always coun-
terposes the light of dawn. Whereas this god's Japanese style amounts to
a dilettantish interest in minor details, slimy lichens that conceal the clean
edge of the rocks, Pound reveres the imagistic clarity and totality of the
Noh drama as well as the samurai warrior ethos. Besides usury, the god's
anal aggression consorts with the bellicose and calumniating traits of the
Allies in Canto 72.

Having in Cantos 14 and 15 (the Hell *Cantos*) portrayed what Eliot
objected to as a hell for "the *other people*,"[7] Pound was now in the midst
of the inferno of World War II. Unlike most of *The Cantos* up to this
point, but anticipating the Pisan *Cantos*, Canto 72 (and less noticeably
Canto 73) is a first-person narration. Though Pound has sought to ap-
proximate Dante's narrative form and at points his hendecasyllabic
meter, he writes not only in correct Tuscan but in a "rough idiom" infrequently sprinkled with dialect. He does not himself undertake an otherworldly journey but is visited by three spirits: Marinetti; Manlio Torquato Dazzi, a literary friend of Pound's; and Ezzelino da Romano, the
medieval tyrant.

Pound's dialogue with Marinetti is his tribute to a writer whom he
admired as a creator of futurism and vorticism and as the chief aesthetic
proponent of Italian fascism. To be sure, during his early career, Pound
had dismissed Marinetti, for like his Vorticist colleagues he wanted to
deny that vorticism was in many ways a reactive imitation of futurism.
By the early 1930s, after having moved to Italy in 1924, Pound came to
praise Marinetti as a polemicist and agitator while acknowledging his
influence on vorticism. Although Pound never embraced or admired the
futurist aesthetic, his visit to Marinetti in Rome in 1932 helped transform
him into an active supporter of fascism.[8] In Canto 72, Marinetti is a
ghost, having recently died after his return from long service on the Russian front (he was sixty-eight), an act of patriotism commemorated in

Canto 92: "and ministri went to the fighting line / as did old Marinetti" (p. 621). Marinetti announces that he wants to continue fighting rather than go to Paradise and then asks for the use of Pound's body. Replying that his body is old, Pound proposes that Marinetti take over the body of some "cowardly and stupid kid" so as to instill him with valor. Marinetti may thus enjoy a "second-birth" as a "panther" and die on the battlefield instead of "*old* in bed." Bitterly denouncing the traitors who engineered the capitulation or "crash," the purgatorial experience Marinetti now suffers, Pound tells Marinetti to make of himself "yet another hero, among so many," whereas Pound's part is to explain the "eternal war / between light and mud," this being an allusion to a canzone by Guido Guinicelli to which Pound also alludes in Canto 51. Pound bids Marinetti farewell, telling him to return as it occurs to him, to which Marinetti responds with the military: "PRESENT!" (*PRESENTE*).

Bacigalupo rightly finds unintentionally comic Pound's suggestion that the soul of Marinetti enter the brain of a young imbecile.[9] Yet this proposal would help to fulfill a chief aim of fascism, namely, the transformation of the masses, which Pound dismissed as "malleable mud" (L, 181) and Mussolini as "human material,"[10] to a mechanical instrument mobilized by the Fascist elite. For the most part, though, Pound's proposal bespeaks his and Marinetti's fear that fascism is no longer a "continuing" revolution of creative youth. As is well known, Italian fascism announced itself as a young man's movement. Having promised in his futurist polemics that youth would make a new Italy, Marinetti called for "the Exciter" (*Eccitatorio*), a permanently energizing political body formed of students and Futurist *Arditi* (former shock troops). He warned of the grave dangers of letting such a body grow old. During the 1930s, Marinetti and many other Fascists worried that Mussolini's regime had become complacently middle-aged or bourgeois.[11] The same ideal of fascism figures in the radio broadcasts, which portray World War II as a struggle between youth and age.[12] By contrast, Canto 72 implies Pound's awareness that the Salò Republic, despite Mussolini's continuing appeal to youth, had great difficulty in finding recruits.[13] By that time fascism was at best senescent, with Marinetti dead, Mussolini sixty-one years old, and Pound fifty-nine. Desperation motivates Pound's notion that Marinetti might metamorphose himself into a panther and know a second birth—an allusion not only to the "twice born" Dionysus, Pound's god of vital energy to whom he compares Mussolini at the opening of Canto 74, but to his predatory feline attendants. On the other hand, Pound alludes to the mechanized *Panzer* (panther) divisions upon whom the fate of Italian fascism really depended.

Marinetti's unwavering loyalty to fascism is expressed in his "strong cry" of "PRESENT," capitalized for emphasis. This word recalls the original title of Canto 72, "Presenza," which means "appearance" or "manifestation" and which appropriately introduces a poem filled with apparitions. "Presenza" and "Presente" also have religious associations, as is suggested by the fact that Pound sent the Italian *Cantos* to his daughter as a gift for the Feast of the Epiphany,[14] which evokes the idea of the apparition of flamelike spirits. However, "Presente" exemplifies fascism's attempt to replace Catholicism with its own secular religion, complete with saints, martyrology, and sacrificial rites. Herman Finer observes that during the roll calls that accompanied fascist rituals the participants proclaimed the word "Present" literally to bring to life the "martyrs" of the fascist revolution.[15] Thus, Marinetti asserts the presence of the Fascist dead and of himself, as he has joined their ranks. In Canto 91, Pound covertly identifies himself as a Fascist martyr, or "martire" (p. 614); and in Canto 78, alluding to Mussolini, he writes: "Those words still stand uncancelled / 'Presente!'" (p. 479).

Descending into a bitter, self-condemnatory speech, Marinetti rebukes himself for "much . . . empty vanity," the love of spectacle over wisdom, and for ignorance of the ancients as well as of Confucius and Mencius, whose teachings Pound viewed as the antidote to the crisis of the West. Marinetti adds that, whereas he sang of war, Pound sang of peace. There follows an obscure passage in which Marinetti draws inward. During his self-absorption, Pound hears "another tone of the spectrum," as if this wartime radio propagandist were switching radio bands. The next speaker is Manlio Torquato Dazzi, who was alive in 1944 and whose inclusion in Canto 72, like the slogan "Present," suggests the mingling of the living and dead. Dazzi recites a line of poetry—"*The nostrils belch spirits of flame*"—whose source Pound recognizes as Dazzi's translation of Alberto Mussato's thirteenth-century Latin drama *Eccerinus*, whose eponymous character is Ezzelino da Romano. Pound takes Dazzi to task for having come to "lullaby [him]" (*ninnanannarmi*) with antiquarian verses. Dazzi and Marinetti made a pair: "You both loved in excess, he the future / And you the past." Then, referring to Marinetti, Pound observes that "super-willing produces super-effect / Unfortunately too much," for Marinetti "wanted to destroy / And now we see more ruins than in his willing."

Although Pound invites us to do so, we should not exaggerate the differences between him and Marinetti, whom Pound called "bro. [brother]" in a letter of 1936.[16] In *Jefferson and/or Mussolini*, Pound defends Marinetti's "mass record" against those who would dismiss him as a mere publicist or stuntman (p. 107). Like Marinetti, Pound envisioned in fascism an alliance between the aesthetic and political avant-garde, whereby art would become an instrument of politics and politics an instrument of art.[17] If for Pound the state was concentrated in those "few" who can move from "thought" to "the mobilization of other people's activities" (*SP*, 312), so for Marinetti the people must yield to "those who, like us, have the right to make the Italian revolution."[18] These attitudes reflect both writers' voluntarism and idealism, their characteristically fascist rejection of materialism in favor of what Pound calls "energia e volontà."[19] Marinetti and Pound furthermore admired the machine as the symbol of dynamic modernity, an essential assumption of futurist theory that consorts, at least superficially, with the technocratic elitism of Fascist ideologues.[20] Like many Fascists, both writers derided Christianity as obsolete.[21] Yet, despite their loyalty to fascism, Marinetti and Pound were outsiders within the movement, and few took them seriously. Pound was even mistrusted.[22]

In condemning Marinetti's passion for destructiveness, Pound refers undoubtedly to his attack on *passéisme*: the veneration of museums, cultural traditions, indeed history itself, all of which Marinetti proposed to destroy in the interests of a programmatic modernism. Marinetti even happily envisioned the transformation of humanity into machinery, an essential part of this project being the eradication of *amore*, romantic love.[23] By contrast, for all their interest in machine forms, Pound and his Vorticist colleagues respected cultural tradition and never embraced programmatic modernism.[24] Nor would Marinetti's contempt for *amore* have attracted Pound, whose erotic mysticism plays a central role in Canto 72. The Italian *Cantos* implicitly denounce Marinetti's urge to destroy insofar as they protest the obliteration of ancient monuments, a cultural desecration to which Marinetti indirectly contributed in helping to create a cultural environment in which such acts were considered permissible.

No less self-incriminating is Marinetti's remark that, unlike Pound, he sang of war. In his futurist polemics, Marinetti anticipated the martial ethos of fascism in extolling war as the "world's only hygiene," as the "only thing worthy of man, that beast of prey"; he even asserted that "no work without an aggressive character can be a masterpiece."[25] Such thinking was for the most part unappealing to Pound and the Vorticists, for though their art was aggressive in intent, they viewed war as a symptom of cultural disease and generally refused to glorify it.[26] Yet for all of Pound's avowals of pacifism here and elsewhere, his writings often celebrate warriors, and his identification of Marinetti with bellicosity is thus partly a projection typical of a poet often lacking in self-knowledge.

Pound's most serious criticism of Marinetti is that he never absorbed Confucian and Mencian wisdom. Perhaps the closest Marinetti comes to

Confucianism is in honoring the Fascist dead as if, to quote the sage, "they were present in person" (C, 145). But unlike Marinetti, Confucius was traditionalist and largely pacifist; and whereas Marinetti proclaimed the end of the family, Confucius saw it as the fundamental social institution.[27] So too, Confucius demanded the harmonization of nature with culture rather than its subjection and exploitation by man. Although Pound never fully achieved this ideal, his sensibility resisted the blatantly antinatural aggression manifest in Marinetti's image of the "swift machines that deflower the earth, the sea, the clouds."[28] No less damning, Marinetti sometimes saw in anarchy the potential, through violence, for cultural renewal.[29] It must be emphasized, though, that despite Pound's admiration for the tranquil civility of the Confucian mandarins, he too was attracted to this kind of thinking. In the radio broadcasts he acknowledged that the Vorticist magazine BLAST only made "a bit of a stir, mebbe on the surface" (p. 107), yet he contends in Guide to Kulchur that in a "dead" nation like England a "great energy" like that of the arch-Vorticist Wyndham Lewis is "beyond price," as "something might come of the disorder" he created (p. 106). This statement casts considerable light on Pound's desperate strategy in the Italian Cantos, in which the renewal of fascism depends on the initial violent increase in disorder commanded by Ezzelino da Romano.

According to Pound, Marinetti's "super-willing" produced destruction. Such disorder invites evaluation by the Confucian–Mencian standard because Confucius's idea of the "unwobbling pivot" informs Pound's conception of personal action. Following Confucius, Pound holds that all successful action depends on "sincerity," the "precise" definition of reality as well as of one's true relation to it.[30] The next step is voluntary, steadfast action toward the "good" thus defined. Pound explains this activity not only in Confucian terms but also according to Dante's definition of the *directio voluntatis* (direction of the will) as the heart's steady pursuit of rectitude.[31] Pound agrees with Confucius and Mencius that a person possessed of such a will has attained inner integrity and "calm," standing at the very "center" or "axis" of his being; moreover, that he is in harmony with the "unchanging" or "calm" principle of the universe, the unwobbling pivot, or *chung yung*, that Pound often described as an axis.[32] Obedience to or identification with this principle is "sincerity." And insofar as Pound also identified this pivot with the Axis alliance, Confucianism may explain Marinetti's inner withdrawal: "And he was talking to me / Only in part, nor to anyone near, / One part of himself was talking with himself / And not with the center of himself." Having failed to rest on his central axis, and thus afflicted by a disordered will, Marinetti is engaged in an internal dialogue between the divided parts of his being. He is unwittingly following the Confucian injunction that Pound inscribed on the banners he made for the Salò Republic: "The archer who misses the bull's-eye seeks the cause of the failure in himself."[33]

III

Resuming his conversation with Dazzi, Pound is interrupted by Marinetti, who has renewed his fascist enthusiasm. Pound hears Marinetti's voice as it had once resounded in "Lungotevere, in the Piazza Adriana," perhaps a recollection of their meeting in 1932, when Pound returned from Rome laden with fascist and futurist pamphlets.[34] Marinetti shouts: "Go! go! / From Makalle the extreme edge / Of the Gobí, white in the sand, a skull / SINGS." Mentioning El Alamein, the scene of Italy's defeat in 1942 and a turning point in the war, Marinetti twice proclaims: "We will return!" He envisions the recovery of an Italian or Axis empire, extending from Makale in Ethiopia—relinquished by Italy in 1896 and 1941, the second time to the British—to outer Mongolia. The singing skull evokes a return to origins in the *arditi* and *squadristi*, those progenitors of Italian fascism who paradoxically bore a skull insignia. No less typically fascist is Pound's reply to Marinetti's optimism: "I believe it." As elsewhere, Pound expresses his faith or "*fede*," one of the slogans of Italian fascism.[35]

Gratified by Pound's avowal, Marinetti vanishes in "peace." Then Dazzi returns to his translation, reciting the line "a little smaller than a bull," a reference to the ferocious despot Ezzelino. In an unexpected fulfillment of Pound's idea of translation as necromancy, Dazzi's recitation is interrupted by Ezzelino's ghost, who remains unidentified for fifty-two lines. Causing the air to tremble and the shadow to shatter, Ezzelino is compared to thunder, storm, and a torpedo, the last image perhaps inspired by Pound's hopes for the resurgence of the Italian fleet. In his subsequent speech, Ezzelino leaves no doubt of his "fascist" allegiance. Remarking that the "shit" of the Allies has advanced to Bologna "with rape and fire," he adds that they have brought with them "Moroccans and other garbage." In the radio broadcasts, Pound similarly vilified the French for stationing black troops in Germany after World War I, something the Nazis never forgot (pp. 269, 270). Ezzelino seems no less a mouthpiece for Pound in referring to the "half-foetus" who "sold all Italy and the Empire"—the extremely short Victor Emmanuel III, whom Pound had described as recently as 1941 as a Confucian sovereign.[36] More than a sympathizer, Ezzelino is a sort of fascist *avant la lettre*, for in commenting on World War II he asks us to view it as a continuation of conflicts begun in his own time. This idiosyncratic notion is inexplicable apart from Ezzelino's historical role and Pound's Dantescan interpretation of fascism.

Born into an aristocratic family, Ezzelino became, in 1233, the ally of his father-in-law, Frederick II Hohenstaufen (1194–1250), Holy Roman Emperor and king of Sicily and Germany. By then engaged in his lifelong struggle with the papacy, Frederick claimed imperial primacy in politics and stood for centralization and secularization. Ideologically, the pope's claim to temporal primacy rested heavily on the so-called Donation of Constantine and more practically on his Guelf supporters. According to Ernst Kantorowicz's *Frederick the Second*, a work Pound owned and probably knew well, Ezzelino based his power "wholly on terror" and was the "ancestor" of the ruthless Sigismundo Malatesta and Cesare Borgia, both of whom Ezzelino mentions in Canto 72.[37] Like Frederick II, Ezzelino was excommunicated and accused of abominations, among them Mussato's charge, mentioned in Canto 72, that his father was Orcus, or Satan. However, historians doubt the horrifying tales surrounding Ezzelino.[38] In view of Ezzelino's attempt in Canto 72 to deny or minimize his crimes, it appears that Pound wanted to rehabilitate him. All the same, he remains a figure of violence, the tutelary spirit of neofascism.

Notwithstanding the fact that Ezzelino's reputation won him a place in the twelfth canto of the *Inferno*, Pound rightly identifies him with the Ghibelline, or imperial, cause advanced in Dante's *De Monarchia*. As Dante wrote *De Monarchia* in part to resolve the Guelf–Ghibelline conflict, so Pound applies its argument to World War II, in which the Allies and Axis correspond, respectively, to the Guelfs and Ghibellines. Insofar as the original Ghibellines consisted chiefly of the aristocratic defenders of the emperor, they stand in Pound's eyes for chivalric valor, feudal largesse, and troubadour poetry. The Guelf supporters of the papal cause primarily represented the urban and commercial middle class, thus signifying for Pound the rise of usury. By Dante's day these allegiances had become blurred, and Dante was first a White Guelf (with ties to the old Ghibellines); but after the propapal Florentine Black Guelfs sent him into exile, he came to support the traditional Ghibelline cause. Outraged by civic turmoil, rising political nationalism, and the papacy's hunger for wealth and power, Dante argued in *De Monarchia* that peace, justice, and the unity of mankind require an empire, for only an emperor, as the legal possessor and ruler of everything, is free of those partisan interests that produce greed, or *cupiditas*. The imperial title having been transferred to Germany, Dante thinks of his emperor as German; as he inherits the Roman Empire, he is to unify Italy and rule from Rome. Although Dante was vague on jurisdictional details, he conceived of a European system in which the emperor adjudicates on major issues but in which local laws and customs prevail within their traditional boundaries. In accordance with his view of human nature as *duplex*, earthly and heavenly, Dante's emperor has absolute primacy in the political sphere, thus rejecting the papacy's temporal power.[39] Although Dante condemned the cruelty and paganism of Frederick II, he saw him as a just claimant to the empire.[40]

As early as 1914, Pound observed that Dante's "ghibelline speculations," his "propaganda for a great central court, or peace tribunal," contributed to the Renaissance awakening to the "great Roman vortex" (*LE*, 220). In Canto 5, Pound alludes to *Paradiso* 18, where the radiant eagle symbolizes justice and the Holy Roman Empire. In surrounding this allusion with Venusian themes he anticipates his conjunction of "Roma" with "Amor" (*SP*, 327). Although Pound acknowledged Dante's condemnation of Frederick's heresies, and although he rejected Luigi Valli's contention that Dante, Cavalcanti, and their poetic associates sought to restore Catholicism to an ascetic ideal which they expressed in poetic code, Pound agreed with Valli that the "best poets" up to Dante had aristocratic and "ghibelline" sympathies. Pound traced these sympathies to their light worship, free thinking, empiricism, pagan sensuality, love of political justice—in short, an opposition in one way or another to the Catholic church.[41] All of this bears upon Cantos 72 and 73, whose poetic form is indebted, respectively, to Dante and Cavalcanti and the first of which cites a canzone of Guido Guincelli, Valli's "fiercest" Ghibelline, on the war between light and mud.[42] Pound's "ghibelline" allegiance was strengthened too by his increasing admiration for the Roman imperial ideal, whose later permutations figure in *The Cantos* as a recurrent attempt to establish, free of clerical interference, political and economic justice.

Pound's concept of empire culminated in Italian fascism, which he, like some Fascists, saw as a return to the values of *De Monarchia*.[43] Identified in Canto 41 with the imperial "eagle" (p. 204), Pound's Mussolini is the nemesis of *cupiditas*, who, to quote Canto 77, fights only to achieve the "just price that wd. obstruct future wars" (p. 474). He has the Dantescan *directio voluntatis*, a will toward justice and order.[44] Pound also honors fascism with Ghibelline associations, as in his admiration of Admiral degli Uberti, descendant of the Florentine Ghibelline Farinata degli Uberti, to whom Pound links Mussolini in Canto 77 and with whom Pound twice identifies in the Pisan *Cantos*. Pound even claims that Mussolini has inspired a cultural revolution, which must continue "until we have regained the full force of . . . the ghibelline poets" (*SP*, 335), the larger intention in the Italian *Cantos*.

As Dante prophesies a German emperor ruling from Rome, so the Axis alliance (among other reasons) required Pound to glorify Nazi imperialism and, after 1943, to accept Hitler's primacy. If, as Pound contends, Hitler had the *directio voluntatis*, it was because Germany "was nearer [than England] to the center of that Imperium," namely, Rome (*RB*, 156). Hitler inherited the tradition of medieval German emperors if not European supremacy. However, as the war dragged on, Pound realized that the Axis was an unequal partnership. As in his later broadcasts, Pound, in a 27 February 1944 letter to a Salò minister, implicitly recognized Italy's subordination to the Nazis: "The Germans . . . believe they can create a new order . . . a just peace for a thousand years to come."[45] Yet in keeping with his Dantescan paradigm, Pound's new fascist empire was no dictatorial German monolith but a federation, with Germany acting as primus inter pares. Impressed by Quisling's proposal for a "nordic world federation" (*RB*, 404), Pound also asserted in the broadcasts that Hitler's allies will remain faithful because they know "that Germany will need and want collaboration from men of good will" (p. 309).

Thus, Ezzelino, ally of Frederick II, stands for Italy's current collaboration with Frederick's avatar, Adolph Hitler. As Ezzelino guarded the Brenner Pass, his neofascist successors will prevent the Allied penetration of the Alps. Nor are these neofascists deluded pawns contriving their own subjection. Their relation to the German master is, like Ezzelino's, that of vassal to lord, a feudal arrangement in which, as in fascism and medieval political theory, faithful service receives its just compensations. As Pound says in *Guide to Kulchur*, Frederick II was generous to his retainers (p. 261).

Ezzelino's speech begins with a denunciation of fascism's Italian enemies: "Guelf calumny, and always their weapon / Was calumny, and it is, and not since yesterday. / Fury the ancient war in Romagna." It is not altogether anachronistic for Pound to characterize fascism's enemies as Guelfs, for "Guelfism" resurfaced during the Risorgimento and the Italian fascist era. Centering on Gioberti, the nineteenth-century neo-Guelf movement vainly hoped for papal supremacy in a unified Italian state. Under fascism the title of Guelf was adopted by northern Italian political groups that resented Mussolini's suppression of Catholic prerogatives and organizations. Although the Guelfs were silenced in the early 1930s, they revived in 1938, when Mussolini's imposition of racial laws alienated many Catholics from his regime and subsequently from the war effort.[46] Since Ezzelino proves as anti-Semitic as Pound, he too must resent Catholic pro-Semitism as injurious to fascist solidarity. Ezzelino's anti-Guelf fulminations probably reflect the fact that pro-Catholics played a major role in the resistance, that Catholic prelates protested neofascist brutality, and that the ecclesiastical authorities barely recognized the Salò Republic, all of which hurt it deeply. Richard Webster further notes that the most savage violence between Catholic and Fascist forces occurred in Florence, where "ancient feuds revived"—an allusion to the Guelf–Ghibelline vendettas.[47] However, Ezzelino identifies the Guelfs not with military prowess but with calumny, accusations such as he and Frederick II suffered, while in blaming propapal liars for Italy's disintegration he seeks to exculpate Mussolini.

Uncertain of Ezzelino's identity, Pound asks him if he is Sigismundo Malatesta—an understandable assumption because Ezzelino had previously lamented the supposed destruction of the Tempio Malatestiano: "Who will see any longer the tomb of Gemisto / Who was so wise . . . Down are the arches and burnt the walls / Of the mysterious bed of the divine Ixotta." A Christian Church transformed by Malatesta into the virtual equivalent of a pagan temple, the Tempio celebrated sexual love and in particular Malatesta's mistress, Ixotta degli Atti. Besides Ixotta's tomb, the Tempio contained that of Gemisto Plethon, a Greek philosopher whose paganism Sigismundo admired, as did Pound, as the antidote to Christianity. Ezzelino's allusion to the "mysterious bed of the divine Ixotta" implies that she, like Galla Placidia in Canto 76, is only resting, that her sexual energies remain latent. Pound's notion of coitus as the "mysterium" (*SP*, 70) figures too, inseparable from his belief that fascism will revive pagan vitality and beauty after their millennial suffocation by Hebraized Christianity and usury. Not surprisingly, Ezzelino reveals his own paganism, as one might expect from the ally of Frederick II and the brother of Cunizza da Romano, whom Pound, following Dante, places in Paradise in the Heaven of Venus.[48] Not only does Ezzelino renounce the Bible—"I am that Ezzelino who did not believe / That the world was created by a jew"—but he fondly mentions the myth of Venus and the ultimately resurrected Adonis, which figures in Canto 47: "The handsome Adonis died of a boar / To make the beautiful Venus [*la Ciprigna bella*] weep."[49]

The resemblances between Ezzelino and Malatesta run deeper, for Malatesta hovers over Canto 72 as another model for fascist intransigence. Although Malatesta cannot be described as a Ghibelline, like Ezzelino he locked horns with the papacy, his chief enemy having been Pope Pius II, who denounced the Tempio as a pagan temple. Malatesta has imperial associations not only through the Tempio, "past ruin'd Latium," but in the fact that he was "knighted" by the Holy Roman Emperor and more memorably by his vision of an eagle before a battle, a sign that, says Malatesta, the Romans would have judged an "augury."[50] Rather than representing the final defeat of Malatesta's outnumbered forces by papal troops, Pound focuses in Canto 10 on their last victory and includes an abbreviated Homeric catalog of Malatesta's officers. In Canto 72, Ezzelino recites a five-line catalog of Italian Fascist generals killed at the front. Like Ezzelino, Malatesta is an outsider and scapegoat entangled in betrayals and false accusations. Whereas Ezzelino insists that Mussato "betrayed" him in describing him as the "son of Orcus," Pound shows that Malatesta's monstrous reputation stems largely from the lies spread by Pope Pius II, who envied his domains and stirred up hatred against him. Another victim of Guelf calumny, Malatesta is a precursor of Mussolini.

For it is Mussolini who stands behind Ezzelino and Malatesta. Mussato's description of Ezzelino as "little smaller than a bull" calls to mind Pound's affectionate characterization of Mussolini in *Jefferson and/or Mussolini* as, variously "bull," "bos" (Latin for bull), "bo," and "boss," the leader of a "live nation on its toes like a young bull in the Cordova ring" (pp. 66–67, 99). Detailing Malatesta's contribution to the "Mussolini mystique" in *The Cantos*, Peter d'Epiro notes that both rulers are political outsiders, "factive," "volitionist" personalities, brilliant opportunists and improvisers acting supermorally if not amorally. Just as Malatesta aestheticizes his regime, so Mussolini appreciates Pound's aesthetic "dimension of quality" and seeks to transform Italy into an "enormous Tempio."[51]

Canto 72 asks us to think of the resemblance between Malatesta and Mussolini as regionally founded. Each is a son of the Romagna, a province of Italy that Pound mentions in Canto 72 with a full awareness of its associations both in history and his poem. Malatesta's Romagnole accent is reproduced in Canto 11, and in the manuscript to Canto 30, Pound laments the artistic decline of the Romagna under papal rule.[52] The story in Canto 28 of the tough Romagnole god fashioned from mud is apposite to Canto 72, where the divine light wars against the mud. Pound notes Mussolini's Romagnole origin in *Jefferson and/or Mussolini* (p. 65), and he reproduces his accent in Canto 41, where Mussolini says "qvesta" for "questa," a linguistic peculiarity remembered in Canto 80 (p. 519). Although not of Romagnole origin, Ezzelino, in line 155, says "qvesta" for "questo," repeating Mussolini's usage in Canto 41. Malatesta and Mussolini are rooted in a region famed for its independence, anticlericalism, and ferocity.[53] Pound captures the Romagnole savagery in *Jefferson and/or Mussolini* and in Canto 41, where the *commandante* of Rimini says: "Noi ci facciam sgannar [Romagnole for *scannar*] per Mussolini" (We fascists would let ourselves be butchered for Mussolini, p. 202). All of this is context for Canto 72, in which Pound speaks in Romagnole dialect of the "ziorni [for *giorni*] del crollo (days of the crash) and Ezzelino com-

ments on "ancient war" in Romagna. Yet the theme of Romagnole ferocity culminates in Canto 73, which tells of a girl from Rimini who
sacrifices herself to kill twenty Allied soldiers.

IV

Not yet revealing his identity, Ezzelino rages on against the corruptors of
the Catholic church: "the whole rotten gang," "fat by usury and the best
contracts!" The key to Ezzelino's obscure diatribe is in his later reference
to Dante's discussion of imperial and ecclesiastical prerogatives in the
third book of De Monarchia and especially his attack on the Donation
of Constantine: "If ever the Emperor made that gift, / Byzantium was
mother of the confusion / Made it without form and against law, / Breaking itself up, from itself and from the just; / Nor did Caesar put himself
into splinters, / Nor was Peter the rock before Augustus / Had all virtue
and function. / Who gives in law is the sole proprietor, / And the Florentine knew well the Ghibelline case." Purportedly leaving the governance
of Rome and the imperial provinces of Italy and the West to the popes,
the Donation raised the Holy See above imperial authority while endow-
ing it with temporal (and material) power.[54] Having the benefit of hind-
sight, Pound knew that the Donation was a forgery exposed by Lorenzo
Valla.[55] However, Dante condemns the Donation on different grounds,
which Ezzelino (and Pound) accept. Arguing that the essence of the imperium is the unalienable unity of its temporal rule, Dante holds that, just
as Constantine had no right to give away the empire, so the church had no
right to receive it, for Christ said that his kingdom was not of this world,
and therefore the church is not entitled to hold property.[56] Like Pound,
Dante saw the Donation as a chief cause of the church's corrupting en-
tanglement in politics and cupiditas.[57] Insofar as, for Dante, the emperor
is the sole proprietor of the inherited earth, all possessions are imperial
fiefs, and ecclesiastical property is by definition stolen from the imperial
patrimony. The church must divest itself of permanent possessions and
regard its property as a sacred trust intended for redistribution.[58]

Ezzelino argues that, even if the Donation were authentic, it is legally
invalid because it violates the "law" and "form" of the empire, its incon-
testable authority and unity in the temporal sphere. In challenging the
empire's legal right to sovereignty, the Donation divides the empire "from
itself" and thus impedes its primary function, the dispensation of "the
just." Not only had Constantine betrayed Caesar, who maintained the
integrity of political authority but, as Dante also argues, the Catholic
church (Peter, or the "rock") owes its existence to the empire initiated

by Augustus. Ezzelino reiterates Dante's position that he who lawfully "gives" material possessions—that is, the emperor—is their "sole proprietor." However obscurely, the passage implies that the Catholic church, mired in *cupiditas* and thus tied to the plutocratic Allies, has conspired to sabotage the Axis.

"Sooner will the Holy See be cleansed / By a Borgia than by a Pacelli." Ezzelino thus castigates Eugenio Pacelli, Pope Pius XII (1939–1958), whom Pound correctly saw as Mussolini's natural enemy. It could not have helped Pacelli in Pound's estimation that he came from the Roman "black" aristocracy, nostalgic for papal rule in Rome and hence the object of disdain in Canto 28 and *Jefferson and/or Mussolini* (p. 30). In Canto 100, Pound notes: "Durch Bankhaus Pacelli kompromittiert [because of the Bankhaus Pacelli compromised]" (p. 719). Writing to Elizabeth Winslow in 1953, Pound mentions Pacelli's connection with the Bankhaus and contends that the papacy remained a great financial power.[59] Apparently, the Pacelli family's demonstrably close ties with the Bank of Rome (presumably the "Bankhaus") were for Pound sufficient proof of the papacy's affiliation with the plutocratic warmongers Pound saw as undermining Mussolini. Ernesto Pacelli, the uncle of Eugenio, was the aggressive head of the Bank of Rome and helped to stir up the Libyan war (1911–1912); Francesco Pacelli, whose name many Italians associated with the Bank of Rome, was the Vatican's first representative in the negotiations toward the Lateran accords of 1929.[60] Such facts might suggest to a highly suspicious mind that the Vatican had mercenary motives in reconciling with the Italian state. Pound's allegations, moreover, are inseparable from anti-Semitism, for he claimed in the radio broadcasts that the Vatican had been infiltrated by the international Jewish usurocracy.[61] He thus attributed the Vatican's infuriating lack of patriotism— its aloofness from the regime, its failure to support the war effort, its disapproval of Mussolini's racial laws—not to moral scruple but to its secret alliance with Jewish bankers.

Pound's Machiavellian inheritance is implicit in Ezzelino's statement that the Holy See would sooner be cleansed by a Borgia. Often citing Machiavelli's apothegm that "humanity lives in a few [*gli uomini vivono in pochi*]," the rest being "sheep" (*LE*, 83), Pound also admired the "Latin clarity" of the statement "who wills the end, wills the means" (*J/M*, 34), an amoral prescription consistent with Machiavelli's (and Mussolini's) opportunistic politics. In *The Discourses*, Machiavelli denounces the papacy's hunger for political and material power as the chief cause of foreign intervention and the political disorder of Italy. In *The Prince*, he laments the death of Cesare Borgia, who had seemed on the verge of unifying Italy's fragmented states, of driving off the foreign intruders, and of eliminating the papacy's divisive political influence.[62] Pound's view of Borgia probably owed something as well to Jacob Burckhardt's observation that Machiavelli's "secret sympathy" for Cesare reflected his hope that "this great criminal" would "annihilate the Papacy." Cesare meant to keep the Pontifical States "at any cost," a goal that, after his "enormities," would have forced him to "secularize" them. "In pursuing [the] hypothesis" of Cesare becoming pope, writes Burckhardt, "the imagination loses itself in an abyss"—precisely one's sensation in reading the Italian *Cantos*.[63]

Having vilified the "deniers" of Peter, Ezzelino says that they "come now to bellow that [Roberto] Farinacci / Has rough hands, because he eats the leaf." The colloquial "eats the leaf" (*mangiafoglia*) means "smells a rat," "is onto something." Ezzelino corrects himself in adding that Farinacci has "*one* rough hand" but that he "gave the other," pre-sumably a heroic act for which Ezzelino honors him with inclusion in a catalog of Italian generals killed at the front. Well known as the party boss of Cremona, Farinacci was one of the most prominent "fascists of the first hour," an organizer of those violent *squadristi* who paved the way for Mussolini's dictatorship. As the leader of Italian fascism's intran-sigent right wing and hence "more fascist than the Duce," Farinacci most completely exemplifies, in the words of Harry Fornari, the "fascist drive to power through any and all violent means." Standing from first to last for revolutionary fascism, the control of every aspect of social life, in-cluding the church, by a totalitarian police state, Farinacci increasingly criticized the regime for its loss of revolutionary dynamism.[64] In the 1920s he denounced the church hierarchy; the Masons, whom he ac-cused of financial conspiracy and control of the press; and Jewish bank-ers. In 1926, Mussolini dismissed Farinacci from the party secretaryship, annoyed by the bad publicity resulting from Farinacci's failure to control *squadristi* violence and from his anticlerical polemics. In 1935, Farinacci returned to Mussolini's good graces and served in the Ethiopian cam-paign. As for the hand he "gave," he lost it not in battle but in an accident while fishing with grenades in Ethiopia—an unsportsmanlike method that speaks volumes about the man.[65]

During the late 1930s, Farinacci was perhaps the most fervent Italian Fascist supporter of Mussolini's alliance with Hitler and of his anti-Semitic racial laws. He harped on such Poundian themes as the Jewish international conspiracy, Geneva as world government, Jewish Bolshevik leadership, Jewish financial opposition to fascism, and *The Protocols of the Elders of Zion*. Again running afoul of the Catholic hierarchy, which rejected anti-Semitism as contrary to Christianity, Farinacci countered with the fascist totalitarian argument that the church is subservient to the state. He also claimed, as Pound does, that true Christianity is racially anti-Semitic, so fascism had supposedly put Christianity into practice. Farinacci insinuated that the church's "philo-Semitic" policies resulted from its infiltration by Freemasons, democrats, and Jewish finance; his antipapalism in the 1930s and 1940s is virtually synonymous with anti-Semitism. Always on excellent terms with the Nazis, whom he extolled for creating a genuinely totalitarian, revolutionary state, Farinacci abstained on the night of the Grand Council's vote to overthrow Mussolini and found himself persona non grata under the Salò regime. Nonetheless, he continued to make propaganda and to polemicize against the church. Executed by the partisans in 1945, Farinacci believed an Axis victory might yet be achieved through unified German command, solidarity *jusqu'au bout* with the Nazis, and a superhuman effort by the Italians—just what Pound calls for in Canto 72.[66]

When, in *Jefferson and/or Mussolini* (1935), Pound praised Mussolini's suppression of Farinacci's violence, he meant to portray *il Duce* as a moderate ruler worthy of comparison with Jefferson.[67] But Pound said in 1953 that Farinacci's publications served as a "laboratory of ideas."[68] Pound's affinity with Farinacci emerges in *Guide to Kulchur* (1937) in his reference to Farinacci's "demand for the condemnation of Toeplitz" (p. 274). In 1925, Farinacci had accused Giuseppe Toeplitz, Jewish chairman of the Bank of Milan, of financial maneuvers detrimental to the Italian government and demanded his arrest. Three years later he began a conspiracy of innuendo against Toeplitz and the Catholic church, alleging that "many parasites" were concealed in the "crevices" of the Duomo of Milan.[69] To judge from *Guide to Kulchur*, Pound gave credence to these insinuations. During the early 1940s he too thought that fascism was endangered by traitors and double agents: Jewish infiltrators of the church, the Masons, and the "Italian-Jewified plutocratic press."[70] When Ezzelino says that Farinacci "smells a rat," he probably means that Farinacci has uncovered the unholy marriage between Jewish finance and the Vatican.

In stating the "Ghibelline case," Ezzelino means to implicate Dante's conception of church and state as prefiguring fascism, a view that cannot pass unchallenged. As noted, Dante separated church and state into parallel spheres, one spiritual and the other secular, each supreme in its own jurisdiction yet coordinated with the other. This follows from man's nature, which is earthly and heavenly. By contrast, Mussolini aimed not merely at the elimination of the papacy's temporal power but at its integration within his totalitarian state. He sought to supervise or banish church activities and institutions, to use Catholicism to bind Italians to his regime, and to enlist it in national expansion.[71] After the Lateran accords, Mussolini angered the Vatican in declaring that, had it not been for the Roman empire, Christianity would have "perished" in Palestine among a host of irresponsible and politically divisive sects; moreover, that Catholicism had been traditionally subordinate to the empire, being its mere "by-product."[72] Nonetheless, the Lateran accords conceded considerable privileges to the church, which the Fascists largely failed to penetrate.[73]

Although Pound claimed to defend the "Ghibelline case," many of his statements on the relation of church and state conform not with *De Monarchia* but with the fascist position. His approval of the church's relinquishment of the "Temporal Power" after the Risorgimento and the Lateran accords might seem "Ghibelline" in supporting the separation of church and state into parallel, coordinated spheres, neither impinging on the other (*GK*, 76). However, by the late 1930s, Pound was using the word "totalitarian" in the fascist sense of an all-inclusive political and cultural organism (*SP*, 158)—what he described in 1944 as an "absolute" fascist state (*SP*, 306). At the same time, Pound charged that Christianity's primary interest in self-examination and personal salvation in the next world rendered it socially and politically irresponsible.[74] Being originally Jewish and therefore subversive, Christianity needed the support and protection of the Roman Empire to develop from a "seditious" sect into a "bulwark of [public] order" (GK, 43). Pound thus described the true form of Christianity as "something NOT evolved without Constantine and Justinian" (SP, 90). That is what Ezzelino means in Canto 72: "Nor was Peter the rock before Augustus." Moreover, Pound holds that in its ideal form the papacy is "equivalent to the ideal of the empire" (*SP*, 67). When he says that the church's values are "in large part STATAL" (*SP*, 63), he means that the church should "function" organically (*GK*, 258), like any other institution, as an instrument of state.

After Ezzelino breaks off, Pound hears "fused voices" that remind him of radio transmitters operating simultaneously and then birds making counterpoint as on a summer morning. It is as if his desire for renewal had lifted him out of the nightmare of war into the world of troubadour poetry. Next he hears the words: "I was Placidia, I was sleeping under the gold." Sounding like the "notes of a well-stetched string" (*note di ben tesa corda*) and thus expressed in those clear sharp sounds that Pound identifies with cultural excellence, this is the voice of Galla Placidia, the late Roman aristocrat whose tomb at Ravenna Pound thought mistakenly to have been destroyed in an air raid. Disturbed, like Ixotta, in her place of rest, Galla Placidia represents the pagan aestheticism and eroticism Pound imagined fascism to uphold. Apparently moved by this decadent theme, Pound extemporizes a poem: "Melancholy of woman and the sweetness" (*Malinconia di donna e la dolcezza*). But before he can continue in this nostalgic vein, ill-becoming a Fascist, he is interrupted as Dazzi was earlier interrupted by Marinetti and again by the still more urgent Ezzelino—a narrative doubling suggesting that Pound, rather than balancing past and future, shares something of Dazzi's antiquarianism. It is Ezzelino who interrupts Pound, holding him "like a nail in the wall" in the iron grip of a disembodied hand. Reminiscent of Farinacci's lost hand, this image represents fascist tenacity beyond death. Ezzelino speaks as one who explains to a "raw recruit" what to do in battle: "The will is old, but the hand is new. / Take heed! Mind me, before I return / In the night. / Where the skull sings / The foot-soldiers [*fanti*] will return, the banners will return."

Canto 72 thus concludes with a profession of faith (*fede*) in the resurgence of fascism. The singing skull again symbolizes the *arditi* and *squadristi*, Fascists of the first hour, and implies that fascism will recover its originating energies. Avatars of Malatesta's "fanti" in Canto 9 (p. 11), the foot-soldiers are the neofascist legions. As for the banners, the true Fascist regards them as the "center of loyalty," or, to quote the constitution of the Fascist party, the "emblem of the Fascio and the symbol of the Faith."[75]

V

Whereas the form and meter of Canto 72 are roughly Dantescan, the subject matter, staggered lines, and crisp occasional rhymes of Canto 73 loosely imitate the canzone and ballata forms of Guido Cavalcanti. Its structure is thinner than that of Canto 72, its themes, allusions, and grammar less complex, and its narration much more straightforward and often close to propaganda. In the opening lines, Pound tells how, having slept, he awakened to see in the "lost air" Guido Cavalcanti on horseback. Cavalcanti laments the condition of Italy, then celebrates an act of fascist heroism.

It gives him no pleasure, says Cavalcanti, to see his "line" (*stirpe*) dying out, "besmirched with shame / Governed by swine," these being Roosevelt, Churchill, and Sir Anthony Eden, whom Cavalcanti either equates or affiliates with "bastards and little jews / Gluttons and liars," adding that the people are "squeezed out completely / and idiotic!" *Stirpe*, meaning "stock" or "race," was a fascist code word and the name of an Italian fascist journal. In describing the people as "besmirched," Cavalcanti implies the defeat of light by mud. The "swine" encompass not only the Allied leaders but the Jewish (and Gentile) "loan-swine" and "gun-swine" of the radio broadcasts and Canto 52 (p. 258); their characterization as Jews typifies Pound's habit of describing as Jewish anyone he dislikes. Conjoined with a Poundian contempt for the mass of "idiotic" Italians, Cavalcanti's profascist diatribe is fueled by his knowledge that Florence, his city, had fallen to the Allies.

Pound told Romano Bilenchi that fascist doctrine passed to him "by way" of Guido Cavalcanti.[76] Although Cavalcanti was a White Guelf, Pound emphasizes his Ghibelline and hence "proto-fascist" associations. He notes that Cavalcanti's father and Frederick II, as epicurean heretics, occupy the same circle of the Inferno, where they seem to be awaiting Guido, and that Cunizza was welcomed by the Cavalcanti.[77] In keeping with contemporary views of Cavalcanti,[78] Pound's conception of the poet as a chivalrous Ghibelline aristocrat is evident in Canto 73, in which Cavalcanti, riding above the mud, refers to his own "proud" (*altiero*) spirit. In describing himself as "riding" (*cavalcante*), Cavalcanti punningly calls attention to the aristocratic and equestrian origins of his own name. Pound may even have found imperial associations in Cavalcanti's name, for in *Convivio* 4.9.10, Dante described the emperor as the "rider of the human will" (*cavalcante de la umana voluntade*).[79]

For Pound, Cavalcanti typifies those "Ghibelline" values for which fascism is supposedly fighting. Pound's essay on Cavalcanti identifies him with a healthy pagan sensualism, the worship of light as the ordering intelligence of the hierarchical cosmos, a rationalistic empiricism or "natural philosophy" rebellious against Catholic dogma, and an anti-dualistic appreciation of sexual love, whereby love itself becomes a means of visionary illumination.[80] It is therefore appropriate that Cavalcanti mentions Pound's love for the "clarity" (*chiarezza*) of his understanding, thus calling to mind Cavalcanti's sonnet in which the beloved makes the air "tremble with clarity" (*fa di clarità l'aer tremare*) (PC, 42–46). Having known the "brightness" of Venus while alive, Cavalcanti has descended from the Third Heaven, which he shares with Cunizza. Just as Pound's fascist voluntarism consorts vaguely with Cavalcanti's concept of the loving will that acts from "overplus," so Pound's political elitism finds an affinity with his aristocratic poetic ethos.[81] Nor is there any doubt that Cavalcanti in Canto 73 is an anti-Semite, since Pound defines his values as the antithesis of the ascetic, repressive "Hebrew disease" (*LE*, 154).

Like Ezzelino, Cavalcanti interprets World War II in terms of Guelf–Ghibelline conflicts. Describing Florence as *la città dolente*, he identifies it with Dante's Hell, adding that it has been "ever divided." As in Cavalcanti's time, Florence's internal divisions have undermined its defense against foreign invaders. No doubt Cavalcanti also expects us to know that Dante, prior of Florence in 1300, had no choice but to send Cavalcanti, his "first friend" and fellow White Guelf, into exile at Sarzana, where he contracted malaria in the same year, dying soon after his recall to Florence; thus, Canto 73: "Death that I was at Sarzana." Insofar as The Cantos identify the malarial swamp with usury, mental confusion, and all sorts of cultural disease, Cavalcanti's premature death signifies his defeat by the negative principle. He is yet another Ghibelline-Fascist maverick, a scapegoat destroyed by calumny.

Canto 73 gains added significance in connection with Pound's little-known opera *Cavalcanti*, the last (historically inaccurate) scene of which finds the poet on his deathbed at Sarzana, attempting to teach his canzone "Perch'io non spero di tornar gia mai" (Because I do not hope ever to return again). Within the opera the poem expresses Cavalcanti's despair that he will never return (*tornar*) to Florence; as for the melody, it contains, in code, an important political message that the poet's page is to transmit to the White Guelfs. But before he can teach the melody, Cavalcanti dies.[82] Canto 73 thus enables Cavalcanti to "turn again": "I have returned [*Io tornato son*'] / . . . To see Romagna / . . . during the uprising." Now, moreover, Cavalcanti's message is neither forestalled, as Pound transmits it in a fascist newspaper, nor coded, since Pound has cast Canto 73 in the more accessible manner of Cavalcanti's pastorellas, some of which resemble folktales.

Cavalcanti tells how, while passing through the Romagna, he encountered the spirit of a Romagnole girl singing with "joy." "A little stocky but beautiful," she strolls arm in arm with two German soldiers, her lovers. But though the girl awakens Cavalcanti's sexual passion, he is equally impressed by her patriotism. Having been raped by Canadian soldiers, she subsequently lured a whole troop of Canadians into a field her brother had set with mines. The minefield is located "there towards the sea," "where was the Temple / Of the beautiful Ixotta." Twenty Canadians were killed, with the girl, but the Canadians' German prisoners escaped. Cavalcanti responds: "Glory! glory! / To die for one's country / In Romagna! / The dead are not dead."

Pound's acceptance of the subservience of the Italians to the Germans is suggested by the fact that an Italian girl not only is literally in bed with Nazis but kills herself that they may survive. But for Pound the girl proves the persistent vitality of fascism, not least through her power to sexually arouse the middle-aged Cavalcanti. Canto 73 thus surmounts the anxieties of the preceding canto, in which Pound fears that fascism is old—the worst fate for a movement obsessed with sexual potency. When Cavalcanti says that the girl has hit the target, she exemplifies the undivided fascist will, for in finding the Confucian "bull's-eye" that Marinetti had missed, this archer need not look within for the cause of her failure.

However, the girl's ultimate significance is that her *fede* confirms fascism as a sacrificial "religion."

The girl must also be seen in relation to *The Cantos'* themes of love and violence as embodied in Pound's favorite goddesses: Aphrodite, who attracts and terrifies, and Artemis, or Diana, who in Canto 30 punishes Nature's desecrators. These, moreover, are cognate figures, as Cavalcanti's reference to a *diana*, or reveille, also refers to the star of Venus (Diana) while connoting Diana the Roman version of Artemis. Not only is the girl's promiscuity Venusian, but as if she bore Artemis's vengeful arrows, she punishes those who have profaned the bed of the divine Ixotta. Indeed, the retribution is suffered at the site of her tomb. As for Cavalcanti's implausible notion that the temple-minefield stands "toward the sea," it calls to mind the statue of Aphrodite that Pound would erect at Terracina, with her eyes "white toward the sea." [83]

Canto 73 concludes with Cavalcanti's paean to the neofascist recruits whose winter "uprising" portends the certain rebirth of fascism in the spring. Yet Pound acknowledges that rhetoric is not Cavalcanti's mode,[84] and this prophecy is unconvincing. On the whole, Cantos 72 and 73 suggest that mud is defeating light, that fascism is old, unpopular, and suicidal. When, in the opening of Canto 74, Pound finally acknowledges defeat, portraying the war as an apocalyptic event whereby the world ends not with an Eliotesque "whimper" but with a "bang" (p. 425), he probably alludes to the explosion in Canto 73. Nonetheless, Pound's fascist optimism in the Italian as in the Pisan *Cantos* is not simply whistling in the dark. In defining the "repeat in history" (*L*, 210) as a structural pillar of *The Cantos*, Pound refers to their emplotment of history as the recurrence of archetypes. Thus, if Pound must sing of the perpetual war against usury ("Bellum cano perenne," he announces in Canto 85), this war, though never quite won, is never quite lost; for the eternal impulse that fascism exemplifies always reemerges. In the Pisan *Cantos*, Pound assuages the pain of defeat by interpreting fascism in the light of the African myth of the city of Wagadu, which was four times destroyed and as many times rebuilt, its creators having risen spontaneously from the earth.[85] Yet these configurations of fascism had been anticipated in the Italian *Cantos*, where history records both a "filthy series" of Guelf calumnies and the recurrent exemplars of the imperial cause.

These variations of the verb *tornare* (to turn) form the densest semantic complex in the Italian *Cantos*. Pound asks Marinetti to return, after which Marinetti twice announces: "We will return." After Marinetti's second speech, Dazzi "returned" to his "little song" (*ritornello*). Ezzelino speaks of his returning, adding that the foot-soldiers "will return, the banners will return." Cavalcanti speaks of his "return," alluding implic-

itly to "Perch'io non spero di tornar gia mai." However, the most significant instance is the passage in which Ezzelino wishes for the resurrection of fascism: "So that the buried may bind the dust together / In the
depths, and move, and sigh, / And, to hunt down the foreigner, thirst /
To return alive." This image imports fascism, since "bind" (s'affasca,
probably a misspelling of s'affascia, from s'affascere) here means to
bundle into a fasces.

Pound had observed that Dante's *Inferno* evoked the "aimless turmoil
and restlessness of humanity" in the "whirling and smiting wind" beating
upon those who had failed to govern their emotions (*SR*, 133, 130).
Given that Dante stands behind Canto 72, that Ezzelino is likened to a
storm, and that Florence is "la città dolente," the action of both poems
forms part of a larger tornado-like motion—in short, the war. Confucius
celebrated the man who stands "firm in the middle of what whirls without" (*C*, 113); Pound likewise sought his unwobbling pivot amid the
whirlwind of World War II.

Finally, this whirling motion recalls Pound's concept of the "vortex."
Whether aesthetic or natural, objective or subjective, Pound's vortex is a
"patterned energy" characterized by the organization of dynamic forces
into an intense formal unity focused on a single point or node. Although
the unwobbling pivot qualifies as a vortex, its best-known example is the
"rose in the steel dust," the transformation of dead iron filings into a
beautiful form through the "driving" agency of a magnet.[86] This symbolizes the mind's capacity to create form and the formative potential in
external reality. As a chief manifestation of the medieval world of "moving energies, . . . magnetisms that take form," Cavalcanti had this ability
to create (and find) pattern (*LE*, 154). In the broadest sense, though, the
vortex manifests the *forma* or "immortal *concetto*," which Pound also
compares to the rose pattern formed from iron filings. The *forma* is an
essential pattern that persists through various historical permutations
and thus, like the rose, always "rises from death" (*GK*, 152). One thinks
of Ezzelino's image of the buried Fascist dead "bind[ing] the dust together," then moving, breathing, and returning. Pound envisions fascism
as a patterned energy reemergent through the undying and magnetizing
fascist will. This patterned energy also signifies the *forma*, for in recov-
ering its form, fascism would exemplify that "persistence of pattern" in
nature that no "cataclysm" can "shake" or destroy (*LE*, 155).

It is a commonplace of Pound criticism that after World War II Pound
retreated to a "paradise within" while seeking to shape a lasting utopia
from the fragmentary remains of millennial civilizations: Confucian
China, Byzantium. This shift in the direction of *The Cantos* is usually
explained by Pound's shattering incarceration as a U.S. Army prisoner at
Pisa and his subsequent thirteen-year confinement in an insane asylum in

Washington, D.C. Less frequently, but more accurately, this shift is explained by the collapse of fascism. For this reason the omission of the Italian *Cantos* from Pound's epic seems especially deplorable. Insofar as they show *why* Pound could no longer invest his hopes in Mussolini, whose utopia had been rejected by history itself, Cantos 72 and 73 indispensably mark the major turning point of the entire poem. Yet when Hugh Kenner describes the long-standing absence of these cantos as defining a kind of structural "fault line," he implies formalistically that the shape of *The Cantos* has less to do with politics than with the impersonal, unblamable forces of inorganic nature. Fault indeed, but on Pound's part and that of his protectors. First the suppression of those works and then their undeserved neglect has helped to underwrite the now untenable position that *The Cantos* are at worst a marginally fascistic poem. This is not to imply that proof of Pound's fascism requires even one citation from the Italian *Cantos*. Nonetheless, these works are remarkable in Pound's poetry for the violent clarity with which they reveal both his political ideology and its inextricable connection with *The Cantos* as a whole. In a moment of historical and personal crisis, when Mussolini's and Hitler's prospects could not have been less promising, Pound pledged them his absolute loyalty. The completeness of his allegiance is evident not simply in his celebration of the values and exemplars of Italian Fascism but in his decision to express himself in its language. For those who continue to doubt the reality and centrality of Pound's fascism, here is the smoking gun.

Appendix: Ezra Pound's *Cantos LXXII–LXIII*
Presence
Cavalcanti—Republican Correspondence
(translated from the Italian by Robert Casillo and John Paul Russo)

CANTO LXXII

That one may begin recalling the shit war
Facts of the case will arise. In the beginning, God
The great aesthete, having created heaven and earth,
After the volcanic sunset, after having painted
The rocks with lichens in the Japanese manner,
Shat the great usurer Satan-Geryon, prototype
Of Churchill's bosses. And now it comes to me to sing
In a rough idiom (and not singing in Tuscan) because
After his death Filippo Tommaso came to me, saying:
　　"Well, I'm dead,
But I do not want to go to Paradise. I want to keep fighting.
I want your body, with which I could keep fighting."

And I replied: "My body is already old, Tommaso,
And then, where would I go? I am in need of my body.

But I will give you a place in the Canto, to you will I give the word;
But if you want to keep fighting, go, get some young man;
Get some cowardly and stupid kid
And put a little courage in him, give him some brains,
Give Italy yet another hero, among so many;
  So you can rise again, so become a panther,
So you can know the second-birth, and die a second time,
Not to die *old* in bed,
  rather to die at the sound of battle
To reach Paradise.
  Purgatory you've already done with
After the betrayal, in the days of September (Year 21),
In the days of the crash.
  Go! Go and make yourself a hero again.
Leave the word to me
Let me explain
  that I may make the song of the eternal war
Between light and mud.
  Farewell, Marinetti!
Come back and speak when you'd like to."
  "PRESENT"
And, after that strong cry, he added sadly:
"In much I followed empty vanity,
I loved spectacle more than wisdom
Nor did I know the wise ancients and I never read
The words of Confucius or Mencius.
I sang of war, you wanted peace,
Both blind!
  I lacked within, you in everyday things."
  And he was talking to me
Only in part, nor to anyone near,
One part of himself was talking with himself
And not with the center of himself; and from gray
His shadow turned grayer
Until another tone of the spectrum
Issued from the diaphanousness of the empty cavity:
  "*The nostrils belch spirits of flame.*"
And I:
  "Have you come Torquato Dazzi to
      lullaby me with verses
That you translated twenty odd years ago to wake Mussato?
You make a pair with Marinetti
  You both loved in excess, he the future
And you the past.
Super-willing produces super-effect
Unfortunately too much, he wanted to destroy
And now we see more ruins than in his willing."
But the first spirit, impatient
As one who carries urgent news
And cannot put up with matters of less urgency,
Began again, and I recognized the voice of Marinetti

As once heard on Lungotevere, in the Piazza Adriana:
    "Go! go!
From Makalle on the extreme edge
of the Gobí, white in the sand, a skull
        SINGS
And does not seem tired, but sings, and sings:
        —Alamein! Alamein!
             We will return!—
        WE WILL RETURN!—"
"I believe it," I said,
And it seemed that with this reply he found peace.

But the other spirit returned to his little song
With:
        "a little smaller than a bull" . . .
        (which is a line from the *Eccerinus*
Translated from the Latin).
        He did not end
The line.
        Because all the air trembled, and the whole shadow
With a shattering
And like thunder which obtrudes in the midst of rain
Was firing sentences without sense. Until with squeaking,
As in a submerged hull when a ray finds it
Which anticipates perhaps death
        and in any case great pain,
I heard a crackling in the screeching:
        "Guelf calumny, and always their weapon
Was calumny, and it is, and not since yesterday.
Fury the ancient war in Romagna,
The shit rises to Bologna
With rape and fire, and where the horse pisses
Are Moroccans and other garbage
Which to mention is shame,
        So that the buried may bind the dust together
In the depths, and move, and sigh
And, to hunt down the foreigner, thirst
To return alive.
I saw plenty of filth in my time.
History exemplifies in a filthy series
Who betrayed cities or a province
        But that half-foetus
Sold all Italy and the Empire!
Rimini burned and Forlì destroyed,
Who will see any longer the tomb of Gemisto
Who was so wise, even if he was a Greek?
Down are the arches and burnt the walls
Of the mysterious bed of the divine Isotta . . ."

        "But who are you?" I cried
Against the fury of his storm,

"Are you Sigismundo?"
    But he did not listen to me,
Raging on:
    "Sooner will the Holy See be cleansed
By a Borgia than by a Pacelli.
Son of a usurer was Sixtus
And the whole rotten gang,
Worthy followers of Peter the denier,
Fat by usury and the best contracts!
Who come now to bellow that Farinacci
Has rough hands because he eats the leaf.

He has *one* rough hand, but he gave the other,
Thus having honor with the heroes,
So many of them are there: Tellera, Maletti,
Miele, de Carolis and Lorenzini,
Guido Piacenza, Orsi and Pedrieri,
And Baldassare, Borsarelli and Volpini,
To name only the generals.

Son of a banker was Clement, and born
Of a usurer was Leo X . . ."
    "Who are you?" I cried
"I am that Ezzelino who did not believe
That the world was created by a jew.
If I were guilty of any other outrage,
    it little matters now.
I was betrayed by the one whom your friend translated.
That is, Mussato, who wrote
That I was a son of Orcus,
And if you believe in such nonsense,
Any carrot can make an ass of you.
The handsome Adonis died of a boar
To make the beautiful Venus weep.
If I made a toy of reason,
I would say that a bull for the butcher,
Or for the zoologist, is worth a pigeon.
Anyone who takes pleasure or joy from the legends
Will say that the animal does not make the religion.
One false deed punishes the world
More than my rages: all of them! Trap, wretched trap!
Remove the wild beast from its hole,
If not this:
    Does the human beast love its shackles?
If ever the Emperor made that gift,
Byzantium was mother of the confusion,
Made it without form and against law,
Breaking itself up, from itself and from the just;
Nor did Caesar put himself into splinters,
Nor was Peter the rock before Augustus
Had all virtue and function.

Who gives in law is the sole proprietor,
And the Florentine well knew the Ghibelline case."

And as waves coming from more than one transmitter
I then heard
Fused voices, and with broken phrases,
And many birds making counterpoint
In summer morning,
        among which squeaking
In a sweet tone:
        "I was Placidia, I was sleeping under the gold."
It sounded like notes of a well-stretched string.
        "Melancholy of woman and the sweetness . . . "
                         I began
But I felt my skin shrinking
Between my shoulders
        and my wrist taken
In such an iron grip
        that I could not move
Either hand or shoulder, and gripping my wrist
I saw a fist
        and I did not see the forearm
Which held me like a nail in the wall;
Anyone who hasn't felt it would doubt me.
And then the voice who was raging before,
Said to me ferociously, I say ferociously, but without hostility,
Rather it was almost paternal, as one who explains
In the midst of battle what a raw recruit should do:

        "The will is old, but the hand is new.
Take heed! Mind me, before I return
In the night.

           Where the skull sings
The foot-soldiers will return, the banners will return."

CANTO LXXIII

And then I slept
And waking in the lost air
I saw and heard,
And the one I saw seemed to ride on horseback,
And I heard:
"It does not please me
That my line die out
                    besmirched with shame
Governed by swine
                  and perjured.
Roosevelt, Churchill and Eden
                    bastards and little jews
Gluttons and liars all of them
             and the people squeezed out completely
                        and idiotic!

Death that I was at Sarzana
                    I await the reveille
                                        of the uprising.
I am that Guido whom you loved
                                for my proud spirit
And the clarity of my understanding.
Of the circle of Venus
I knew the brightness
                    already riding
                                        (never postillion)
Through the streets of the Borgo
                                otherwise known as
The doleful city
                (Florence)
                                ever divided,
An irascible, frivolous lot
                                what a race of slaves!
I passed through Arimnio
                    and encountered
                                        an emboldened spirit
Who was singing as if bewitched
                            with joy!
It was a country girl
A little stocky but beautiful
                            two Germans on her arms
And she was singing,
                    singing of love
                                without needing
                                        to go to heaven.
She had led the Canadians
                            onto a minefield
Where was the Temple
                    of the beautiful Isotta.
They were walking in fours and fives
                            and I was hungry
        for love still
                    despite my years.
Thus are the young girls
                    in the Romagna.
The Canadians were coming
                            to 'wipe out' the Germans,
To ruin what remained
                    of the city of Rimini;
They asked for the way
                to the Via Emilia
                                                    of a girl,
                                    a girl who'd been raped

    By one of their gang a little earlier
        —Well, you know, soldiers!
                            This is the street.

Let's go, let's go
　　　　　　to the Via Emilia!—
She went along with them.
　　　　　　Her brother had dug out
The holes for the mines,
　　　　　　there towards the sea.
Towards the sea the girl,
　　　　　　a little stocky but beautiful,
led the troops.
　　　　　What a brave girl! what a brave young girl!
She was playing her game
　　　　　　out of pure love,
　　　　　　　　what a heroine!
She defied death,
She overcame her uncertain
　　　　　　fate.
A little stocky but not too much
　　　　　　she hit the target.

　　　　　　　　　　　　　　　What splendor!

To hell with the enemy,
　　　　　　twenty of them killed,
The girl herself dead
　　　　　　among that rabble,
The prisoners were rescued.
　　　　　　The bold spirit
　　　　　　　　of the young girl
Was singing, was singing
　　　　　　enchanted by joy,
Right now on the road
　　　　　　that goes down to the sea.
　　　Glory to the fatherland!
　　　　　　　Glory! glory
To die for one's country
　　　　　　in Romagna!
The dead are not dead,
I have returned
　　　　　　from the third heaven
　　　　　　to see Romagna,
to see the mountains
　　　　　　during the uprising,
What a beautiful winter!
　　　　　In the north the fatherland is reborn.
What a girl!
　　　　what girls,
　　　　　　what boys,
　　　　　　　wear the black!

JANET PÉREZ

Fascist Models and Literary Subversion

Two Fictional Modes in Postwar Spain

At the close of the Spanish civil war, the Franco regime sealed the borders and began a systematic campaign of reprisals against those who had served the Republic. Those who had been unable to escape into exile were in effect trapped, as *escuadras negras* (death squads) went from village to village, rounding up even postal workers and other civil servants whose employment dated from the monarchical period prior to inception of the Republic. Depending on circumstances (and especially whether they had friends or relatives on the winning side), such persons were either summarily executed or jailed as political prisoners. Some were tried and later executed, others sentenced to death but eventually pardoned, and others released after serving sentences of varying lengths. Immediately following the cessation of hostilities, all bookstores in Spain were closed for a period of two to three weeks while their shelves were purged of a long list of texts unacceptable to the new regime. Destroyed or confiscated were all foreign works (except those by German, Portuguese, and Italian Fascists) and the majority of modern Spanish works, including nineteenth-century realists and naturalists, the members of the "Generation of 1898" and "Generation of 1927," especially Modernists, vanguardists, and experimentalists whose aesthetic criteria were anathema to the Nationalists. Not only were Spanish readers and would-be writers of rising generations cut off from contemporary European writing, but they also were deprived of their own immediate past and literary traditions. As a consequence, those postwar writers not educated prior to the war received not so much a formation as a deformation: they were maintained in an artificial state of "innocence," ignorance, and literary naiveté.

The Franco censorship, already functioning in Burgos well before the end of the civil war, operated out of a bureau of the Ministry of Information euphemistically dubbed Servicio de Libros (Book Service). Officially nonexistent, it was extraordinarily effective. Everything printed in the country—even matchbooks, playing cards, and magazine covers—had to be approved and licensed by the censorial triumvirate consisting of three different and separate censorial entities: political, religious, and "moral." The most important and potentially most dangerous was the political censorship; writers who offended in this area could be summarily jailed and sometimes were. In other cases, their homes were searched and other manuscripts seized. Because the censorship's existence was denied, writers were aware only in the vaguest way of what might or might not be permissible. Obviously, no criticism of the government, its functionaries, or the Falangist party was allowed; nor was it feasible to portray the police or military in any negative fashion. Sympathetic portrayal of the Republic and its supporters was out of the question, as was depicting the losers' view of the civil war. Nor could the recent conflict be called "civil war"; official rhetoric demanded that it be styled "our glorious Nationalist uprising" or "our glorious National crusade." Other banned subjects included documentation of poverty, ignorance, economic stagnation, social injustice—the problems and inequities the Republic had barely begun to combat. Nor was it thinkable to attempt to publish writings favoring divorce, abortion, birth control, or euthanasia; justifying adultery, premarital eroticism, sexual license, prostitution, or "career women"; or portraying women as satisfied in roles other than wife or mother. Second in order of stringency was the religious censorship, exercised by priests, who kept watch over the orthodoxy of any mention of the church, its functionaries, and dogma and ensured that any sins portrayed were punished by fulminating retribution before the text's conclusion. Finally, the so-called moral censorship dealt primarily with the use of profanity and obscenity and constituted the only case where a few exceptions might be made (usually for the purpose of demonstrating official "tolerance"). Status as a legal nonentity enabled the censorship to be arbitrary and capricious, and much of the individual writer's difficulty in dealing with it derived from the absence of known rules and guidelines. Censorship varied from genre to genre (being more stringent in proportion to the larger size of anticipated circulation), from author to author, and moment to moment, as political and social circumstances fluctuated.[1]

The immediate postwar years have subsequently been dubbed the period of *triunfalismo*, a label encapsulating the orgy of self-glorification by the victorious Falangists, the exalting of Franco, of the Nationalist triumph, of militarism, and of fascist values. Combined with the foregoing was the most rabid anticommunism, with all those who had opposed

Franco—regardless of ideology—indiscriminately labeled *rojos* (Reds) and routinely portrayed as villainous. The resulting texts, anything but subtle, were imbued with the full range of fascist myths and aesthetics (exalted patriotism, heroism, duty, honor, the cult of machismo and virility, courage, youth, force, discipline, violence, and brutality) and the corresponding horror and disgust toward Masons, Jews, homosexuals, perversion, drug addiction, pacifism, intellectualism, and freedom of the press. In Spain, given the immediate past, the list of anathema was extended to include local autonomy, separatism, and regional cultures, with the vernacular languages being outlawed; the patriarchal family became quasi-sacrosanct, protected by a series of laws intended to prevent married women's working outside the home, to put an end to feminist emancipation, and to encourage the production of large families for the fatherland. Legally a perpetual minor, the married woman became a ward of the husband, and to keep her busy, the Franco regime instituted prizes for fertility and the largest number of offspring.

Writers who did not choose to write within the pro-Franco, profascist vein of *triunfalismo* were obliged to exercise extreme caution in their choice of subjects, characters, and vocabulary, and they soon began to cultivate a neobaroque complexity and obscurity of style as one means of obfuscation. Most pro-Republican writers were dead or in exile; a few (e.g., the poet Miguel Hernández) were soon to die in prison. Of the many new or relatively unknown writers who came to the fore in the postwar years, the majority were either nonaligned or tacitly opposed to Franco. It is this group, improperly and indiscriminately grouped under the rubric of *franquismo*, that produced nearly all significant literature of the postwar period, as with few exceptions the works of *triunfalismo* were propaganda or pamphleteering, lacking in literary value and all but forgotten within less than a decade of their composition. The *franquista* label is misleading insofar as it denotes the period but not necessarily or even usually the writer's ideological stance. The writings grouped under the rubric of *franquismo* comprise a broad spectrum of attitudes, from lukewarm tolerance or acceptance of Franco as a lesser evil to outright opposition camouflaged in various ways to hoodwink the censors.[2]

The difference between the pro-Franco, Falangist writers of *triunfalismo* and the nonaligned or opposition writers grouped by later critics under the rubric of *franquismo* comprises an enormous aesthetic distance that can best be apprehended through examination and comparison of sample writings by a representative writer from each group. It must be remembered that both groups were subject to censorship, and it cannot be assumed that the writings of either were published in exactly the form submitted by the writer. Indeed, García Serrano—the author chosen to represent the pro-Franco, Falangist writers of *triunfalismo*—complained to this critic (during an interview at García Serrano's home in Madrid in the spring of 1962), that the censors were more permissive with the "others" (i.e., the opposition) than with the Falangist faithful. If the party stalwarts were expected to serve as models, it may be that the censors demanded some cosmetic cleanup of certain passages or language, but it is doubtful that any saw their works banned completely for political reasons.

Rafael García Serrano (Pamplona, 1917—), a novelist, essayist, and journalist, founded the Falangist S.E.U., a profascist syndicate of university students and the only student organization legalized by the Franco government. García Serrano, a student at the war's outbreak, volunteered for the Franco army and spent some five years in hospitals following the decisive battle of Teruel. His first novel, *Eugenio o la proclamación de la primavera* (Eugene or the Proclamation of Springtime; 1938), was written early in the war and lyrically exalts Falangist heroics and the warlike spirit. Characters are abstract and idealized, and the entire work abounds in demagoguery. Typical of *triunfalismo*, also, is García Serrano's first postwar novel, *La fiel infantería* (The Loyal Infantry; 1943),[3] which paints a crude and dramatic portrait of life in the Nationalist trenches. Too skewed to be taken seriously as a historical document, it is more valuable as a testimony of moral and psychological attitudes. Literary limitations aside, *La fiel infantería* received the National Literary Prize "José Antonio Primo de Rivera" (named for the founder of the Falange) in 1943 and represents García Serrano's most significant critical and popular success. For these reasons, his second novel will be examined in more detail shortly as a representative text of *triunfalismo*.

Plaza del Castillo (The Castle Square; 1951), set in the author's native Pamplona immediately prior to the outbreak of hostilities, is more controlled in its passion and probably constitutes his best literary achievement. Other treatments of the war by the same writer included *Los ojos perdidos* (Lost Eyes; 1958), wherein combat and wartime tensions are relegated to the background during a sentimental interlude; and *La paz dura quince días* (Peace Lasts Two Weeks; 1960), a novelized chronicle with considerable autobiographical input that presents the Seventh Navarre Brigade during a brief respite following successful conclusion of the Nationalist campaign in northern Spain during the fall of 1937. In these and the remainder of at least fifteen volumes of fiction, as well as more than a dozen movie scripts, García Serrano portrayed his personal recollections of historical events, thinly disguised as fiction or presented as confessional testimony. His personal view of art and literature downplayed such elements as the well-constructed narrative and convincing, rounded characters in favor of the apologia of war and violence.

García Serrano, who was for a time director of Madrid's Falangist daily *Arriba*, authored thousands of newspaper articles and reports, a sampling of them being collected in volume form in *El pino volador* (The Flying Pine [Madrid: Editora Nacional, 1964]). Because of the absence of any literary pretense, the volume provides an especially clear sampling of García Serrano's ideological discourse. The tone is typically, truculently pro-Franco and pro-Falangist. The title essay's point of departure is the death of a stately pine, after which the writer nostalgically evokes and contemplates the four and a half centuries of Spanish history supposedly witnessed by the tree. Like many other events reported by García Serrano, this happening in the present becomes simply a pretext for a sentimental historical extravaganza, idealizing the past and glorifying the Spanish empire. Other pieces in the collection contain variations on the same theme, each dealing with some great patriotic moment or hero of Spain's history and yearning for bygone times. The author vents his hostility against the United Nations and excoriates France and England for their roles in Spanish setbacks in the eighteenth and nineteenth centuries. Exalted patriotism, nationalism, conservatism, and isolationism are joined by militarism in several pieces on the history and traditions of the Spanish infantry, sprinkled with more recollections of the author's wartime experiences. García Serrano's accounts of events preceding and during the civil war are models of biased reporting: all noble traits and motives are ascribed to the Falange, with only pejoratives describing the *rojos*. Ideology notwithstanding, the author's emotion is manifestly sincere and at times comes close to lending an epic tone to his otherwise arrogant and aggressive evocations.

Examination of the language of *La fiel infantería* reveals immediately that the rhetoric is imbued with fascist ideology, from the overall conception down to the level of metaphor, image, and vocabulary, with militarism implicit in even unrelated rhetorical figures. For example, in the opening pages, in a section setting the scene of the hero's immediate past and describing an afternoon in spring, there is an abundance of martial terminology: "April *triumphed* over the boulevards and the women" (p. 22, emphasis added). "Mario, noting the virility of his twenty years" (ibid.), "it wasn't a rebellious afternoon, of combative springtime" (p. 23). After the once uncommitted hero has experienced his conversion and finds himself in the trenches, he initially imagines the war as a belligerent variant of Olympic Games: "a decorative struggle, to delight the century. . . . Decoration of warriors and poets fallen from heaven amidst a soiled society which knew nothing but eating, holding elections and sleeping with prostitutes" (p. 29). Other volunteers sleeping in the trenches near him are described as "those who always awaited the battle with the impatience of an amorous rendezvous" (ibid.). The day following the outbreak of the war, when the clandestine Falangists have taken to the streets, Mario likewise goes out "to display before the early morning sun his blue [Falangist] shirt, his title to manliness" (p. 31). The first day of the uprising in the hero's hometown is described thus: "That 7:00 A.M. was the most glorious ever witnessed by the cloudless sky" (p. 34).

Fascist ideology is very much in evidence, not only on the rhetorical level, as demonstrated above, but in the action itself. Thus, the password for the guard when the hero is in the trenches is "Hitler, Huesca" (p. 34), and when he first joins a company of volunteers, the author takes the opportunity to exalt discipline: "Mario felt a sudden respect for the soldiers. He was doing what he wanted, they obeyed" (p. 34). Distribution of individual first-aid kits provides an occasion for a show of machismo as the hero advises his friend that it's more "literary" to use his shirt for a bandage, and proclaims, "I only recognize one class of wounds: minor. Anything else is a passport [to the other world]" (p. 37). Much attention is given emblems, as there are repeated instances (e.g., pp. 33–34, 38) in which Falangist thugs tear down Republican flags and beat up those who do not rush to salute the Sindicalist banner. Similarly, the author/narrator describes with great enjoyment a Falangist vandalizing of a Republican newspaper: "We went to occupy a Leftist newspaper. I don't know what fever took hold of us: we deliberately broke everything and then threw it out the windows. A soldier was breaking light bulbs with his gun butt" (p. 56).

The music of a military band announcing the arrival of rebel General Mola provides García Serrano a pretext for indulging his heroic rhetoric:

We looked straight ahead, eyes damp and filled with the pride of centuries. Hadn't the man of Flanders [i.e., Spanish soldiers of the wars of Counter-Reformation], arrogant in battle, known a similar day, with his moustache still wet from blond beer, or the blonde bourgeois girl of the kermesse? Didn't the veterans of Italy form one day for the first time, fed up with turning back the French, liberating the Pope, and even with locking him up? And didn't the knights of America experience their military baptism to the tune of a harangue, those enchanters of the world who rendered miracles insignificant? (p. 40).

The moment of leaving for the front unleashes another torrent of militaristic lyricism: "At the moment of marching to the music, drunk on flags and history—those family histories of the grandfather who died in another war, or the father who has a medal—mad with virility, a man thinks that there's nothing comparable to being a soldier and dying for the Fatherland" (p. 43).

Arriving in Castilla as the rebellious forces march on Madrid, the hero/narrator describes being pinned down under enemy fire in these terms: "By now we could no longer see where our shells were exploding, and frequently the pebbles shattered at our feet. In the distant rocks fleeting shadows scurried: they were Reds. Now I don't remember, but then we must have been furious at not having shotguns. Nothing is so satisfying in combat as emptying the magazine at a human target behind the bushes" (p. 71). Emphasis is given to the religious practice and observances of the Falangists in the trenches, and after taking a well-defended valley that had slowed their advance, the hero-narrator comments, "Upon praying the rosary, we gave thanks and didn't ask for anything: that night we had everything" (p. 77).

An attitude of scornful superiority is displayed toward all, not merely the enemy and the more or less uncommitted populace, but even those who apparently cheer them on their way, once they have entered Republican territory: "even while savoring the honey [i.e., cheers] with which the local political bosses and cowards regaled us as we passed, we were all sure—all of us—that one day we'd turn our rifles against their applause, because their will was that of filthy lucher" (p. 79). There are long discussions on patriotism (e.g., pp. 103–106) and religion but little novelty as the narration progresses. About all that changes are the seasons, and from time to time the narrative consciousness, as one of the transitory narrators is killed (cf. the section entitled "Bienaventurados los que mueren con las botas puestas: Ramón, Miguel, Matías" [Blessed are those who die with their boots on]). The narrative covers only the first year of the war, from the spring or early summer of 1936 to that of the following year, with primary emphasis on the early weeks of the conflict. Throughout, the idealistic Falangists are confident that the war will be over in a short while, at first days, then weeks; this note of confidence in the imminent fall of Madrid is the note on which the novel ends as the spring of 1937 begins.

Gonzalo Torrente Ballester was for many years considered a pro-Franco writer, although careful analysis of any one of his works will suffice to demonstrate the error of such attribution. A one-time member of the Galleguista party (Galician independence movement), he was in France on a study grant, gathering materials for a dissertation, when the war erupted. Separated from his family by the hostilities, he returned surreptitiously, making an illegal entry after jumping ship in a Nationalist-held port. As he was young enough to have no political record on file, he decided to camouflage his outlawed Galleguista affiliation by joining the Falange. At the time that Torrente was active in the Falange—as a non-combatant and mainly during the war years—some branches retained a certain intellectual respectability and moral integrity, especially the group headed by the late Dionisio Ridruejo (to whom Torrente dedicated his first novel and who was condemned by the Franco regime to internal exile shortly thereafter).

The war years and the decade immediately following in Spain comprised a period of intense mythmaking by the Falange and Franco regime, as both José Antonio Primo de Rivera (founder of the Falange and executed by the Republicans in the early stages of the war) and Franco himself were mythologized. The term is appropriate, for Torrente's work throughout his career evinces a deep and abiding interest in the relationship between man and myth, between the real, human figure and the glorified distortion mythified by history.[4] Several points made by Roland Barthes in *Mythologies* (trans. Annette Lavers [New York: Hill & Wang, 1972]) are pertinent here: "myth is a language" (p. 11) and a "type of speech . . . a mode of signification, a form. Myth is not defined by the object of its message, but by the way in which it utters this message: there are formal limits to myth, there are no 'substantial' ones" (p. 109). So conceptualized, myth has a great deal to do with rhetoric, but, as emerges from the analysis by Barthes, it is by no means confined to speech and speech acts; it "can consist of modes of writing or of representations, not only written discourse, but also photography, reporting, sport, shows, publicity, all these can serve as a support to mythical speech" (p. 110). Myth's province is that of the media, and in a totalitarian state like Franco Spain, with a controlled media, myth was likewise controlled. Its nature is affected by slants and selectivity, hype, censorship, and the whole gamut of specifically ideological factors. "Shows," as Barthes uses the term, would include parades, public appearances by the dictator, ideological theater and film, and, in the case of postwar Spain, almost all public information, official photography, painting, posters, rituals, and symbols such as the yoke and arrows (ubiquitous emblem of the Falange). Although Barthes's primary interest is the role of media-propagated myth in consumerism, many of his observations apply equally well to the management of information under Franco. The French critic even indicates that myth is politically conservative: "Statistically, myth is on the right. There it is essential. . . . It takes hold of all aspects of the law, of morality, of aesthetics, of diplomacy, of household equipment, of literature, of entertainment" (p. 148).

Implicitly, Barthes recognizes that the victors in historical conflicts replace the myths of the vanquished with their own: "There is no fixity in mythical concepts: they come into being, alter, disintegrate, disappear completely. And it is precisely because they are historical that history can very easily suppress them" (p. 120). This is perhaps the most significant point of confluence between Barthes and Torrente: each reacted similarly to the same phenomenon, management of information by the media. The preface to the first (1957) edition of *Mythologies* leaves little doubt as to Barthes's attitude and purpose: "In the account given of our contemporary circumstances, I resented seeing Nature and History confused at every turn, and I wanted to track down . . . the ideological abuse which, in my view, is hidden there" (p. 11). Curiously enough, Barthes's recommendation for combating myth is a variant of the method adopted by Torrente more than a decade earlier:[5] "The best weapon against myth is perhaps to mythify it in its turn, and to produce an *artificial myth*" (p. 135). Rather than creating an artificial myth, a countermyth, Torrente selects extant myths and intertextual precedents that parallel the structures or reflect motifs of fascist or Falangist myth and subverts them. This procedure, which Torrente termed "destripar el mito" (disemboweling the myth), exemplified to perfection in his *Ifigenia* (1949), typically involves preserving the outer structure or shell of the plot, yet so changing the motivation or modifying circumstances that what originally seemed a heroic deed becomes a vile or cowardly one. At other times, however, Torrente does create artificial myths with similarly subversive potential; like the classical myths selected for reworking, these too embody a cluster of values that closely coincide with those promulgated by the Franco regime. Perhaps because the censors were not literary critics but bureaucrats, untrained in the detection of irony and parodic subversion, they failed to perceive the demythologizing charge of Torrente's writing. However, the subtlety that the censorship required Torrente to exercise seems to have concealed his messages from the critics and the public as well (for self-evident reasons, of course, the "friendly" critic who detected a subversive message in a published text would be unlikely to call attention to it).

A closer look at Torrente's demythologizing is in order before detailed examination of his story, "Gerineldo,"[6] which has received no critical discussion to date and exemplifies writing originally deemed *franquista* literature, as well as the aesthetics and the subversive charge with which such writing was often endowed by writers whose sympathies lay more with the opposition than with the regime. Torrente's first novel, *Javier Mariño* (1943), vaguely modeled on the *Odyssey* in a manner reminiscent of James Joyce's *Ulysses* (much admired by Torrente), is something of a tongue-in-cheek imitation of fascist and Falangist novels of "conversion," in which the hero, originally living an escapist or bohemian existence, experiences an epiphany that results in his embracing the Franco cause and going to Spain to fight, thereby also resolving any and all religious, emotional, and other quandaries. As was Torrente himself, Javier is living as a Spanish student in Paris, deeply involved in the intellectual and literary life of the capital. But the putative motivation for his conversion is insufficient (Javier is more or less assigned the role of patriot, Falangist, and Catholic by those around him, who take for granted that he fits a cultural stereotype and will act in accord with it). And Javier is not an attractive hero: pedantic, overly literary, and superficially academic, he is too self-centered to commit himself either to love or fully to a cause. Ostensibly returning to Spain to volunteer (less because of enthusiasm for the Franco cause than because he is too diffident to bring himself to undeceive those who assume this will be his course of action), Javier also manages by his timely departure to extricate himself from a love affair grown unmanageable. The work as originally conceived was substantially different, emphasizing the feminine love interest (Torrente planned to title it "París. Magdalena,"[7] but he was forced to make extensive revisions after the first version was banned). The revision satisfied neither its author nor the regime, which withdrew *Javier Mariño* from circulation less than two months after publication.

El golpe de estado de Guadalupe Limón (The "Coup" of Guadalupe Limon; 1945),[8] is a burlesque chronicle of revolution and counterrevolution in a nameless South American country during the 1820s. Neither time nor place should be taken at face value: temporal and spatial exoticism were frequent devices for circumventing the Franco censorship, and the fate of *Javier Mariño* would logically make Torrente more cautious. The revolution is as much a result of feminine rivalries and intrigues as it is of ideology or concern with freedom and the country's plight. The plot per se is less important than Torrente's focus on the process of mythification—first of the country's murdered liberator, Clavijo, and later of the heroine, Guadalupe, who becomes the martyr of the revolutionary movement. It must be borne in mind that Spain was then undergoing mythification of the "savior" Franco and "martyr" José Antonio. Furthermore, the postwar struggle for power within the Falange may have served as Torrente's model for the jockeying for power in the banana republic's revolutionary ranks (the same kind of infighting that led to the exile of Dionisio Ridruejo, mentioned above). Such themes are clearly seditious and potentially dangerous for the writer but less so than an even more explosive parallel: the novel's major event is a revolt against a tyrranical dictator who has led a military uprising against the lawfully constituted government of the republic. The reflection of Franco's revolt against the Spanish republic could hardly be more evident, but apparently readers were fooled by the change of time and place, the heightened visibility of feminine roles, and the jocular tone. Nor did the Spanish censors realize that censorship also played its part in *Guadalupe Limón*: the four daily newspapers of the fictitious republic, initially at variance over revolutionary events, end by publishing the same, identical versions of the fall and death of the liberator once the new regime's censorship is in place. Torrente risked serious consequences for this portrayal of the muzzling of a free press by dictatorial censorship, governmental management of the news, and the use of disinformation. He incurred equally serious risk through depiction of the ways and means whereby historiography is controlled by the victorious faction, thus favoring those in power (the central theme of one of his least-understood later novels, *La rosa de los vientos* [The Compass Rose; 1985]). The use or abuse of history as indoctrination is a primary theme also of *La princesa durmiente va a la escuela* (Sleeping Beauty Goes to School; 1983), written in 1950 but withheld from publication until after the death of the dictator and the transition to democracy. *Guadalupe Limón* was published during one of the Franco regime's most vigorous campaigns to discredit its former foes, when what Barthes would term the myths of the Republic were being reversed and suppressed. As Barthes said of myth, "its function is to distort, not to make disappear" (p. 121), and the *rojos* were indeed officially distorted.

Torrente's novelette *Ifigenia* (1949)[9] demythologized the sacrifice of Iphigeneia on the altar of Diana at Aulis (a sacrifice intended to placate the goddess and obtain favorable winds so that the becalmed Greek fleet might sail to Troy). Extrapolating and exaggerating unworthy motives already implicit or explicitly present in Euripides' portraits of Agamemnon and Achilles, Torrente makes both incarnations of *philotimia*, egotistically preoccupied with how future historians will immortalize their actions (i.e., how their respective form of mythification will ensure future glory). Torrente also uses a minority, dissenting version of Iphigeneia's parentage: she is revealed as the daughter of Helen and Theseus, the fruit of an affair before the former's marriage to Menelaus. The result is no longer a tragedy but more of a satiric drama of intrigue. And Iphigeneia, no virgin victim, is several months pregnant with Achilles' child, so disillusioned with her first deception in love that she welcomes death. In the case of other major characters, heroic and tragic motives are similarly removed and selfish or vengeful ones substituted. Torrente thus preserves the outer shell of the myth and its essential action but provides a radically skeptical view of personalities and motives that transforms the inner essence of events. His prologue to the new edition of this work, in *Ifigenia y otros cuentos* (Barcelona: Destino, 1987), confesses that *Ifigenia* "was, in its day, although no one realized it, a book of political intent" (p. 9). The one major character invented by Torrente becomes especially interesting in this regard: Calcas, soothsayer of the Greek army, is an aging, embittered intellectual, vitally and erotically frustrated, who manipulates most of the remaining characters. Recalling the fascist distrust of intellectuals, it seems probable that Calcas was intended as a "red herring" to distract attention from the satiric, reductive, and subversive treatment of other characters and values. Calcas was/is the ostensible villain who camouflages the "disemboweling" of a myth embodying such values as exalted nationalism, close union between religion and the state, the concept of war as glorious, violence, militarism, idealization of the homeland, and the sacrifice of the individual to the interests of the state. The myth also portrays an established religion or its representatives adopting a partisan stance, in effect intervening in a political event (a transparent allusion to the Spanish church hierarchy's support of Franco). Corresponding fascist myths—patriotism, honor, glory, heroism—are undermined in a veiled but mordant political satire.

Many of the same techniques appear in *La princesa durmiente va a la escuela*,[10] which was conceived as part of a series of four, including *Ifigenia* (the others were never published and perhaps never finished, as Torrente clearly despaired of being understood by readers of the day). The countermythification process is applied to the well-known fairy tale, the basic premise being that Beauty has been sleeping for five centuries instead of one, awaiting the prince's kiss. Using the mock heroic mode, Torrente targets the pomp and circumstance of state ceremonials and vulgarization of traditions and complexities of protocol, as well as speculation and profiteering by highly placed government officials (at a time when many Franco minions were becoming millionaires in the black market). In this text also, Torrente introduces a specious villain, the diabolical "psychiatrist," Dr. Motza, a charlatan and homosexual, another ostensible red herring or target of ridicule intended to divert attention from the shocking violence of the outcome and the immolation of Sleeping Beauty. Written some three years after promulgation of the Spanish "organic law of the State" established a monarchical succession for Franco, the work portrays a constitutional monarchy whose king is a helpless figurehead at the mercy of the party in power, unable to make the simplest decisions for himself, such as what newspaper to read. Because the choice of this fairy tale as mythic model is unlikely to have been gratuitous, Torrente may have wished to suggest that those who believed that Franco would actually relinquish his power were as much in need of reeducation as the heroine. The central premise is that the princess, having fallen into her enchanted sleep before Luther or the Reformation, will awaken in the twentieth century with the mentality of the fifteenth, making it imperative to prepare her psychologically. Torrente satirizes not only historiography but the many interest groups controlling its texts, as the operation of educating the princess is disputed by several vested interests aspiring to control her indoctrination. Reawakening the princess might also be an allegory for the regime's alleged goal of revitalizing the glorious Spain of bygone eras. The whole affair is turned into a Hollywood extravaganza, complete with the world press and diplomatic corps. If the princess is an allegory for Spain, this work is still more daring than

Ifigenia: as her indoctrination goes awry, Beauty makes common cause with the proletariat, marching on the palace with them. She and the prince—who dies trying to protect her—are machine-gunned by professional agitators hired by the party in power to prevent the king's contact with the populace. Here Torrente alludes obliquely to the fascist doctrine of excessive force.

"Gerineldo," published in some long-defunct periodical in 1944 and lost for many years, subverts another "classical" model, in this case the chivalric tale or epic. Torrente alludes in particular to Charlemagne, Roland, the Carolingian empire, and the "doce pares de Francia" (twelve peers of France). The numerous deliberate anachronisms include some moderately plausible ones that might easily go undetected by readers unversed in medieval French history; but other anachronisms are too outrageous to overlook: for example, the emperor and his secretary fret over the probability of a "popular revolution." The language is deliberately sprinkled with archaic forms (e.g., address of the emperor as *vosotros*) and epic tag lines intended to evoke oral origins, and it is strewn with malaprop proverbs in the manner of Sancho Panza. The ironic, humorous, understated, vaguely condescending tone of narrative discourse accommodates these and other intentionally incongruous elements. A seemingly omniscient third-person narrator exposes the thoughts of the characters, offering such editorial comments as "It was very moving" (p. 165) and metaliterary observations: "It was an irreproachable scene" (ibid.). The basic quest pattern is modified: instead of following the hero, Torrente has the narrative consciousness remain on the home front. The first part provides an exposition of the emperor's discovery of the loves of his daughter Berta and the page Gerineldo. Torn between paternal love and outraged honor, he turns for advice to his secretary, Eginardo (another intellectual and once again the specious villain of the piece, whose false motives derive from his own unrequited love for Berta). Concealing his desire for revenge, Eginardo advises the emperor to marry the pair and make Gerineldo a peer of the realm. In the second part, a "messenger" from the empire's easternmost extremes begs aid against the barbarians. Following Eginardo's suggestion, Gerineldo is entrusted to command the defending army—a convenient, "honorable" means to eliminate him. Time passes, and in the absence of news, rumors circulate of Gerineldo's fabulous victories, but the supposedly spontaneous popular ballads commemorating his heroic deeds are composed, suspiciously, "in good university Latin with reminiscences of Virgil" (p. 168). Concern among the Twelve Peers leads some to advocate ennobling Gerineldo to make him one of them (and so appropriate his heroic achievements), but another expresses doubt as to the authenticity of the reported victories.

A strange messenger reports overwhelming victory by Gerineldo and death of the enemy leader. The final part depicts the return of the arrogant, victorious "hero" Gerineldo, who recounts his search for a phantom enemy, leading to eventual accidental discovery that the whole affair was a ruse to discredit him in Berta's eyes. Enraged, Gerineldo slew the herald who had inadvertently revealed the plot, overcoming his desire to burn Paris to the ground in vengeance, and convinced his men that they "should plunge into the frozen lands of the steppes and seek out the enemy in their homes" (p. 172). Gerineldo is proclaimed a count and peer of the realm and marries the princess.

The obvious superficial resemblances to the quest pattern model of the fairy tale and chivalric romance are calculated once more to suggest the absence of relevance for the Spain of here and now. Success of the stratagem is evinced by the tale's approval for publication in the popular press, the most heavily censored of the media. Political implications remained undetected, perhaps due again to the presence of the red herring or ostensible villain in the form of Eginardo, a calculating, clever, and conceited intellectual who manipulates almost everyone. One ideological target, perhaps the most evident, is the control of information (i.e., censorship), including the "management" of news and use of disinformation, all exploited by Eginardo to control public opinion in Paris and create a false aura of superhero, which would render Gerineldo an impostor if he lived to return. Less evident but still more devastating is the fact—evident upon reflection—that the putative savior and heroic "defender" of the fatherland who overcomes the trap set for him to return in triumph has, in fact, attacked the peaceful citizens of another country and slaughtered them in their homes, with no motive other than personal aggrandizement (one possible allusion is to Hitler). Seemingly sanctified by formulaic presentation, Gerineldo's is in fact just one more tale of murder and pillage. Oblique allusions to the medieval glorification of war and militarism (e.g., "Blessed be the Lord of Hosts, who has sent to us an enemy" [p. 168]) suggest that those espousing similar beliefs in the present are modern barbarians.

Other examples might be adduced, not only from Torrente's remaining early fiction but his theater, and even so recent a novel as *La rosa de los vientos* (Barcelona: Destino, 1985), which treats in greater detail than any previous work the processes of mythification and the implications thereof for historiography. The foregoing should suffice, however, to indicate the range and variety of Torrente's countermythic techniques and the forms appropriated for his subversive ends. His basic patterns involved selection of a myth or "classic" model containing a nucleus of values closely approximating fascist dogma or Falangist myths, which were abstracted and subverted, either through altering motivations or modifying circumstances sufficiently that acts formerly perceived as heroic are stripped of hypocrisy and self-serving camouflage and revealed in their all-too-human dimensions. The reader has only to juxtapose Torrente's countermythic versions of fascist myths and Falangist heroics with García Serrano's depiction of the Nationalists in *La fiel infantería* to receive the full impact of the writer's satiric, sardonic wit.

RICHARD J. GOLSAN

Henry de Montherlant
Itinerary of an Ambivalent Fascist

A lthough Henry de Montherlant continues to be regarded as a major writer and even a "classic" in his native France,[1] interest in his work in this country has been until recently in sharp decline. Known primarily as the author of a number of misogynistic novels written during the 1920s and 1930s and a series of anachronistic plays produced during the 1940s, 1950s, and 1960s, Montherlant was largely ignored by American critics, who found his writing rigidly traditional and his values offensive. His plays occasionally appeared in anthologies, and his novels were infrequently reissued for what remained of their shock value.[2] Otherwise, Montherlant was all too often dropped from course syllabi, and his works gathered dust on library shelves.

When the scandal surrounding Paul de Man's wartime journalism for the collaborationist Belgian press broke and critics began lining up to defend or attack the distinguished deconstructionist, Montherlant's name resurfaced. The notoriety he achieved, however, was less than flattering. On 11 November 1942, de Man reviewed Montherlant's *Le solstice de juin* in his weekly literary column in the collaborationist newspaper, *Le Soir*.[3] In his review, de Man attacked *Le solstice*, a collection of thirty-one brief essays dealing for the most part with France's recent defeat at the hands of Nazi Germany, for its superficiality and the presumption of its author in discussing events the nature and importance of which were beyond his competence. He also criticized *Le solstice* for the narrowly individualistic ethic it proposed, concluding with a prediction that the book would soon be totally forgotten.

De Man's defenders, among them Jacques Derrida and J. Hillis Miller, have seized upon de Man's review of *Le solstice de juin* in an effort to show that in attacking a "political book" by a "collaborationist writer," de Man was, in fact, performing an act of resistance. If this is so, then charges of collaborationism and fascism against de Man need to be reconsidered, if not dropped altogether.[4]

This reading of the review of *Le solstice* is highly problematic in a number of ways. First, it implies that de Man objected to collaborationist attitudes expressed in *Le solstice*, which is certainly not the case. In later columns in *Le Soir*, de Man praised *Le solstice* for precisely these sentiments.[5] More significantly, it reduces Montherlant and his book to the status of exemplary figures of collaborationism, yardsticks against which others and their works can be measured. I do not wish to deny that Montherlant was a collaborator or that *Le solstice de juin* merits in many ways the label assigned it by Jeffrey Mehlman, namely, a "manual of collaboration."[6] I will argue, however, that to assess fairly and understand Montherlant's collaborationism, a close look at his writings and activities during the Occupation, as well as his intellectual itinerary leading up to the war, is in order. Like de Man, Montherlant deserves better than a hasty and ill-informed condemnation.

False Itineraries: Montherlant's "Mémoire"

In 1948, Montherlant published a "Mémoire," or "statement of accounts," in which he attempted to explain and justify his activities during the Occupation period. In a preface to the "Mémoire," he notes that an earlier, less detailed version of the document was prepared to accompany his official dossier as it passed through the various purge committees established following the Liberation. Montherlant had been accused of publishing a number of pro-German texts, including *Le solstice de juin* and articles in the collaborationist press, between 1940 and 1944. With one exception, these purge committees found Montherlant innocent of all charges. In October 1946, he was condemned by the Comité National d'Epuration, a committee composed of the writer's peers, and forbidden to publish in France for one year. The sentence was retroactive, however, and therefore interfered in no way with his life or literary career. In Montherlant's view, the conviction was one of "pure form," which had nothing to do with his actual activities during the Occupation. Instead, he attributed it to the Parisian literary community's desire to punish a writer they had always disliked and to the climate of the times themselves. In the postwar period, Montherlant states, "every Frenchman is an accused" (M, 274).[7]

The rhetorical flourishes with which the preface concludes, clearly designed to stir the reader's sympathy and promote a sense of complicity with the writer, give way in the "Mémoire" itself to a sober, detailed account of Montherlant's activities during the Occupation and his political *engagements* in the interwar period. The image Montherlant seeks to create of himself in the pre-Occupation itinerary is that of a dedicated patriot deeply concerned with the security of his country. A volunteer soldier during World War I, Montherlant notes that he was seriously wounded at the front and that the wound he received required medical attention until 1936. He argues as well that he emerged from the war convinced that nothing had been resolved and that another war between France and Germany was inevitable. This concern, he writes, is evident in his first book, *La relève du matin*, published in 1920, and continues as a major theme in works published throughout the interwar period. Unlike other French writers, who refused to "face up to reality," Montherlant was willing to play the role of Cassandra during the 1920s and 1930s, repeatedly calling on France to develop "a taste for force and courage" in order to confront its traditional enemy.

As to his politics between the wars, Montherlant claims to have been essentially "apolitical." By this he does not mean that he had no political opinions but that he shared sympathies with both the Right and the Left. This attitude, moreover, is consonant with his philosophy of *alternance*, according to which all doctrines—political, religious, and otherwise— are equally valid and deserving of respect. During the 1930s, Montherlant notes, he contributed to both the left-wing weeklies *Vendredi* and *Marianne* and to the right-wing reviews *Candide* and *Revue des deux mondes*. Solicited by the Left to speak on behalf of the Spanish Republic, he was also invited to the Nazi Congress in Nuremberg in 1929. A speaker at a meeting of the extreme-right Rive Gauche group, he authored as well the anti-Munich essay *L'equinoxe de septembre* (1938), for which the Communists alone praised him.

Although these details, taken at face value, might lead one to conclude that Montherlant was a patriotic, open-minded Frenchman unlikely to betray his country in a moment of crisis, closer inspection puts this inference in doubt. First, Montherlant's service during World War I in no way precludes collaboration during the Occupation. Marshall Pétain himself, head of the collaborationist Vichy government, was, of course, France's greatest military hero of World War I; and French Fascists such as Joseph Darnand, head of the Milice, and Marcel Bucard, leader of the Francistes, were decorated veterans. Second, Montherlant's call for France to develop an ethic of "force" and "courage" led him eventually to embrace profascist and anti-French positions. Finally, Montherlant's account of his journalistic career is misleading in that it fails to mention his contributions to *Je suis partout*, the most notorious profascist weekly published in France in the interwar years. In keeping with the spirit of the newspaper, these contributions stress the sanctity of war and violence, emphasize the survival of the fittest, and condemn French decadence.[8]

The second and lengthiest section of the "Mémoire," focusing on the Occupation itself, deals with three main topics: Montherlant's relations with Vichy, his dealings with the German authorities, and the contents of *Le solstice de juin* and other supposedly incriminating writings on which the charges of collaboration were based. Montherlant's strategy in all of these areas is ultimately to deny any guilt and to claim, despite all appearances, that he was at least a spiritual *résistant* before the idea had even occurred to the majority of his countrymen.

An early supporter of Vichy, Montherlant states that he had become disillusioned with the Pétain government by December 1940. A two-day visit to Vichy had convinced him of the pettiness of the regime as well as its incapacity to rejuvenate a moribund nation. Subsequently, he refused to write a monograph in praise of Pétain's politics for the publisher Grasset (M, 290), and in *Le solstice* and elsewhere he openly criticized Vichy's organization for war veterans, the Légion, its cult of youth, and the vulgarity of its propaganda (M, 288). As to his occasional praise of Pétain in *Le solstice*, which was published in October 1941, Montherlant claims to have left these compliments in the text out of personal gratitude to Pétain for releasing, at Montherlant's request, a schoolteacher jailed for unpatriotic statements (M, 287).

In discussing his relations with the Germans, Montherlant notes that, unlike other well-known writers accused of collaboration, Drieu la Rochelle and Brasillach among them, he refused on two occasions, in 1941 and 1942, to attend the Nazi-sponsored European Writers Congress in Weimar. Similarly, he declined to contribute to the German-language Parisian daily *Pariser Zeitung* or to write the text for a photo album of the work of Arno Breker, the Nazis' favorite sculptor. When *Le solstice de juin* was published, he refused to autograph copies on sale at the pro-German Rive Gauche bookstore.

The German response to these rebuffs, according to Montherlant, was increasing impatience, which eventually yielded to suspicion and hostility. Nine of Montherlant's articles for the Parisian press were censored by the German authorities (M, 302), and in March 1944, the Gestapo came to his residence, searched the premises, and questioned him concerning possible ties to the Resistance (M, 302). For those suspicious of his account of the Gestapo raid, Montherlant provides the name of a witness, attached to the German embassy at the time, who would be willing to testify to the truth of his claims (M, 302).

Although many of the details Montherlant offers concerning his dealings with Vichy and the Nazis are accurate, others are highly misleading. For example, Montherlant understates his initial enthusiasm for Vichy in the "Mémoire" and describes his one trip there in negative terms. In his recently published correspondence with Roger Peyrefitte, he offers a very different view of his journey and especially of his final impression, in a letter dated December 1940: "I leave Vichy drunk with enthusiasm for what I've seen there: high morale, order, and an atmosphere devoid of petty interests. Truly the New Regime has won me over."[9] The letter to Peyrefitte suggests as well that he was not disillusioned with Vichy as early as he claims in the "Mémoire."

Montherlant's account of his dealings with the Germans suffers less from inaccuracies than from a number of important omissions. Although it is true that he declined invitations to the Weimar Writers Conference, the clandestine newspaper *Les lettres françaises* reported in April 1943 that he had actively solicited the invitation of 1942 and had declined it only after learning of initial Russian victories on the eastern front.[10] As to his refusal to sign copies of *Le solstice* at the Rive Gauche bookstore, this decision may have been prompted at least partly by the fact that the bookstore displaying Montherlant memorabilia at the time was bombed by the Resistance in November 1941.[11] Finally, although Montherlant claimed accurately that he did not contribute to the *Pariser Zeitung*, he did publish a tribute to his friend and translator Karl-Heinz Bremer, killed on the Russian front, in the German language *Deutschland Frankreich*.[12]

Montherlant was not accused by the purge committees of fraternizing with the enemy, and he chose to downplay personal and social contacts with the Germans in the "Mémoire." Pierre Assouline, among others, has pointed out, however, that Montherlant frequented the German Institute in company of André Thérive, Jacques Chardonne, and Drieu La Rochelle, all well-known pro-Fascist writers.[13] In his own article in the collaborationist and pro-Nazi weekly *La Gerbe*, Montherlant speaks of social evenings spent in the company of Nazis such as Karl Epting. These were the very contacts with the Germans that led Céline to announce to his lawyer that Montherlant was "a thousand times more of a collaborator" than he was.[14]

If the inaccuracies and omissions in Montherlant's account of his activities and attitudes toward Vichy and the Nazis suggest an effort to whitewash a past more compromising than commonly assumed, his readings or, more precisely, misreadings of *Le solstice* and other writings published during the Occupation only serve to confirm this impression. Despite Montherlant's claims to the contrary, these texts reveal not only the nature and extent of his collaborationism but also the fascist impulses and sympathies that motivated him to compromise himself.

Montherlant's defense of *Le solstice de juin* as a book undeserving of the charges leveled against it begins with the assertion that the book was initially censored by the Germans and that the issue of the *Nouvelle revue française* containing the title essay of the collection was suppressed as well (M, 298). Karl Epting and Karl-Heinz Bremer eventually had the censure lifted, although Montherlant asserts that the Germans continued to object to both pro-English statements made in the text and calls for France to regenerate itself. Criticism of Pétain's *Ordre nouveau*, referred to earlier, were also not well received, either by the Germans or by Vichy itself.

Also shocking to the Germans, according to Montherlant, was an essay titled "La sympathie," in which the writer expressed solidarity with the Parisian workers after attending a ceremony at the Mur des Fédérés in 1936 during the Popular Front period. The text, Montherlant claims, is openly favorable to "the ideas being fought against" by the Nazis (M, 300) and appeared, moreover, at a time when a German victory seemed assured.

A close reading of "La sympathie" confirms that it does not conform in its entirety to the description provided in the "Mémoire." Montherlant does indeed express sympathy for the workers' demands for better pay and living conditions, but his sense of solidarity is attenuated by his belief in his own social and natural superiority. When one of the workers, addressing him as *comrade*, uses the polite form *vous*, Montherlant reflects: "This 'comrade' linked to 'vous' was most profound. The 'vous' recognized the fatal inequality of conditions within society as within nature herself; the 'comrade' joined to 'vous' indicated that with a little intelligence, good will and generosity, camaraderie could exist beyond this inequality" (E, 929).

Camaraderie between the two men can exist, then, as long as it is founded on a recognition of social and natural differences between individuals that can never be and *should* never be challenged. It is hard to imagine why social conservatism and natural elitism of this sort should offend the Nazis.

One passage that went unnoticed by the Nazis and to which Montherlant attributes an extremely subversive intent deals with the notion of heroism. Asked to compose "20 lines on heroism" by the Vichy Ministry of Youth, Montherlant offered the following in the pages of *Le solstice*: "Civic heroism. Its multiple forms. I am nevertheless drawn to only one of these. That of the individual who through fidelity to his ideas, his beliefs, or his style of life, accepts, in the France of 1941, to remain isolated; or that of the group which for the same reason, accepts its status as a minority" (E, 932–3).

Montherlant provides the following gloss on this passage in the *Mémoire*: "I wrote these lines in March 1941 and since the armistice, I had resided exclusively in the Free Zone. The only group which, in France and most particularly in the only France I knew at the time, that of the Free Zone, was a minority, what did it consist of, if not those who resisted the politics of Vichy?" (M, 209).

It is hard to imagine that during a period that *preceded* the publication of Montherlant's most procollaborationist and indeed profascist writings (the most incriminating pieces in the collaborationist press appeared in *La Gerbe* from August 1941 to January 1942), he was busy writing subtle apologies for the Resistance. A more plausible interpretation of the passage is that the group in question consisted of Montherlant, Peyrefitte, and their circle of adolescent homosexual lovers, which Montherlant referred to fondly as a "chivalric order." (The initial essay in *Le solstice*, "Les chevaleries," is, in fact, a veiled and highly embellished description of the group). During the Occupation, both Montherlant and Peyrefitte were arrested for homosexual activities, and their correspondence contains numerous references to their persecution at the hands of the Vichy authorities. It is this group, then, "isolated" in the France of 1941 but faithful nevertheless to a "style of life," to which the passage on heroism most likely refers.

If the texts that Montherlant would have the reader believe are subversive do not stand up to close inspection, many of the other essays in the collection do not allow for alternative readings of this sort. They are overtly procollaborationist, anti-French, and ultimately pro-Nazi. Montherlant admits in the "Mémoire" that he strongly supported the signing of the armistice in 1940, and in *Le solstice* he calls for France, like a vanquished athlete, to sit down at table with its conqueror and help celebrate his victory. As painful as the debacle of 1940 was to the French, the metaphor of the athletic competition employed by Montherlant is largely innocuous and in no way denigrates the loser. This cannot be said, however, of Montherlant's choice of metaphors in other essays. In "Les chenilles," he compares the defeated French to the caterpillars on which he urinated to entertain himself during pauses at the front in 1940, where he served as a war correspondent. He states: "I liked to contemplate them, while they convulsed interminably in bouts of agony; these creatures usually so nonchalant, at present tied in knots, exhibiting in their contortions a white belly I didn't know they possessed; stretching their heads towards the sun in a movement both pathetic and ludicrous" (E, 952). Montherlant proceeds to acknowledge that he permitted those who withstood the onslaught to survive out of a sense of *fair play*! Not only does "Les chenilles" suggest a darker side to Montherlant's analogy between sport and war, but it casts the French people in the most abject and humiliating role imaginable.

The title essay of the collection, which deals directly with France's military defeat, also denigrates the French while singing the praises of its conquerors. Montherlant disdainfully dismisses the French army as composed of "skinny officers wearing glasses", "overweight bourgeois," and "hysterical women" (E, 957). The society that spawned these pathetic men is described as a "hollow sham" where all is "facade" and "superficiality" (E, 957). The German soldiers are, by contrast, "large schoolboys" with muscular, naked legs, playing harmonicas as they advance. These "invaders from Clovis's kingdom" possess all the vitality and joy of youth and easily overrun their French counterparts.

The oppositions Montherlant establishes in these descriptions are consistent with the rhetoric of prewar fascism in France and with that of the most fervent collaborators during the Occupation. For Robert Brasillach, the intellectual darling of French fascism between the wars, the movement's appeal resided precisely in its spirit of joy and its exaltation of youth and vitality. The democracies, and specifically the French Third Republic, were, by contrast, exhausted, decadent societies corrupted by bourgeois values and an indifference to physical well-being. Montherlant taps into this rhetoric in Le solstice and exploits it to create a vulgar and offensive epic of the Nazi victory, which he likens finally to the victory of Pan over "the Galilean" (E, 954), paganism's conquest of Christianity. He blames the latter, in fact, for developing among the French "a taste for weakness" and making them "anemic." That he wishes to identify himself with the powerful "pagan" victors is evident in his appropriation of the swastika to his own principle of alternance: "The victory of the solar wheel [the swastika] is not only the victory of the sun, of pagan life. It is also the victory of the solar principle that nourishes me, that I have celebrated and that I feel governs all my life" (E, 960).

If Montherlant's reading of Le solstice in the "Mémoire" is selective and gives a false impression of the work as a whole, his discussion of his contributions to the collaborationist press is even more evasive and misleading. Montherlant's major journalistic contributions during the Occupation were written for the weekly La Gerbe, created by Alphonse de Chateaubriant, author of the 1937 panegyric to Hitler, La gerbe des forces, and funded by the Germans.[15] According to Robert Paxton, the journal was specifically created by the Nazis to provide a major outlet for their favorite writers, most notably Montherlant.[16]

In his "Mémoire," Montherlant describes La Gerbe as the "most literary" of the Occupation weeklies. Although he admits to having written several articles for the journal and to having had an interview published there, he denies any deep ideological connection with La Gerbe and its publisher. The journal's indifference to him, he argues, is evident in the editor's choice not to review *Le solstice de juin* when it appeared. In any case, Montherlant claims to have quit writing for *La Gerbe* at the end of 1942, when the German invasion of the Free Zone made publishing in the collaborationist press "indecent" (M, 302).

On all counts, these statements are misleading and false. Although Montherlant, Céline, and other procollaborationist writers published in *La Gerbe*, their contributions were for the most part hardly "literary." On 13 February 1941, Céline published an "Acte de Foi" (Act of Faith) in the policy of collaboration. Montherlant's contributions included the most offensive essays published subsequently in *Le solstice*, such as "Les chenilles," as well as other strongly procollaborationist items. Besides these "literary" works, *La Gerbe* published a steady stream of the crudest pro-German and anti-Semitic propaganda as well as items of "scientific" interest, including articles by the notorious anti-Semitic professor Georges Montandon, with titles such as "Physical Traits of the Judaic Type."[17]

La Gerbe, moreover, was hardly indifferent to Montherlant. Although no review of *Le solstice* was published (perhaps it seemed redundant, since so many of the essays in *Le solstice* had already appeared in *La Gerbe*), reviews of other books by and about Montherlant appeared regularly, as did essays in praise of the writer. On 23 April 1942, for example, Montherlant is described as a writer whose works paved the way for the "European renewal," and he is championed as the ideal "man of the new France."

Despite the "indecency" of writing for the collaborationist press after the invasion of the Free Zone, Montherlant published in *La Gerbe* well beyond the end of 1942. The post-1942 articles include more or less innocuous items such as a meditation on the lessons of the Persian poets, as well as more compromising political articles and interviews. The last of these, an interview with Christian Michelfelder, was published on 16 December 1944.

Montherlant's statements in *La Gerbe* are generally consistent in tone and degree with the collaborationist rhetoric of *Le solstice*, but two items in particular surpass even the most offensive essays in the 1941 collection in their disdain for the French, admiration for the Germans, and strongly fascist sympathies. In an essay entitled "Le goût d'attaquer," published on 28 August 1941, Montherlant describes an evening spent before the war with Karl Epting, then director of the German student house in Paris, at a boxing competition between French and German students. Montherlant notes that the French students failed to win a single match and then offers the following explanation of their humiliating defeat: "They thought it [the competition] was a joke. They refused to train. Then there were Marcelle and Germaine, those perfect emptiers [*videuses*] of men, and the long besotting in the cafés. As to 'national prestige,' they couldn't give a damn." It is no wonder, he concludes, that "la 'doulce' France," whose youth was raised on "a hatred of force" and a love of a soft, decadent existence, should be crushed in war by their virile enemies.

The humiliation of the boxers is no more offensive than that of the caterpillars of "Les Chenilles," and the "lesson," so to speak, is quite similar to that of the title essay of *Le solstice*. In "Le goût d'attaquer," however, Montherlant openly flaunts his personal connections with the Nazis and embraces a fascistic misogyny strongly reminiscent not only of French Fascists such as Drieu La Rochelle but of the Freikorps soldiers so vividly described by Klaus Theweleit in his celebrated study, *Male Fantasies*.[18] Women drain men of their vitality and force and in so doing threaten their very existence. It is the Frenchman's willingness to have commerce with them that has undermined the nation and brought about its destruction.

The second item, an interview with Michel B. de la Mort, was published on 8 January 1942. Asked to offer a postscript to *Le solstice*, Montherlant took the opportunity to present a new characterization of the conflict raging in Europe: "The struggle against the average Europeans (of course, this means the lower Europeans) has commenced. The struggle between the heroic elite of the new European civilization and the lower Europeans: the struggle of the heroes against the slaves." And he adds: "Let us note quickly that the heroic values [of this new elite] do not coincide necessarily with moral values: these heroes are not all just men."

For Montherlant, the heroic elite struggling to create a new European civilization are the Nazis and those who measure up to them, and the "slaves" are those who resist them. The Nietzschean language not only confirms the extent of his admiration of these new masters but suggests his readiness to acknowledge in them a superior *race*. The use of the term "lower Europeans" for Germany's enemies reinforces the racist slant of the description because it suggests an opposition between the northern European, "Aryan" Germans and the darker, southern races they dominate.

Montherlant insists, moreover, that this new elite must not be confused with moral elites of the past, those who would, for example, be wedded to Christian values and virtues. Although he fails to identify the heroic virtues that animate them, he does specify that the new heroes are by no means all "just" men. Given the context of his Occupation writings, one would assume that heroic virtues consist primarily of the force and virility of the conqueror. In the new European civilization, these virtues take precedence over "moral values" and "justice," which have weakened France and Christian Europe in the past. In condemning justice and championing force, Montherlant condones the brutality of the Nazi New Order.

The most shocking passage in the interview, however, concerns the responsibility of the heroic individual in the current situation: "When certain communities will have shown that their nature is that of the slave, the heroes belonging to these communities will know, when necessary, to detach themselves and join up elsewhere."

Although the "communities" in question remain unidentified, Montherlant's intention is clear: If France fails to measure up to the "new European civilization," if it proves to be a nation of "slaves," then its heroic individuals, including Montherlant himself, must cast their lot with the Germans.

Montherlant's "Mémoire" concludes with an apology to the reader for the "dryness" of the text, a shortcoming he justifies on the grounds that his purpose has been to remain objective and present all of the essential facts of the case. The "statement of accounts" and the political itinerary it seeks to establish, however, fail to hold up. Behind Montherlant's facts and the textual interpretations he offers are other facts, other interpretations, which point to an itinerary whose final destination is very different from the one Montherlant proposed in the "Mémoire." The intellectual *résistant avant la lettre* gives way to the "hero" who condemns and belittles his country and arrogantly announces his readiness, indeed his obligation, to make common cause with the heroic elite of the New Europe, the Nazis themselves. Montherlant's affinities with the Nazis and with fascism in general are, moreover, readily apparent in these essays and articles. He shares their disdain for the "decadence" of bourgeois democracies in general and of republican France in particular. He also condemns Christian morality and ethics, which, he believes, engender spiritual and physical weakness; and he loathes and fears women who, in his view, emasculate men and drain them of vitality. At the same time, he shares the Nazis' elitism, which, in the interview in *La Gerbe* at least, assumes overtly racist dimensions. Their cult of virility and force and their emphasis on youth are among his most central and abiding concerns.

It is tempting to conclude, on the basis of the wartime essays and journalism examined here, that Montherlant was simply another "integral" fascist,[19] an older Brasillach perhaps, whose reactionary views led logically to collaboration after June 1940. His own evasiveness and distortions in the "Mémoire" serve only to reinforce this impression. Nevertheless, the particulars of Montherlant's case are not that simple, his itinerary not that direct. Although the conclusion of the essay "La Sympathie" reaffirms social and natural hierarchies, Montherlant's sympathy for the worker's plight in 1936 should alert us to impulses in his character that his fascism can neither explain nor accommodate. Montherlant frequently compares these impulses to Christian charity and a concern for the downtrodden. They appear alongside more properly fascistic exaltations of youth, virility, and misogyny in Montherlant's work, especially his fiction, throughout the prewar period and into the Occupation itself. As one might expect, the marriage of the two extremes is not a happy one. They finally confront each other in Montherlant's most accomplished artistic achievement during the Occupation, the 1942 tragedy *La reine morte*. Their history, the history of "charity" and "force," and their final confrontation in *La reine morte* must be examined before any final conclusions on Montherlant's politics during the Occupation can be drawn.

Force versus Charity: From Fascist Fictions to *La reine morte*

Montherlant established his reputation as a novelist during the 1920s with the publication of two highly autobiographical works, *Le songe* (1922) and *Les bestiaires* (1926). The hero of both novels is Alban de Bricoule, an arrogant young aristocrat intent on testing his strength and courage in life-and-death situations. The first novel, dealing with Alban's experiences as a soldier during World War I, focuses on the theme of male camaraderie, *l'ordre mâle*, at the front, but it also examines Alban's love affair with Dominique Soubrier, a young athlete whose discipline and independence appeal to him. The relationship, although unconsummated, thrives until Dominique, overwhelmed by her love for Alban, begins to forsake her independence in an effort to secure a stronger commitment from him. Alban, horrified by her passion, sentimentality, and, in his view, her loss of dignity, begins to detach himself. His affection for her remains, the narrator informs us, but "the highest part of his being was drawing back from the young woman, drawing back out of a superior disesteem" (R, 181). At the end of the novel, Bricoule abandons Dominique and happily returns to the "masculine order" and violence of the front. It is this life of unbridled force that, after all, appeals most to him: "Something inside of him cried out that the life of the predator coincided best with his nature, that he would be happier tomorrow fighting—unjustly this time—against innocent Arabs [in the colonies] than he would ever be happy sitting in town" (R, 139).

Les bestiaires was published four years after *Le songe*, but its subject is the prewar apprenticeship of an adolescent Alban in the bullfighting rings of Spain. Once again, the novel focuses on the "masculine order" of courage, violence, and death, this time in a struggle against beasts instead of other men; and once again this masculine order is set in opposition to a feminine world of sexual passion and sentimentality. Bricoule's romantic interest in *Les bestiaires* is the haughty Soledad, who refuses to give herself to Alban until he has conquered the fiercest of bulls, the "Bad Angel." Testing his courage, resolve, and strength to the limit, Alban vanquishes the beast but then rejects Soledad, realizing that to involve himself with a woman would be to betray all that he has accomplished in the masculine order. The novel closes with Alban exulting in his victory over the "Bad Angel" and celebrating the rites of the ancient god Mithras, whose bull-killing exploits he has imitated so well.

Despite major differences in historical setting and geographical locale, the thematics and plot structures of the Alban de Bricoule novels are remarkably similar. The young hero must prove himself in the masculine world of violence and death, and his superiority is ultimately a function of his physical prowess in dominating man and beast. He reaches maturity when he understands that his true nature coincides with that of the predator and that the exercise of force is good in itself and needs no justification. In *Le songe*, Alban longs to fight and dominate the Arabs after the war, even though he understands that such a course of action is unjustified. But no matter. The apotheosis he seeks, the god he wished to become, is, like Mithras, a divinity whose sole qualification is his capacity to dominate and destroy.

The apotheosis of sorts that Alban achieves at the end of both novels is, moreover, accomplished at the expense of women. Dominique and Soledad are both sacrificed to the hero's quest to attain a virile ideal, and each ultimately embodies the negative principle itself. Simone de Beauvoir has argued that in Montherlant's work, woman is "night, disorder, and immanence,"[20] and in *Le songe* and *Les bestiaires*, women fail to escape these categories. Dominique is proud, autonomous, and essentially virile at the outset, but as she succumbs to her feminine passion for Alban, she becomes despicable and is compared to those women who cling to their lovers' arms and resemble "creatures without spines . . . large slugs in disguise" (quoted in Beauvoir, p. 59). The image of the slug suggests not only filth but the formless abjectness of subhuman existence.

Soledad hardly fares better. She too is stripped of her humanity in being reduced to the status of a mere obstacle in the hero's quest for transcendence. Her refusal to give herself to Alban is intended not to spur him on but to remind him of his weakness. In fact, according to de Beauvoir, Montherlant's women do not wish their men to succeed, to surpass themselves. They wish instead to close men in, to limit them, because they "are incapable of feeling a man's thirst for transcendence, of sensing his grandeur" (Beauvoir, p. 59).

Although Alban's mistresses are the targets of hostility in *Le songe* and *Les bestiaires*, other women in different roles also come under fire in Montherlant's early works. In the play *L'exil* (1914) and the semifictional tribute to sports, *Les olympiques* (1924), it is the mother who impedes her son's self-fulfillment, in the first instance by preventing him from joining *l'ordre mâle* at the front and in the second by refusing to allow him to test himself on another masculine proving ground, the soccer field.

But as Beauvoir points out, the mother is also guilty of another and more profound sin, that of being responsible for her son's birth. The god-like, masculine heroes Montherlant's protagonists seek to become resent owing their existence to anyone because a true divinity is self-created: "A god is not engendered; his body, if he has one, is a will transformed into hard and obedient muscles, not a flesh dumbly inhabited by life and death; this perishable, contingent, and vulnerable flesh that the god renounces, it is his mother he holds responsible for it" (Beauvoir, p. 58).

As Alice Kaplan has explained, this need for self-generation, this desire to eliminate entirely the role of the female in the process of procreation, is frequently a part of what she describes as "fascist fantasy narratives." In Marinetti's epic *Mafarka*, the hero's greatest accomplishment is the engineering and construction of his son, Gazouramah.[21] Although Montherlant does not share the Futurist's fascination with modern technology, he too dreams of an ideal race of men completely independent of feminine intervention.

Despite the obvious fascistic overtones of Montherlant's early fiction—the fascination with violence and death, the idealization of the virile male, and the hatred and fear of women—the works in question are devoid of any social or political context that would allow these predilections to assume overtly political or ideological dimensions. This is perhaps most suprising in *Le songe*, where the historical setting of the Great War would seem to lend itself to the nationalistic exaltations that appealed so much to German writers like Ernst Jünger.[22] Nevertheless, by the early 1930s Montherlant was ready to engage in social and political issues for the first time in his fiction. The result is *La rose de sable*, a contemporary novel set in French North Africa and completed in 1932.

For those accustomed to the celebration of force and violence in *Le songe* and *Les bestiaires, La rose de sable* comes as a complete surprise, in terms of both the human values it celebrates and the political views it espouses. Summing up the novel three years after its completion, Montherlant described it as a work "whose central fire is charity" (*E*, 505) and whose aim was to criticize "the colonial principle" and to speak out for the downtrodden and exploited Arabs.

Despite the length of the novel, its plot is quite simple. Michel Raimond describes it as follows: "A young lieutenant, enamored of patriotic and colonialist principles, gradually discovers the Arab world, comes to question the legitimacy of the French presence, contests the value of military operations, and decides not to participate in what his heart and mind condemn."[23]

The young lieutenant, Auligny by name, also discovers in the desert the love of an Arab girl, Ram. It is the tenderness he feels for her that initially awakens in him a realization of the sufferings of the Arabs and the cruelty of the French and finally leads him to abandon his post.

In every important way, *La rose de sable* breaks with Montherlant's earlier fiction. The exaltation of force, violence, and virility, the "Nietzschean Mask" as Raimond describes it (p. 130), drops away and is replaced by sympathy, selflessness, and charity, none of which had appeared in Montherlant's earlier works. Woman is no longer an obstacle to overcome but a catalyst that allows man to form a more equitable and generous vision of the world.

Two factors are responsible for the complete reversal in Montherlant's perspective. The first, described in the foreword to the 1936 collection of essays, *Service inutile*, concerns a change in attitude toward violence itself: "At war, in the stadium, I had witnessed only violence between equals: healthy violence. In North Africa, I saw violence exercised by the strong, the European, against the weaker native: I think that the experience disgusted me with violence for life. And I started to love the vanquished" (*E*, 575). Second, in 1928, Montherlant had discovered Sainte-Beuve's history of Jansenism, *Port-Royal*, and was profoundly impressed with this most austere form of Christianity and the virtues it espoused. Although he could not share the Christian's faith, "I shared to a large degree their sentiments; I remained outside religion but I respected it" (*E*, 578).[24]

Having spent the first two years of the decade in North Africa writing *La rose de sable*, Montherlant returned to France in April 1932, intending to publish the now-completed manuscript. Shortly after his arrival, however, he changed his mind, reasoning that the "debilitated" state of the nation would make the publication of a novel critical of France and French colonialism untimely and ultimately damaging to national morale. In 1932, Montherlant published, in the pages of the newspaper *La Liberté*, the following impression of the nation he found on his return from North Africa:

Our country is subverted from within, attacked from without. The Foreigner is in our home, by subterranean infiltration. I see the national spirit weakened or indecisive, the total absence of public spirit, a conformism of disorder which possesses all the stupidity that it tries to attribute to a conformism of order. No indignation, no strong reaction from anyone: France is a soft cheese which one can enter and cut up as one pleases. I've been reproached at times for not having enough love, but I have indignation, which is a form of love. (*E*, 586).

Montherlant concludes by noting that the country's elite, unlike its German counterpart, had done nothing to bring about the nation's renewal: "While Germany's elite has saved it from the consequences of its defeat, France's elite has greatly contributed to the sabotage of our victory."

Once again, a complete reversal. The sympathy for the native, for the "other," in *La rose de sable* is replaced by a paranoid denunciation of the outsider who has insidiously invaded *La patrie* and is contributing to its destruction. Weakness, disorder, and indifference prevail in a country gone soft, a country whose elite does not measure up to the Nazi elite across the Rhine.

The article in *La Liberté* is significant not only because it reaffirms a reactionary, fascistic ethic in which force and toughness are implicitly championed but because it inserts this ethic in a context that is openly ideological. A fierce and indignant nationalism and a call for order are now linked to the manly virtues espoused in *Le songe* and *Les bestiares*. The whole passage, moreover, smacks of the critique of French decadence found in *Le solstice de juin* and other wartime writings. Missing only is the misogyny of the Alban de Bricoule novels, but this too returns with a vengeance in Montherlant's *succès de scandale* of the mid-1930s, the quartet of novels titled *Les jeunes filles*.

It is tempting to conclude that Montherlant's decision in 1932 not to publish *La rose de sable* represents an effort on his part to suppress that side of his nature susceptible to charitable, selfless, or, as Alban de Bricoule would say, "sentimental" urges. While such crude psychologizing is risky, Montherlant's actions in 1932 confirm the tension between the two extremes, a tension that apparently could not be eased simply by "alternating" them. In any case, the political implications of the author's suppression of *La rose de sable* are clear: given the choice between what he perceived to be the interest of justice and the interests of the nation, Montherlant opted for the latter. But the nation he chose was not the pluralistic, democratic society of the Third Republic but an idealized, forceful nation uncorrupted by foreigners and controlled from above by its elite. Montherlant's preference in the 1932 article of a strong authoritarian state over the ideals of justice and democracy ominously foreshadows the political choices he made after the French defeat of 1940.

The individual titles of the series *Les jeunes filles*—*Les jeunes filles* (1936), *Pitié pour les femmes* (1936), *Le démon de bien* (1937), and *Les lépreuses* (1939)—reveal a strong animosity toward women that the works' contents bear out. The haughty, condescending tone of the first two titles, "The Young Girls" and "Pity for Women," gives way in the final volume, "The Leprous Ones,"to an image intended to evoke corruption, contamination, and horror. The plots of the novels follow the romantic adventures of the writer-hero Pierre Costals, but the real aim of these works is to provide a unilateral condemnation of women and their corrupting influence on contemporary French society. Costals is involved with three women: Thérèse Pantevin, a hysterical religious fanatic who confuses her love for Christ with her passion for Costals; Andrée Haquebaut, a frustrated provincial intellectual who cannot accept Costal's sexual indifference to her; and Solange Dandillot, a wealthy bourgeoise who alone appeals to Costals because she is the most "natural." Considered together, the three women sum up and express for Montherlant the vices not only of the female sex but of a French society that has been corrupted by the nefarious influence of women. Women are no longer simply a threat to the individual, as they are in the Alban de Bricoule novels, but to the fabric of culture itself. According to Henri Purruchot, these corrupting vices include sentimentality, gregariousness, and *irréalisme*, an incapacity to see and accept things as they really are.[25] They also comprise a sterile intellectualism and strong religious sentiments, both of which weaken the spirit and the will. Many of these elements reappear in Montherlant's attacks on French decadence during the Occupation.

On a personal level, Montherlant exorcises his own "demon of goodness" by attributing charitable urges associated with religious sentiments to the women that the novels condemn. Thérèse Pantevin, whose single-minded religiosity resembles the devotion of the Jansenists themselves, slowly loses her mind and is dismissed by Costals. The respect for Christian sentiments, which Montherlant claims to have discovered in the late 1920s and which inspired the writing of *La rose de sable*, is suppressed in *Les jeunes filles*.

The only woman who escapes a complete condemnation in the novels is Solange Dandillot, and the reasons she is exceptional are most revealing. The narrator describes her as being completely "natural," by which he means that she is entirely inconsistent and whimsical. She lacks both a strong will and the intellect to provide a coherence to her character, and this is precisely why Costals is so taken with her: "I can't stand women who possess their own will and that's why you're made for me for all eternity" (*R*, 1096). Of necessity, Solange seeks authority and direction outside herself, so she is drawn to the Right. As the narrator informs us, she has even belonged to "a group of the extreme-Right," but he refuses to identify the group out of a sense of delicacy, since Solange has previously slept with one of the group's members.

Although Costals ultimately rejects her, Solange does represent the only female *type* the fictional writer and his real-life creator find acceptable. Devoid of a will and an identity of her own, she seeks to be dominated by a strong male and finds security in an authoritarian political order.[26] She is the object of Costals' lust, but she never achieves the status of an independent *partner* in their lovemaking because that would imply a form of equality Costals cannot abide. He decides definitively to leave her when she seeks to tie him down in a stultifying, bourgeois marriage, for acceptance of the marriage would acknowledge her dignity, her humanity, which Costals is unwilling to do, and it would also entail a concession, disastrous in its consequences, to a decadent French society destitute of redeeming, manly virtues. In breaking with Solange (and the other women who pursue him), Costals, and Montherlant through him, announce their liberation from a culture gone soft and reaffirm their commitment to the phallocentric and Nietzschean values of Montherlant's early fiction. Moreover, these values are now moored to a cultural critique that is clearly reactionary and fascistic in its essence. *Les jeunes filles*, therefore, sets the stage for the pro-Nazi, Occupation writings to come.

If *Le solstice de juin* and the articles in *La Gerbe* were all that Montherlant produced during the Occupation, it would be easy to conclude that the struggle between force and charity, so evident in the writer's prewar itinerary, had concluded with the defeat of the latter and resulted, finally, in an outright and unequivocal commitment to fascism. The presence of the dramatic masterpiece *La reine morte*, however, renders such a conclusion simplistic and premature. Produced in December 1942, *after* the publication of Montherlant's most politically compromising essays and articles, the play stages a "return of the repressed," charity, and dramatizes its direct confrontation with its opposite. Moreover, the struggle is played out in a specifically political context. Thus, the drama provides a crucial, final piece of evidence in establishing the contours of Montherlant's wartime politics and their relation to his prewar itinerary.

Taking place in Portugal "in bygone times" (*T*, 105), *La reine morte* examines the political and human crises surrounding the marriage of the Portuguese prince, Don Pedro. Ferrante, the prince's father and the play's protagonist, wishes his son to marry the infante of Navarre, a proud, arrogant, and strong woman who cares nothing for human emotions and is, in her own terms, "born to rule" (*T*, 148). Such a marriage, in the king's view, not only would benefit Portugal directly by furnishing it with a powerful ally in Navarre, but it would provide a strong partner for his son, who lacks strength and the will to rule. When Ferrante demands of Pedro that he marry the infante, the prince refuses, confessing his love for another woman, Inès de Castro. Illegitimate and a foreigner, Inès is the infante's opposite in every way: she has no interest in politics and is a creature of remarkable generosity and kindness. In her own words, "all I know how to do is to love others" (*T*, 151).

When Ferrante learns from Inès at the end of the first act that she and Pedro have been secretly married for a year, he imprisons his son and tries to persuade Inès to accept a divorce, with the understanding that she can continue to be his mistress. Although he wishes to break up the marriage, Ferrante nevertheless is drawn to Inès and wishes to protect her in a political situation in which she is the most vulnerable player. Inès refuses, and the infante, impatient by nature, leaves Portugal and returns home.

In the final act, Inès, who has become more and more intimate with Ferrante during the course of the play, confesses that she is carrying Pedro's child, a son. Ferrante, seeing all of his political plans come to ruin, orders Inès's execution. Torn apart by the political and personal quandaries surrounding Pedro's marriage, Ferrante witnesses the dissolution of his own identity ("I have melted away like the wind in the desert" [*T*, 161]) and dies in his throne room. Pedro enters accompanied by courtiers bearing the body of Inès. Pedro places a crown on her chest, and all present kneel around her, ignoring the body of the dead king.

Given the action of the play and the characters presented, *La reine morte* lends itself to a variety of political readings. It could be argued, for example, that the infante represents the virile German conqueror who is ultimately rejected by a French nation seduced by the charms of the soft and decadent Inès, an *illegitimate* intruder. Such a reading would be consistent not only with Montherlant's most avowedly pro-Nazi writings in *Le solstice* and *La Gerbe* but with his 1932 attack on the decadence of the French nation in *La Liberté*.

Another scenario, proposed by Simone de Beauvoir after the war, also paints *La reine morte* as a profascist drama, in which Ferrante is Heinrich Himmler and Inès a victim of Buchenwald (Beauvoir, p. 69).

Both of these readings are, however, one-sided and inadequate. Whatever the ultimate fate of the characters, they are all presented in a sympathetic light at one point or another in the play. This is especially true of Inès, whose generosity and goodness powerfully affect all of the other characters, including the infante herself. To find in her a personification of the decadence Montherlant attacks in his earlier writings is simply untenable. Similarly, Beauvoir's reading of Ferrante as a cold-blooded Nazi exterminator cannot be supported in the text. In the second act, he refuses to execute Inès even though his councilors make a good case for such an option; he relents and orders her death only when he has lost his grip on the kingdom and on himself.[27]

Perhaps *La reine morte* should be read less as a political allegory per se than as a meditation on the destructive potential of the struggle be-tween force and charity when cast in a political context. Giving full ex-pression to both extremes for the first time in a single work, Montherlant exposes the cost in human and political terms of a conflict in which nei-ther side wins. Inès's love, though not vanquished, costs her her life as well as the life of her unborn son. On the other hand, *raison d'état* and the use of force and violence necessary to sustain it fail to achieve their aims, as neither Pedro's imprisonment nor Inès's murder secure for Fer-rante the alliance he desires.

A pro-Resistance play? A pro-Nazi play? *La reine morte* is ultimately neither. Instead, it exposes the bankruptcy of politics as a means of cop-ing with human dilemmas and constitutes as such a belated recognition on Montherlant's part of the personal cost of his own fascist commit-ments. But this does not entail a political reversal so much as a spiritual withdrawal. In its geographical setting and deliberately vague time frame, *La reine morte* is already a retreat into *inactualité*, a withdrawal from the present. Henceforth, the Fascist "hero" who continues to write for *La Gerbe* will be less the committed ideologue than the empty suit of armor sitting on the throne that Ferrante describes to Inès in *La reine morte*.[28]

In the final analysis, *La reine morte* raises more questions than it an-swers. What accounts for the political nihilism of the play after the pro-fascist acts of faith in *Le solstice de juin* and *La gerbe*? It is tempting to conclude that Nazi military reversals in late 1942 chastened Montherlant and led him to conclude that the wiser course would be to tone down his procollaborationist stance. What better way to accomplish this than in a dramatic work (and not a political essay) that takes place in a vague and distant past, a drama, in other words, that would be unlikely to arouse Nazi suspicions? Such expediency, given Montherlant's record, is cer-tainly not out of the question. A more plausible and more lenient view, based on Montherlant's prewar itinerary, is that those charitable, hu-mane urges that had led him to political positions opposed to nazism and expressed in *La rose de sable* could not be definitively repressed, if for no other reason than that they nourished his artistic inspiration.

Does *La reine morte* make Montherlant any less of a collaborator? Certainly not, but it does challenge the view, implicit in Derrida's and Hillis Miller's defenses of de Man, that Montherlant was an exemplary literary collaborator whose "crimes" far exceeded those of de Man. In fact, Montherlant's wartime record ironically resembles the young Paul de Man's: both men compromised themselves most thoroughly by writ-ing for collaborationist publications, and the most profascist articles by each man appeared in 1941 and 1942.[29]

What *La reine morte* does suggest is that Montherlant came to understand the cost in human terms of the political choice he had made. Rather than reverse his field, he simply withdrew. The political and philosophical nihilism of the 1942 play would dominate his work more and more in the postwar period and contribute finally to his suicide in 1972.[30]

Fascists on Film

The Brasillach and Bardèche *Histoire du cinèma*

D espite Robert Brasillach's avowed fascist leanings—and his execution as a collaborator in 1945—the *Histoire du cinéma* he
wrote with Maurice Bardèche[1] has somehow managed to escape
the political label that has attached itself to his other work. Brasillach's
marginal politics did not seem to interfere with the work's reputation as
a first major effort to write an international history of film: Iris Barry,
director of the newly established film archives of the Museum of Modern
Art, rushed to translate it into English in 1938.[2] Nor did Brasillach's condemnation for collaborating with the Nazis hinder the French republi-
cation of the encyclopedic work, constantly updated by his devoted
brother-in-law, Maurice Bardèche. In his introduction to the *Histoire du
cinéma* in Brasillach's complete works, Bardèche takes pains to stress that
the work bears little relationship to Brasillach's other, more ideologically
oriented writings or to the events of its time. Calling it a "foreign plant"
among "the habitual preoccupations and thoughts of the author," Bardèche goes on to say that the work, "indifferent to events and catas-
trophes, . . . dove and surfaced periodically as if it had had its own existence, without any relationship to our lives."[3] The only trace of contemporary events or ideologies (which he euphemistically terms "l'air du
temps") to be found in the work, Bardèche asserts, is a two-page summary of an anti-Semitic pamphlet written by Lucien Rebatet, which appeared only in the 1943 edition, published during the Nazi occupation.
Most subsequent readers have seemed to concur with Bardèche's view.
When the American translation was reprinted in 1970, reviews described
the work in completely apolitical terms, calling it "one of the early and
now classic motion picture histories which is still widely read, largely for
a French view of the American motion picture."[4] Even William R.
Tucker, in his "political biography" of Brasillach, is content to mention

the *Histoire du cinéma* merely as a biographical anecdote, an outgrowth of Brasillach's youthful passion for the movies.[5]

My own initial reading of Brasillach's film history also seemed to bear out Bardèche's contentions. I had expected a Fascist of Brasillach's political stripe to hold up Leni Riefenstahl's *Triumph of the Will* as a standard of cinematic excellence and to denigrate filmmakers of Jewish background, like Charlie Chaplin or Fritz Lang. It was rather a surprise, then, to find that this is not at all the case: Brasillach and Bardèche's judgments of significance and quality are not radically different from those of more recent French film historians, even the Marxist Georges Sadoul. Completed in 1935, the first version of *Histoire du cinéma*, perhaps understandably, fails to recognize the artistic merits of sound cinema, then only recently introduced, and it underestimates the importance of certain directors, like Jean Renoir, who had not yet produced their major works. But on the whole, the judgments of Brasillach and Bardèche have been echoed by later critics, and their appreciation of Méliès, Eisenstein, Chaplin, and René Clair and their understanding of the qualities of German expressionism and American comedy, have remained largely unchallenged.

It is true, as Alice Yaeger Kaplan has pointed out, that the 1943 edition,[6] updated by Brasillach alone and published under German censorship, had modified earlier judgments to reveal an overt anti-Semitism, clearly in accord with Nazi policies and just as clearly in line with Brasillach's own statements in *Je suis partout*, the notoriously anti-Semitic newspaper with which he had been involved for several years. In some cases, the 1943 modifications signaled by Kaplan radically altered earlier views, as in the case of Charlie Chaplin, for whom the 1935 edition had expressed unreserved admiration despite his partially Jewish ancestry. The 1935 reference to "a strangely human note to his [Chaplin's] misfortune" becomes, in 1943, "a strangely Hebraic note."[7] In the climate of the time, the change from "human" to "Hebraic" could hardly be a more radical reassessment. In other cases, Kaplan finds anti-Semitism functioning to flesh out a previously unexplained aesthetic judgment. Brasillach and Bardèche's original opposition to sound is now articulated in terms of their fear of the introduction of an "unstable Jewish accent" as against the notion of "a mother tongue, properly enunciated on the sound track."[8]

However, these overtly anti-Semitic references are absent from the original 1935 edition, the one translated into English by Iris Barry and reedited by Bardèche. Thus, the *Histoire du cinéma* with which most readers are familiar has managed to escape the contamination of Brasillach's fascist politics by appearing to remain safely in the realm of aesthetics.

In Brasillach's other work, however, I have often found it difficult to establish a neat line separating the political from the aesthetic. Other commentators seeking an understanding of Brasillach's politics have experienced similar difficulties: Tucker concludes that "[Brasillach's] intuitive approach to politics prompted an awareness that fascism was as much a response to the movement of time, a style, and a feeling of exhiliration, as it was a political creed."[9] Brasillach contributes to the confusion by stating openly in his memoirs that, for him, fascism was not a political or economic doctrine but "a spirit," a form of youthful joy.[10] In fact, he concluded in a later text, it was "a form of poetry—the poetry of the twentieth century."[11]

Reading Brasillach's explicitly political texts against the background of the *Histoire du cinéma*, I have been struck by the fact that the same terms Brasillach uses to describe the cinema also appear in his discussions of political phenomena. Speaking of the Belgian Rexist movement of Léon Degrelle, which provided his first serious contact with a Fascist group, Brasillach wrote: "We will have understood that the success of nationalism in those years came from its power of proposing images to the masses and being, for better or worse, a *poetry*."[12] Reading such a description out of context, it would seem that Brasillach was discussing the work of a poet or even a filmmaker rather than a politician. The same sort of evaluation extends to Brasillach's image of Fascist Italy, characterized in his novel *Les sept couleurs* almost uniquely by scenes of singing youth that seem more appropriate to one of René Clair's musical comedies than to Mussolini's Blackshirts. Tucker observes that Brasillach in Italy seems to have been impressed by "little more than the stage decor."[13]

Brasillach's descriptions of Nazi Germany are even more cinematic and, in fact, evoke comparisons with Leni Riefenstahl's propaganda film, *Triumph of the Will*. Brasillach had certainly seen the film prior to his own attendance at the 1937 Nuremberg congress: he described *Triumph of the Will* as "monotonous and at times magnificent" (p. 397) in the 1935 edition of *Histoire du cinéma*, and it is possible that it may have shaped his response to his own experience. His journalistic account of the 1937 Nuremberg congress presents a succession of visual images similar to those in the film, from the picturesque views of ancient German architecture to the sea of undulating Nazi banners.[14] Even Hitler himself is not analyzed as a political leader or the exponent of an ideology; Brasillach focuses his description on Hitler's eyes, whose mysterious sadness is reminiscent of an expressive close-up from the silent films Brasillach knew so well. In his memoirs, Brasillach describes Hitler, like his favorite filmmakers, as "a poet," and this indeed seems to have been the place occupied by Hitler in Brasillach's system of thought. Reading Brasillach's account of fascism, it is not difficult to see how a number of critics, following the lead of Walter Benjamin, have seen fascism as an aestheticization of politics.[15]

If Brasillach's political thought reveals a confusion of political and aesthetic categories, can this confusion have failed to affect his work of an overtly aesthetic nature? Can we really maintain Bardèche's view of the 1935 *Histoire du cinéma* as a work unaffected by the political climate in which it was written? Although the *Histoire du cinéma* continues to be accepted by readers who would condemn Brasillach's fascist politics, the work does possess, as one American reviewer enigmatically expressed it, a "frequently unique viewpoint."[16] To attempt to articulate the nature of this uniqueness may provide a way of understanding the relationship of the *Histoire du cinéma* to other aspects of Brasillach's work, as it may illuminate the responses of two young members of the French Right to the new mass medium.

One element of Brasillach and Bardèche's judgments that immediately raised readers' questions was their violent opposition to the transition to sound film. This opposition was, for obvious reasons, particularly evident in the 1935 edition.[17] At that time, of course, such an aesthetic preference for silent film was not as eccentric as it seems today: Brasillach and Bardèche were articulating sentiments shared by other intellectuals devoted to film, most notably René Clair, whom they quote freely on this subject. Kaplan points out that in the 1935 edition of their work, Brasillach and Bardèche seem strangely unable to articulate their objections to sound.[18] The judgments they quote from Clair do not aid in this explanation but merely support their premise that true cinema is in essence a visual art.

Even in 1938, however, their American translator, Iris Barry, was puzzled by their attitude. On the basis of her own considerable knowledge of film, she felt that Brasillach and Bardèche's hostility to the early sound films and their nostalgic admiration for the silent films of the 1920s bore no relation to reality: "Actual examination of the production," she comments, "suggests no such conclusion."[19] Despite Brasillach and Bardèche's failure to articulate their arguments, Barry is quick to perceive a reason behind their preferences, in the devastating effect the advent of sound had had on the French cinema industry: "It is difficult to reject the suspicion that the sad state into which the French film industry had fallen at the time this book was written may account to a very large extent for the pessimistic note on which the authors closed."[20]

The "sad state" to which Barry refers was, in part, a function of the poor quality of some early French sound films. Later film historians seem, indeed, to concur with Brasillach and Bardèche's condemnation of these films, many of which were simply adaptations of theatrical productions. But Brasillach and Bardèche's opposition to these debased examples of the cinematic art is hardly sufficient to explain their hostility to the principle of sound itself, especially since they were willing to recognize that sound had also contributed to a number of outstanding films, including several by their favorite contemporary director, René Clair. Their rejection of the sound film on grounds that purport to be purely aesthetic seems, as Iris Barry suspected, to mask concerns that were not unrelated to the economic plight of the French film industry.

Brasillach and Bardèche indicate their awareness that, by 1935, the major French production companies had reached a state of financial collapse: the Pathé company had gone bankrupt in the midst of a financial scandal, and the other major French firms had gone into decline. This financial disaster was brought on, at least in part, by the advent of sound technology, which was entirely in the hands of American and German corporations. As Brasillach and Bardèche take pains to point out, the French had once pioneered the development of synchronized sound, but their inventions had never been commercially developed. Now, not only were French companies obliged to pay large sums to acquire the new technology, but much of the film production in France itself was taken over by foreign firms. Both the American Paramount and the German Tobis set up studios in Paris, where, in the absence of sophisticated dubbing techniques, they mass-produced several versions of the same film in different languages, with foreign casts and foreign directors. Sadoul reports that many French directors were alienated by the frantic commercial pace of these enterprises and were driven to leave France for better working conditions in England.[21] According to Roy Armes, in 1934, 20 percent of French films were made abroad and an additional 20 percent were made in France by foreigners.[22]

Such transgression of national boundaries was clearly abhorrent to Brasillach and Bardèche. It violated not only their sense of French pride but their entire view of the nature of the cinema, which, for them, was closely tied to the concept of national character. As Kaplan has noted, *Histoire du cinéma* is carefully organized in terms of national cinemas, and some editions even include a film bibliography in which films are listed under national rubrics.[23] As logical as such organization might at first appear, its appropriateness could easily be questioned at a time when, for some years, filmmakers had been moving from country to country, lured as much by the promise of political and religious freedom as financial reward. At the moment Brasillach and Bardèche were preparing their first edition, many filmmakers were fleeing Hitler's Germany, a phenomenon discussed quite openly in *Histoire du cinéma*. But such transcendence of national boundaries did not lead Brasillach and Bardèche to question their principles of nationally based organization. It becomes apparent that, for them, the divisions along national lines were more than a convenient way of arranging material: conformity to a "national character" was indeed a fundamental principle of their aesthetic judgment.

This is apparent even in their discussion of very early films. Brasillach and Bardèche rejoice over the "ethnic and national character" of one of the first German films, a short scene of young people on bicycles: "In this simple little film the whole pictorial sense of the Germans . . . [is] already to be detected" (p. 20; Barry, p. 8). And, indeed, they will continue to praise this trait in later German films. They go on to note with pleasure that the Russian cinema, even before World War I, was dominated by "certain important national elements" (p. 73). Particularly important to the character Russian cinema was to take, in their view, was the nature of Slavic theater, with its ability to express the reality of the crowd; this is the quality they would continue to find throughout the history of Russian film, culminating in the much-admired Eisenstein. Swedish cinema, too, was to be praised for understanding "the function that national legends and the national character were to play, as material fitting for translation into visual imagery and rhythm" (p. 77; Barry, p. 58). Even the Americans—who do not rank high on Brasillach and Bardèche's list of preferred nations—were at their best when, prior to World War I, they confined themselves to making Westerns because this genre was "so purely local and autochthonous" (p. 85; Barry, p. 65) and was inspired by America's own "national mythology" (even so, Brasillach and Bardèche cannot refrain from adding that this mythology was of a "somewhat barbarous naiveté" [p. 87; omitted from the American translation].)

Aesthetic value, for Brasillach and Bardèche, is so closely linked with "national" characteristics that it seems to be rooted in the native soil. Thus, when major German directors of the 1920s left for Hollywood, their departure not only devastated the German film industry but also, in the eyes of Brasillach and Bardèche, destroyed the quality of their own work: "When they left home the German directors clearly lost their originality in trying to cater to an international audience" (p. 289; Barry, p. 259). Similarly, they found René Clair's work lacking in interest when he left France in the latter half of the 1930s. The only figure with enough individual talent to escape this problem of transplantation from the native soil seems to have been Eisenstein—but, of course, the country he left was the Soviet Union.

As individual filmmakers could be destroyed by leaving their native soil, the film production of a nation could be undermined by the infiltration of foreigners. This, in their view, was a major factor in the decline of the German cinema in the 1920s: "A considerable number of foreigners had rapidly crept into the German studios and denationalized them; they obviously cared for nothing but making money" (p. 289; Barry, pp. 258–59). Such infiltration by what they here term "foreigners" seemed to Brasillach and Bardèche to have also been responsible for the current problems of the French cinema. They note that in the 1920s the "pillar of the French film industry," the Pathé production company, was bought by the Natan brothers, who are described in the 1935 edition as Rumanians. The Natans' management of Pathé corresponds, for Brasillach and Bardèche, to a period in which not a single film of value was produced and that plunged the French cinema into "abjection" (p. 254). In later editions of their *Histoire du cinéma*, Brasillach and Bardèche are more explicit in decrying the presence of Jews in the French film industry. Brasillach later claimed to have become anti-Semitic only in 1936, in response to the "excessive" presence of Jews in the Popular Front ministries,[24] but even in 1935, it is not hard to see behind the "foreigners" who had denationalized the formerly creative German cinema—the "Rumanians" who were responsible for the "abjection" of the French film industry—the hidden presence of Jews.

Imbued with the principle that good film is related to its national background, Brasillach and Bardèche are, as can be imagined, greatly preoccupied by French film. Their *Histoire du cinéma* is, in its inspiration, a profoundly chauvinistic text. An important hidden agenda of Brasillach and Bardèche seems to be the documentation of the early achievements of the French cinema and its decline at the hands of its enemies—a project strangely like that of the French Right of the 1930s, which continually lamented the decadence of a once-great country.

Indeed, for Brasillach and Bardèche, the history of the cinema is a story of confrontation between nations, a story of victory and defeat that parallels the broader sweep of political history. The central events of these histories are often the same, for it was World War I, in their view, that precipitated the downfall of the previously unchallenged French cinema: "It is the war that marks the date of the American victory on world screens, it is the war that marks the date of the French defeat" (p. 115; omitted from the American translation). Although the *Histoire du cinéma* was written by two different authors and covers a great diversity of material, it reveals a remarkable unity of conception. Despite its pretense to being merely an account of moments in the development of the various national cinemas, *Histoire du cinéma*, in fact, tells the story of the rise and fall of the French cinema, and that story takes on the overtones of tragedy. Indeed, Brasillach had a penchant for setting the events of his own time in the framework of classical tragedy: in his novel, *Les sept couleurs*, he placed an account of the development of European fascism within the structure of Corneille's tragedy, *Polyeucte*.

The form of the modern-day technological tragedy Brasillach and Bardèche fashion from the history of French film is immediately apparent in the story of Georges Méliès that Brasillach recounts in his memoirs. Méliès is portrayed at length in *Histoire du cinéma* as one of the founding fathers of world cinema. In the early 1930s, however, Bardèche had found the internationally known filmmaker dying in obscure poverty in an old-age home in Orly. In his memoirs, Brasillach presents a vivid image of the downtrodden Méliès, who had seen the bankruptcy of his film production company and had been reduced to selling toys at the Gare Montparnasse. Brasillach describes the appearance of the impoverished genius at a gala given for him by the film industry in 1928, surrounded by the disdainful and mocking figures who now dominated the cinematic world: "Fat gentlemen in top hats, Jews and Aryans, enormous caricatures of capitalism, with indulgent smiles watched this little bearded old man do his tricks. They had the money, the power, they were the cinema, and there was some contempt in their way of looking at this poor man who had found a way of not getting rich by making films." [25] In his humiliation and in the characterization of the forces that crush him, the once-great Méliès could stand as the emblem of French cinema itself as it is portrayed in *Histoire du cinéma*.

If we are to believe Brasillach and Bardèche, all important technological advances in the early years of the cinema had their origins in France. By their account, the work of the Lumière brothers predated Edison's American film patent. Even synchronized sound—a technology that in the 1930s was dominated by American companies—was first developed in 1910 by the Frenchman Gaumont, at a time when, they claim, Edison was "vainly seeking the secret of coordinating sound and picture" (p. 71). The American edition translates this passage rather differently: "Edison in New York had also, though less successfully, run synchronized film-and-photography talkies" (Barry, p. 54). On the basis of their interpretation, Brasillach and Bardèche joyfully conclude: "We can see that sound cinema . . . is really a French invention" (p. 71; omitted from American translation). To Méliès, of course, goes credit not only for creating the first film studio but for realizing the capacities of the new medium to create a world of magical fantasy that predated and made possible the work of the better-known American, Walt Disney. In their presentation of the "classic age of silent movies," Brasillach and Bardèche proudly assert: "Méliès had discovered virtually the whole of [the cinema's] primitive alphabet" (p. 254; Barry, p. 225).

As Méliès represents, in this narrative, the great moment of invention in the French cinema, his abject state in the 1930s is an image of its subsequent decline. For despite the presence of vigorous creators like René Clair in the 1920s and 1930s, French cinema as a whole, in the view of Brasillach and Bardèche, was losing ground. They accuse the French film industry, as early as the 1920s, of giving way to a base commercialism and to American financial pressure: "In the end everything was subordinated to catering to the lowest and most ridiculous public taste; then came loss of money and finally the dollar triumphed" (p. 254; Barry, p. 226). And they end their history on an even blacker note: in 1935, the year in which they were writing, they report, "the French film industry practically disappeared" (p. 384; Barry, p. 226). The reaction of Brasillach and Bardèche to this financial disaster, however, is strangely ambivalent. While lamenting the success of the American takeover, they do not seem unduly upset by the demise of what they had long deemed a mediocre French production. In fact, they are able to perceive a ray of hope in the collapse of the large companies, believing that real progress was to be found in smaller, independent filmmakers. Their ambivalence about French commercial success suggests a parallel with the attitude of the young Facists of the 1930s, who, even as they claimed to support French interests, yearned for the collapse of the decadent French Third Republic.

Other film historians have described the invasion of the French film industry in the 1930s by both American and German companies. It is interesting to note that Brasillach and Bardèche refer only to American domination. In fact, although they eagerly condemn the mediocrity of American-controlled production, they fail to mention that all of their admired René Clair films of the early 1930s were made in the studios of the German firm Tobis.[26] *Histoire du cinéma* is permeated by such blatant anti-Americanism: the chapters on the American cinema, most of which were written by Maurice Bardèche, spend more time decrying the vulgarity and crass commercialism of such figures as Cecil B. de Mille than analyzing important American films. In his memoirs, Brasillach is honest in stating that "Americanism" had seemed to be the chief danger facing France in the early 1930s.[27] Indeed, this feeling seems to have been widespread among French intellectuals, who realized that world War I, which had taken a heavy toll on France and other European countries, had actually contributed to U.S. industrial development.

The opposition of Brasillach and Bardèche to American domination of the cinema, however, seems to go beyond mere chauvinism: for them the

American film industry appeared to incarnate the very spirit of industrial capitalism, to which they and others of the French Right were vehemently opposed. Their opposition to Hollywood-style capitalism cannot merely be seen as a preference for the creative individual as opposed to large-scale production, as might appear from some of their comments on the French cinema, because they do not seem opposed to large production companies in other national contexts. They are lost in admiration for the organization of the state-run and ideologically monolithic Soviet cinema of the 1920s, and they seem to look with some favor on the centralized German film industry, especially after its appropriation by Hitler.[28] Their opposition to the American cinema industry seems to be based on other considerations, never articulated in coherent fashion. At certain points they link Hollywood production to liberal democratic values in its preoccupation with "pleasing the greatest number"—a standard Brasillach and Bardèche consistently reject for reasons they obviously consider beneath serious discussion. Bourgeois democracy, as epitomized by the United States, was, of course, despised by the elitist Brasillach and other French Fascists of the 1930s, and this condemnation clearly extended itself into the aesthetic realm.

The discussion of the American film industry in *Histoire du cinéma* is focused more on the production companies than on the films themselves, and in describing the formation of the early film companies, Brasillach and Bardèche take particular delight in showing that the people involved are "really" furriers or haberdashers. Their real condemnation of the American film industry would thus seem to be twofold. Having been founded by men whose training and interests were commercial rather than purely artistic, the American cinema is dominated by the crass commercialism Brasillach and Bardèche never fail to condemn as inimical to aesthetic considerations. Such commercialism seems, for them, a central trait of the American national character. Moreover, behind the "haberdashers" and "furriers" can be discerned without much effort a Jewish presence, although explicit objections to Jewish domination of the large American film companies do not appear in the work until 1943.[29] Thus, the constant denigration of the American film industry—which, of course, does not extend to a devaluation of all American films—reflects not only a nationalistic commitment to French preeminence but also an antipathy to liberalism and capitalism and a barely disguised anti-Semitism, all of which trace their origins to the thought of the contemporary French Right.

The right-wing ideological premises I have thus far identified in *Histoire du cinéma* find their expression primarily in the analysis of the cinema industry rather than in judgments of individual films, although

Brasillach and Bardèche do not hesitate to denigrate the work of emigrant filmmakers and to condemn the whole enterpise of sound cinema. Their standards seem to become less ideological when they discuss the films themselves. In analyzing the criteria, aesthetic or otherwise, that provide Brasillach and Bardèche with reason to value an individual work, it would be useful to begin by considering not the objects of their derision but, rather, their cinematic heroes, Méliès and René Clair.

Méliès is the first heroic figure to make an appearance in *Histoire du cinéma*. The chapter that describes his early work is entitled, in the French edition, "Finally, Malherbe Arrived," a reference to the man who brought order to the Renaissance chaos of the French language.[30] For Brasillach and Bardèche, Méliès bears the primary responsibility for the early development of French film. To Méliès are applied the epithets of highest approval in Brasillach's aesthetic judgment. He is, above all, an "inventor," in the true sense of the word—a creator, who stamps his work with his own distinctive mark: "the one man who brought to this new technical invention an immense number of really original ideas, and who finally made of the film something other than a mere offshoot of photography" (p. 22; Barry, pp. 9–10). The individual contribution of Méliès is of a nature particularly appealing to Brasillach and Bardèche, for they see him as having moved French cinema away from photographic realism. The early cinematic images produced by the Lumière brothers were indeed of a realistic nature, although other critics have pointed out that these films did much more than merely record events in a photographic way, as Brasillach and Bardèche seem to imply.[31] But, while not denying their pioneering role in the technical development of cinema (Brasillach and Bardèche stress the extent to which the Lumiére brothers were ahead of the American Edison), they find the Lumière films to be of little artistic interest.

It is evident that the subjects of the Lumières' short films did not appeal to Brasillach's world of values: the shots of workers leaving a Lyons factory provided a vision of proletarian life that had no counterpart in Brasillach's own view of social reality; the train arriving in the station suggested a world of modern technology that Brasillach tended to condemn (except, perhaps, in its cinematic form); and the scenes of the Lumière family at home evoked a world of bourgeois values against which he had consistently proclaimed his rebellion.[32] In her American translation, Iris Barry inserts a footnote to express her amazement that Brasillach and Bardèche, who commonly see indications of a "national character" in the early productions of other national cinemas, had failed to recognize "how beautifully French" (p. 8) the Lumière films revealed themselves to be. Many film critics have seen in the contrasting styles of the Lumière brothers and Méliès a prefiguration of the tensions between realism and fantasy that were to characterize the further development of French film. It is clear that, against the "realism" of the Lumière films, Brasillach and Bardèche preferred Méliès's world of magical illusion.

If the hero of the early years of French cinema is Méliès, the central figure of its later development, for Brasillach and Bardèche, is René Clair. The important position occupied by René Clair in the 1935 edition of *Histoire du cinéma* does not, even today, appear without justification. In 1935, Clair would have seemed uncontestably the leading figure in French cinema. He had made the transition from the avant-garde of his early *Entr'acte* to a more commercially viable cinema without losing his personal vision; and despite his stated aversion to sound, he was one of the few French filmmakers to make the transition from silent to sound production successfully. As Brasillach and Bardèche were among the first to point out, Clair's musical, *Sous les toits de Paris*, used sound in original and creative ways, often as a counterpoint to image.

Yet the admiration Brasillach and Bardèche showed for the work of René Clair is not without its subjective elements. As the reasons for their preference for Méliès become clear when his work is contrasted to the implicit social realism of the Lumière films, the qualities they value in René Clair become apparent in their concomitant devaluation of Jean Renoir. Later criticism, particularly that of the Nouvelle Vague, has tended to elevate Renoir to the position of giant of the French cinema in the 1930s; but at the time the first edition of *Histoire du cinéma* went to press, Renoir's major works still lay ahead of him. Thus, Brasillach and Bardèche's initial discussion of Renoir is based largely on his rather uneven career in silent film, and their judgment that Renoir, in 1934, had not yet given his full measure was, in fact, quite perspicacious. The way they evaluate Renoir's existing production, however, sheds more light on the nature of their own aesthetic standards than on the films themselves. Rather surprisingly, their greatest praise is reserved for *La petite marchande d'alumettes*, Renoir's adaptation of a Hans Christian Andersen fairy tale. This short film made them believe that a new poet of the cinema had been born, but this mistaken impression was soon to be rectified. For Renoir's subsequent works—*La chienne, La nuit du carrefour, Madame Bovary* and *Toni*—Brasillach and Bardèche have, in fact, little patience, briefly praising only their pictorial qualities, their "beautiful images." Their brief impressions of these films, several of which have been highly praised by later critics, help to explain their judgments. For *La chienne* they reserve the adjective "excellent"—but only because its naturalism is "redeemed" by its "pictorial sense." Naturalism thus clearly constituted for Brasillach and Bardèche an aesthetic flaw, for which only Renoir's considerable artistic gifts could hope to atone. This is hardly surprising in view of the identification of naturalism with its founder, the hated Emile Zola, champion of Dreyfus and avowed enemy of the French Right. After years of neglect, naturalism was, in fact, coming back into vogue in the early 1930s.[33] This was particularly true in the films of Renoir: his adaptation of Zola's *Nana* received short shrift at the hands of Brasillach and Bardèche, who later also seemed incapable of appreciating his 1938 adaptation of *La bête humaine*. Brasillach's articulated hostility to the naturalist novel and its more recent "populist" offspring,[34] as well as his implicit aversion to the realistic aspects of Renoir's work, might be located in the fact that such works often constituted a critique of the existing social hierarchy and presented a vision of social conflict, a view of society to which Brasillach's own fiction reveals him to be resolutely opposed. It is to Brasillach and Bardèche's credit that they do not simply dismiss all of Renoir's work for these reasons. Instead, recognizing its artistic merit, they prefer merely to misread it. They describe Renoir's disquieting *Toni*, which deals with the condition of Italian immigrant laborers in southern France, as a "peasant film," thus erasing any possible social commentary. In the 1943 edition, Brasillach goes much further, reading Renoir's militantly antiwar film, *La grande illusion* as, rather surprisingly, a positive vision of the youthful camaraderie of war.

In their aversion to the suggestion of class conflict in French society, Brasillach and Bardèche tended to minimize its presence in film as well. Where such social antagonism was evident in works that they found, for other reasons, worthy of admiration, Brasillach and Bardèche chose to ignore it altogether or to discuss it in purely aesthetic terms. They praise Fritz Lang's *Metropolis*, with its powerful images of oppressed workers confined in a subterranean city, for its ability to create a world; but they find Lang's vision of social conflict clearly repugnant: "The confused ideology of Lang, the contrast between the fortunate beings who live in the sunlight and the unfortunate ones who live in the darkness, are disconcertingly childish" (p. 290; Barry, p. 260). Their description even avoids the language of class conflict through the use of socially neutral terms like "fortunate" and 'unfortunate." In *Metropolis*, they find that such oppositions, when read on a purely aesthetic level, can become "useful and striking" (p. 291; Barry, p. 260). It is through a similar process of aestheticization of ideological content that Brasillach and Bardèche are able to read Eisenstein's *Potemkin*, a film in which they, rather surprisingly, manage to find "a total absence of visible ideology" (p. 304; Barry, p. 291). Instead, they find a highly organized series of powerful dramatic scenes that tell a "universal human story" of a struggle between oppressors and oppressed.

In contrast to the all-too-realistic vision of Renoir, Lang, and Eisenstein, René Clair seems to offer, for Brasillach and Bardèche, a poetic vision of a harmonious world in which social conflict is soon resolved. Even the apparently chaotic images of Clair's avant-garde *Entr'acte* are, when read by Brasillach and Bardèche, governed by a "mysterious" order that creates "a sort of harmony," (p. 273), which they contrast to the disordered avant-garde films of the left-wing Luis Bunuel. They continue to find this harmony in Clair's feature-length films, which nevertheless appear to touch on contemporary social reality. But the poor people of Paris in *Sous les toits de Paris* lead their lives to the rhythm of accordion music, and in *A nous la liberté*, when confronted by a shower of bank notes, the characters perform a graceful dance rather than running off with the money. (Brasillach and Bardèche comment, "If the members of the crowd at the inauguration were simply running after the bank notes, that would be the end of them; they would vanish along with their booty. As it is, they reappear, running here and there all over the factory without apparent aim but not without order" [p. 369; Barry, p. 331]).

Although his films have been described as anarchistic, Clair himself insisted he had no social program,[35] and he has not been identified with any ideological stance. He consistently chose to set his films in clearly unrealistic decors, and he once stated that a good (silent) film had the ability to transport its spectators into a world of dreams, to make them lose their "sense of reality."[36] Whereas Clair seemed able to distinguish the reality he created in his films from the world outside the movie theater, Brasillach, as he confesses in his memoirs, sought in the world around him the vision he had discovered on the screen: "Attentive to what René Clair's films taught us, we looked around us at the lower-class neighborhoods, the strange, simple little figures."[37] In Brasillach's memoirs, as in his novels, Paris ceases to be a large anonymous modern city; it becomes a series of picturesque "villages," each with a life of its own, as in Clair's *Sous les toits de Paris*. Although Brasillach's own Vaugirard district was filled with small factories and strikers in the Depression years, he never seems concerned by any of its social problems: it is as if he were living in a Paris of cardboard stage sets like those in which Clair's movies were actually filmed. Even the social upheavals that followed the election of the Popular Front government in 1936 assume, in Brasillach's memory, a reality reminiscent of cinema: in the occupied factories he is aware only of "very photogenic groups with accordion players straight out of Russian films."[38]

For Brasillach and Bardèche, Clair's films are modeled on the ballet. A world in which each dancer in his or her assigned role contributes to the beauty of the overall performance, the ballet offers an implicit ideal of social organization, one not unlike that proposed by Brasillach in his own novel, *Le marchand d'oiseaux*: "The important thing was to accept, to play one's mysterious role."[39] This vision of a society where differences are subordinated to a higher order is also an essential element in Brasillach's concept of fascism: in *Notre avant-guerre* he stresses the importance to "young fascists" like himself of an almost mystical social unity: "From the independent researcher to the captain of industry, the poet, the scholar, the worker, the nation is a single entity, like an athletic team."[40] Although Brasillach never attempted to relate Clair's films to his own political beliefs, his admiration for Clair's harmonious and ordered cinematic world reveals the aesthetic preferences that also underlay his political vision.

It is possible that Brasillach's personal brand of fascism represented an attempt to restructure political reality in aesthetic terms, as Walter Benjamin would have it, an attempt to force the real world of contemporary society to conform to the vision of order and harmony he found in a film of René Clair. It would be more accurate to point to the inextricable mingling of political and aesthetic elements in all of Brasillach's work. If his political statements may be seen as a potentially dangerous aestheticization of politics, his forays into cinematic criticism must be recognized as an equally questionable politicization of aesthetics. It has, I believe, become clear that in their study of film, Brasillach and Bardèche were heavily influenced by what can only be termed a political vision: their emphasis on national character, their inability to tolerate "foreign" influences, their blanket condemnation of American capitalism, even their consistent preference for a "poetic" vision over a realistic one, can be seen as related to an agenda of anticapitalism, anti-Semitism, and mystical national unity, factors commonly associated with right-wing politics of the 1930s and explicitly with fascism. If their *Histoire du cinéma* continues to be read, it can no longer be seen simply as a record of idiosyncratic French views on the cinema; rather, it shows its readers how films look when viewed through the lens of a particular right-wing ideology.

Style, Subversion, Modernity
Louis-Ferdinand Céline's Anti-Semitic Pamphlets

If you give a German and not a collective interpretation to the Nazi horror, you reduce the man in Belsen to regional dimensions. The only possible response to this crime is to turn it into a crime committed by everyone. To share it. Just like the idea of equality and fraternity. In order to bear it, to tolerate the idea of it, we must share the crime.
—Marguerite Duras, *The War: A Memoir*

I n a 1957 recording in which he commented extensively upon questions of style, French novelist Louis-Ferdinand Céline decried modern literature's lack of emotion and chastised his contemporaries for their obsession with rational "ideas." Judging the creative efforts of fellow writers uniformly "useless," Céline vaunted his own literary achievements and represented himself to the postwar listening audience declaring: "There's nothing more vulgar than ideas. Encyclopedias are full of ideas, there are forty volumes of them, enormous ones, brimming with ideas. Very good ones no less. Excellent. That have served their time. But this is not the question. That's not my domain, ideas, messages. I am not a man of messages. I am not a man of ideas. I am a man of style."[1]

Although Céline no doubt subscribed in earnest to the aesthetic principles he champions in what he terms his "great attack on the Word," it must be recognized that statements such as these are also a central feature of what Philippe Alméras has called Céline's postwar "disinformation" campaign:[2] a strategy of self-rehabilitation and obfuscation by which the author sought to fashion a literary persona whose artistic stature would entirely eclipse the racist and reactionary substance of the political message he had delivered with such venom on the eve and in the early period of the Nazi occupation of France. Though Céline makes no mention here of the political persecution he incessantly claimed to have suffered following the war, an earlier treatise on style, *Entretiens avec le Professor Y* (1955), provides some sense of the motivations he may have had for belaboring his contributions as a stylist. In a tone conveying a significant degree of recovery from the morose self-pity in which he so lavishly indulged in his postwar prison narrative *Féerie pour une autre fois* (1952) and once again with the same comic verve animating his work of the early

1930s, Céline marvels at his own ingenious discovery: a miraculous literary technique allowing him to reproduce the affective charge of spoken speech in writing. Expounding on the merits of this style, one whose force he compares to the electrifying movement of the modern subway, Céline describes the nebulous essence he so greatly reveres and laboriously pursues in his fiction: "[E]motion can only be captured in the spoken word . . . and reproduced in writing at great pains and with immense patience that a jerk like you couldn't even imagine . . . [. . .] I'll explain the trick to you later! for right now just keep in mind that emotion is finicky, ephemeral, supremely: evanescent."[3] Céline's narrator goes on to surmise in *Entretiens* that the galvanizing effects of his poetry in motion so directly challenged the foundations of modern rationalism that it ultimately posed far too great a menace to the established order to be legally countenanced. He substantiates this claim by pointing out that writers who have never practiced such willful subversion of prevailing literary norms have, quite unlike himself, never found themselves in prison. "[B]ut the Delly's![4] Take a look at the Dellys! . . Who are earning a hundred million a year, without publicity, without critics. . . ! Are they searching for "the emotion of the spoken word"? Them? Poppycock! . . And they never go to prison, they don't. They're doing just fine!"[5]

In the prolific correspondence[6] and other commentaries in which he inveighed against the adversaries he deemed responsible for his ostracized status in French postwar letters, Céline seldom makes direct reference to his three pamphlets *Bagatelles pour un massacre* (1937), *L'ecole des cadavres* (1938), and *Les beaux draps* (1941), polemical works that communicated very precise ideas regarding ethnic difference and delivered an incendiary message of racial hate just prior to European civilization's most barbarous assault on the principle of cultural diversity. Despite rather imaginative claims that it was solely the seditious character of his style that drew him into the juridical maelstrom of the postwar purges, it was, in fact, the political content of these texts that formed the basis of the criminal indictment on charges of collaboration and high treason that was handed down against him in late 1945.

Although they have not been published since the Occupation and thus remain inaccessible to the public at large, Céline's anti-Semitic pamphlets have, over the past few decades, generated a variety of commentaries, ranging from exhaustive inventories of political content[7] to more probing semiotic and cultural critiques exploring their relationship to the formal innovation with which he is widely credited. Julia Kristeva remarks, for instance, that Céline's pamphlets "carry on the wild beauty"[8] of the quasi-psychotic style he introduced in *Voyage au bout de la nuit* (1932) and *Mort à crédit* (1936). His indefensible political opinions notwithstanding, she concludes, Céline's borderline narrative subjects and the fractured, lyricized voice in which they speak constitute a formal menace to monotheistic symbolism and the societal institutions it sustains. In her study of the cultural and aesthetic values of Fascist intellectuals in interwar France,[9] however, Alice Y. Kaplan cautions against the ahistoricism of Kristeva's psychoanthropological reading. In striving to capture the rhythmic drive and vocal immediacy of vernacular French, she asserts, Céline crafted a language whose populist appeal was immensely useful to France's more resolute Fascists and contributed much to their utopian celebration of "phonocentric" art forms. Citing such traits as a violent rejection of all institutional authority, an imperious disdain for modern mass culture, and an egomaniacal, anti-intellectual nihilism, François Richard[10] argues in yet another political vein that Céline was an indomitable nonconformist. He must thus be placed squarely in a French genre of right-wing literary anarchism whose elitist tenets and reactionary vision are at great odds with the progressive, egalitarian ethos of a more readily identifiable leftist variant in the tradition of Mikhail Bakunin and Pierre Joseph Proudhon.

For readers familiar with the inconsistencies in the wide range of heretical views Céline held on the modern world, the lack of consensus among these critics is not in the least bewildering. Although Céline adopted many of the same negative stances taken up by France's fascist-leaning groups in the final years of the Third Republic,[11] his pronouncements in the pamphlets often overtly contradict themselves and are so ludicrously totalizing that they defy reason altogether, rendering it impossible to gauge precisely or definitively stabilize the author's political identity.[12] Or to invoke Philippe Muray's very apt metaphor, Céline's writing, much like a directional compass at the North Pole, sends the instruments of conventional political understanding into a veritable craze, provoking in even the most astute reader a somewhat maddening loss of ideological orientation.[13]

And yet, given the virulence of his attack, in the pamphlets, on the European Jewish community and considering the historical setting in which it occurred, it is not surprising that Céline is often either instinctively associated with fascism or even emphatically identified as one of its major proponents.[14] It was, after all, a racist discourse much like Céline's that propelled the deadly expansionist force of fascism in its most pernicious form: German Nazism. In France of the interwar period, however, racialist doctrine did not figure prominently in the rhetoric or political agenda of an insurgent Right bent chiefly on crushing the republic it despised and combating what it perceived to be a mounting threat from the Socialist and Communist Left. Only late in the 1930s, a decade of great political strife and economic chaos, would the far Right in France thematically brandish anti-Semitism and this, historians observe, more out of nationalist sentiment than racist conviction.[15] But unlike his cohorts on the anti-Semitic Right, who generally rebuffed apocalyptic racialist scenarios, throughout this period, Céline engaged in a single-minded effort to rid the European continent of Jews, an ethnic minority he believed was ravaging the biological vigor and emotive force of France's "Celto-germanic" Aryan race.

Curiously, although Céline's political allegiances and collaborationist activities have been scrutinized for some time,[16] his racist convictions and the complex racialist thought supporting them have not, until very recently, been given the critical attention they merit.[17] Nor has Célinian scholarship extended its analytical reach across disciplinary boundaries to reflect in concrete historical terms on the broader cultural setting in which the pamphlets circulated and on the attitudes and values to which these texts gave voice, albeit in wildly distorted and exaggerated form. Considered for generations a refuge from authoritarian repression, France in the 1930s was a foundering republic whose egalitarian ideals and tradition of tolerance were being undermined by political turmoil and economic rigors that fanned the fires of xenophobia and ethnocentrism. Foreign nationals immigrating to France late in the decade—many of whom were Jews fleeing persecution in Central and Eastern Europe—would find themselves in great disfavor, encountering an atmosphere much less hospitable than was surely imagined from afar.[18] The influx of Jewish immigrants also aroused resentment toward France's population of native-born Jews, who since the Great Revolution of 1789 had celebrated emancipation, embraced assimilation, and wholeheartedly accepted what in terms of cultural identity and integrity were the very exacting conditions of full-fledged citizenship in the French nation.[19] Cognizance of these historical circumstances is crucial to understanding the resurgence in interwar France of discrimination against Jews that, except for the short-lived outburst of bigotry during the Dreyfus affair at the end of the nineteenth century, had generally been held in check in the modern era by the universalist norms of republican reason.[20]

The discovery following World War II of the genocide practiced on European Jews in the hinterland of the Third Reich's conquered territories in the East renders it perhaps difficult today to fathom the relatively high threshold of tolerance for ethnic prejudice that constituted the societal norms of the time. Not solely the animus of hatemongers on the extreme fringes of the political Right, the rapidly growing Jewish population in France, composed in its majority of new or recent arrivals, was the focus of much governmental debate and the source of considerable collective angst. Anti-foreign sentiment coalesced with vestiges of more traditional Christian Judeophobia to heighten social tensions and cultural antagonisms in a situation that was rapidly deteriorating both domestically and internationally. The election in May 1936 of SFIO chief Léon Blum, France's first Jewish prime minister of its first government of the Marxist Left, did little to allay conservative fears concerning the erosion of traditional French values, the bold challenge to established authority erupting in the lower ranks of the social order, and what was increasingly viewed as the destabilizing influence in French society of "foreign" elements.[21] France's strained relations with its Jewish community just prior to and especially during World War II have been illuminated in the impressive body of historiography now available to students of the period.[22] These accounts go far in describing a cultural ambiance and mentality with respect to ethnic difference that must surely have acted as an inducement to Céline the racial purist, giving him at least tacit license to unleash his latent anti-Semitism in 1937 with *Bagatelles pour un massacre*, a publication that enjoyed astonishing commercial success.[23]

In *Toward the Final Solution: A History of European Racism* (1978), George L. Mosse notes that studies of the Third Reich have often failed to examine the genealogy of Western racism and the racialist thought that was such an integral component of Nazi ideological discourse and political practice.[24] Ignorance of this legacy has fostered the postwar notion that Hitler's relentless biologically motivated persecution of Jews was the product of a depraved political mindset and ultimately but a pathological aberration of history. Aware of the historical influences on the development of Nazi racist thought, Enzo Traverso recognizes, however, that "[r]acial anti-Semitism, elaborated in Europe at the end of the 19th century and transformed into State ideology by Hitler and Rosenberg in national-socialist Germany, would simply be inconceivable outside of the long history of oppression, pillaging and domination of colonized peoples and of the destruction of their cultural otherness."[25]

The scientific claims of racialism—that corpus of the late-nineteenth-century anthropological, linguistic, and historical thought asserting the biological superiority of white Europeans over peoples of color—have since the midtwentieth century lost all intellectual credibility.[26] But while the notion of race "as a meaningful criterion within the biological sciences has," as Henry Louis Gates, Jr., points out, "long been recognized to be a fiction,"[27] the language of difference it generated continues to shape Western beliefs and value systems in subtle but significant ways. Even the most superficial reading of cultural codes in any number of postwar Western societies reveals that unlike fascism's spectacular mass political formations, the racist impetus driving the Nazi movement has not entirely dissipated. The trajectory charted from the European colonial enterprise to the racialist doctrines of the Third Reich has particular relevance to the discussion of Céline's pamphlets, for the vile racial slurs he hurls at Jews often metaphorically communicate equal disdain for the colonized peoples of Africa and Asia, offering a particularly crude example of the continuity Lorenzo stresses between colonial ideology and modern anti-Semitism.

The training Céline received as a medical doctor no doubt prepared his reception of the hygienist racial principles, whose scientific pretensions derived much from nineteenth-century French sources. The writings of Comte Arthur de Gobineau, author of the voluminous and, by today's standards, supremely arrogant *Essai sur l'inégalité des races* (*Essay on the Inequality of the Races* [1853–55]), were crucial to the establishment of the hierarchical classifications and aesthetic notions that became grounds for much modern racial stereotyping and primed the cultural terrain for the eugenics vogue that followed.

But Gobineau's theories of race were ultimately more influential on the German than the French Right, whose conservative Catholicism, although fiercely anti-Semitic at the end of the century, was averse to racialism's biological determinism, which essentially denied the redemptive spiritual powers of baptism.[28] In this regard, the social biology Céline espouses in the pamphlets more closely parallels the hygienist preoccupations of the Nazi regime than the anti-Semitism promoted by even the most inspired of French Fascists. In the late 1930s, Céline, in typical maverick fashion, was one of the few cultural figures of prominence over whom racialist thought held sway. Even Robert Brasillach, one of the most important Fascist intellectuals of the period, was reticent in the late 1930s to laud Céline's political efforts in *Bagatelles* and *L'école*, considering his anti-Semitic diatribe far too ideologically and stylistically extravagant.[29] And while idealists like those gathered at *Je suis partout* sought to promote broad social, cultural, and political change in France with utopian visions of authoritarian fascist renewal dancing in their heads, Céline focused his energies obsessively and with a sense of urgency on the "Jewish Question." When, for instance, in the early 1940s, governmental officials did not implement racial policies as expeditiously as he would have liked or when the collaborationist press failed, in his view, to publicize sufficiently the Jewish menace, Céline coined the pejorative term "rapprochistes" (reconciliationists), which he frequently invoked in this period to designate fellow anti-Semites who had, in his view, no true understanding of the biological imperative on which immediate action needed to be taken. The correspondence and interviews printed in the pro-German press in the early period of the Occupation[30] are documents that show Céline at his most activist, dispensing racist wisdom and assessing the political possibilities of the moment. In a letter to Alain Laubreaux published in *Je suis partout* in November 1942, Céline wrote: "Reason of race must take precedence over reason of the state. No explanation to furnish here. It's very simple. Fanatical total racism or death! And what a death! They're waiting for us! Let the mongoose spirit incite us, fire us up."[31] And in a letter to Jacques Doriot published earlier that year in the columns of the *Cahiers de l'émancipation nationale*, he laments:

While you are away in the Army, some very nasty things are happening. Just between the two of us, quite frankly, we are witnessing right now very loathsome workings; the systematic sabotage of racism in France by anti-Semites themselves. They can't manage to get along. A very French spectacle. How many anti-Semites are there all in all on our soil? I'm not talking about loafers. Hardly enough to make up a little Prefecture! . . . and, among these enthusiasts how many are leaders? valid, armed, suitable? A dozen or so. In this decisive, inspirational, mystical moment, to what task do we see them passionately devoting themselves? To shooting themselves in the foot![32]

The fact that Céline's views on race were particularly extremist and by his own admission shared by only a small band of zealots[33] does not mean that the society at large was averse to racially motivated anti-Jewish sentiment. Indeed, the conservative Vichy regime adopted discriminatory legislation in October 1940 and relied on hereditary rather than religious or cultural criterion in ascertaining which individuals were to be subjected to the spate of new laws imposing severe restrictions on the cultural, economic, and social life of all Jews residing in France. Enacted not as a result of German mandate but rather on the Vichy government's own initiative, this legislation established a definition of Jewishness that was even more rigorous and inclusive than that applied in the Nazi regime's 1935 Nuremburg racial laws. This is not to suggest, however, that prior to or following the Franco-German armistice of June 1940 the French public was massively swayed, as was the case in neighboring Germany, by mystic "volkish" notions of racial grandeur calling for the purge of "degenerate" foreign elements. Rather, the refugee crisis of the late 1930s, a situation that extreme-rightist agitation and Hitler's continued expulsion of Jews from invaded territories greatly exacerbated, in tandem with the humiliating military defeat in 1940, conspired to render many of the French simply indifferent to the plight of Jews now desperately struggling to survive in their midst. Perhaps it is the interwar and Occupation experience that best illustrates Jean-Paul Aron's precept concerning the limits of humanitarian goodwill in France and, during World

War II, one must hasten to add, in a host of other democracies with liberal pretensions: "In France, we esteem others provided we have nothing to do with them." [34]

George L. Mosse maintains that it was the tremendously uprooting and alienating experience of industrial urban existence that compelled European masses to embrace fascism's authoritarian and, in Germany, ethnocentric solutions to the economic and social ills of the time. Although this view fails to consider the manner in which fascist movements that rhetorically impugned modernity actually came to reconcile themselves with technology, recuperating its possibilities rather artfully to their own political advantage,[35] it does accurately describe the forces contributing significantly to the genesis of Céline's racism. The pamphlets, of course, raise a vast range of aesthetic, cultural, sociopolitical, and historical issues, but it was, I propose, the deep abiding resentment he had for the rationality of the modern mechanized world and for the disaffection it produced in human culture that most actively stirred Céline's political passions.

Chronologically speaking, *Mea Culpa*, the terse but tempestuous denunciation of Soviet communism he authored in 1936, actually initiated Céline's foray into political writing. Announcing many of the themes and concerns addressed in the tracts that followed, *Mea Culpa* also decisively and bitterly marked the closure of a brief period of flirtation between Céline and the French Left. Traveling to the Soviet Union in 1936 on proceeds from the Russian translation of *Voyage au bout de la nuit*, Céline had the opportunity to observe firsthand a revolutionary society in the making. Very little is in fact known about Céline's activities during his unceremonious visit to Leningrad in the late summer of 1936, where he spent the entirety of his monthlong stay.[36] Upon returing to France, however, Céline was quite vocal about his views on the Socialist fatherland. To Cillie Pam he wrote: "I've returned from Russia, What a horror! What a vile masquerade! what a dirty stupid fabrication! It is all so grotesque, theoretical, criminal!" [37] To Karen Marie Jensen, the Danish friend to whom he would entrust a stash of gold during the war and in whose Copenhagen apartment he was arrested in late 1945, Céline communicated a vision of the Soviet Union that foreshadows both the acerbic tone and the totalizing rhetoric in which he would express abhorrence for the Soviet experiment in *Mea Culpa* and again a year later in *Bagatelles pour un massacre*: "I was in Leningrad for a month. All of this is *abject, dreadful,* inconceivably *filthy.* You have to see it to believe it. A horror! *Dirty, poor—hideous.* A prison of larva. Everything is police, bureaucracy and filthy chaos. Everything is sham and tyranny" (Céline's emphasis).[38]

The fact that Céline's trip to the Soviet Union took place in 1936 at the height of the Stalinist purges no doubt greatly encouraged Céline in his impression of generalized repression and of the Soviet leadership's reliance on an omniscient police presence for the maintenance of public order and of its own political authority. But judging from *Bagatelles pour un massacre* and most particularly *Mea Culpa*, an essay that Philippe Muray argues must be considered an integral part of the pamphleteering episode in the author's career,[39] Céline's grievances against Soviet socialism extended far beyond the terror visited upon the Soviet population by Stalin's secret police. It is rather the rationalization of the entire biopolitical space[40] of postrevolutionary Soviet existence that Céline finds insufferable and whose attendant evils he strives in these writings to bring to the attention of the French public.

Michel Foucault has argued[41] that when the liberal regimes of the modern era extended civil rights to populations in the West, the expansion of freedoms was accompanied by the rise of more insidiously coercive strategies of normalization that introduced into a wide variety of institutions (prisons, psychiatric institutions, schools, hospitals, the industrial workplace) practices allowing for a continuous regulation of the social body and mastery of its movements. In this critical light, it becomes more fully apparent that what Céline reviles most in the socialist experiment he observed was the intensification of normalizing and disciplining techniques whose reach, he feared, was being extended over an ever wider terrain of human existence. *Bagatelle*'s repeated and derogatory references to Stakhanovism, a doctrine exalting the productionist achievements of the model Soviet worker, is one of the more prominent examples of the parallels Céline draws between modern methods of disciplining masses devised in the industrial West and the Soviet application of analogous principles. In a strident attack on productionist ideals and materialist values in general, Céline boldly declares in *Mea Culpa* that "all Fords are alike, Soviet or not"[42] and decries the continued enslavement of both Communist and capitalist workers to modern industrial technology and machinery. Céline best depicted the dehumanizing effects of these labor practices in the Detroit episode of *Voyage au bout de la nuit*, a passage of his spectacularly successful first novel that led many in the early 1930s to believe his political sympathies were with the revolutionary anticapitalist Left:

It's sickening to watch workers bent over their machines, intent on giving them all possible pleasure, calibrating bolts and more bolts, instead of putting an end once and for all to this stench of oil.
[. . .] All outside life must be done away with, made into steel, into something

useful. We didn't love it enough the way it was, that's why. So it has to be made into an object, into something sold. The Regulations say so.

[. . .] Nobody spoke to me. Existence was reduced to a kind of hesitation between stupor and frenzy. Nothing mattered but the ear-splitting continuity of the machines that commanded all men.[43]

In *Bagatelles pour un massacre*, Céline draws the then rapidly mechanizing Soviet Union into the scope of his antimodern invective, charging that the Soviet state was engaged in an implacable quest for absolute conformity and uniformity in its Communist subjects. But a similar initiative had also been launched, he observed, by French captains of industry and this, of course, at the behest of Jews whose principal aim it was to transform the French masses into automatons. While Céline's mission in the pamphlets is clearly that of halting the march of material progress and of resisting the normalization of everyday life, he also resigns himself in *Bagatelles* to the fact that the French have already been thoroughly "robotized":

France, [which has been] materialized, rationalized, perfectly muzzled, perfectly subjugated, by Jewish villainy, alcoholized right down to the marrow, [rendered] absolutely barren of all lyricism [. . .] is doomed to destruction, to an enthusiastic massacre by the Jews.[44]

Standard in everything, this is the panacea of the Jew. No more revolts to fear from pre-robotic individuals that we are, our furniture, novels, films, cars, language, the vast majority of modern populations are already standardized. Modern civilization is total standardization, souls and bodies under the Jew. (*BPM*, 158)[45]

The robot [. . .] is the end result of so many "rational" civilizing efforts . . . admirably naturalist and objective (still a Robot stricken with habitual drunkenness! to date, the Robot's only human trait) . . . Since the Renaissance, we have ventured to work more and more ardently for the advent of the Kingdom of Science and of the social robot. The starkest . . . the most objective of languages is the perfectly objective journalistic Robot language . . . We are in the midst of it . . . There is no longer any need to have a soul in front of gaping holes to express oneself humanly . . . Only volumes! [..] and advertisement! . . . and just any robotic twaddle triumphs . . . We're in the midst of it! (*BPM*, 142)[46]

If the layer of racist scapegoating is stripped away in these texts, one can credit Céline with a certain lucidity in his understanding of the modern techniques of social control, for he perceptively identifies the normalizing or, as he would have it, "standardizing" effects of what Foucault has called disciplinary power, recognizing that it operates essentially through a subtle process of internalization that induces docility and conformity. Like the mechanisms governing the gestures of a robot, this wholly new type of power imperceptibly controls the body and automatically generates desired movements and behaviors in its subjects. In Céline's mind, despite their declared antagonism, Western liberal capitalism and its Soviet Communist rival, both functioning under the aegis of Jews, had discovered the efficacy of this mode of regulating the social body and increasing its productivity.

Remarkably, Céline also grasped in *Bagatelles* the political import and manipulative powers of the modern media. Unlike wily Fascists who scampered to seize upon the political potential cinema, radio, and journalism offered, however, Céline entirely repudiated these forms of mass communication, which he considered culturally ruinous. And as one might expect, his understanding of the uses and abuses of the new technology is not without its racist twist:

Observe that all French, English and American films, that is to say Jewish films, are infinitely biased, always, from the most innocuous to the most amorous! . . . from the most historical to the most idealist . . . They exist and are propagated for the glory of Israel . . . under various disguises: democracy, equality of the races, hate of "national prejudices," the abolition of privilege, the advance of progress, etc . . . [. . .] Their goal is strictly to daze the goy ever more, to lead him as quickly as possible to repudiate all of his traditions, his sorry taboos, his "superstitions," his religions, in short, to make him renounce his entire past, his race, his own rhythm to the benefit of the Jewish ideal. To create in him, through film, the irresistible taste for all things Jewish to be bought, goods, luxuries that the Aryan then manufactures for himself, switches so he can whip himself, chains so he can shackle himself, the entire apparatus of his bondage and stupefaction for which, to top it off, he by the way pays with what an exorbitant "surplus." (*BPM*, 190)[47]

Once again, if the adjective "Jewish" were deleted from these texts, one might find in the above statements not simply a litany of the principal themes of reactionary discourse in Europe in the late 1930s (antidemocracy, antimaterialism, racism, nationalism, etc.) but also an incisive and indeed prescient view of the lucrative commercial use to which advanced monopoly capital in the West would so effectively put the visual and audio mass media in bolstering its postwar consumer economy. The author claims here that film and its beguiling imagery were promoting the demise of an authentically "emotive" cultural life and that Jews were responsible for this irrevocable loss. But for Céline, the signifier *juif* actually functions rhetorically in this context, as it often does in the pamphlets, as a metaphor for capitalist modernity, which he cannot, it seems, bring himself to name. The thought of challenging the legitimacy of an entire economic order that systematically cultivates acquisitive values and capitalizes on the homogenized desires it creates in its largely unpropertied masses would, however, have been entirely antithetical to the petty bourgeois conservatism Céline so consistently displayed in his writing. In his final pamphlet, *Les beaux draps* (1941), Céline in fact goes so far as to formulate his most radical vision of social change, "Labiche Communism," in which, contrary to the Soviet model, property rights prevail and all natives are given the opportunity to elevate themselves to the status of small property owners.[48] His scatological language and Bohemian persona aside, Céline was, it appears, decidedly middle class in his revolutionary aspirations.

Although less so in France than in other Western economies, the deep crisis of capitalism in the 1930s had created immense hardship for the popular classes, and Céline's vociferating in the pamphlets is surely in some part a response to that suffering. Indeed, the admiration he expresses for Hitler in *L'école des cadavres* stemmed not only from the Führer's racist fervor but also from his successes in eradicating unemployment in the Reich, a feat accomplished primarily through the savage repression of trade unions and the wholesale militarization of the German economy. But in 1937, Céline, the famed pacifist of *Voyage au bout de la nuit*, refused to recognize the bellicose designs from which Hitler's economic policy derived. Rather, he searched for an identity upon which to project blame for both the economic woes and threat of war France faced, quickly settling on the nation's minority population of Jews. As Paula Hyman has so perceptively remarked and as Céline's pamphlets amply demonstrate, Jews residing in France in the 1930s and 1940s, many impoverished immigrants, were to suffer immensely for the coincidence of the emancipation of French Jewry during the Revolution of 1789 and the rise of laissez-faire capitalism, a fiercely competitive economic order whose social ills and class inequities were often handily imputed to Jews, bourgeois and proletarian, propertied and unpropertied alike.[49]

At first glance, it might appear that Céline practices a thoroughly unimaginative racism when he globally projects onto Jews responsibility for the sorry state of affairs in "Aryan" France. Upon closer observation, however, there is a far more elaborate construction of difference taking place here. In a twist of logic that perhaps seems preposterous today but which was, historians observe, not so aberrant in his day, Céline proclaims in *Bagatelles pour un massacre* that France, one of the great colonial powers of the time, was itself becoming a Jewish colony. Language invoking the colonizer/colonized dichotomy abounds in *Bagatelles*, with French terms implicitly designating the subordinate status of peoples in the colonial setting (i.e., "indigène" and "autochton") frequently used in reference to the French. In the absence of a full-scale rebellion against Jewish power, the French would, he reasoned, find themselves experiencing the same exploitation and human indignities to which the French governing élite had for over a century subjected the conquered peoples of its overseas possessions, a brutal reality Céline knew well since he had carried out medical research in French colonial Africa in the 1920s. The Paris Exposition of 1937 provided ample proof to Céline that the indenture of the French was closely at hand: "[T]he Exposition of '37 brings us [. . .] a magnificient, overwhelming demonstration of this Jewish colonial fury, [one that is] less and less concerned about the resentments and reactions of the natives, more on top of things, more brash every day while commensurately the natives [are] more submissive, crawling more viscidly, more cowardly" (*BPM*, 107).[50]

But the signifier *juifs* occupies a highly unstable position in Céline's colonial discourse, constantly and paradoxically shifting from the space of colonizer to that of colonized. With their towering economic might and unbridled cultural influence, he argues, Jews imperiously govern the French masses whom they have successfully transformed into a horde of feeble natives laboring robotically to fill the coffers of their omnipotent masters. Lost souls now stripped of their authentic emotion and innate lyricism, the French wander about modernity's cultural wasteland in a drunken stupor. Alternatively, an inherent racial inferiority, like that which colonial ideology attributed to the indigenous peoples of color it subjugated, makes Jews entirely unworthy, biologically speaking, of the supremacy they enjoy over Aryans. Céline incessantly reinforces the latter notion by fusing Jewish identity at various moments with that of Africans, Arabs, and other peoples of the Near and Far East, many of whom were directly or indirectly ruled during this period by Western powers and for whom he quite obviously had the greatest contempt. In other words, in his construction of Jewish identity, Céline collapses two distinct subjectivities, one endowed with the capacity and ambition to disempower the French entirely and the other stimulating a white supremacist impulse to reassert mastery over what nineteenth-century Western expansionist doctrine deemed the legitimately colonizable other.

It is readily apparent that the subject interpellated in Céline's political discourse is positioned in the middling ranks of a social hierarchy composed not only of class gradations in France proper but also encompassing differentiations of human worth throughout the entire scope of its colonial empire. Céline the pamphleteer is thus able to tap rage that seethed in this period against France's social elite (ritually referred to by the Left during the 1930s as the "200 Families") without directly challenging the structural foundations on which the edifice of class privilege actually rested. He does so by displacing the resentment and class animosity he sparks in dispossessed, downwardly mobile Frenchmen into the arena of colonial signifying practices. There he conjures the specter of an inverted hierarchical paradigm in which white Europeans are ruled by Jews—Jews who have been orientalized and negrified so as to intensify racist affect—and does so with an excess of style that invites racial violence against the alterity he has constructed. In this context, such aggression would be viewed not as an abhorrent assault on enlightened liberal principles of inalienable human rights but rather legitimized as part of the colonial regime's requisite coercion of non-European peoples that was at this time a rather normal feature of Western empire-building around the globe.

Like many contemporaries on the Right who vilified modernity's depersonalized forms of existence and the insipid democratic culture it was said to have spawned, Céline turned nostalgically to a premodern, preindustrial past in search of a remedy to the social ills he diagnoses in the pamphlets. In *Mea Culpa*, for instance, Céline finds an approximation of the social harmony he envisions in medieval days of old, a time when the poetic, it would seem, transcended the political, and sameness prevailed over difference: "Politics have rotted Mankind even more profoundly in the last three centuries than during all of Prehistory. In the Middle Ages we were nearer to being united than today . . . a common spirit was taking shape. The tall tale was a much better "poetry high," more intimate. It exists no more." [51] Céline's yearning for the songful essence of a bygone era is, quite clearly, as reactionary in social as it is in temporal terms, for he is essentially lamenting the demise of what he imagines to have been a homogeneous community unadulterated by the politics of racial, ethnic, class, and other forms of cultural difference, thereby allowing the subject he fashions to revel in symbiosis and poetic rapture. Although Céline's aim here is ostensibly to depoliticize and repoeticize French cultural life, it is obvious that reviving the kindred spirit of this paradise lost is as much a political as it is an aesthetic undertaking. For Céline, such a project would entail nothing short of incinerating the entire materialist status quo that over the previous three hundred years of modernization had, he believed, sapped the culture of its primordial emotion, stripped human communication of its intimacy and left but the cerebral artifice of highbrow rationalism. *Bagatelles pour un massacre* adequately demonstrates that in Céline's mind, the restoration of this tradition also required the distinction and separation of the human races of which presumably only select groups, "Aryans" of northern European stock, were capable of resurrecting the lyrical past and experiencing its emotive highs. In the period immediately preceding and especially during the war, preserving what little remained of that bio-poetic heritage would become the author's mental fixation, convinced as he was that "[w]hen you mix two bloods haphazardly, one poor the other rich, you never enrich the poor one, you always impoverish the rich." [52]

In reverting to what he believed was the previous order of things but in a thoroughly modern mode of writing, Céline produced a discourse of extraordinary political ambivalence. Having spurned refined patterns of bourgeois expression in favor of a highly volatile, elliptical utterance that simulated popular oral speech, Céline had, in his first two novels, made a revolutionary break with conventional narrative forms. In the political writings that followed, he carried that innovation to even greater verbal extremes and stylistic heights but did so in the plainly reactionary hope of excluding identities whose mere distinctiveness threatened his own and with the aim of arresting the proliferation of difference in a democratizing modern world he loathed. As such, the stylistic audacity that ultimately secured Céline's place in the modernist canon is not without concrete political and historical implications.

In one sense, Céline's avant-garde aesthetic practice can be considered a mode of resistance to the normalizing logic of the modern industrial world. The surplus of meaning and feeling generated by his rhythmically charged, telegraphic sentences did indeed exceed the limits of and thus directly challenge the institutionalized literary and political discourse of the time. Robert Brasillach's review of *Bagatelles pour un massacre*[53] clearly suggests that Céline's wild distortion and overstatement of the Jewish threat, largely an effect of his stylistic verve, surpassed by far what he and no doubt other more sober anti-Semites on the fascist Right considered to be the bounds of verbal propriety in expressing one's bigotry. Céline's racist frenzy might, he feared, become a liability to the far Right in France, where Brasillach, the refined Normalian, surely recognized the importance of operating culturally and politically within Cartesian norms of moderating reason. While they held the modern liberal order in equal contempt and energetically promoted its demise, Céline differs markedly from extreme rightist politicos of Brasillach's genteel sort in that he invariably chose to occupy a radically marginal position with respect to the numerous societal institutions he opposed, intent upon violating the conventions of speech that purveyed and sustained their authority.

Alice Y. Kaplan notes that "anti-modern modernism," reactionary discourse of the type Céline enunciated in his highly disjunctive, effusive style is one of several important oppositions fascist ideology collapsed in the "polarity machine" it so successfully operated in its mobilizing stages.[54] In addition, Céline's nostalgic desire to poeticize the daily life of French masses, his will to efface all difference in order to achieve euphoric collective oneness, and of course, his racial anti-Semitism also echo important themes and mirror the aesthetic vision shaped in various strains of European fascism. But there are, critics have noted, crucial elements of Céline's political thought that do not conform to the fascist formula including, among others, his vehement hostility to Italian fascism, a steadfast antimilitarism, total cynicism with respect to the cult worship of the authoritarian leader, and an eternal pessimism running counter to fascism's thrill-seeking pursuit of direct political action and to its grandiose schemes of refashioning human existence.[55] While the fascist motifs that can be culled from Céline's texts clearly point to the dangers of uncritically celebrating his stylistic innovation and subversive posture vis-à-vis the modern world, his ideological idiosyncrasies also make it difficult simply to relegate his writings and their complex web of political meanings to the refuse heap of fascist collaboration.

It is perhaps more in the anecdotal than the purely analytical domain that one can grasp a sense of the inveterate recalcitrance and contentious demeanor toward any and all established authority that made Céline a highly combustible political item in the late 1930s and under the Occupation. One such incident involved a dinner invitation to the German embassy in 1941 during which officials of the occupying power sought to test the ideological waters and no doubt curry favor with Louis-Ferdinand Céline, France's most renowned anti-Semite. In the company of artist Gen Paul and Fascist writer Drieu La Rochelle, Céline, it was subsequently reported, scandalized his hosts by brooding through much of the dinner, only raucously interjecting his views on current affairs. At the close of the evening, François Gibault relates, German ambassador Otto Abetz, beside himself, was obliged to ask servants to leave the room when Céline began to lambaste Drieu la Rochelle, bellowing "in terms rarely employed in embassies" that surely "the Germans were going to lose the war." Attempting to contain the effects of such flagrant heresy, Abetz sheepishly advanced: "But it is well known that you, Mr. Céline, do not like the Germans."[56] Céline vigorously objected to this characterization, inviting his cohort Gen Paul to display their mutual admiration for the occupiers by treating the ambassador to a Chaplinesque impersonation of Adolf Hitler. Plainly ruffled by these antics, the other dinner guests rushed to inform the ambassador that Céline was not at all well and to suggest he be immediately escorted back to his residence.

It would thus appear that Céline was as "abject" in his personal and political life as Julia Kristeva claims he was in his writing, forever disturbing "identity, . . . system, order" and resisting "limits, borders, positions, rules."[57] In *Powers of Horror*, Kristeva largely brackets the substantive political issues the pamphlets raise in order to hearken to the musicality of Céline's polyphonic narrative voice, one that glides the word across the page like the evanescent footsteps of the ballerinas the author idolized. It is impossible not to hear, she asserts, "the liberating truth of such a call to rhythm and joy, beyond the crippling constraints of a society ruled by monotheistic symbolism."[58] Ironically, in attributing an emancipatory quality to Céline's writing, Kristeva echoes Céline's own assertion that he had been indicted by the postwar powers not for political beliefs espoused and activities in which he engaged during the war but for his seditious assault on the literary, cultural, and political establishment of his time.

In assessing the validity of these claims, it is useful to invoke here a key passage of Michel Foucault's essay, "What is an Author?" in which he reflects upon the dynamics of discourse, asking:

[h]ow can one reduce the great peril, the great danger with which fiction threatens our world? The answer is, one can reduce it with the author. The author allows a limitation of the cancerous and dangerous proliferation of significations within a world where one is thrifty not only with one's resources and riches but also in the proliferation of meaning. . . . We are accustomed to thinking that the author is so different from all other men and so transcendent with regard to all languages that, as soon as he speaks, meaning begins to proliferate indefinitely. The truth is quite to the contrary: the author is not an indefinite source of significations which fills a work; the author does not precede the work, he is a certain functional principle by which, in our culture, one excludes and chooses: in short, by which one impedes the circulation, the free manipulation, the free composition, decomposition and recomposition of fiction.[59]

Foucault is referring specifically in this context to the menacing character of literature, but in the final years of the Third Republic and under the subsequent Vichy regime, similar "functional principles" can be seen operating in relation to the political text. From a very different perspective from the self-serving one Céline adopted after the war, it could indeed be argued that the postwar politico-juridical machinery sought principally to reduce and confine the meanings of texts by writers, Céline among others, in order to contain the broader significations that might have emerged following the war as French and much of European society confronted the genocidal consequences of the racist and ethnocentric discourses that had proliferated in the period immediately preceding and during World War II.

The following excerpt from a 1949 letter to Albert Paraz provides a sense of Céline's own understanding of the meaning at stake in the representations of the interwar, Occupation and immediate postwar period. Fulminating against his political adversaries and proclaiming his innocence in the face of what were indeed very serious criminal charges,[60] Céline snarled: "[W]hat can you cling to in the midst of this madness? Bagatelles came out before the war—expulsion meant *Palestine*— *Nothing more*—and to stop them from invading us from Poland— Where's the crime? I don't see it. I see only that I myself have been persecuted, robbed, plundered, chased from my home, from my *birth place*, from my livelihood. That's all. I never asked that they be *treated* the way I am being *treated*, never" (Céline's emphasis).[61] Along with the grotesque insensitivity Céline displays in his equation of the tragic fate of European Jewry during the war with the personal hardships he faced in de facto political exile after the war, he also performs a skillful sidestepping of the central political and ethical issues his pamphlets raised in the postwar era, texts that preached a virulent hatred for minority social groups and, as he acknowledges himself, called for their exclusion. But for readers aware of the historical setting and anti-Semitic feeling that pervaded French society in the late 1930s, Céline's statement also recalls the precise terms in which broad segments of the public formulated the resentment harbored against foreign Jews immigrating to France before the war, animus that stemmed more from xenophobic than racist impulses but that nonetheless came during the war to influence the standing of a well-established and assimilated community of native-born Jews.

In gauging the extent to which anti-Semitism had permeated French society on the eve of the war, Marrus and Paxton rightly situate writers like Céline at the extreme limits of racist speech and thought. As it circulated in the public arena, they note, bigoted discourse of this sort tended by its very excessiveness to make open expression of the ethnic and anti-foreign prejudice building in mainstream society appear all the more temperate and respectable. But in the aftermath of the war, that same verbal excess, coupled with the stature it had brought him in French prewar literary culture, would make Céline especially vulnerable to absorbing responsibility for a complex signifying system whose hierarchical tenets had long justified and secured Western mastery of peoples it deemed other and whose obscene cultural arrogance he displayed in all of its aggression before the civilization that spawned it.

Of the writers and intellectuals charged with collaboration and high treason following the war, Louis-Ferdinand Céline was undoubtedly the figure who in the decade preceding the war had achieved the greatest celebrity. That renown derived not only from the acclaim *Voyage au bout de la nuit* had won in 1932 but also from the controversy that raged over the stylistic liberties he had taken in this and especially his subsequent novel *Mort à crédit*. As the passages of the pamphlets and wartime correspondence cited above clearly establish, in the late 1930s and early 1940s, Céline devoted his immense creative energies and talents to disseminating the racialist beliefs to which he now openly subscribed. These writings speak volumes not only on the crisis of modernity and the bitter political struggles waged in the late 1930s in response to it but also on the entire tradition of Western racism to which Céline appealed in formulating, with characteristic verbal abandon, his own understanding of the ruin into which France was about to fall.

As a cultural figure of distinction and, no doubt, influence in the 1930s, Céline surely bore ethical responsibility and was, in the end, held legally accountable for promoting the racial prejudice that became so massively destructive during the war.[62] Céline's admirers and detractors have for decades debated the judiciousness of these postwar legal proceedings, focusing primarily on questions of personal guilt and innocence and on the appropriateness of his sentence. But structurally speaking, it might be said that the criminal indictment of Céline the author provided the postwar era with an effective mechanism for containing what Foucault describes as the "dangerous and cancerous proliferation of significations" texts are capable of producing. In the context of World War II and the experience of Vichy France, perhaps that peril involved the indictment of a far broader cultural text, whose exclusionary impulse was expressed in more banal, circumspect forms than in its Célinian counterpart but that also contributed in important ways to the smooth functioning of numerous institutions that were indispensable to the operation of the bureaucratic machinery of genocide set in motion during the war. In focusing public discussion on the juridical guilt of a writer such as Céline, one whose legendary misanthropic character and explosive, transgressive style accommodated the finger-pointing exercise especially well, the society at large was able to deflect attention away from such complicity. More important, however, the "author function" to which his bigotry is generally reduced has, in effect, hindered a thorough critical assessment of the more subtle, widely shared notions of ethnic difference and cultural worth that continue to generate in the contemporary Western world, well beyond the era of fascist and collaborationist evil, meanings that echo the racist voice of Louis-Ferdinand Céline.

If Looks Could Kill

Louis Malle's Portraits of Collaboration

scandalize [MF *scandaliser, to cause to stumble, shock, fr. Gk* skandelon, *stumbling block, offense*] 1: *to speak falsely or maliciously of.*
scandalous 1. obs: *constituting a spiritual or moral lapse endangering by example faith or morals.*

—Webster's Third New International Dictionary

After all, the fundamental question of philosophy (like that of psychoanalysis) is the same as the question of the detective novel: who is guilty?
—Umberto Eco, *Postscript to the Name of the Rose*

In 1987, Marguerite Duras was subpoenaed to testify for the defense in a trial that was notorious before it began: that of Klaus Altmann-Barbie for crimes against humanity. Duras, the personal friend of François Mitterand, whom she knew as Morland when the two worked together in the Resistance; Duras, whose husband, a political prisoner, was spirited back from a concentration camp just in time to prevent his death from starvation and whose painful recovery she documents in excruciating detail in the title story of her 1985 book, *The War*.[1] Duras respectfully declined the court's invitation. Citing Article 331 of the penal code, which limits witnesses' testimony to the facts of the case and the personality of the accused, she declared that she had no firsthand knowledge of the facts, and she was pleased never to have met Klaus Barbie.

It was not the story about her husband that inspired the defense attorney, Maître Jacques Vergès, to request Duras's testimony but rather another piece in *The War*, in which Duras describes the inner turmoil of Thérèse, a young Resistance woman presiding, just after the Liberation, over the interrogation and torture of a petty informer. Thérèse is fictional, but Duras makes no bones about admitting that the incident is drawn from personal experience. Maître Vergès no doubt hoped that her testimony (along with that of others, such as Regis Debray and Raymond Aubrac) would demonstrate that Barbie's atrocities should be classified not as crimes against humanity but as war crimes, and as such they resembled those committed by many French people during the Occupation, the post-Liberation *épuration*, and the Algerian conflict. He thus insinuated that if Barbie were to be found guilty, then a large number of French men and women would be implicated as well. Vergès had clearly not read

Duras's story closely enough to perceive its suggestion that torture, no matter who inflicts it, is a horror, even for the perpetrator. Nevertheless, he was all too well aware of the collective uneasiness about other possible revelations that made the trial of Barbie such a focus of anxiety and scandal.[2]

It is not difficult to discern the factors contributing to what amounts to a widespread, if ambivalent, return to (or of) the period 1940–1944 in French public life and cultural production of the 1980s. In addition to the Barbie trial, preceded by his sensational extradition from Bolivia, we can cite the Mittérand government itself—the first socialist government since Léon Blum's and the first Président de la République to have bona fide Resistance credentials without the investment (or with a negative investment) in continuing to endorse the official Gaullist myth of the Resistance. Records about the Occupation have been largely inaccessible, and those about the *épuration* became available only in the 1980s.[3] Even the 1989 bicentennial showed signs of having been mediated by memories of history more recent than the Revolution: the celebration incorporated a mock trial (a replay of the Revolutionary Convention) in the form of a televised public referendum on the execution of Louis XVI. Louis fared better this time around: the good citizens of Paris voted to acquit the king. Their collective gesture can be seen, I think, as a ritual of self-accusation and self-forgiveness for national crimes in Revolutionary times and since. Such an interpretation is suggested by the fact that Louis's defense was argued by none other than Jacques Vergès. By comparing World War II with the Algerian conflict and the *épuration* and then, implicitly, with the Terror, Vergès strategically blurred categories and glossed over historical differences, making it more difficult than ever to come to terms with France's collaboration with nazism.

These incidents are emblematic of the peculiar dynamic of confession and invention, of guilt and desire for absolution, of evasion and a will to knowledge to be found in some recent fictions that try to construct a discourse about World War II and France's murky role in it. The obsessive insistence with which memoirs and fictions return to stories about the war makes it clear that national and individual collaboration remains a scandal, understood both as an outrage and in its etymological sense of *skandalon* (see my first epigraph). The fear of being accused (or suspected) of complicity with the Nazi program remains an important stumbling block in French identity and in scholars' attempts to understand postwar French history. Deriving from religious usage and designating a temptation or leading astray by example, the term is also usefully identified as a recurrent trope that suggests the presence of a historical disease or contagion.

This return to the period of the Occupation is particularly remarkable in the work of certain artists, associated with the New Novel and New Wave filmmaking, who, from the mid-1970s to the mid-1980s, have moved from the experimentation and self-reflexivity on which they built their reputations to an overtly historical mode. Duras, whose work has always been intensely personal, became more explicitly autobiographical with the appearance of *The Lover* in 1984 and *The War* in 1985; Alain Robbe-Grillet's two volumes of memoirs appeared in 1984 and 1987. Nathalie Sarraute published her memoirs in 1983.[4] Among the filmmakers, most notable are François Truffaut (*The Last Metro*, 1981) and Louis Malle (*Au revoir les enfants*, 1987). These works do not for the most part analyze or comment openly, nor do they evoke public events on the panoramic scale of the Barbie crimes and trial or the Revolutionary Convention. Rather, they are personal stories of private betrayal and loss recounted against a historical backdrop that is sketchy at best. Rather than reinterpretation of the events themselves, what seems to be at stake in such stories, as in the earlier work by the same artists, are the problematic nature of representation and the questions of how the self constructs itself historically and, conversely, how historical knowledge is shaped by private circumstance and mediated by writing or filming.

In many fictions of World War II, from William Styron's *Sophie's Choice* and Elie Wiesel's *Night* to the books by Robbe-Grillet and Duras, memories are organized around a focal scene that appears in some ways to be the origin or crux of the story. Such paradigmatic moments or primal scenes function as metaphors of a trauma so mysterious as to evade representation. In this they resemble what Robert Jay Lifton has called an "image of ultimate horror." Noting that most of the Hiroshima survivors he interviewed suffered from the persistence of "a specific image of the dead or dying with which the survivor strongly identifies himself, and which evokes in him particularly intense feelings of pity and self-condemnation," Lifton described such images as "a type of memory which epitomizes the relationship of death to guilt." Further on, Lifton renames such obsessive scenes "residual image[s]" and describes them as "the pictorialization of [the individual's] central conflict in relationship to the disaster."[5] Lifton's formulation lends itself to use as a model of the relationship between film and memory, a model in which the disaster is not pictorialized directly but is mediated by rhetorical conventions and personal psychic configurations. I want to use one film—Louis Malle's *Au revoir les enfants*—and in particular one scene in the film, as an example of just such a process of pictorialization and to theorize the relation of image making to a personal sense of guilt.

In a statement accompanying the published script of his film, Louis Malle says that the story was

. . . inspired by the most tragic [*dramatique*] memory of my childhood. In 1944, I was eleven years old and boarding at a Catholic school near Fontainebleau. A new boy joined us at the beginning of the year. A brilliant student, he intrigued me. He was different; his background was mysterious. He didn't talk much the first few weeks. Little by little we became friends, when, one morning, our small world collapsed.

That morning of 1944 changed my life. It may have triggered my becoming a filmmaker.[6]

Yet Malle did not make a film about the incident until 1987: forty-three years (and twenty-eight films) later, at the age of fifty-four. "I should have made it the subject of my first film," he remarks, "but I preferred to wait." My own questions are, Why did he wait so long? What connects the "tragic memory" depicted in *Au revoir les enfants* to Malle's choice of filmmaking as a career? What finally made it possible or necessary to make this film, and in the images he chooses? And what is the truth value of the memory depicted; that is, what exactly is the experience that is being represented, given Malle's repeated statements that the movie doesn't depict the memory the way it happened at all and, in particular, that the crucial scene is pure invention?[7]

The anecdote of *Au revoir les enfants* is deceptively straightforward and realistic: the action takes place over a few weeks in the winter of 1944 at a Catholic boarding school. The head priest, Père Jean (who is active in the Resistance), hides three Jewish boys in the school under assumed names. Julien Quentin, Malle's autobiographical persona, becomes friends with one of the new boys, Jean Bonnet (Kippelstein), who also rivals him as best student in the class. Julien applies his academic acumen to deciphering the enigma of Jean's identity. Meanwhile, war intrudes on the isolated school in the form of air raids, a kitchen helper's dismissal for black market activities, the lawless behavior of *miliciens* harassing on elderly Jewish gentleman in a restaurant and more pervasively in the rationing of heat and food and in the boys' conversations, which incorporate overheard and half-understood remarks about Pétain, "les collabos," the militia, the Russian front, the Service de Travail Obligatoire (forced deportations to work in Germany), the Allies' advance, and so on. On the fatal day, the regional Gestapo chief descends on the school, arrests Jean Kippelstein and the two other Jewish boys, along with Père Jean, while the school proctor, also a Resistance member, escapes across the roof. The final frame is accompanied by an adult first-person voiceover, telling us that all three boys perished in the camps. The voice, presumably that of the filmmaker himself, adds: "Over forty years have passed but I will remember every second of that January morning until the day I die."

At first, *Au revoir les enfants* seems a tale of resistance and heroic defeat. In harboring the three boys, the headmaster's actions are courageous; Julien's brother matures from playing annoying pranks on German soldiers (he gives misleading directions so that they will lose their way in the town) to a tentative decision to join the Maquis. The boys themselves are stoically "resisting" wartime conditions of deprivation and family separation. Julien's friendship with Jean grows apace with his progressive understanding of his friend's perilous situation. The film's narrative line is sustained by a detective plot, mirrored internally by the two boys' shared reading of Sherlock Holmes. Julien deciphers clues: an overheard midnight prayer, a family photograph hidden in a locker, an erased but faintly legible name in a schoolbook, and his friend's evasion of certain questions about his birthplace, the whereabouts of his parents, and his dietary habits. When he pieces together, finally, the puzzle of his friend's Jewish identity, he refuses to understand it: "What's a Jew?" he asks his brother, who answers that it is someone who doesn't eat pork. "You're putting me on," Julien retorts. "What exactly do people blame them for?" (p. 39). The spectator, from a vantage point that is both more adult and historically retrospective, has understood from the beginning but nonetheless identifies with the unintended but sinister irony of the young boy's questions. Julien's conscious attitudes and deliberate actions, as they naively deconstruct the very notion of racial/religious difference by rendering it ludicrous or meaningless, constitute an act of resistance.

A deeper look reveals, however, that the film is haunted by small as well as flagrant acts of collaboration and of foolish risk-taking that betrays. The extent to which collaboration is the ambiguous subterranean trauma of *Au revoir les enfants* can be discerned in certain similarities with Malle's 1974 film about the Occupation, *Lacombe Lucien*. The earlier film portrays a sullen and doltish teenage boy's descent into brutality and recounts the conflict between his activities on behalf of the local Gestapo and his growing attachment to a Jewish tailor and his daughter, France. When the German police come to arrest France (having already taken her father), Lucien kills the German, and he and France live a brief life as fugitives until the war ends. A final subtitle informs us of Lucien's postwar trial and execution for collaboration.

Both films take place in 1944 and portray an adolescent boy, present in virtually every scene, who befriends and acts as would-be protector of a Jew. Both show history to be largely the sum of chance events: collaboration is portrayed (entirely in the early film, episodically in the later one) as occurring when characters succumb to small thoughtless actions that would be insignificant in normal times but that result here in tragedy: Lacombe drinks too much and gossips about a schoolteacher, who is then captured and tortured by the Gestapo; in *Au revoir les enfants*, Père Jean refuses communion to a Jewish boy, thereby revealing the limits of his Christian charity and his religious training. He similarly protects his middle-class charges by dismissing Joseph, the kitchen helper, using him as a scapegoat for collective misbehavior. Spiteful and destitute, Joseph will turn informer. Most centrally, Jean Bonnet/Kippelstein's arrest follows directly from an inadvertent gesture on the part of Julien himself. In both films, a final voice-of-God conclusion announces the subsequent death of a protagonist in direct consequence of the events we have just witnessed.

Lacombe Lucien emerged from Malle's research into the psychology of the traitor. He decided to incarnate that interest in the story of a collaborator only after considering and rejecting a string of subjects: the Mexican *halcones* (police stooges who infiltrated student rebel groups in 1968), a young French accountant-turned-torturer Malle had interviewed in Algeria, Algerian *harkis* who aided the French army, and Lieutenant Calley of the U.S. Army, in prison at the time for torturing Vietnamese villagers.[8] Even before its precise historical context, then, the genesis of *Lacombe Lucien* foregrounded Malle's fascination with collaboration in the more general sense and with unquestioning obedience to authority as forms of human behavior. Lucien's actions are explained psychologically: they result from character weaknesses—in particular, a craving for adult identity and authority—and from situations that lead Lucien inexorably down what one could call the path of least resistance.

The film's ambivalence about Lucien—a sympathetic portrayal of a person engaged in detestable behavior—is reflected in the scandal it unleashed. The press at first unanimously hailed the film as a masterpiece, only to execute an abrupt about-face a month later and condemn it. All sides found fault with the representation of the collaborator as unremittingly stupid and proletarian. The Right criticized it for painting French fascism's adherents as a band of marginals devoid of ideological commitment and driven by a latent brutality only waiting for the opportunity to express itself. Lucien is not even an antihero: he becomes what he is by chance, his collaboration is unknowing and almost inadvertent; he simply follows the drift, drawn along by events he doesn't understand. The Left criticized Malle for making a film about a collaborator at all, for disculpating a soundrel (that is, for implicitly making a case for compassion or even amnesty), and for portraying the *résistants* as murdering marauders.[9] The controversy revealed a deep unwillingness, at every point along the political spectrum, to demystify the Resistance or to delve into the psychic or even the political logic of collaboration. One scene shows Lucien idly chatting with a tortured Resistance prisoner chained to a radiator. Angered because the man calls him *tu*—that is, treats him like a child—Lucien tapes his mouth shut. I like to read this scene as emblematic of the censorship still in place in 1974 on representations of the Occupation.

Perhaps because of its abstract and philosophical genesis, *Lacombe Lucien* executes a variety of maneuvers that systematically distance the protagonist and protect the audience from too-direct involvement with Lucien; despite his boyish charm and his status as protagonist, he remains remote from his typical audience because of his class situation and his unthinking and instinctive responses. Although he is present in every scene, his visual point of view is never that of the film. He is opaque, his thoughts are enigmatic, and as spectators, we watch him, not *with* him; he (and by extension collaboration) remain in the sphere of spectacle. At the same time, he is not unappealing as an awkward and desiring adolescent, and the interest of the film lies in the scandal—tragic in its inexorability as it is presented—of his stumbling descent into brutality.

In exploring psychological dimensions of collaboration, *Lacombe Lucien* goes a step beyond Sartre's 1939 portrait of the budding Fascist in *L'Enfance d'un chef*,[10] whose protagonist, it will be remembered, was also named Lucien. Malle's portrayal is less Manichaean; he injects notes of pathos and tragedy into the collaborator's itinerary; in so doing, Malle makes his Lucien more troubling. In falling in love with a woman whose name—France—is certainly allegorical, Lacombe identifies himself with—even as—a victim. Sartre's Lucien was more intellectual and cosmopolitan, and he chose evil more lucidly. Although his development is nonetheless believable, Lucien Fleurier is not a sympathetic character, and Sartre makes no excuses for him.

The critical response to *Lacombe Lucien* obliges us to revise the truism that Marcel Ophuls's *The Sorrow and the Pity* unmasked the myth of the Resistance and opened the way for responsible reexamination of the Occupation. In truth, the floodgates of memory (especially memories of collaboration) were more like a revolving door, opening in stages. Ophuls's film marks a double scandal: first for what it attempted to reveal and then for the fact that it took the French government ten years to accord it the screening it deserved in France; for although Ophuls's film was released in 1971, it was banned from French television until the Mittérand Ministry of Culture finally reinstated it, amid renewed controversy, in 1981.[11] The delay in its release and the magnitude of its effect measure the strength of the resistance to it, for what Ophuls's documentary challenged was the tremendous investment in the official Gaullist construction of history, according to which national unity in resisting the occupier was marred by only a handful of traitors, cowards, and fools.[12]

Even more persistent was the belief that collaborators and *resistants* were themselves two clearly defined and completely distinct groups. *The Sorrow and the Pity* shatters such Manichaean views of the Occupation and delineates instead a complex array of degrees and forms of collaboration and resistance.

Moreover, if *The Sorrow and the Pity* showed the French public that Germans and a few French lackeys were not the only villains of the Occupation, Ophuls's most recent film, *Hotel Terminus: The Life and Times of Klaus Barbie* (1988) traces the responsibility for Barbie (and tracks Barbie himself) from Germany and France to Latin America by way of the United States. Ophuls's film, like so many stories about the Holocaust—including *Au revoir les enfants*—is a monstrous postmodern detective story, in which there is a detective (Julien in Malle's film and Ophuls himself in *Hotel Terminus*) but from which the crime, the criminal, and even the trial are missing. Moreover, although there is no real "solution" at the end of either film, the criminal's guilt was manifest from the start; and what is spellbinding is how many others (individuals, governments) are implicated. Curiously, Barbie's itinerary, traced by Ophuls, also provides a map of Malle's own travels in his quest of a nationality for his collaborator: from France to Latin America (add Algeria) to the United States and back to France. So it is no simple cinematic tribute but rather an ironic commentary that in *Au revoir les enfants*, when Julien and Jean and the others are treated to a movie, the schoolmaster's choice is Charlie Chaplin's *The Immigrant*, in which we watch with the schoolboys the scene in which the Little Tramp arrives in view of the Statue of Liberty.

What is evident now in the succession of Ophuls's relentless documentaries are the stages in an epic scandal that threatens to include an everwidening number of participants in the spiraling taint of nazism; for when categories break down, as the distinctions between resistance and collaboration do in *The Sorrow and the Pity*, who is to say what the definition of a collaborator is? The prophylactic spell of the Gaullist narrative is broken: anyone might be guilty, even those whose only role was to witness the events, so complacent distance is no longer possible. The critical controversy surrounding *Lacombe Lucien* and the intervening censorship and rerelease of *The Sorrow and the Pity* no doubt had their effect on the greater complexity of the psychological portraits and the subtlety of the representation of collaboration in *Au revoir les enfants*.

The differences between Malle's two films serve to measure his evolution from 1974 and 1987. Awareness of the contagious nature of guilt for collaboration and an attempt to take responsibility for it account for the distance between *Lacombe Lucien* and *Au revoir les enfants*, a distance that can be discerned in the structure and techniques of narration. The extradiegetic statement that concludes both films has a very different impact in each. The narrator who emerges at the end of *Au revoir les enfants* speaks from a split consciousness; the film is unveiled as autobiographical and retrospective. The adult remains scandalized and contaminated by his childhood experiences, haunted by a conflict he came to understand only much later. This self-reflective dimension is totally absent, on the other hand, from *Lacombe Lucien*, which is a prospective story with a voice-of-God narrator who announces (in subtitles) the sequel to the story but not its effect on the present.

There are significant differences in the portrayal of collaboration as well. *Au revoir* foregrounds the death of the *victim* of collaborationist policies, whereas *Lacombe Lucien* sketches a portrait of the collaborator *as* victim of the *épuration* as well as of his own latent brutality and of history itself. And in *Au revoir*, collaboration is not conceived as inherent in the character of the protagonist; it is not even a slippery slope of incidental or unknowing small choices. Even the kitchen helper makes a deliberate decision to seek revenge by denouncing the school. The two films also deploy different answers to the question: collaboration with what? Lucien is accomplice to torture of individuals in the Resistance; at stake in *Au revoir les enfants* are acts of complicity with genocide.

The most disturbing and complex moment in *Au revoir* involves Julien himself in a decisive moment of collaboration. What is troubling and courageous in Malle's portrayal here is that collaboration is not an *essence*; it is an *act*. The traumatic memory for Julien Quentin, on that morning in January 1944, is the arrival of the Gestapo at his school to arrest his friend. But the way the scene is played out implicates Julien as more than a spectator, or rather, implicates him *as* a spectator. The boys are in a classroom listening to a teacher who, with the aid of a map of Europe and a set of blue and yellow pins, is giving an update on the progress of the Allies. He has just stepped away from the map and begun a geometry lesson when a Gestapo officer, Dr. Muller, marches into the classroom, accuses the fathers of hiding Jews in the school, and demands to know which student is Jean Kippelstein. The boys freeze and lower their eyes. After a stunned moment of silence, the teacher states that there is no one by that name in the school. Muller then steps impatiently to the map and begins angrily to pull out the colored pins. During the instant while his back is to the class, Julien turns furtively to reassure himself that his friend Jean is there. His glance is intercepted by Muller, who strides directly to Jean's desk. Slowly and with dignity, Jean puts away his writing materials, takes his coat, and begins to shake the hands of his classmates, bidding them good-bye one by one.

As if there were any doubt about the gravity or the choreography of the gesture, it occurs twice, in slightly different contexts, with Julien playing different but related roles. A few moments after the scene just described, the boys are all gathering their belongings, the school having been peremptorily and punitively closed. From the classroom, Julien has gone to prepare his own knapsack and thence to the infirmary, where he will help a sick classmate pack his things. Meanwhile, the Gestapo officers search the school for the two other Jewish boys. With the proctor's help, Négus, one of the remaining Jewish boys, takes refuge in the infirmary, posing as a patient under the covers in one of the beds. When the two Gestapo officers burst into the room, Julien looks on as a nurse gives the boy away wordlessly, with a glance in the direction of the bed.

Julien Quentin is thus not simply a witness to Jean's arrest. It is his own act, however inadvertent, that gives his friend away, just as fatally as the nun's deliberate betrayal of Négus; motivation makes no difference whatsoever in the outcome. Despite Jean's reassurance that "they would have caught up with me in any case" (p. 71), the fact remains that Julien is not innocent. Thus is collaboration figured as a specular drama: a moment of active looking that causes the death of another. This intercepted glance provides a rhetorical or geometrical (triangular) figure for the structure of collaboration and indeed even as its definition. Given the Catholic school setting and the film's incessant use of religious motifs, it is not out of place to call this look a Judas kiss: the juxtaposition of the two scenes cleverly and accurately conveys the dynamic of denunciation and counterdenunciation that characterized the anarchic final months of the Occupation. Julien plays the collaborator's role in the first scene. He is witness to an act of collaboration in the second. These are truly looks that kill.

I submit that it is this moment of Julien's glance that constitutes the primal scene or, in Lifton's words, the "*residual image*—the pictorialization of [the individual's] central conflict in relationship to the disaster" that haunts the narrator in the final voiceover, presumably Malle himself. The distance between intention and outcome is thematized in the difference between looking *at* (betraying) and looking *with* (protecting); viewing the Chaplin film together, the two profiles of Jean and Julien are framed side by side in extreme close-up, transfixed by a cinematic image that provides for them, in the words of André Bazin describing Chaplin, "unlimited imagination in the face of danger." [13] These words can be understood to reflect Malle's optimism about the function of cinema in general and perhaps his hopes for this specific film vis-à-vis a French public still reluctant to confront the dangers of memory. Within a politicized thematic of looking, watching a film can itself constitute a political choice, Malle seems to suggest: because of Chaplin's politics and his Jewish origins, *The Immigrant* would, in 1944, have constituted an obvious contrast with the anti-Semitic propaganda films that might have been screened in other schools.

In glancing at Jean and thereby inadvertently identifying him as a Jew, Julien performs the fundamental anti-Semitic act as it is defined by Sartre in *Réflections sur la question juive* (*Anti-Semite and Jew*, written in 1944 and published in 1946). Sartre's essay (like his later essay on racism, *Black Orpheus*) is permeated with a vocabulary of visibility and looking: in times of persecution, the Jew seeks invisibility; it is the anti-Semite's fear and hatred, concretized in his/her eyes and gaze, that constitutes the Jew as such. So powerful is the anti-Semite's hatred and the look that embodies it, and so clearly does it preexist the social identity of the Jew, Sartre argues, that it is the anti-Semite who creates the Jew; and "if the Jew did not exist, the anti-Semite would have to invent him." [14] With its emphasis on eyes and the power of the glance, it is as if Malle's film were a fictionalized demonstration of Sartre's argument.

But perhaps I am unfair. After all, Julien is clearly not an anti-Semite—quite the contrary. His fatal gesture is motivated not by betrayal but the opposite: a desire to reassure himself that his friend is safe. And in any case, how guilty can a twelve-year-old be? And of what, exactly? It becomes important to point out that, in contrast with the narrator's backward quest revealed at the end, and until the Gestapo arrives, *Au revoir les enfants* is much less concerned with nazism than with adolescent sexual curiosity. Julien is both a naive Sherlock Holmes discovering the murderous mysteries of nazism and an adolescent boy in search of sexual secrets. The scene immediately preceding Dr. Muller's arrival in the classroom shows Jean and Julien in the dormitory late at night, reading together by the light of a pocket lamp. Julien is reading aloud an erotic passage from *The Arabian Nights*: "And with a quick motion she threw off her veils and disrobed completely to show herself in her native nakedness. . . . Truly, she combined the lascivious movements of Arab girls with the heat of the Ethiopians, the startled candor of the Franks with the consummate science of the Indians, the coquetry of the women of Yemen" (p. 67). Et cetera. The boys nod off to sleep, and abruptly the film cuts to the fatal classroom scene. Malle's editing shows that it is precisely when and because history intervenes that sexual investigation is displaced. The confession scenes are particularly ironic; being asked to admit to euphemistically evoked sexual "mauvaises pensées" seems especially ludicrous within the atmosphere of mortal danger and real evil that prevails and that is the substance of the film's overall confessional project. [15]

Given the juxtaposition of erotic and political curiosity—and the inherent voyeurism of the camera eye, which can make all taboo subjects interchangeable—it would have been easy to let one become a metaphor for the other, but Malle did not choose this path. Instead, the film shows how each shapes the other: circumstances dictate that for Julien (as for Lucien, for that matter) sexual and political awakening are intermeshed, and there is a corresponding loss of innocence in both domains. The best visualization of this is again to be found in Jean's and Julien's furtive nocturnal reading of *The Arabian Nights*. As is evident in the passage quoted above, that book serves both as an improvised sex manual for adolescents and a lesson in (spurious) racial differentiation. So it is that when, to his acute embarrassment and fear, Julien is ordered to drop his pants, it is not sexual but racial difference and survival that are being determined. *The Arabian Nights* are also, of course, a tale of captivity and a storyteller's attempt to outwit death. Thus, Jean signals his defeat (and perhaps transfers responsibility to his friend) by giving the book to Julien before he departs.

The intertwined quests for political and sexual knowledge are also foregrounded in Julien's conversations with his older brother. François is interested in girls, though, whereas Julien is still passionately caught in the coils of the family romance. The film opens in a train station on the scene of mother and son's tearful farewells. Julien's declaration to his mother that he wishes to stay in Paris to live with her (pleading that his father needn't know) recalls the incestuous mother and son of Malle's 1971 *Souffle au coeur* (*Murmur of the Heart*). Both of these films (and others such as *Pretty Baby*) are punctuated by the child's suspicions or discovery of maternal unfaithfulness. In *Au revoir les enfants*, the superimposition of Malle's family romance motif on the equally triangular intercepted gaze of collaboration yields a multiply determined figure of guilty memory. It is this guilt that is the object of the adult filmmaker-detective's backward glance.

And it is in this sense that we can read the crucial moment of *Au revoir les enfants* as a primal scene and begin to understand it as a fictional construct. In his case study of the Wolfman, Freud narrates the psychoanalytic project as a detective plot: he investigates how the self is constituted by an act of traumatic and inadvertent looking.[16] Geraldine Pederson-Krag, comparing Freud's case study to detective story readers in her attempt to explain the irresistible appeal of the genre, isolates common elements that describe just as well the memory quest of *Au revoir les enfants*: a secret scene of wrongdoing, an anxious but curious detective/child who retains a submerged memory but only partial understanding of a scene witnessed, the child's uncertainty as to whether he has simply witnessed or actually been a participant in the scene.[17] Geoffrey Hartman, too, stresses that detective fiction shares with the psychoanalytic understanding of sexual curiosity a witnessed wrongdoing, what he calls a "heart of darkness scene" or a "scene of suffering" that is understood to enfold some primal mystery. As readers or writers of such fiction, according to Hartman, we are motivated by a "reality-hunger, our desire to know the worst and the best."[18]

Guilt, like curiosity, is contagious. As Freud understood in his analysis of the Wolfman's primal scene (and as Alfred Hitchcock also knew when he made *Rear Window*), Malle demonstrates in *Au revoir les enfants* that looking is an act that truly implicates the spectator in a way no other figuration of guilt could achieve. In the fatal classroom scene, the gazes of character (Julien), camera, and spectator converge to indicate the Jew for the Nazi. This sort of suture-shot establishes the spectator's direct complicity (though as involuntary as Julien's), all the more so because we have been induced, both narratively and visually, to identify with Julien. Thus, Malle's film not only portrays a mechanism of involuntary complicity but also enacts it.

The figure of the fatal intercepted glance ensnares the profession of filmmaking as well; here the traumatic memory, "pictorialized" as a guilty glance, offers an insight into Malle's vocation as a filmmaker. Is the making of fictional images symptomatic of a repressed trauma that gets repeated and transformed as it inevitably returns? Is the cinematic eye a detective (a "private eye") or a psychoanalytic quest for an original but submerged scene of wrongdoing? Is filmmaking an opportunity to expiate the criminal look with a healing one? Perhaps all of these, but in any case, *Au revoir les enfants* reveals the danger of looking and its power to define and even construct social categories and to position individuals in history. In particular, Malle shows that the act of looking is as heavily bound up with racism as with filmmaking.[19]

In Malle's film, historical memory is not, as I have said, simply a displacement or reworking of the family romance. Recent writings on primal scene theory question the archaeological/referential model of psychoanalysis and emphasize instead the displacement whereby the child witness to the primal scene or "secret wrongdoing" unconsciously constructs guilty memories in which he assumes the guilt of the fathers.[20] There are three sets of fathers in *Au revoir les enfants*: Julien's real father is conspicuously absent; the school fathers mean well, but their authority is ultimately ineffectual and illusory. Finally, of course, it is the intervention of the Nazi authorities themselves (with the word *Halt*, the "nom/non du père") that marks the end of childhood. Not "au revoir les enfants" but "au revoir l'enfance," good-bye to childhood. The child detective is left with the bag and with the question of where real agency is located, who is guilty. The story is not a confession of responsibility for a past wrongdoing. Rather, the act is invented to account for the guilt.

In its figuration of guilt as a furtive glance backward, I believe that *Au revoir les enfants* paints a portrait of a generation and reveals the particular images in which its memories are cast. Julien, like Malle and others of his generation—such as Truffaut, who was born the same year—was too old in 1944 to be oblivious and too young to be responsible. That Julien's awakenings to the primal mysteries of sexuality and history coincide suggests the necessity of reexamining the connections between nazism and eroticism as these have been configured by Michel Foucault and Susan Sontag, among others,[21] who analyze the appeal of nazism through adult understandings of sexuality and power. Hayden White has shown how narrative history is "emplotted" according to the generic conventions of storytelling: tragedy, comedy, farce, irony.[22] Malle's films—and his career as a filmmaker—suggest that we also may need to investigate the ways in which historical memories are mediated by psychic mechanisms and developmental narratives, with their concomitant guilts and censors, desires and displacements, and, of course, their gender specificity. If this is the case, then the representations of collaboration—and the interpretation of those representations—are just beginning.

STEVEN UNGAR

Scandal and Aftereffect
Martin Heidegger in France

The works that are being peddled about nowadays as the philosophy of National Socialism but have nothing whatsoever to do with the inner truth and greatness of this movement . . . have all been written by men fishing in the troubled waters of "values" and "totalities."
—Martin Heidegger, *An Introduction to Metaphysics*

To articulate the past historically does not mean to recognize it "the way it was" (Ranke). It means to seize hold of a memory as it flashes up at a moment of danger.
—Walter Benjamin, "Theses on the Philosophy of History"

I. Fishing in Troubled Waters

Jean-Paul Sartre wrote in 1960 that the case of Martin Heidegger (1889–1976) was too complex for him to explain. What Sartre did not—could not? would not?—address at the time has returned as scandal and aftereffect. Until recently, the reception of Heidegger in France bordered on the reverential. His books were read as works of art, his every pronouncement scrutinized and debated at length. In postwar France, the effects of this reverence promoted a cult following. Over nearly four decades, Heidegger personified the philosopher-poet whose conception of language and practice of writing earned him a following among writers, intellectuals, and artists including Sartre, René Char, Georges Braque, Jacques Lacan, Michel Foucault, and Jacques Derrida. George Steiner helps to explain this appeal by remarking that Heidegger "belongs to the history of language and of literature as much (some would say more) than he does to that of ontology, of phenomenological epistemology or of aesthetics."[1]

To be sure, reverence toward Heidegger has never gone uncontested. Alternative receptions inside and outside France have ranged from the skeptical to the frivolous. Philosophers of language such as Rudolf Carnap, A. J. Ayer, and W. V. Quine have objected to Heidegger's pseudo-statements as "irrelevant to the legitimate practice of philosophy." Others have dismissed Heidegger more or less outright as "the best comic example of the philosophical quack." An editorialist has quipped that analytic philosophers tend to divide into two camps: those who believe Heidegger's writings are largely gibberish and those who believe they are entirely gibberish.[2]

The challenges against Heidegger's writings are not confined to the peculiarities of language and style. Philosophers in the analytic tradition scoff at obscure and irrational writings they nonetheless continue to read. Why, then, do so many readers—especially informed readers who presumably know better—seemingly take the trouble? Once again, Steiner expresses a commonly shared opinion when he writes that "the question of whether Martin Heidegger is saying anything substantive and arguable *at all*, of whether his voluminous pronouncements upon man and *mundum* are anything but tautological incantations, lies deeper" (Steiner, p. 38). But while many reactions to Heidegger are cast in an ironic mode, it would also be a mistake *not* to question the more serious concerns and ambivalence such irony expresses. Much of the hostility directed toward Heidegger's writings can be explained by the fact that they raise the issue of limits between philosophy and nonphilosophy or, as some might state it, between philosophy and its others. In addition, they do so in ways that consistently elicit affective responses where one might otherwise expect other responses. The quips and swipes aimed at Heidegger only strengthen the provocation his writings exercise, especially among readers who see them as exemplary of what philosophy should *not* be.

Well before the recent controversy surrounding the nature and extent of Heidegger's involvement with National Socialism, resistance to his writings pointed to the various kinds of mediation at work in their reception. To restate this somewhat differently, Heidegger's reputation had been that of a "difficult" writer long before recent debate revised this difficulty from the perspective of National Socialism. Part of the problem was archival, involving inadequate or blocked access to materials and the existence of texts in multiple versions. Even now, the appearance of sixty-five volumes suggests that a complete edition of Heidegger's writings is unlikely to occur for years, if ever at all! In such terms, the history of French receptions of Heidegger's writings is very much an account of corrections and supplements that never fulfill the ambition of definitive access. Christopher Fynsk identifies some terms and assumptions on the basis of which this reception has occurred when he holds that the corpus of Heidegger's writings is "a construct that has won apparent unity and coherence of meaning through a conflictual process of differentiation and exclusion—a process that always leaves its marks in the form of gaps, inconsistencies, aporias, etc."[3] The charges of difficulty made against Heidegger's writings are inappropriate if and when they reduce language and style to surface effects. Moreover, they are often nothing more than elaborate attempts to justify a refusal to take seriously writings that fail to conform to certain conventions of clarity and rigorous argument. Perhaps, as Fynsk proposes, reading does not begin until the surface intelligibility of the writings is broken in order to follow "not the content, a series of propositions or theses (or even a series of what may seem to be poetic figures), but the very movement of thought in its becoming-other" (Fynsk, p. 15).

What might be the terms and the ambitions of a protocol of reading that would engage Heidegger's writings without either trivializing them or simulating their tone and style? My approach in what follows derives from what I see as the motivations contained in claims and counterclaims concerning the status of Heidegger's writings. Should these writings be taken seriously? If so, how might such seriousness relate to issues concerning their status as philosophical texts? Apart from what Heidegger may or may not have intended, the issues raised by such questions go beyond the attributions of authority associated with possession ("Heidegger's philosophy") and type ("Heideggerian philosophy"). Nor is it just a matter of relating philosophy to other academic disciplines such as literature and history. For to do so is to start from assumed distinctions that assert the priority—if not the privilege—of thought over language and other practices of representation. A final caveat: my presentation of Heidegger's writings is intended to introduce the various ways they have been read and reread—by Heidegger himself, among others. Only by looking first at these appropriations and how they evolve over time can any sense of current debate be understood beyond topicality and polemic. Only then might it be possible to situate—if not also to correct—the logic at work in strong and productive misreadings that have made Heidegger's writings the test case of a received modernity that is presently under intense critical revision. Not, then, Heidegger's writings as *Urtext*, but instead as one prototype of a conception and practice of philosophical writing that is only now coming to be understood some fifty to sixty years after the fact.

II. Correction

Well before recent attempts to collapse conventional distinctions between disciplines and genres, Heidegger's writings broke the illusion of a pure thought distinct from representation. In place of philosophy as a discipline distinct from literature and/or history, I want to explore how Heidegger's early writings raised the question of what philosophy is and what it *was* at the time, as well as claims regarding what it might become. The initial formulation of these claims occurred with the 1927 appearance of *Being and Time* (*Sein und Zeit*). Heidegger's desire that the book be read as an ontology of *Dasein*—that is, as a philosophy of what he termed Being's being—marked his view of it as the first in a series of critical engagements with a metaphysical tradition whose essence he saw as anthropocentric. Heidegger wanted to situate himself both within and at a critical remove from this tradition. In so doing, he wrote in the shadow of Friedrich Nietzsche, whom he later referred to as the last metaphysician. The project announced in *Being and Time* was a polemical response to both the epistemological concerns of neo-Kantians such as Ernst Casirer and the phenomenological concerns of Heidegger's former teacher, Edmund Husserl.

In a strict sense, *Being and Time* inscribed human agency within what Heidegger termed the disclosure of the essential truth of Being. Those who approach Heidegger's writings of the 1920s and 1930s from the perspective of his postwar texts often dehistoricize this disclosure. They cite his dismissal of the rectorate period—"the greatest stupidity [*die grösste Dummheit*] of my life"—in order to avoid serious consideration of his ontology in terms of German politics of the period. Recent allegations suggest that the extent of this avoidance may be greater than most of Heidegger's readers thought. The hypothesis opposes received opinion in order to reconsider the extent to which Heidegger's interwar and wartime writings were already marked with signs of historical and political thinking either he or his followers displaced if not also suppressed. What might such a hypothesis imply about Heidegger's personal agency and/or intentions? How might it promote fuller understanding of the ontology set forth in *Being and Time*? Finally, what might it suggest concerning the evolving postwar reception of Heidegger's writings in France and elsewhere?

It is tempting to see *Being and Time* as the product of an existential involvement that takes place prior to Heidegger's 1929 conflation of philosophical theory with ideological motifs. The priority of the existential over the political should not be misconstrued as a simple or direct consequence of chronology. It bears on a conception of agency and on specific actions that Heidegger subsequently undertook during the National Socialist period. Three to four years *before* he became rector under the Nazi regime in April 1933, Heidegger was already considering how he, as a professor of philosophy at the University of Freiburg, could contribute to the disclosure of *Dasein*. Jürgen Habermas notes that "the switches are set for a national/revolutionary interpretation of what in *Being and Time* was a self-heeding and self-assertion sketched in existential terms. Thus Heidegger, who had opted for the Nazi party before 1933, could explain Hitler's successful power-grab in terms of concepts *retained* from his own analytic of *Dasein*."[4]

Being and Time announced the ambitions Heidegger (already) held for philosophy in the late 1920s. Its acclaim—some might describe it instead as notoriety—also derived from Heidegger's skill at imposing a controversial philosophical position against which subsequent positions were defined and evaluated. It supports the view that by the mid-1920s Heidegger was already adept at manipulating controversy in order to legitimize a powerful personal identity within the German university system that he saw as a prime site for the spiritual and social changes he described in the 1933 rectorate speech. If, as Heidegger and many exegetes have since claimed, *Being and Time* is an attempt to overcome metaphysics in the name of an ontology, its disclosure of the social and/or political implications of this overcoming was partial if not oblique. In retrospect, *Being and Time* lays the foundation of an ontology whose relation to the political and social issues of the period is disclosed only in part.

Is the ontology set forth in *Being and Time* (already) political? Pierre Bourdieu drops the distinction between philosophical and political approaches to Heidegger's writings when he refers to corresponding social and mental spaces:

The singularity of Heidegger's enterprise resides in the fact that it tends to *make exist* within the very heart of the philosophical field—and by means of a philosophical power play—a new position in relation to which all other positions would need to define themselves. . . . In order to bring off such an overthrow of power relations at the heart of the philosophical field and to give a form of respectability to a position that was heretical, it was necessary to associate the "revolutionary" dispositions of the rebel with the specific authority that is guaranteed by the accumulation of a significant amount of capital at the very heart of the field.[5]

If the ontology in *Being and Time* is already political, any attempt to set it within a discourse of "pure" philosophy promotes the very ambiguities Heidegger exploited throughout his career, from the rectorate period of the mid-1930s through the 1966 interview with *Der Spiegel* published after his death ten years later. The initial obstacles to proving the hypothesis of political ontology are textual. It is not merely that different readers perform different readings, as though literary and philosophical readings excluded each other. Beyond differences between readers and readings, the textual and semantic density of the writings promoted a disparity among divergent readings that rendered them inadequate and open to revision. As a result, the disclosure conveyed by the Heideggerian text extends from exposition to demonstration and performance. It collapses the distinction between the disclosure of Being designated by Heidegger's use of the Greek term *aletheia* (especially, but not only, in "The Origin of the Work of Art") and the mastery of disclosure performed by textual effects that depart from conventions of conceptual and logical rigor shared by many philosophers.

Issues related to ambiguous disclosure also broach more delicate matters of agency and the uses to which Heidegger's writings have been put. As with Nietzsche, it is unclear to what extent appropriation after the fact extended beyond what Heidegger may have intended. Nevertheless, it is no coincidence that the literary ("poetic") qualities admired by many of Heidegger's French readers are often at the forefront of debate. As with Nietzsche before him, Heidegger is often dismissed as a "dangerous" philosopher whose ideas advanced the political ends of National Socialism. Ongoing debate in Germany, France, and the United States supports serious consideration of this view and of a revisionist approach to the interwar period of Heidegger's career, whose consequences we have yet to understand in full.

The stakes for critical understanding played out in terms of the historical turn and the new historicism are not simply theoretical. We will have learned little of value until we take a longer and harder look at a certain cultural past than many of us seem willing to do. Reference to philosophy in terms of national practice can border on caricature. But it also asserts that philosophy is not merely the tradition of texts and issues composed of "great books" and/or "great ideas." Philosophy is undeniably this, but it is also a set of practices and institutions that regulate how books and ideas circulate in the public sphere. Despite my misgivings over the validity of reference in terms of national practice, my inquiry into Heidegger derives from a conviction that the fate of a German philosopher in France constitutes an especially instructive example of how revision promotes a critical and historical understanding of French modernity of the past half-century.

III. A Scandal of a Book

Debate since 1987 has focused on *Heidegger et le nazisme* (*Heidegger and Nazism*), the translation into French of a text written in Spanish by Victor Farías, a one-time student of Heidegger. (A translation into German appeared in 1988 and another, into English, a year later.) The circulation among languages and cultures illustrates the geographic scope of intellectual debate over Heidegger. It supports my sense of the multiple resistances with which interpretation of Heidegger or of Farías must contend. These, in turn, impose strategies of reading and understanding against received notions. Even in its current disarray, debate discredits this standard ("orthodox") reading by substantiating the view that Heidegger's allegiance to National Socialism lasted well beyond the rectorate period. It also credits the thesis that Heidegger's postwar silence concerning the Third Reich is nothing less than the result or effect of a coverup.

To my knowledge, the first of Martin Heidegger's writings to be published in France was a 1931 translation of "What Is Metaphysics?" that appeared in *Bifur* (No. 7) alongside "La Légende de la vérité" (The Legend of Truth"), a philosopher's tale by the young Jean-Paul Sartre.[6] Fol-

lowing the Liberation, some thirteen years later, the divergence between
Sartre's 1946 *Existentialism Is a Humanism* and Heidegger's 1947 "Letter on Humanism" moderated an influence Sartre had acknowledged in
his 1939–1940 war diaries and in the section of *Being and Nothingness*
on "The Three H's": Hegel, Husserl, and Heidegger.[7] A decade later,
Heidegger's participation in a 1955 Cerisy-la-Salle colloquium organized
in his honor led to a cult following that remained more or less intact until
1987, when Victor Farías argued at length that Heidegger's commitment
to National Socialism was longer and more substantial than had been
previously thought.[8]

Much, though certainly not all, of the controversy surrounding the
Farías book masks what is perhaps all too evident, namely, that Heidegger's involvement with National Socialism is not news.[9] But if this is so,
then why all the fuss? Why is debate surrounding *Heidegger and Nazism*
so vehement and so sustained? In France, the prevailing reverence toward
Heidegger has never gone uncontested, especially among those philosophers who tracked his interwar and wartime activities firsthand: "The
French press has spoken of Heidegger as a Nazi; it is a fact that he was a
party member. If one had to judge a philosophy by the political courage
or lucidity of the philosopher, that of Hegel would not be worth much.
It happens that the philosopher is unfaithful to his best thought when it
becomes a matter of political decisions. . . . Yet it is the same man who
philosophizes and who chooses in politics." Without further explanation,
one might easily mistake this passage as written in the wake of *Heidegger
and Nazism*, when, in fact, it appeared just after the Liberation.[10] Nonetheless, one should consider the difference of the intervening forty years.

French debate surrounding Heidegger *after* Farías has at times resembled a mock trial played out in popular memory as a historical return
of the repressed. Even earlier in the decade, press coverage of the New
Philosophers (*nouveaux philosophes*), Jean-Marie Le Pen's National
Front party, and the New Right (*nouvelle droite*) had promoted an obsession with parallels—both real and imagined—between the cultural
politics of the 1930s and those of the more recent "post" age. Such parallels did not, however, account in full for the recent furor in France over
Heidegger, especially when, as noted above, his involvement with National Socialism had already been known. In this sense, much of *Heidegger and Nazism* drew on existing sources, such as Guido Schneeberger's
anthology, *Nachlese zu Heidegger* (Berne: Suhr, 1962), and the articles
by Hugo Ott recently published in book form under the title *Martin Heidegger: Unterwegs zu seiner Biographie* (Frankfurt: Campus, 1989).[11]
The debate over *Heidegger and Nazism* has come about as a *succès de
scandale* fueled by a media orchestration aimed at shocking a general

public that had never fully confronted the extent of Heidegger's Nazi ties.[12] This predisposition lent itself exactly to an aftereffect Farías exploited to full advantage, as though the allegations against Heidegger extended to his readers via a logic of contamination that was all-encompassing. The result was an atmosphere in which debate focused less on engaging ideas than on judging—and presumably condemning—the alleged actions of an individual or group.

Because I take the current calls for accountability to be serious, I also see the inordinate desire to achieve closure on debate in the wake of Farías as an instance of the trope of anticipation known as prolepsis. In regard to Heidegger in particular, this anticipation engages a disclosure that is integral to the notion of truth as unconcealedness (*aletheia*) referred to above. Aside from its occurrence within the mid-1930s period of Heidegger's writings known as the turning point or shift (*Kehre*), the interplay between closure and disclosure in "The Origin" is itself inscribed within the same sorts of social instabilities that dominate the revisionary atmosphere of recent debate. In some instances, the will to closure is clear and visible, as though the irruption of a suppressed or repressed past justified suspicion and what Herman Rapaport has referred to as the hermeneutics of detection.[13] The greater the resistance to the past, the more forceful its inevitable return. My intention here and in what follows is neither to condemn Heidegger nor to dispute or explain away the allegations against him. Instead, I want to assess what the return of a certain past might imply for our understanding of literary and philosophical modernity in interwar and postwar France. Rather than filling in the blanks, we need to understand where the blanks come from and why we are only now beginning to see them.

The allegations in *Heidegger and Nazism* illustrate how aftereffect can transpose a name and a corpus. In this sense, the extent to which Farías has reopened debate is surprising, especially when so much of the material he provides is biographic. Seemingly, Heidegger's mythic stature raises the stakes of interpreting his writings, rather than vice-versa.[14] Farías seldom moves beyond biography. He uses the seventeenth-century Viennese court preacher Ulrich Megerle (also known by his pseudonym, Abraham a Sancta Clara) as the model figure around whom he constructs his account of Heidegger's spiritual and ideological evolution between 1910 and 1964 (Farías, especially pages 39–55 and 292–301). In so doing, he implements a logic of prefiguration that sacrifices the specificity of Heidegger's evolution in favor of biographic closure. Presumably, Farías begins and ends by invoking Megerle because he wants to show the constancy of anti-Semitism within Heidegger's writings. But he does little to help his reader understand whether this attitude derives from the peasant's traditional mistrust of urban worldliness or from an overt political discourse within Heidegger's philosophical vision before, during, and after the Third Reich.[15]

Farías tries to insert his reading of Heidegger within a number of historical contexts, but his dependence on chronology imposes a structure and a continuity—of the life, of the work—that are belied by the internal breaks undermining his implicit claim to systematic understanding. We may, for example, attribute a coherence to writings whose evolution we fail to recognize because we reduce them to tentative or partial expressions of a predetermined whole. Thus, we tend by habit to impose identity and repetition over difference. In so doing, we displace, deny, and suppress difference to a point where scandal and controversy are the marks of its infrequent return—with a vengeance. The results are open to further revision. As long as doubt and uncertainty remain, allegations such as those made in *Heidegger and Nazism* will continue to receive a minimal degree of serious consideration. Whether they are stated convincingly and whether they further understanding—or Heidegger, of Nazism, of modernity—are separate matters.

IV. Getting Serious

My interest in Heidegger derives from a belief that the irruption as aftereffect of a certain past imposes a rethinking of issues at work in current debate over Heidegger's writings of the 1930s. The debate over Heidegger is scandalous in a limited sense; it serves as a scandalous instance— "scandal" from the Greek *skandalos*, meaning obstacle or trap—but should not be taken as the full force of the aftereffect I am exploring. *Heidegger and Nazism* is meaningful not only in what it says about Heidegger but also in what it implies about the French reception of Heidegger. My remarks to this point suggest that questions concerning Farías on Heidegger also beg the question of historical understanding. In this sense, the issue of "Why Heidegger and the Nazis?" might be rephrased as "Why Heidegger and the Nazis . . . *now?*"

The question of how seriously one should take debate over Farías transcends the merits and liabilities of his book on Heidegger. I see it as equally important to consider the social, political, and institutional conditions that make the (serious) reception of a book like *Heidegger and Nazism* possible; for what we regard as meaningful and important depends not only on historical context but also on a recognition that this context is itself problematic. Rüdiger Bubner raises the point in discussing the evolution of modern German philosophy well beyond Heidegger: "The historicity of contemporary philosophy finds its expression in the shape of its problems. In the range of the problems that are recognized as actual, contemporary philosophy defines itself as against tradition and at the same time puts itself into a relationship to it."[16] In such terms, the problems of philosophy are not just those that are legitimized by tradition but also and especially those that are unforeseen and for which there may be no simple or immediate solution. Whatever the outcome, the suspicion that Farías projects onto the "other" Heidegger—that is, the Heidegger who seems *not* to have retreated from politics after the rectorate period—carries over into practices of denial and repression that occur fully in the present.

Debate over Heidegger also engages issues of revision and, in particular, the extent to which the claims made by and for Farías alter our understanding of the recent past. Once again, revision may lead to multiple consequences; it affects not just what we may or may not learn about Heidegger but how we view those whose intellectual debts to Heidegger are seemingly compromised. On this side of the Atlantic, Richard Rorty asserted the preeminence of moral concerns that bear on any revision in the wake of the Farías book when he asked, with provocative irony, why anyone should care whether Heidegger was a self-deceptive egomaniac:

A good reason for caring about such matters is that the details about the attitudes of German intellectuals toward the Holocaust are important for our own moral education. It pays to realize that the vast majority of German academics, some of the best and brightest, turned a blind eye to the fate of their Jewish colleagues, and to ask whether we ourselves might not be capable of the same sort of behavior. . . . A bad reason for caring is the notion that learning about a philosopher's moral character helps one evaluate his philosophy. It does not, any more than our knowledge of Einstein's character helps us evaluate his physics. You can be a great, original, and profound artist or thinker, and a complete bastard.[17]

Rorty clearly describes the moral stake in debate over *Heidegger and Nazism*. Nonetheless, his desire to reject Heidegger the rector and Nazi party member in order to retain ("save") the philosopher and author of *Being and Time* simply does not hold. What remains unquestioned is the perceived exemplarity of Heidegger's writings over and above their author. Even if Heidegger had willfully sought to dissociate his philosophy from his political views or from the politics of Third Reich and postwar Germany, their articulation could not be dismissed as neatly as Rorty suggests.

To a certain extent, Rorty seems to take a cue from Farías. Throughout *Heidegger and Nazism*, Farías discusses only those texts that substantiate a stable identity built on a chronology that is incomplete at best a reductive at worst. His attempts to use chronology to reconstruct Heidegger's philosophical vision are belied by the internal breaks undermining the claim to consistency and stable identity that chronology implies. It is always possible to "find" consistency in writings when we reduce them to variations of a predetermined whole. Thus, we tend by habit to impose identity and repetition over difference. In so doing, we displace, deny, and suppress the latter to a point where aftereffect and scandal are the marks of its return.

How seriously are we to take the Farías allegations and, by extension, Heidegger's writings in their wake? How might we read the texts in question without either dismissing them because of political views on the part of their author we may find loathsome or reducing them to hermetic and untimely meditations? These questions are raised by the rapid appearance in France of close to a dozen studies and dossiers. Some readings openly take position for or against Farías; others use the Farías book to develop their own projects. Most contain a little of both approaches. Luc Ferry and Alain Renaut argue in *Heidegger and Modernity* that the Farías Affair is a consequence of a Heidegger revival whose ties with a disenchanted Left they view with bemusement. By what strange inversion, they ask, has someone who was more than a fellow-traveler of the Nazis become today the principal philosopher of the Left? The question is provocative; I also see it as disingenuous and polemical.

Ferry and Renaut locate debate over *Heidegger and Nazism* within an ongoing critique of modernity whose philosophical model finds initial—and exemplary—form in Heidegger's writings:

The deepest significance of the debate, for which the Farías book and even the Heidegger case are merely the occasion, becomes clear: it hinges on—we can see this clearly in Derrida—the criticism of modernity, and what defines it philosophically, culturally, and no doubt also politically, namely the outbreak of subjectivity and the values of humanism. The Heidegger controversy merely stands in the foreground of a controversy that has a quite different impact, involving nothing less than the significance attributed to the logic of modernity; if we argue so much about it today, isn't it because Heidegger's deconstruction of modernity provided a considerable part of the French intelligentsia with the bases and style of its criticism of the modern world? [18]

For Ferry and Renaut, Heidegger's attitude toward modernity is divided from within. It is postmodern in that the call to Nazi revolution promotes an end—and potential transcendence—of modernity; and it is antimodern in its call for a return to the Greek tradition as a reaction to European decadence. Both positions are taken as critiques of modernity and, in particular, of its political expression in democracy. Next, Ferry and Renaut trace what they take for the political consequences of the postmodern/antimodern split within Heidegger's writings. Where the former liquidates subjectivity by passing from democracy toward authoritarian movements, the latter supplements a vision of decline with laments of rootlessness and lost traditions.

The critiques Ferry and Renaut attribute to Heidegger tell us little more than that what is set forth as philosophical often takes on ideological, if not openly political, status. And although they state that the time for polemicizing is over, Ferry and Renaut often seem more concerned with the new-look Heideggerians they want to discredit than with the philosophical issues they claim to address. This fall into polemic is a symptom of place and time. It points, in turn, to a wider coming to terms with a political past visible in Heidegger's writings but certainly not limited to them. Current debate is serious in a positive sense if and when it forces us to rethink assumptions concerning the cultural practices associated with interwar and postwar periods. Seriousness in this sense depends very much on tone and rhetoric. Where Rorty takes Heidegger's philosophy seriously over and against the man who wrote it, Ferry and Renaut seem more interested in upbraiding self-styled Heideggerians whom they seem to take almost *too* seriously! The result in both instances misses the mark.

The institutional origin of Philippe Lacoue-Labarthe's *La Fiction du politique: Heidegger, l'art et la politique* is significant. The book began as a statement he was asked to write by the committee of examiners to which he had submitted his candidacy for a doctorate on the basis of cumulative work (*sur travaux*). The French context also transforms what might otherwise be misconstrued as a statement of faith (*profession de foi*) into a reflection on the claim to philosophize Lacoue-Labarthe questions by staging his engagement with Heidegger's writings as a test case and potential measure of philosophy's limits. Attentive readers will recognize the gesture as deconstructive in that it posits the provisional end or closure that Derrida and others have modeled on Heidegger's notions of *Destruktion*, *Zerstörung*, and *Abbau*. The gesture is neither respectful homage nor stylistic indulgence; it is most certainly not arbitrary. For the question of determining philosophy's limit points directly to the ambitions that Heidegger holds for philosophy from the late 1920s period of *Being and Time* through the 1966 interview in *Der Spiegel*.

Lacoue-Labarthe directs the question of philosophy's limits toward the institution of the university: "And it is outside the University, or on its fringes that at the same time an imitation twice removed has assumed the title of philosophy (Sartre) and that thinkers of an otherwise rigorous exigency and of a completely different sobriety have continually tested, at its limit, the capacity-to-philosophize [*le pouvoir-philosopher*] (Benjamin and Wittgenstein, Bataille and Blanchot, for example)"[19] Two remarks are in order. First, the spatial metaphor associated with terms "limit" and "fringe" in the preceding passage characterizes legitimation as centrifugal rather than centripetal, decentered rather than centralized. Second, legitimation is tied to practices of autobiography and confession that elide the very distinction between "man" and "work" that Farías—and Rorty, in his wake—seem intent on maintaining.

Early in his account, Lacoue-Labarthe identifies the origin of his own (modest) claim to philosophize when he writes that a reading of Heidegger gave him a first jolt (he uses the French term *choc* and adds *Stoss*, the German term for "push" or "shove" that he borrows from "The Origin of the Work of Art" (Lacoue-Labarthe, p. 11). At about the same time, he learned that Heidegger had been a member of the Nazi party. From the start, then, Lacoue-Labarthe reads the Heideggerian text in view of a political commitment that he cannot abide. This means also that he refuses both to separate the political from the philosophical and to reduce the former to the status of an aberration. How, then, does Lacoue-Labarthe describe the articulation of the political and the philosophical?

My hypothesis is as follows: it lies, on the one hand, in the tenor and style of the commitment of 1933 which are precisely (because it is a commitment that is involved) philosophical, and as a consequence produce statements that are philosophical in type and can be located as such in the tradition. The commitment of 1933 is founded on the idea of a hegemony of the spiritual and the philosophical over the political itself (this is the theme of *Führung* of the *Führung*, or of the *Führer*) which leads us back at least to the Platonic *basiléia*, if not to Empedocles. His statements (on Germany, on work, on the University, etc.) are purely and simply programmatic and are, moreover, organized in a number of "Appeals." On the other hand, if it is true that certain of these calls (the most immediately political or the least removed from the National-Socialist program) will subsequently be unequivocally abandoned and repudiated, in its deep intention and the essential nature of its aspirations, the injunction of 1933 will be maintained to the end. (Lacoue-Labarthe, p. 13)

These remarks start by reasserting that a serious commitment to National Socialism pervades the 1933–1934 rectorate period that some, including Heidegger, have trivialized as a lapse. Yet the status of the period in question remains ambiguous. For while the seriousness of Heidegger's commitment has been documented over and above his own statements to the contrary, it has also been invoked to dismiss Heidegger's writings outright and thus precisely in order *not* to read them. In both instances, a gesture of avoidance forecloses textual analysis on the basis of criteria that are motivated at least as much by moral as by historical and/or political concerns. Lacoue-Labarthe's conclusion is unequivocal: in 1933, Heidegger neither slips nor falters. He willingly commits himself to the rectorate and to what he might accomplish by making the university a prime site of National Socialism's transformation of Germany society: "In 1933 Heidegger is not mistaken [ne se trompe pas]. But he knows in 1934 that he was mistaken [s'est trompé]; not about the truth of Nazism but about its reality" (Lacoue-Labarthe, p. 20).

To resume at this point, Lacoue-Labarthe sees Heidegger's gesture of commitment as unequivocal and serious when he made it, even if one limits its direct political expression—that is, its impact on the institution of the German university system—to the ten months of the rectorate. For Lacoue-Labarthe, the rectorate is consistent with a philosophical vision that retained a disposition to the essential truth and greatness of the National Socialist movement long after Heidegger resigned from the rectorship. But what is this disposition and how might an understanding of its expressions and evolution help to account for the intensity of recent debate over Heidegger? More pointedly, was Heidegger's withdrawal from the rectorate only an accommodation that removed him from public view without moderating his support of National Socialism?

Lacoue-Labarthe's view of the coincidence of political and philosophical concerns in Heidegger's writings offers a clear advantage over the more topical concerns of *Heidegger and Modernity*. Yet Lacoue-Labarthe does not follow through the full implications of his argument. He correctly grasps the seriousness and extent of Heidegger's commitment, but his reference to "multiple calls" is surprisingly elliptical. The same holds true for the "deep and essential expectations" of the 1933 injunction. Why does Lacoue-Labarthe stop short at the rectorate period? If Heidegger's commitment to the rectorate was unequivocal and serious when he made it, what might explain his resignation less than a year later?

Lacoue-Labarthe's answers to these questions are surprisingly indirect and understated. They focus on his sense of the discrepancy between the "truth" and the "reality" of Nazism as he refers to them in the passage quoted above. Presumably, this discrepancy results from Heidegger's recognition of National Socialism as a political *reality* whose philosophical *truth* he had mistaken as compatible with *Being and Time* and his subsequent writings. Such an account is liberal, that is, generous and forgiving almost to the point of apology. It implies that Heidegger's resignation marked a refusal on his part to allow ontology to serve political ends presumably unworthy of it. Thus, self-critique seemingly leads to self-correction and to the withdrawal from politics associated with the *Kehre*. This is certainly not, however, the only way to interpret the 1933–1934 transition, especially if the *reality* of National Socialism were seen as less committed to the political and social changes that Heidegger hoped to enact via the rectorate.

The rectorate speech supports this second approach by asserting the role that the university's self-determination might play in promoting a National Socialist conception of nationhood. In fact, one could also argue—via the trope of crossover known as chiasmus—that Heidegger came to see the philosophical *reality* of National Socialism as inadequate to the *political* truth of *Being and Time.* In such terms, Heidegger might well have become more Nazi than the Nazis and thus a liability because of a political, as opposed to philosophical, extremism that the party could not tolerate. As with the statement from Sartre's *Critique of Dialectical Method* to which I referred at the start of this chapter, the case of Heidegger might have been too complex for the Nazis to explain!

Neither Lacoue-Labarthe's motives nor his fairness strike me as questionable. Yet it often seems as though the personal nature of his narrative imposed accountability on him that ought more rightly to have projected onto the Heideggerian texts. The call to accountability is directed by the institution onto the candidate-critic whose own claim to philosophize sets him into a mediating role between the institution and Heidegger. Given this setting, Lacoue-Labarthe's choice of an autobiographical account internalizes a vulnerability imposed by the institutional setting of the doctoral defense (*soutenance*). The result, in spite of Lacoue-Labarthe's admirable candor, further displaces a direct encounter with Heidegger. In so doing, it inadvertently prolongs the aftereffect he seeks to overcome.

V. No Way Out

Debate surrounding Heidegger has often cast him as a representative figure, as one who stands *for* deconstruction, Continental philosophy, or "theory" and thus *against* analytical philosophy. The displacement expresses a resistance to thinking in historical terms, a resistance that takes on various forms along the lines of aggregate denial. Debate also stages a struggle over legitimation, involving principles and categories that range from canon, genre, and medium to national and regional practices. For some, this struggle is a constant in all cultural discourse. For others, an intense revisionist element raises the stakes of debate in view of political and institutional struggles that are openly polemical. The discrepancy between apparent and true debate is a sign that something is seriously flawed. It is not merely that the wrong kinds of arguments are being used to address the right kinds of issues. In this instance, it also suggests that many who do not know the history of deconstruction might very much like for it to be scandalous.

While I see no simple way to work through or be done with the current scandal of aftereffect over Heidegger, a number of considerations strike me as worthy. To begin, future debate should strive less to determine a definitive meaning than to trace an ongoing movement intelligible through a series of changes. This is not to say that the true meaning of Heidegger's writings will appear only gradually and over time. Nor does it suggest that rereading is always mediated by the passage of time and thus at a necessary remove from an originary meaning. To the contrary, debate over Heidegger is very much of a current affair. It engages the claim to authority that Farías makes against the grain of received opinion. In this sense, Heidegger's writings serve as both pretext and supplement: they are the points of departure for a contest among rival approaches as well as the material evidence to be scrutinized if and when consensus over approach is ever reached.

A second consideration concerns a relation to the past that takes form in the act and products of narration. If history is a kind of narrative, then what is it about? Who narrates it? How and why is it narrated? Hayden White raises these questions in conjunction with some remarks on the authority attached to certain accounts that impose on real events the forms and coherence more commonly associated with stories about imaginary events. The authority of historical narrative arises from a desire to make experience meaningful and coherent, a desire whose origin White locates in wishes, daydreams, and reveries. Historiography allows this desire for the imaginary and the possible to be considered against the imperatives of the real and the actual: "If we view narration and narrativity as the instruments with which the conflicting claims of the imaginary and the real are mediated, arbitrated, or resolved in a discourse, we begin to comprehend both the appeal of narrative and the grounds for refusing it."[20] White reaches no definitive conclusion concerning the function of narration, but the questions he raises concerning the appeal of narration and narrativity in the representation of events construed to be true rather than imaginary bear directly on current debate.

The turn to history I have sketched throughout my discussion of debate over Heidegger should not be mistaken for a historicism with scientistic ambitions of objectivity. This is especially the case because the turn is imposed rather than chosen, a precondition over which we have no control rather than a situation resulting from individual or collective agency. Furthermore, attempts to attain rapid closure derive from claims to mastery and appropriation that are often unexamined. Much of the problem comes from a mentality of detection that is ultimately ineffectual. So many self-appointed prosecutors make their cases against Heidegger in terms of biography. In so doing, they leave more or less unexamined the relevant set of mediations between the philosophical and the political around which more substantial understanding ought to be founded.

Where to go from here? One option, among others, is visible in a play of terms that ought to have alerted Ferry and Renaut to combine the title of their book with that by Farías. By deleting or by placing the centrality of Heidegger under erasure (*sous rature*) they might have addressed the convergence of nazism and modernism that is the pretext of Lacoue-Labarthe's account. This is especially so because Lacoue-Labarthe uses the autobiographical to ground his assessment of Heidegger in terms of the very kind of personal involvement that Ferry and Renaut take to be compromising. The confessional nature of Lacoue-Labarthe's account emphasizes the reality of the relation to—or even *with*—Heidegger in lived and/or existential terms that Ferry and Renaut simply fail to engage.

Though we might prefer to believe otherwise, admitting fascism and/or national socialism as integral to certain conceptions of modernity is one of our big cultural nightmares. It is not just that we might be contaminated at a distance, but that we are already contaminated through Heidegger as well as through all of those who in one sense or another made common cause with the project of a revolution from the extreme right, whether that project be seen as fascist, national socialist, royalist, or simply anti-communist. This is not, I imagine, a message that self-styled liberal or progressive readers would like to receive. Yet it seems that we will learn nothing from the debate over Heidegger until we come to grips with the full implications of what it means to associate fascism with modernity.[21] Ultimately, this means taking a longer and harder look at our cultural past than many of us are willing to do. In the end, the irruption of a certain past surrounding Heidegger is not simply his; through him, it is very much ours as well. This is the primary sense of what it means today to take Heidegger—and the scandal of aftereffect— seriously.

REED   WAY   DASENBROCK

Paul de Man
The Modernist as Fascist

O ver the past several years, controversy has reigned over the implications of the discovery after Paul de Man's death that this famous and revered literary critic, Sterling Professor of Humanities at Yale University, wrote during World War II for a number of pro-Nazi, collaborationist newspapers in Belgium, most notably the daily *Le Soir*, published in Brussels. What strikes me about the controversy, as my title should suggest, is that the discussion has to a large extent focused on a secondary issue: whether de Man's wartime activities have any implications for deconstruction, whether there are any links between fascism and deconstruction.[1] But de Man's fascism cannot be understood by going only forward in time, by returning quickly to the issues and concerns of the present; to understand de Man's fascism, we need to go backward, to understand the intellectual roots of his fascism and of the kind of fascism he espoused before returning to the understandably urgent question of the relation between this and the present. It has been said in defense of de Man both that most of his columns in *Le Soir* concern literary, not political, matters and that the decision on the part of his uncle, Hendrik de Man, to collaborate must have been a major influence on de Man's actions during the war.[2] Both points are true, but in no way do they separate de Man from fascism. His literary journalism, read closely as the apologists for de Man urge, help show precisely what kind of Fascist the younger de Man was; the fascinating life and works of Hendrik de Man help fill out this picture. What emerges is precisely a type of pro-fascist intellectual that should be quite familiar to us in the English-speaking world. My title echoes the subtitle of Fredric Jameson's book on Wyndham Lewis quite deliberately;[3] in their support of fascism, the de Mans resemble pro-Fascist Anglo-American Modernists such as Wyndham Lewis and Ezra Pound in a number of key respects.

Paul de Man is known as a literary critic primarily for his studies of romanticism, so it comes rather as a surprise to note the pattern of interests shown by his wartime journalism before and during the Nazi occupation of Belgium, which is overwhelmingly toward modern, indeed modernist, literature. Before the Nazi invasion, in *Cahiers du libre examen*, de Man wrote a long piece on "Le roman anglais contemporain,"[4] which shows a detailed knowledge of the works of Joyce, Lawrence, Woolf, Huxley, and others. Another preinvasion piece, "André Gide" (30 Nov. 1939, pp. 11–12), compares Gide at length to Huxley. These preinvasion articles, presumably less ideologically motivated and less directed by extraliterary interests than those to follow, show no particular orientation toward German literature and instead a strong commitment to the literature of the contemporary avant-garde.

This is a pattern that continues, with some variations after the Nazi occupation of Belgium, in the articles written in *Le Soir*. It has been pointed out by Jonathan Culler, for example, that Hitler and the Nazi party are almost never directly mentioned in the *Le Soir* articles and that de Man contents himself with vague references to Germany's place in the world.[5] These references are surely not as devoid of political implications as Culler assumes, but even so there is a contrast between de Man's treatment of Germany and German culture and his treatment of another fascist country, Italy. For one of the surprising elements in de Man's contributions to *Le Soir* that has barely been commented on is a series of articles on Italian culture.[6] These articles are surprising in any case for some of the same general reasons as the articles on Huxley and Joyce. De Man's later career evinced no great interest in Italian culture or literature. But they are even more surprising because of the directness with which de Man engages fascist ideas in these articles.

The specific stimulus for de Man's articles was a series of presentations on Italian culture at L'Institut de la Culture Italienne in Brussels. The first three were on contemporary Italian poetry and were given by Professor Donini, director of the institute. These were treated in two articles by de Man that are far more than simply accounts of Professor Donini's presentations. The first of these articles, "Conférence sur la poésie d'Eugenio Montale" (11 Feb. 1941, p. 29), reports on both Professor Donini's first lecture, on Giuseppe Ungaretti, and the second, on Montale. De Man discusses their poetry with obvious enthusiasm, comparing Montale to Proust, and places them in a modernist context: "These are modernists who have broken away from the rules of the traditional technique." But Montale and Ungaretti are both considered explicitly as Fascist poets as well: "Both of these poets belong to the first fascist generation and have undergone analogous influences." One suspects Professor

Donini of some conscious misrepresentation here in presenting both of these poets as supporters of fascism,[7] but de Man's enthusiasm for the notion that these Modernists are Fascists is worth noting. De Man's closing sentence reveals the reason for his enthusiasm: "Here one will have the chance to acquire an overview of contemporary Italian poetry and to see how, in the climate of fascism, a beautiful and original poetry has been able to bloom." Thus, great poetry is being created in a fascist climate in Italy, and the implicit suggestion is that Belgium may have something to learn from the Italian experience.

The article reporting on the final lecture of Professor Donini, "La troisième conférence du professeur Donini" (18 Feb. 1941, p. 32), makes this connection explicit enough. The poets discussed in this lecture, "members of the first purely fascist generation," are much less well known today, if only because these poems do seem truly fascist: "They speak of patriotic and heroic sentiments provoked by the Ethiopian and Spanish wars as well as the current war." And though de Man seems less enthusiastic about these more popular poets, again he has nothing but praise for the social context of literature in Fascist Italy: "The vogue of Montalian sadness and despair proves only one thing: that the fascist regime grants complete freedom to the poet to find his source of inspiration wherever he chooses, even in a domain which seems completely opposed to the civil and warrior spirit dear to the educators of the people." So the regime is to be praised for the climate of openness and freedom it has created, and the piece ends by quoting Mussolini: "It is above all at the present moment that poetry is necessary to the life of the people."

Three more articles follow these two, which, though not on literary topics, still reveal a considerable interest on de Man's part in contemporary Fascist Italy. The next article is on another presentation at the institute, one by Luigi Pareti on "Les systèmes impériaux de la Rome antique" (13 Mar. 1941, p. 48). This was not purely an antiquarian lecture, for Professor Pareti's point is that the genius of Roman organization was not passed down to the modern British or French empires but was being rediscovered by contemporary Fascist Italy: "This conference has clearly shown how and to what imperial system Fascist Italy is linked."

Professor Pareti gave a second lecture, on the Risorgimento, discussed in "Le 'Risorgimento' italien" (17 Mar. 1941, p. 50), and his argument on that occasion, at least as stressed by de Man, was on the national, purely Italian character of the Risorgimento, the movement toward Italian independence and unification in the nineteenth century. The Risorgimento had often been seen as largely influenced by French currents of thought, but Pareti presents the Risorgimento not as a by-product of the French Revolution but as a forerunner of fascism: "A philosophy of the humble was created which exalted labor and the land and emphasized the necessity of improving class relations." In this context, de Man (I would presume following Pareti) revealingly cites Giambattista Vico: "Italian thinkers, and in particular G.-B. Vico in his theories, had long since articulated this desire on the part of Italy to become once again a strong and centralized state." And the point de Man wants to make—whatever relation this has to Professor Pareti's remarks—is made clear enough in the final sentence: "And the lesson is important for Belgians who wish to see their country reconstitute itself: they will see how it is necessary to discover these regenerative forces not in looking beyond the nation's borders but in drawing on specific qualities which have manifested themselves throughout the nation's history." The last of this series of articles is devoted to "La formation de la jeunesse en Italie" (25 Mar. 1941, p. 54), and here de Man's attention is devoted to the educational institutions created by Fascist Italy. De Man's language again seems to endorse Italian fascist ideals: "The harmonious equilibrium obtained by the concerted action of these two [Italian educational] institutions corresponds to fascist principles which demand the creation of good citizens."

Now, these articles do not constitute a large percentage of the 170 articles de Man wrote for *Le Soir*, but I find them worth noting. In them, de Man is explicit about the relation between fascism and the cultural subjects he is discussing, and he is explicit about his enthusiasm for Italian fascism. One does not find de Man quoting Hitler, but here he quotes Mussolini with evident approval and enthusiasm. One does not find de Man referring to the Nazi party, but these articles are strewn with positive references to Italian fascism. How do we explain the difference?

The reason I can find is suggested both by the content of the articles themselves and by what we can infer about de Man's cultural affiliations. One of the obvious differences between Nazi Germany and Fascist Italy were their differing attitudes toward literary and artistic modernity. Nazi Germany, of course, condemned modernism in the arts as decadent and largely Jewish in inspiration, calling for a return to Germanic national traditions in the arts and in literature. The response of artists and intellectuals to this program and to the Nazi regime was overwhelmingly hostile. Even those who supported the Nazis—Heidegger and Webern, among others—were frustrated in their desire to influence Nazi cultural and educational policies. Heidegger's support for nazism is of course a scandal, currently receiving belated attention on the scale of that being paid to the case of de Man, but no one has ever claimed a central role in nazism for Heidegger.[8]

Italian fascism provides a sharp contrast to Nazi Germany in this respect. Literary and cultural modernity—even modernism—didn't seem opposed to fascism in Italy. Futurism, an important movement in modernism before World War I, was an important forerunner of and influence on fascism. Never purely an art movement, it was an important force in the movement calling for Italian intervention on the Allied side in World War I; Mussolini joined the Futurists in that fight, which was an important step in his shift in the political spectrum from left to right.[9] And though futurism did not remain an important artistic force after World War I, a version of it was still active in the 1930s, supportive of and supported by the Fascist regime. For example, Ardengo Soffici, one of the original Futurists, is one of the pro-Fascist poets mentioned by de Man in "La troisième conférence du professeur Donini." Another important precursor of fascism was the novelist Gabriele D'Annunzio's seizure of Fiume in 1919; this crystalized Italian dissatisfaction with the postwar settlement and with the liberal democratic government that had allowed Italy's expansionist claims to be disregarded at Versailles. And though D'Annunzio remained personally ambivalent about Mussolini and the Fascist regime, he has also been called the John the Baptist of fascism.[10] The distinguished Italian philosopher Giovanni Gentile was the minister of education in Mussolini's first government and was the semiofficial "philosopher of Fascism," and though Gentile is not named in the *Le soir* articles, de Man seems cognizant of his educational reforms in "La formation de la jeunesse en Italie" and of his profascist interpretation of Vico in the article on the Risorgimento.

These are the best-known examples, but generally it can be said that Italian fascism enjoyed a broad base of support among intellectuals and artists until the German alliance and World War II (just as it did among the people) and that this involved a much less reactionary attitude toward cultural modernity than did National Socialism in Germany. Even those intellectuals and writers famous for their opposition to the regime—most notably, Benedetto Croce, Ignazio Silone, and Antonio Gramsci—conceded its support among a great deal of the population and of the intelligentsia. And Gramsci's now-famous concept of hegemony, in which coercive power is often less crucial to a government's ability to stay in power than its ability to persuade "the other classes of society to accept its own moral, political, and cultural values,"[11] is best understood as his attempt to explain this puzzling phenomenon.

Moreover, this was also true outside Italy. In contrast to Hitler and the Nazi party before and after their seizure of power, Mussolini and Italian fascism enjoyed a generally favorable press in the English-speaking world for at least the first decade of his regime.[12] Mussolini was remembered with gratitude as one of the key figures in the Italian intervention on the Allied side during World War I; the less than impressive showing of Italian forces in the war suggested to many that Italy needed "shaping up" along the lines Mussolini seemed to be following; and the old cliché that "at least he made the trains run on time" corresponded to a real if shallow perception of Mussolini in Anglo-American culture. Favorable dispositions toward Italian fascism were particularly to be found among the Modernists: Lawrence depicted Italian fascism in a positive light in *Aaron's Rod* and, more obliquely, in *Kangaroo*; Yeats had positive things to say about Mussolini and Gentile's philosophy and sought a comparable "renewal" in Ireland; Wyndham Lewis, in *The Art of Being Ruled*, praised both Russian bolshevism and Italian fascism as alternatives to bourgeois democracy; finally and most notoriously, Ezra Pound was an enthusiastic supporter of Mussolini, comparing him to Thomas Jefferson and broadcasting on Rome Radio in support of the Axis throughout World War II, by which time everyone else in the English-speaking world who had praised Mussolini earlier—including Winston Churchill—had changed his mind. So de Man's combination of enthusiasm for advanced modern literature and Italian fascism is not at all unusual.

Nor is it utterly inexplicable. Of course, different people found different things in fascism, but three key aspects of fascist ideology appealed to intellectuals inside and outside Italy: fascism as a modernizing dictatorship, as a form of socialism critical of Marxism, and as a theory of politics with room in it for art and the artist. The first is probably the least important for literary intellectuals like Paul de Man, though certainly a key aspect of the regime for Pound and probably the aspect of Italian fascism with the greatest relevance to the postwar world. A. James Gregor has, in a series of books and articles, argued persuasively that Italian fascism served as a model for many contemporary third world countries.[13] It is the type of developmental dictatorship, the kind of government that tries to overcome a situation of relative underdevelopment and economic dependence on others by a form of nationalist but socialist dictatorship. Most of the regimes Gregor alludes to see themselves as Marxist, but their thinking is much closer to Mussolini's kind of nationalist socialism than to any pure Marxism. One important flaw in Gregor's case, I think, is that the same could be said of Leninist Russia; but many people in the 1920s—including Wyndham Lewis in *The Art of Being Ruled* and even Pound for a short while[14]—saw Italy and Russia as comparable and in some senses parallel challenges to Western society, not, as we have come to think of them, as polar opposites on a political spectrum.

This leads to the second reason for the appeal of Italian fascism to intellectuals, which is that it presented itself as a form of socialism but one freed of the limitations of Marxism. Mussolini, of course, was a leader of Italian socialism before the war, and he and many of his followers had been part of a syndicalist, anti-Marxist current in Italian socialism. It has been argued—correctly, I think—that the socialist and syndicalist trappings of Italian fascism were simply that—trappings, ideological camouflage for the less attractive, more coercive, and more reactionary realities concealed underneath. But the corporatist ideology of fascism, clearly part of de Man's interest in Italy, has clear socialist roots and explains much of the appeal of fascism to intellectuals. Here, so it was believed, was a radical movement purified of the shortcomings of Marxist thought.

The key problem with Marxist thought for intellectuals and writers was that its economism, its base-superstructure model, seemed to leave no room for ideas or for art. According to Marxism, man's consciousness was determined in the final analysis by his economic circumstances, and the final reason for the appeal of fascism was its reversal of this economism. Going back to Sorel's critique of Marxism for ignoring the role of myths, for ignoring the potentially creative role of beliefs, fascism seemed to give mythmakers, hence artists, an important role in social life.[15] In practice, the fascist political machinery took the mythmaking into its own hands, but fascist theory and the adherence to fascism of such distinguished writers as Pirandello and the others already mentioned seemed to leave an important role open to the artists. It is the last two points that seemed crucial to a W. B. Yeats or an Ezra Pound, concerned as they were with the place of literature in society, and Paul de Man obviously shared their concern and their naive belief in the centrality of literature in Italian fascism.

It is crucial in this context to realize that, in the 1920s and 1930s, Hendrik de Man, Paul de Man's uncle, was formulating a critique of Marxism in a brilliant series of books that in important respects dovetails with this Sorelian critique of Marxism. Hendrik de Man's oeuvre is enormously complex and variegated. Like his nephew, he was multilingual, writing in German, Dutch, French, and English with equal ease. He was a university professor in the United States and later in Germany and Belgium, and he was a formidably erudite and cosmopolitan writer and thinker. But he was also from his youth a committed—if increasingly heterodox—Socialist, an important figure in Belgium's socialist movement, and a minister in the government in the 1930s.[16] Hendrik de Man's key work is *Zur Psychologie des Sozialismus* (written in German and published in 1926), translated into English as *The Psychology of Socialism* in 1928 but in French given the more striking and accurate title *Au delà du Marxisme*.[17] De Man wanted to go beyond Marxism for a number of overlapping and complex reasons. First, he felt that the Marxist

doctrine of class struggle was outdated, both because of the increasing
bourgeoisification of the proletariat and because it didn't take enough
cognizance of the common interests that exist in any nation across class
boundaries. (Here it is relevant that de Man, like Mussolini, fought in
World War I, which provided every combatant with a firm sense of the
limits of proletarian internationalism.) Second, the class struggle and
other aspects of Marxism tended to cause alienation in the workplace.
De Man thought that alienation should be overthrown and each worker
given the kind of joy and pride in his work that medieval craftsmen possessed.[18] Third, the base-superstructure model ignored the role of ideas,
of cultural traditions, and of leaders. All three concerns crystallized in de
Man's reflections on the role of intellectuals in socialism, and for de Man
their role was to lead, not to feel inferior to "true proletarians."[19]

There is much in Hendrik de Man's analysis that is peculiarly and
powerfully his own, but this brief discussion should also help place his
work in context. First, he was working in a tradition of anti-Marxist
socialist thought descending from Proudhon (whom he admired) and
Sorel (whom he didn't mention). Second, there is at least a strong resemblance between much of his work and a tradition in English thought,
descending from Ruskin and William Morris through Guild Socialism
and powerfully influencing Ezra Pound, that stresses the role of the artist
and the sanctity of work and similarly idealizes the Middle Ages. And
third, in his critique of the doctrine of class struggle from a position that
takes account of nationalism, he is close to a line of fascist thought, seen,
for instance, in the lecture on the Risorgimento by Professor Pareti reported by Paul de Man, in which the organization of society into corporations should accomplish a lessening of class tensions and struggle. In
the 1930s, Hendrik de Man returned to Belgium, formulated the *Plan du
travail*, a plan to revive the Belgian economy, and became a minister in a
coalition government. His experiences there, particularly his growing
perception of the malignant power of banks and international finance to
hinder reforms in a small country like Belgium, made him sound more
and more like Ezra Pound, whose focus on the problem of credit—no
matter how right-wing in Pound's articulation in the 1930s—had left-
wing roots in the ideas of Silvio Gesell, a minister in the 1919 Bavarian
revolutionary government, and in those of Proudhon.[20]

So the stage was set in Hendrik de Man's political evolution for this
lifelong Socialist's curious and short-lived attempt to collaborate with the
Nazis when they overran Belgium in 1940. International socialism having
failed, it was time to try National Socialism, he seems to have thought.[21]
But it is also interesting to note, particularly given Derrida's attempt to
assign much of the responsibility for Paul de Man's wartime activity to

Hendrik de Man, that Hendrik de Man broke off his collaboration much sooner than his nephew did. Paul de Man was still writing for the *Bibliographie Dechenne* as late as March 1943, most of the way through the war.[22] By July 1941, Hendrik de Man already was in sufficient conflict with the Nazis that he was prohibited from speaking in public in Belgium. By November 1941, he had left Belgium for France. In June 1942, his *Réflexions sur la paix* was seized and banned by the German military authorities. In November 1942, Hendrik was held for questioning by the Gestapo and, barely eluding Nazi arrest, he escaped to the Alps, where he remained on the Swiss–French border for the rest of the war. Sentenced to prison in absentia for his wartime activities in Belgium, Hendrik de Man would remain in Switzerland until his death in 1953.[23]

The preceding discussion has proceeded, I should admit, on good modernist lines, establishing primarily some suggestive juxtapositions among the various political positions I have been sketching here: the ideological propaganda, if not the actual practice, of Italian fascism; the themes of Anglo-American modernism; the themes of Hendrik de Man's anti-Marxist writing; and the less theoretically explicit positions implied in Paul de Man's wartime journalism. This complex of attitudes, revolving around the place of literature in society, the advocacy of literary modernity, the rejection of the economism of the base-superstructure model, and the need to replace alienation and class struggle by "joy in work" are not at all characteristic of nazism, but they are part of the intellectual heritage of Italian fascism.

Now, this does not constitute a watertight argument labeling all of these as essentially fascist, nor am I sure I would want to make such an argument. It is an open question how much we should infer from Paul de Man's quoting Mussolini and explicit praise of Italian fascism; but since we have been invited to infer charitable, anti-Nazi conclusions from de Man's failure to quote or name Hitler, then we need at least to be aware that he quotes Mussolini. It is another open question how much we should infer from his relationship to Hendrik de Man. But again, given the charitable inferences being drawn from that relationship, the congruence in beliefs is worth pointing out, as is the younger de Man's longer-lasting, if less visible, role in collaboration. Finally, it is an open question how much de Man would have known of the politics of modern literature in English. Surely, he cites Huxley and Joyce more than Lawrence; but again, given that his citation of these figures and other modern writers has been the basis of an argument separating de Man from fascism, it needs to be pointed out that these references bear another construction.

Much that has been cited in defense of de Man's wartime journalism does separate him from a hard-line Nazi position. Norris, for example, makes much of his citing Charles Péguy, a Christian Socialist of the prewar period; he again makes much of his citing Kafka and other modern writers.[24] And Derrida, pointing to this ("Sound," p. 631) and similar instances, argues for the "heterogeneity" of de Man's wartime writing. But much that has seemed heterogeneous and therefore possibly nonconformist in these articles becomes much less heterogeneous given my reading of the kind of Fascist intellectual Paul de Man was. Charles Péguy, a maverick Sorelian Christian Socialist who died at the Marne, is precisely the kind of nationalist Socialist Mussolini liked to point to as a source for fascist ideology, and he is often cited in Lewis's *The Art of Being Ruled*.[25] The young Paul de Man was not torn between fascism and a commitment to modern art; he identified them. And just as important, this is not an idiosyncratic notion on his part. He was in a coherent intellectual tradition when he looked to Italian fascism as a model of a state that gave birth to modern art and gave a role to artists. Seeing de Man in that tradition, as that type of Fascist intellectual—different from the Nazis but no less fascist for all that—makes much in the wartime journalism clearer.

Just the act of working as a journalist becomes much clearer. People who knew Paul de Man later in life or knew his work, which is always difficult and not written for the common reader, have had difficulty coming to terms with his being a journalist, and the contempt shown by Derrida for all of the journalists writing about the case of Paul de Man is only the other side of the same coin. But this contempt shows precisely how far he is from understanding the milieu of modernist fascism. Mussolini, of course, was a journalist when young; Hendrik de Man wrote a good deal of journalism; Ezra Pound's works of journalism number in the thousands. Nor is this a coincidence; as Denis Mack Smith has written, "journalism and public relations were probably the most essential of all professional activities under Fascism."[26] And this is because they were essential to the winning of the acquiescence of the people to the regime, to the construction of hegemony in Gramsci's sense.

But there was always a tension in the journalistic practice of modernist fascism, which is that a desire to reach out to readers goes hand in hand with a disdain for those readers. The pro-Fascist Modernists felt that they were offering the "truth" to the people, but they knew that it was a "truth" not accepted by many of those people, and this situation was one they tended to assimilate to the situation of the unappreciated Modernist artist. This can be seen clearly enough in a figure like Ezra Pound, and here Eliot's complaint to Pound about a piece written for *The Criterion* is apposite: "I asked you to write an article which would explain this subject to people who had never heard of it; yet you write as if your readers knew about it already, but failed to understand it." [27] This contradiction or tension is also found in de Man's journalism. One particularly revealing example is his article written in Flemish, "Cultural Life: Advantages and Disadvantages of the Popular Editions" (*Het Vlaamsche Land*, 20 Oct. 1942, pp. 334–35). This discusses the boom in sales of books written in Flemish during the war. For de Man, this is clearly good for the public but potentially bad for the artist:

The commercial possibilities existing at present should not be an exhortation for every writer to demand an impression of 50,000 copies and for every publisher to aim at such an impression for every manuscript, under the pretext that everything can be sold anyway. Otherwise the popular edition will exert a very bad influence on the literary creation, which is the opposite of the original intention. The writer must not condescend to the people, but the people must rise to the level of the artist. (p. 334)

This is truly an odd argument to make in a piece of journalism unquestionably "condescending to the people," but the cultural elitism on display here is a perspective readily assimilable to that of fascist modernism.

But this is not the only aspect of the journalism that we can understand better by seeing it in the context of modernist fascism. The one article everyone writing on the de Man affair feels compelled to discuss is "Les Juifs dans la littérature actuelle" (4 Mar. 1941, p. 45), and much of the discussion has revolved around the right context in which to place this repellent article. Though its anti-Semitic sentiments are clear, the main thrust of the article is to discuss modern literature, criticizing the notion that it has been poisoned by Jewish influence. As a piece of Nazi anti-Semitic propaganda, it is obviously inept. No Nazi would be concerned with the question of distinguishing modern literature from the Jews: the Nazi line on modern literature was precisely that it was Jewish and corrupted by that Jewishness. But the article makes perfect sense in the context of the ongoing debate within fascism as a whole (a parallel debate was also going on in the Soviet Union in the 1930s) about literary modernity. De Man, in pointing to a number of Modernist writers who had not been corrupted by Jewish intellectualism, is in the Italian tradition of not seeing modernist literature as irredeemably decadent. Now, de Man's list—Gide, Kafka, Hemingway, and Lawrence—has been the subject of some discussion as, except for Lawrence, it is not a list of writers sympathetic to fascism.[28] Derrida uses this list as evidence for his argument that even this piece is an "anticonformist attack" on nazism: "The examples chosen are already curious and insolent because there are no others, because there is no German example, because the French example is

Gide, the American Hemingway, the English Lawrence, and because Kafka is Jewish, but especially because they represent everything that Nazism or the right wing revolutions would have liked to extirpate from history and the great tradition" ("Sound," p. 628). Derrida's specific points here could all be challenged. As Stanley Corngold has pointed out, the source of this list is a quotation from Huxley contained in the pre-Occupation essay "Le roman anglais contemporain," but one clearly Jewish name is left out—Proust.[29] But the most important point to challenge is Derrida's monistic identification of "Nazism or the right wing revolutions." The first of those "right wing revolutions"—Italian fascism—showed absolutely no desire to "extirpate" the forces of modernism; it sought instead to harness those forces in support of fascism. However one interprets the specific names on de Man's list, the space between de Man's defense of modernism and Nazi attacks on modernism does not automatically prove that de Man is antifascist, for that ignores the different fascist tradition, that of Marinetti, of Céline, of Pound, a tradition of fascist modernism or modernist fascism. Futurism, in fact, is named in the next paragraph of the essay as one of the revolutionary movements de Man is thinking of; and not long after this essay was written, the founder of futurism, F. T. Marinetti, was taking part in the Nazi invasion of the Soviet Union. De Man's defense of modernism unfortunately does not in any way establish some subtle antifascist strategy at work in these deplorable writings.

This placing of de Man's wartime journalism in what I think is its proper intellectual context raises at least as many questions as it answers, questions both about de Man's route to that fascism and about subsequent developments. There are larger questions lurking here as well. If so many Modernists were Fascists and so many Fascists were Modernists, is modernism itself a form of fascism? Obviously not, for the Nazi attack on modernism was a real one, and central Modernists like Joyce have impeccably antifascist credentials. So what is the place of modernism, and what place does or should modernism have in our intellectual landscape? It is beyond the scope of this essay to answer such questions here. But obviously, the case of Paul de Man has irrevocably changed the landscape in which we discuss the politics of modernism. No longer can critics like Fredric Jameson confidently evaluate modernism from without, using poststructuralist methodologies, for de Man's intellectual and political history shows us what any reader of the texts of Derrida and Barthes should have known already, that poststructuralism is deeply rooted in modernism.

This is not to label poststructuralism or deconstruction unproblematically fascist, since modernism isn't unproblematically fascist. It is just to say that contemporary critical theory is part of a history that includes modernism and fascism (we should have known this already too, given Nietzsche and Heidegger). These all belong together in problematic and disquieting ways, and they have all helped create the intellectual landscape in which we live and work. Pangloss is of no help here, and the strategy of seeing no evil and speaking no evil of de Man's defenders doesn't work. But neither does it work to ascribe all evil to another, whether that other is modernism, fascism, or deconstruction. We live in a postfascist culture as surely as we live in a postmodernist culture. It was disquieting enough to realize that some of our best writers were Fascists, more disquieting yet for some to realize that some of our best philosophers and critics were Fascists as well. If, as I have argued elsewhere,[30] the lesson we should draw from the case of Ezra Pound is that poets aren't, as Shelley would have it, the unacknowledged legislators of the world (or if they are, they shouldn't be) because they are no wiser about politics than anyone else, the lesson we should draw from the case of Paul de Man is that theorists aren't (or shouldn't be) the unacknowledged legislators of the world either.

Notes

Introduction (pp. ix–xviii)

1. Robert Soucy, *French Fascism: The First Wave, 1924–1933* (New Haven, Conn.: Yale University Press, 1986), xi.

2. Extreme-right-wing groups in Europe and the United States deny, for example, the existence of death camps and crematoriums while attempting to exonerate Hitler and other Fascist leaders. For a complete discussion of these groups and their activities, see Gill Seidel, *The Holocaust Denial: Antisemitism, Racism and the New Right* (London: Beyond the Pale Collective, 1986).

3. For a discussion of the debate over the relationship between fascism and culture in the interwar years in the Italian context, see Jeffrey Schnapp and Barbara Spackman's introduction to the special issue "Fascism and Culture," *Stanford Italian Review* 8, nos. 1–2.

4. Zeev Sternhell, "Preface to the English Edition," in *Neither Right nor Left: Fascist Ideology in France* (Berkeley: University of California Press, 1986), ix–xvi.

5. For a discussion of these contradictory tendencies in French fascism, see Alice Kaplan, *Reproductions of Banality: Fascism, Literature, and French Intellectual Life* (Minneapolis: University of Minnesota Press, 1986), 25–28. See also Robert Soucy, "Drieu la Rochelle and Modernist Ant-Modernism in French Fascism," *MLN* 95, no. 4 (1980): 922–38.

6. Isaiah Berlin, "Joseph de Maistre and the Origins of Fascism I–III." *New York Review of Books*, 27 Sept., 11 Oct., 25 Oct., 1990.

7. See Noel O'Sullivan, *Fascism* (London and Melbourne: J. M. Dent and Sons, 1983).

8. Robert Musil, "Ruminations of a Slow-witted Mind," *Critical Inquiry* 17 (Autumn 1990): 51–52.

9. Susan Suleiman, "Malraux's Women: A Re-Vision," in *Witnessing André Malraux: Visions and Revisions*, ed. Brian Thompson and Carl A. Viggiani (Middletown, Conn.: Wesleyan University Press, 1984), 140–58.

10. Russell Berman, "Modernism, Fascism, and the Institution of Literature," in *Modernism: Challenges and Perspectives*, ed. M. Chefdor, R. Quinones, and A. Wachtel (Champaign: University of Illinois Press, 1986), 94–102.

11. See "Fascinating Fascism," in Susan Sontag, *Under the Sign of Saturn* (New York: Vintage Books, 1981), 73–109.

12. In this context, see Michael North, "The Public as Sculpture: From Heavenly City to Mass Ornament," *Critical Inquiry* 16 (Summer 1990) 860–79.

13. Blanchot's involvement with the neofascist review *Combat* during the 1930s in France was revealed in an article by Jeffrey Mehlman entitled "Blanchot at Combat." Mehlman's insistence on a link between Blanchot's fascist past and his postwar critical practice aroused a storm of controversy and prompted an angry denial from Blanchot himself. For the article and the details of the affair, see Mehlman's *Legacies of Anti-Semitism in France* (Minneapolis: University of Minnesota Press, 1983). The publication of Robert Casillo's *The Genealogy of Demons: Anti-Semitism, Fascism and the Myths of Ezra Pound* stirred controversy because of Casillo's insistence on the centrality of Pound's fascism to his poetry. Pound's commitment to the Axis powers was already well known.

14. For Sternhell's discussion of the diversity of French fascism, its political weakness, and the necessary link between the two, see the Introduction to *Neither Right nor Left*.

15. For a detailed discussion of the Faurisson affair and the trial in particular, see Seidel, *The Holocaust Denial*, 99–111.

16. See "Qu'est-ce qu'un collaborateur?" in Jean-Paul Sartre, *Situations III* (Paris: Gallimard, 1949).

17. In this regard, see especially Duras's *La douleur* (Paris: P.O.L. editeur, 1985), Modiano's *La ronde de nuit* (Paris: Gallimard, 1969), and Tournier's *Le roi des Aulnes* (Paris: Gallimard, 1970).

Epic Demonstrations (pp. 1–37)

1. "Arte e civiltà," delivered on October 5, 1926, reprinted in Benito Mussolini *Opera omnia* (Florence, 1951–1963), 22:230.

2. On the *Critica Fascista* debate, see J. Schnapp and B. Spackman, "Selections from the Great Debate on Fascism and Culture," *Stanford Italian Review* 8, no. 1/2:235–72.

3. Margherita Sarfatti, "Architettura, arte e simbolo alla Mostra del Fascismo," *Architettura: Rivista del Sindacato Nazionale Fascista Architetti* 12 (Jan. 1933), fasc. 1, p. 1. This article has now been reprinted in *Storia moderna dell'arte in Italia 3: Dal Novecento ai dibattiti sulle figure e sul monumentale, 1925–1945*, ed. Paola Barocchi (Turin: Einaudi, 1990), 222–227.

4. The full passage reads:
La Mostra dimostrativa della Rivoluzione, è dunque, non solo come cornice, ma nella sua essenza, opera d'arte e opera di architettura; fu ideata, vagliata, eseguita e composta da artisti, con coraggio di scelta, responsabilità di direttive e libertà di invenzione; insomma con l'ingegno, con l'audacia e anche con il cuore; così, come solo si possono fare le opere d'arte. Non è una raccolta di materiale storico, ma storia in atto, attraverso la trasformazione mitica e pur verace—anzi, la sola verace—in simbolo e allegoria. (Sarfatti, "Architettura, arte e simbolo," 5)

5. There is some dispute about total attendance figures. In his graphically opulent *Italiani e stranieri alla Mostra della Rivoluzione Fascista* (Turin: S.I.A.E., 1935), Francesco Gargano claims a total of 3,854,927 visitors. Most Archivio

Centrale dello Stato (ACS) records, however, mention the figures of either 3,701,818 or 3,708,214.

6. I am aware of ongoing research on the subject by Professor Borden Painter and of dissertations by Marla Stone ("The Politics of Cultural Production: The Exhibition in Fascist Italy, 1928–1942," [Princeton University, 1990]), and Libero Andreotti ("Art and Politics in Fascist Italy: The Exhibition of the Fascist Revolution [1932]" [Massachusetts Institute of Technology, 1989]), which I was able to consult only after completing this essay. All references to archival documents in the Archivio Centrale dello Stato in Rome are listed by the abbreviation ACS, followed by the name of the precise inventory, the envelope number (b.) and, when appropriate, the fascicle number (f.).

7. A detailed plan was printed in June 1928 by IFCM for distribution to members of the overseeing committee. Designated as confidential, this *Prima bozza del piano generale per la Mostra del Fascismo* is found in ACS: Mostra del Fascismo, b. 274.

8. "La Marcia su Roma sarà considerata nella Mostra, non già come un semplice fatto storico, ma come la sintesi e la risoluzione di un'epopea, l'inizio di una nuova storia" ("Una lodevole iniziativa dell'Istituto Fascista di Cultura: La mostra storica del Fascismo [Nostra intervista con l'on. Alfieri]", *Il Popolo d'Italia*, 31 March 1928).

9. In his interview with *Il Popolo d'Italia*, Alfieri justified the full year of preparations by stating that IFCM's ambitious plan required "uno studio minuto e particolareggiato, una richiesta paziente e minuziosa dei documenti, la cui raccolta vuole tempo, che infine il materiale statistico e fotografico deve esser curato in modo da rispondere bene allo scopo di raggiungere l'immediata evidenza di ciò che deve rappresentare" ("Una lodevole iniziativa").

10. ACS: PNF–Carteggio del Direttorio, b. 274 ("Sottocartelle della M.R.F."). The passage is excerpted from a memo dated "Rome, October 12, 1928" and signed by Alfieri.

11. "Per mettere in rilievo un fenomeno storico e la grandiosità di un'opera non è necessario affatto ricorrere a tutti i più infimi particolari ... basta uno sguardo d'insieme per afferrare il fenomeno" (Alfieri, "Una lodevole iniziativa").

12. Cited from Alfieri, "Una lodevole iniziativa."

13. The original plan had been to close after one month, even though in his 31 March interview Alfieri did not discount the possibility that the exhibition might become permanent: "chi potrà dire quali saranno gli ulteriori sviluppi della nostra iniziativa?"

14. A 20 November 1928 press release printed in *Il Popolo d'Italia* speaks of the "Secretary" of the PNF, either Turati or Marinelli, initiating the move to the Roman Palazzo Regina Margherita "dove la mostra potrà avere più alta consacrazione e più vasto successo." Four days later, a second release attributes the transfer to *il Duce*, adding that no delay will ensue ("non dovendo il lavoro d'organizzazione subire il minimo ritardo" [*Corriere della Sera*, 24 Nov. 1928]). Both releases indicate that the collecting and sorting operation would be moved to PNF headquarters at the Palazzo Littorio.

15. In late December 1928, Starace had visited with IFCM in order to examine "alcuni aspetti del problema culturale del Fascismo milanese ravvisando l'opportunità che le varie forme di attività svolte dai numerosi organismi culturali cittadini siano coordinate e disciplinate per evitare dispersione di forze e per raggiungere più facilmente il fine che essi si propongono ("Nel Fascio Milanese: La giornata dell'on. Starace," *L'Ambrosiano*, 29 Dec. 1928, p. 4). An article in

L'Ambrosiano dated 19 April 1929, openly criticized IFCM for its insufficient "discipline" and called for coordination of the activities of local cultural institutes under the aegis of INCF.

16. It is worth noting, once again, that (a) IFCM's *Prima bozza del piano generale per la Mostra del Fascismo* contained only one passing allusion to Mussolini in nine pages, and (b) it proposed neither a room dedicated to the memorabilia of *il Duce* nor a recreation of the offices of *Il Popolo d'Italia* on Via Lovanio or on Via Paolo da Cannobio (all three would become central components in the 1932 Mostra). In his 31 March interview, Alfieri had mentioned the desirability of staging the exhibit at the actual offices of *Il Popolo d'Italia* but pointed out the many technical obstacles.

17. Com'è noto, si era pensato, in un primo tempo, di far coincidere la celebrazione del decimo annuale con l'inaugurazione della Mostra nazionale storica del Fascismo. Per ragioni indipendenti della volontà degli organizzatori e anche per dare alla Mostra quella risonanza che merita per il suo valore storico essa è stata rinviata sine die.... si è verificata una nobile e spontanea gara tra tutti i cittadini nell'offrire al partito, per l'Esposizione, cimeli e documenti storici. Le offerte hanno inoltre dimostrato che la Mostra avrà un'ampiezza non prevista all'inizio dell'organizzazione, e richiederà la scelta di un apposito, amplissimo locale. ("Il X Annuale dei Fasci di Combattimento," *Corriere della Sera*, 6 Mar. 1929, p. 1)

18. "Far cosa d'oggi, modernissima dunque, e audace, senza malinconici ricordi degli stili decorativi del passato" (Benito Mussolini, cited from Alfieri and Freddi's preliminary guidebook, *La Mostra della Rivoluzione Fascista*, [Rome: PNF, 1932, pp. 8–9). The theme would continue in Mussolini's later pronouncements: "Voglio una mostra palpitante di vita virile e anche teatrale . . . non fatemi qualcosa che assomigli alla palandrana di Giolitti" (reported by F. T. Marinetti in "La Mostra della Rivoluzione Fascista segna il trionfo dell'arte futurista," *La Gazzetta del Popolo*, 29 Oct. 1932, p. 3).

19. The precise title of the event would vary over the following months. As late as 30 April 1932, *Il Popolo d'Italia* could speak of the exhibition as the Mostra Politica del Fascismo, presumably to differentiate it from the Mostra delle Realizzazioni (scheduled for the following year). An emendation follows on 10 June: "Il Capo del Governo, inoltre, in considerazione che la Mostra della realizzazione [*sic*] del Fascismo è stata rinviata di un anno, ha deciso che la Mostra comprendente la parte storico-politica e che si inaugurerà il 28 ottobre debba più opportunamente chiamarsi 'Mostra della Rivoluzione Fascista'" ("Il Duce impartisce le direttive per la Mostra della Rivoluzione Fascista," *Il Popolo d'Italia*).

20. The document, titled "Appunti sul programma della Mostra del Fascismo" and later distributed to the heads of government agencies, begins as follows:

È anzitutto opportuno considerare la Mostra del Fascismo non semplicemente come una rievocazione storica, fine a sè stessa, ma come mezzo, il più facilmente comprensibile e percettibile, di rappresentare la somma di tutte le complesse attività svolte e delle realizzazioni compiute dal Fascismo. Senza voler far paragoni con altri Paesi, i quali hanno commemorato con grandiose e solenni manifestazioni i loro più importanti anniversari politici, è sommamente utile che il Fascismo, nel decimo anniversario della sua assunzione al potere, sosti un momento per dimostrare all'Italia e al mondo quanto esso ha saputo compiere nel campo materiale e spirituale. Non quindi "esposizione" o "mostra," nel senso abituale della parola, ma rassegna di attività e di forze, bilancio dei primi dieci anni al potere, dal quale bilancio nasce implicitamente il programma avvenire. (ACS: PNF–Carteggio del Direttorio, b. 273 ["Alfieri"])

Once distributed through internal government channels, this document was published in different versions as a pamphlet (Barabino & Graeve: 1932) and in *Il Popolo d'Italia* (15 July 1931 and 30 April 1932).

21. The document speaks of "la sintetica visione dei successivi avvenimenti" and of the "periodo eroico che va dal 23 marzo 1919 al 28 ottobre 1922" ("Appunti sul programma," pp. 2–3).

22. "La Mostra avrà una brevissima parte—una specie di introduzione—dedicata alle manifestazioni interventiste e alla guerra; introduzione che sarà assai efficacemente rappresentata dalla fondazione del *Popolo d'Italia*, che può legittimamente considerarsi l'espressione più genuina e più sintetica del grande movimento rinnovatore" ("Appunti sul programma," p. 3).

23. La varia e complessa attività svoltasi in questi dieci anni dal Regime . . . sarà rappresentata a mezzo di quadri raffigurativi a base statistica, a mezzo di documenti e soprattutto a mezzo di segni in cui la genialità dell'artista dovrà tradurre ed esprimere nella forma più vivace e convincente, anche il materiale più arido . . . tutta la varia e complessa attività del Regime nel campo della vita e del pensiero, vi dovrà trovare adeguata raffigurazione, così che dal paragone di ciò che l'Italia era, dieci anni addietro, balzerà spontanea la imponenza delle realizzazioni compiute dal Fascismo e sopratutto si potranno considerare nella guista prospettiva le enormi difficoltà superate, gli sforzi compiuti, i risultati raggiunti. ("Appunti sul programma," p. 4)

24. That the admittedly conventional language of Alfieri's "appunti" refers to a Modernist ideology of design is confirmed by a later document, in which he explains to the PNF secretary Starace that the postponed Mostra della Realizzazioni ought to take "una forma *spettacolare* [emphasis mine], cioè vivace e suggestiva, fatta soprattutto con mezzi di confronto e di paragone e non rifuggendo dalle forme più moderne della propaganda e della pubblicità" (Alfieri to Starace, 28 June 1933, ACS: PNF–Carteggio del Direttorio, b. 273 ["Alfieri"], pp. 2–3).

25. Iti Bacci, vice-secretary of the PNF, sent out two circulars (Nos. 4 and 8) in August 1931 for the gathering of, respectively, historical documents and contemporary materials. The second (dated 22 Aug.) insists "che la raccolta comprenda *tutte* le opere e le realizzazioni del Regime compiute durante il decennio, anche le minori, così che la raccolta sia completa in ogni sua parte e per qualsiasi genere di attività" (ACS: PNF–Direttorio Nazionale, b. 217, f. 2.2.7, pp. 1–2).

26. Freddi published some of his historical outlines, among them one for Room A: *Luglio–Dicembre 1914* (Rome: Tipografia della Camera dei Deputati, 1932). For a brief synopsis of Freddi's prior and later career, see Philip V. Cannistraro, *La fabbrica del consenso: Fascismo e mass media* (Rome: Laterza, 1975), 290–300.

27. The most complete contemporary account of planning and preparation for the exhibition is Gigi Maino's, "La Mostra della Rivoluzione Fascista," which appeared in *Rassegna Italiana (Politica, Letteraria e Artistica)* 16.3 (March 1933):203–11. (Maino was the "historian" of rooms H and I.) Also worth consulting are "I documenti dell'epopea fascista: Come è stata preparata la Mostra della Rivoluzione" (*Corriere della Sera*, 18 Oct. 1932, p. 3), authored by

S[alvatore] A[ponte], and the exhibition catalog by Alfieri and Freddi, *Mostra della Rivoluzione Fascista* (Rome: PNF, 1933), 52–58. As late as 7 July 1932, Alfieri was expressing concerns that (a) the federations were far too slow in sending in documentary materials and (b) the reconstruction of the movement's chronology would prove overly difficult given that this was the first "true" narration of fascism's history (Alfieri to Marinelli regarding funds, ACS: PNF–Carteggio del Direttorio, b. 273 ["Alfieri"]).

28. In a meeting called on 9 June 1932, Mussolini was presented by *Il Popolo d'Italia* as formulating the directives for the Exhibition: "Il Capo del Governo . . . ha tracciato le direttive storico-artistiche, affinchè la Mostra risulti un quadro completo e fedele della Rivoluzione delle Camicie Nere" ("Il Duce impartisce le direttive per la Mostra della Rivoluzione Fascista"). It appears that it was in the course of this meeting that Alfieri complained about the fiscal constraints imposed by Marinelli.

29. I lavori sono iniziati il 5 agosto 1932 e terminati il 28 ottobre. Quindi le giornate lavorative sono state 85 corrispondenti a 2,040 ore. Dal 5 agosto a tutto l'8 settembre il lavoro preparatorio è stato compiuto solo di giorno da una media di 107 unità operaie. Dal 9 settembre al 28 ottobre i lavori sono stati condotti di giorno e di notte, con un aumento di unità operaie che ha culminato sino a 520 operai di giorno e 230 di notte. Il totale delle ore lavorative eseguite effettivamente in cantiere dall'inizio al termine dei lavori fu di 305,524. (From the guidebook by Alfieri and Freddi, *Mostra della Rivoluzione Fascista* [Rome: PNF, 1933], 55).

30. Construction materials are covered in pp. 56–57 of the catalog; the electrical and air conditioning system, on pp. 57–58.

31. The press contributed its share in the elaboration of this myth. In its coverage of opening day ceremonies, for instance, the *Corriere della Sera*'s Orio Vergani wrote: "Dino Alfieri . . . ha diretto questa mobilitazione di artisti e di studiosi, e la mobilitazione del piccolo esercito operaio che, in un complesso di 180,000 giornate lavorative, è riuscito a condurre a termine un'opera che, per gli stessi principi architettonici e decorativi che l'ispiravano e rinnovavano tante tecniche di lavoro e di uso di materiali costruttivi, esigeva anche dalla mano d'opera una prova costante di intelligenza, di passione e di capacità interpretative del modernissimo stile" ("Gli eloquenti cimeli dell'appassionata vigilia," 30 Oct. 1932, p. 1). *Il Popolo d'Italia* described the pace of construction as "quella celerità di ritmo che è nello stile fascista" ("La Mostra della Rivoluzione sarà inaugurata stamane," 29 Oct. 1932, p. 2).

32. "Perchè trattarmi così? Forse io demolisco il Regime o contagio l'umanità? Ho una gran voglia di tagliare la corda! Vedo che tutto è inutile" (Freddi to Alfieri, undated, *Il Popolo d'Italia* letterhead, ACS: Ministero Cultura Popolare, b. 171, f. 54). The bulk of correspondence concerning Freddi is found in this same inventory.

33. "Appunto per S.E. Il Capo del Governo," ACS: PNF–Carteggio del Direttorio, b. 273 ("Alfieri").

34. "Questo *spizzico* con continue aggiunte e modifiche rappresenta *un vero disastro finanziario* a tutto beneficio degli speculatori!" (Marinelli to Alfieri, 13 Sept. 1932, ACS: PNF–Carteggio del Direttorio, b. 273 ["Alfieri"]). In a probable reference to Marinelli, Alfieri would later state that "io sono sempre stato tranquillo sul successo della Mostra, anche se in parte c'erano increduli e in parte contrari, tranne Mussolini, che mi ha sempre aiutato" (*Atti del terzo congresso*

degli Istituti Fascisti di Cultura: 24–25 aprile, 1933 [Rome: Istituto Nazionale Fascista di Cultura, 1933], 114).

35. On contemporary economic conditions, see Federico Chabod, *L'Italia contemporanea: 1918–1948* (Turin: Einaudi, 1961), 82–90. Budgetary figures for the 1932 Exhibition are taken from a document entitled "Mostra decennale del fascismo: Schema di bilancio," located in ACS: PNF-Carteggio del Direttorio, b. 273 ("Alfieri"). Dollar equivalents, calculated by extrapolating on the basis of the wages of Mostra personnel, are crudely approximative and are offered only for purposes of comparison.

36. The figures from the "Schema di bilancio" cited above are confirmed by a letter, dated 3 Sept. 1932, from Marinelli to Giacomo Acerbo, the minister of agriculture, which pegs the total cost at "alcuni millioni" and concludes: "quanto si potrà incassare, con ogni migliore previsione, non arriverà a coprire i 2/3 delle fortissime spese occorenti per la Mostra" (ACS: PNF–Carteggio del Direttorio, Servizi Vari, serie 2, b. 332 ["Varie"]). These sums, however, are in sharp conflict with a later document found in ACS: PNF–Carteggio del Direttorio, Servizi Vari, serie 2, b. 330 ("Mostra—Visite collettive—Forfait"), which places the total expenses through May 23, 1933, at 15,051,677 lire.

37. It should also be noted that the promotion of international tourism was a key objective. The Ente Nazionale Italiano per il Turismo (or ENIT) mounted an active publicity campaign abroad that included magazine advertisements.

38. This information is contained in a folder titled "Ispezione della Mostra della Rivoluzione Fascista," ACS: PNF–Carteggio del Direttorio, b. 273.

39. A letter from Marinelli, dated 6 Oct. 1933 and addressed to Guiseppe Cocchia, the Questor of Rome, invites Cocchia to force the firm of Eugenio Risi to desist from publishing and selling "cartoline portanti le fotografie e i disegni della facciata della Mostra della Rivoluzione Fascista," insisting that all rights of reproduction are the sole property of the exhibition itself (ACS: PNF–Carteggio del Direttorio, b. 272 ["Corrispondenza"]).

40. An example of just how strongly the iconographies of railway travel and fascist modernization were linked during this period may be found in the "Polemic on Arches and Columns." Initiated by Ugo Ojetti in early 1933, when Marcello Piacentini, then dean of the Italian architectural establishment, openly supported the Michelucci group's Rationalist design for the Florence railway station, this debate came to a provisional close when Mussolini took sides with the architectural Modernists. The implications of this choice are clear enough: in the early 1930s, Fascist trains and train stations were still meant to signify a rupture with the past, not continuity. On this subject, see the documents collected in *Architettura e fascismo*, ed. Carlo Fabrizio Carli (Rome: Giovanni Volpe, 1980).

41. In an article suggestively placed alongside coverage of the 1932 Mostra, the *Corriere della Sera*, for instance, observed that "dieci anni di Fascismo hanno trasformato il nostro servizio ferroviario da una piaga morale e finanziaria, aggravata da un vero disordine amministrativo, in un esempio di ordine e di progresso tecnico" (Filippo Tajani, "Attivo del Decennale: Risanamento e progresso delle ferrovie," 18 Oct. 1932, p. 3).

42. The quote is from a letter to Alfieri from Freddi, 18 Feb. 1933. Freddi writes: "bisogna invitarlo [i.e., Martelli, the director of railway concessions] a far sì che in tutte le edicole ferroviarie su tutti i carrelli nell'interno delle stazioni, il volume sia permanentemente esposto, possibilmente in numerose copie" (ACS: PNF–Carteggio del Direttorio-Servizi Vari, serie 2, b. 332 ["Alfieri"]). Because of various delays, the catalog did not appear until 23 Feb. 1933.

43. A letter from Alfieri to Marinelli, dated 29 July 1933, envisages "una pellicola sulla Mostra, servendosi naturalmente, di tutto il materiale cinematografico in possesso della Luce. Il montaggio della pellicola deve evidentemente essere fatto da persona pratica esperta e geniale; ed io su indicazione dello stesso Gray ne ho già tenuto parola al Comm. Blasetti, il quale mi ha dichiarato che portrà venire fuori un film straordinariamente interessante" (ACS: PNF–Carteggio del Direttorio, b. 273 ["Alfieri"]). A later note from Marinelli to Giovanni Preziosi, editor of *La Vita Italiana*, states: "si è già provveduto alla riproduzione fotografica di tutte le sale della 'Mostra della Rivoluzione' e del materiale in esse contenuto, e, oltre a ciò, la 'Mostra' è già stata ripresa, per intero, in una dettagliata pellicola cinematografica" (Rome, 30 July 1934, ACS: PNF–Carteggio del Direttorio, b. 272 ["Richieste per invio documenti"]).

44. On this film and the Fascist film industry, see Cannistraro, *La fabbrica del consenso*, pp. 287–88. Information regarding the Ministry of Public Instruction's use of this film is found in ACS: Presidenza del Consiglio dei Ministri, (1931–1933), f. 5.1, n. 7843 ("Film il Decennale"). The film is preserved at Cinecittà in Rome (along with several newsreels concerning the installation and opening of the Mostra).

45. Ada Negri, "Madri di martiri," *Corriere della Sera*, 11 Mar. 1933, p. 3.

46. Sarfatti, "Architettura, arte e simbolo alla Mostra del Fascismo," 10.

47. A letter to Starace dated 12 Jan. 1933, apparently motivated by a slight dip in admissions figures, proposed the following: (1) increased coordination with local Fascist federations, (2) a memo to PNF members, (3) greater press coverage of the Mostra's interior, (4) further distribution of press articles covering the event, (5) a daily radio bulletin on the show, (6) contacts with the Istituto LUCE (presumably leading to photographic documentation and the production of a film), and (7) the placement of new billboards in the principal cities of Italy. See ACS: PNF–Carteggio del Direttorio, b. 273 ("Alfieri"). The proposals were implemented and the resulting influx of visitors would sorely test the Palazzo's ticket machines. A telegram to Marinelli reads: "Guasto automaticket mostra essendo dovuto grande uso . . . richiedere società Milano invio immediato" (Gandolfi to Marinelli, 8 Sept. 1933, ACS: PNF–Carteggio del Direttorio, b. 272 ["Corrispondenza"]).

48. This information is contained in ACS: PNF–Carteggio del Direttorio, b. 273 ("Rapporto giornaliero visitatori"). Detailed records concerning visitors to the Mostra before 9 November 1933 do not seem to exist.

49. Once again, the precise budget figures are confusing. A document in ACS: PNF–Carteggio del Direttorio, b. 271, gives the following figures for 29 October 1932 to 22 November 1933: 28,622,091 lire in "introiti," 13,211,939 lire in "spese," of which 2,754,070 lire went to "allestimento" and 673,886 lire to paying artists. (No explanation is given of how the presence of about 2.5 million visitors could have generated such a large *introito*, although if one assumes, based on the original "schema di bilancio," that 3 lire in railway "diritti di timbratura" were earned per visitor, a figure in the range of 12 million lire is attained.) Another document, signed by Melchiori and dated 7 November 1934, cites a total *introito* of 44,252,044 lire. In any event, by the end of November 1934, well over 7.3 million lire in profits seems to have been distributed to the following public entities: Opera Prevenzione—Giornalisti and MVSN (2.3 and 1.9 million), Ferrovie dello Stato (1.66 million), Comitato Gare e Feste di Roma (250,000), Opera Nazionale per il Mezzogiorno (1 million), and Opera Nazionale Balilla (210,000).

50. "Io conservo la mia convinzione che alla chiusura della Mostra, fissata per il 21 aprile, non solo saranno reintegrate tutte le spese, ma *si otterà un notevole beneficio*" (my italics). Later he continues: "per il successo della Mostra ed i riconoscimenti che continuamente da ogni parte giungono, il problema dell'affluenza e quindi degli introiti diventa una questione puramente di organizzazione nel senso che si potranno portare cento o mille visitatori a seconda del ritmo con cui sarà attuata la campagna di propaganda" (Alfieri to Starace, 12 Jan. 1933, ACS: PNF–Carteggio del Direttorio, b. 273 ["Alfieri"]).

51. The underlying motive seems to have been budgetary; see ACS: PNF–Carteggio del Direttorio, b. 273 ("Richieste agevolazioni varie").

52. The full title of De Grazia's work is *The Culture of Consent: Mass Organization of Leisure in Fascist Italy* (Cambridge: Cambridge University Press, 1981).

53. "Ininterrotto omaggio di folle alla Mostra della Rivoluzione," p. 2.

54. Figures concerning visits on foot and by bicycle are based on the detailed day-by-day records found in ACS: PNF–Carteggio del Direttorio, b. 273 ("Rapporto giornaliero visitatori").

55. ". . . la Mostra della Rivoluzione, che tante ineffabili emozioni ha suscitate, che con tanti ricordi commoventi ha esaltato, infiammato l'animo degli innumerevoli visitatori . . .: quella Santa Rivoluzione che Voi voleste . . . esempio, monito ed incitamento perenne" (Renato Taiuti [?] to Mussolini, handwritten, 9 Oct. 1933, ACS: PNF–Carteggio del Direttorio, b. 272 ["Corrispondenza"]).

56. "Sacrario della nostra Epopea . . . il nostro Altare della Rivoluzione . . . una basilica . . . pellegrini di amore e di fede . . . noi si visiterebbe sempre con curiosità nuova, con passione nuova il reliquario della nostra lotta . . . il nostro Tempio aperto ogni ora, vigilato da Camicie Nere e sempre accogliente come un rifugio di calda passione" (Salvatore Floris to Marinelli, 11 Oct. 1933, Cagliari, ACS: PNF–Carteggio del Direttorio, b. 272 ["Corrispondenza"]).

57. "Lì dove si fa la storia d'Italia, dell'epopea della guerra sostenuta dal popolo d'Italia, i nostri Martiri Fascisti non potevano trovare più degno luogo, più degna esaltazione del Loro sacrificio" (Ezio Silva, Italcable, to Marinelli, 30 Apr. 1933, ACS: PNF–Carteggio del Direttorio, b. 273 ["Richieste agevolazioni varie"]).

58. "La Mostra ha trovato presto i suoi apostoli" (Salvatore Aponte, "Il volto e il cuore della folla alla Mostra della Rivoluzione," *Corriere della Sera*, 11 Mar. 1933, p. 3).

59. The first quote is from Alfredo Panzini, "Storia di diciannove anni" (*Corriere della Sera*, 29 Mar. 1933, p. 3): "Appena varcato l'atrio, la prima sensazione è il silenzio." The second quote is from Salvatore Aponte's "Il volto e il cuore della folla alla Mostra della Rivoluzione": "Una battuta colta a volo nel dialogo fra due custodi all'ingresso della Mostra: 'Entrano come se entrassero in chiesa'."

60. *Corriere della Sera*, 11 Mar. 1933, p. 3.

61. "Ogni sala grida all'anima del popolo nel modo più ardente . . . il messaggio storico di cui è carica" ("Architettura, Arte e Simbolo," p. 10).

62. Louis Gillet, "Rome nouvelle," *Revue des Deux Mondes*, 15 Dec. 1932, p. 810.

63. On futurism, see my "Politics and Poetics in F. T. Marinetti's *Zang Tumb Tuuum*" (*Stanford Italian Review* 5, no. 1 [1985]: 75–92). Marinetti was actively involved in the organization of the Mostra and publicly staked out futurism's claim on the event in "La Mostra della Rivoluzione Fascista segna il trionfo dell'arte futurista" (*La Gazzetta del Popolo*, 29 Oct. 1932, p. 3).

64. Negri, "Madri di martiri."

65. Gillet, "Rome nouvelle," 812.

66. It appears that the only previous such analysis is the extremely brief one found in Giorgio Ciucci, "L'autorappresentazione del fascismo: La mostra del decennale della marcia su Roma," *Rassegna di Architettura* 4 (June 1982): 48–55. All other bibliography makes only passing allusions to the Mostra.

67. The work was published by Vallecchi in Florence and appeared with a prologue by Mussolini. It received considerable attention in the press and appears to have been distributed through the PNF apparatus.

68. The guidebook describes these rooms as "un'anticipazione—schematica, sintetica, a base, si può dire, esclusivamente di diagrammi figurati—sulla Mostra delle Realizzazioni del Regime fascista che si sta preparando" (p. 246).

69. The full quotation reads: "Le fait est qu'on reconnaît dans cette composition terroriste une imagination théâtrale, d'un baroque féroce, un peu tinta-marresque, mais qui fait grande impression. Au fond, toutes les jeunesses d'un même temps se ressemblent. Elles sont nées sous la même étoile. Ce prologue, oserai-je le dire? est un peu bolchéviste pour moi; les emblèmes changés, ce morceau serait applaudi à Moscou" (Gillet, "Rome nouvelle," 809–810).

70. Gillet describes it as "une gueule de fournaise formée d'une série de cintres flamboyants, sous lesquels le visiteur passe comme sous un portique nègre, dans l'assourdissement de ce coup de tam-tam" ("Rome nouvelle," 809).

71. For complete floor plans of the Mostra see Appendix 2.

72. "È come salire dalle catacombe all'aria aperta e al sole" ("Madri di martiri").

73. The alternation is reinforced by its reversibility. After reaching the Sacrarium (room U), visitors were in fact obliged to retrace their steps back through the "Mussolini Room" (T) and the Gallery of Fasci (S) in order to ascend to the second floor. The point of this was to put on display the absolute reciprocity that exists between the heroic subject (Mussolini) and the mass.

74. The point is made frequently in contemporary press coverage of the Garibaldian exhibit as well as of the Mostra: "un'immagine centrale, che da modesta diventa immensa e invade tutto il campo spirituale della mostra: Mussolini. La Mostra della Rivoluzione Fascista è sopra tutto, bisogna dirlo, la Mostra di Mussolini" (Aldo Valori, "Mussolini volto della Rivoluzione," *Corriere della Sera*, 23 Mar. 1933, p. 3).

75. "La sinfonia eroica viene a concludersi qui in un accordo finale che sembra un'eco di paradiso" (Negri, "Madri di martiri").

76. Report by Antonio Pinca, "Organizzazione del servizio della Mostra," 11 Dec. 1940 (ACS: PNF–Carteggio del Direttorio, b. 274, f. "Mostra: Anno XX"). The phrase "totale assenteismo" recurs in numerous other archival documents from the period.

Fascist Modernism, Futurism, and "Post-modernity" (pp. 38–55)

1. The most concise expression of this crisis is to be found in an essay by Hans-Magnus Enzensberger, "The Aporia of the Avant-Garde," in *The Consciousness Industry: On Literature, Politics and the Media*, ed. M. Roloff (New York: Continuum, 1974), 16–41.

2. Renato Poggioli, *Theory of the Avant-Garde*, trans. Gerald Fitzgerald (Cambridge, Mass.: Belknap, 1968), 95.

3. Peter Bürger, *Theory of the Avant-Garde*, trans. Michael Shaw (Minneapolis: University of Minnesota Press, 1984).

4. The best work on the relationship between futurism and fascism can be found in Renzo de Felice, *Mussolini il rivoluzionario* (Turin: Einaudi, 1965), and Renzo de Felice, ed., *Futurismo, cultura e politica* (Turin: Fondazione Giovanni Agnelli, 1988).

5. A strong case for the political overdetermination of the modernist canon in the context of the cold war is made by Jost Hermand, "Das Konzept 'Avantgarde,'" in *Faschismus und Avantgarde*, ed. Reinhold Grimm and Jost Hermand (Königstein: Athenäum, 1980), 1–19.

6. Fredric Jameson, *Fables of Aggression. Wyndham Lewis: The Modernist as Fascist* (Berkeley: University of California Press, 1979).

7. Fredric Jameson, *The Prison-House of Language* (Princeton, N.J.: Princeton University Press, 1972), 45.

8. At this point I should indicate the sense in which Marinetti's name will be evoked here. Although the works cited from futurism are all by Marinetti, I am in a sense using his name as a metonymy for the movement as a whole. My reasons for this will become clear in my refusal to divide futurism into a "heroic" and a decadent stage—a division that, I feel, demands a spurious division of aesthetics and politics. To this extent the name of Marinetti operates as a marker for the continuity of the futurist aesthetic and intellectual project.

9. We should be wary, however, of turning the Nazi public sphere into a monolithic caricature of authoritarianism. See Hans-Dieter Schäfer, *Das Gespaltene Bewußtsein: Deutsche Kultur und Lebenswirklichkeit 1933–45* (Munich: Carl Hanser, 1982).

10. First published by Julie Dashwood, "An Unpublished Letter: Benito Mussolini to Paolo Buzzi," *Italian Studies* 32 (1977):97–99. Dashwood can only estimate the date of the letter, which appears again, dated 21 November 1914, in Alberto Schiavo, ed., *Futurismo e fascismo* (Rome: Giovanni Volpe, 1981).

11. The first to suggest such a division rigorously was Enrico Crispolti, *Il secondo Futurismo: Torino 1923–38* (Turin: Edizione d'Arte Fratelli Pozzo, 1961). He expands upon the problem of periodization in "Appunti riguardanti i rapporti tra Futurismo e fascismo," *Arte e fascismo in Italia e in Germania*, ed. Enrico Crispolti et al. (Milan: Feltrinelli, 1974):7–67.

12. Peter Bürger makes the notion of institutional criticism central to his definition of the avant-garde. He uses the term to identify a critical relationship in which the object is no longer to criticize a specific aesthetic movement or phenomenon (this criticism would be "system-immanent") but rather the very category and institution of art itself.

13. Luciano de Maria, "Introduzione," in F. T. Marinetti, *Teoria e invenzione futurista*, ed. L. De Maria (Verona: Mondadori, 1968), xix.

14. Walter Benjamin, "The Work of Art in the Age of Mechanical Reproduction," in *Illuminations*, ed. Hannah Arendt, trans. Harry Zohn (New York: Schocken, 1969), 217–252.

15. Emilio Gentile, in "Il Futurismo e la politica: Dal Nazionalismo Modernista al Fascismo (1909–1920), in *Futurismo, cultura e politica*, ed. Renzo de Felice, has already pointed out the necessity of differentiating between a traditionalist modernism and Marinetti's brand of nationalism, which he terms "nazionalismo modernista" and which is characterized by the way in which "calls for colonial expansion and the myth of the power of Italy unite with a libertarian nationalism which insisted upon the struggle against German 'barbarism' in the

name of Latin 'civilization.'" Noting the mixture of revolutionary and democratic impulses in this position, Gentile further differentiates it from the modernistic nationalism of such as Corradini.

16. F. T. Marinetti, *Futurismo e fascismo* (Foligno: Campitelli, 1924), 74 (hereafter cited as *FF*). All references to Marinetti's work are from this or the following works: *Selected Writings* (*SW*), ed. R. W. Flint (New York: Farrar, Straus and Giroux, 1971); *Futurist Manifestos* (*FM*), ed. Umbro Apollonio (London: Thames and Hudson, 1973).

17. The debate surrounding the twin fates of cultural modernity and Italian Jewry under Mussolini is well documented in G. Battista Nazzaro's study *Futurismo e politica* (Naples: JN Editore, 1968). Essentially, eventual attacks on futurism coincided with the importation of German notions of racial and cultural purity around the time of the *Entartete Kunst* exhibition in the Third Reich. Marinetti was instrumental in keeping this exhibition out of Italy. His defense of a specifically Italian modernism was coupled with an attack on anti-Semitism as an essentially un-Italian import. The supporters of modernism in the debate—in which aspersions were even cast on the racial purity of the Egyptian-born Marinetti himself—gathered around Sommenzi's journal *Artecrazia*, and it is Nazzaro's belief that the subsequent suppression of the journal marked the death of the avant-garde in Italy.

18. The notion that futurism proposes a fundamental shift in the discursive organization of modernity is proposed most forcefully by Marjorie Perloff, *The Futurist Moment: Avant-Garde, Avant-Guerre, and the Language of Rupture* (Chicago: University of Chicago Press, 1968).

German Primitivism/Primitive Germany (pp. 56–66)

1. Hellmut Lehmann-Haupt, *Art under a Dictatorship* (New York: Oxford University Press, 1954), 79–81.

2. Theda Shapiro, *Painters and Politics: The European Avant-Garde and Society, 1900–1925* (New York, Oxford, Amersterdam: Elsevier, 1976), 265.

3. *Meyers Neues Lexikon* (Leipzig: VEB Bibliographisches Institut, 1974), 10:141–42.

4. Cf. Georg Lukács, *Essays on Realism*, ed. Rodney Livingstone (Cambridge, Mass.: MIT Press, 1980), 76–113.

5. Joseph Wulf, *Die bildenden Künste im Dritten Reich: Eine Dokumentation* (Gütersloh: Sigbert Mohn Verlag, 1963), 50–51.

6. Emil Nolde, *Jahre der Kümpfe: 1902–1914*. 2nd ed. (Flensburg: Christian Wolff Verlag, 1958), 125–26.

7. Max Sauerlandt, *Die Kunst der letzten 30 Jahre: Eine Vorlesung aus dem Jahre 1933* (Hamburg: Hermann Laatzen Verlag, 1948), 72.

8. Nolde, *Welt und Heimat: Die Südseereise 1913–1918* (Cologne: Verlag M. DuMont-Schauberg, 1965), 58.

9. Renato Rosaldo, *Culture and Truth: The Remaking of Social Analysis* (Boston: Beacon Press, 1989), 68–87.

10. Cf. Jean Laude, *La peinture française (1905–1914) et "l'art negre": Contribution a l'étude des sources du fauvisme et du cubisme* (Paris: Editions Klincksieck, 1968), 402–526.

11. Carl Einstein, *Die Kunst des 20. Jahrhunderts* (1926), cited in Reinhard

Wegner, *Der Exotismus-Streit in Deutschland: Zur Auseinandersetzung mit primitiven Formen in der bildenden Kunst des 20. Jahrhunderts*, vol. 27 of European University Studies, series 28 (Frankfurt, Bern, New York: Peter Lang, 1973), 101.

12. Paul de Man, *Wartime Journalism: 1939–1943*, ed. Werner Hamacher, Neil Hertz, and Thomas Keenan (Lincoln and London: University of Nebraska Press, 1988), 216—17.

Gottfried Benn (pp. 67–80)

1. Saul Friedländer, *Reflections of Nazism: An Essay on Kitsch and Death* (New York: Harper & Row, 1984).

2. See Susan Sontag's important article on Riefenstahl in *Under the Sign of Saturn* (New York: Farrar Straus Giroux, 1980), 73–105.

3. This exhibition has been reconstructed as completely as possible (many of the art works were either destroyed or auctioned off or "lost") and shown in Los Angeles and Chicago during 1991. The catalog is excellent (there are several references to Benn): *"Degenerate Art": The Fate of the Avant-Garde in Nazi Germany*, ed. Stephanie Barron (Los Angeles: Los Angeles County Museum of Art, 1991).

4. All in-text references to Gottfried Benn quotations refer by volume and page number to the following standard edition: Gottfried Benn, *Gesammelte Werke in vier Bänden herausgegeben von Dieter Wellershoff* (Wiesbaden: Limes Verlag, 1962): (I) Essays, Reden, Vorträge; (II) Gedichte; (III) Prosa und Szenen; (IV) Autobiographische Schriften. Translations, whenever available, will be marked in text as *PEP*: Gottfried Benn, *Prose, Essays, Poems*, ed. Volkmar Sander (New York: Continuum, 1987). All other translations are the author's.

5. Other essays on this topic are in vol. I: "Züchtung" I and II and "Zucht und Zukunft."

6. Where *was* Benn in 1933 and 1934? The streets were full of uniformed hoodlums in jackboots; parades and flags were ubiquitous; the radio kept blaring out tirades by Hitler and his cohort, inundating Germany with vulgarity, violence, and hatred—the voice of lower-middle-class *ressentiment* resounding through the land. Those were the days of the Reichstag fire and the resulting political witch hunts, the Röhm assassination and bloodbath. Did Benn not look? Not listen? Did he not care to look and listen? Or did he simply not care?

7.   Leben—niederer Wahn!
            Traum für Knaben und Knechte,
            doch du von altem Geschlechte,
            Rasse am Ende der Bahn,

            was erwartest du hier?
            immer noch eine Berauschung,
            eine Stundenvertauschung
            von Welt und dir?

            Suchst du noch Frau und Mann?
            ward dir nicht alles bereitet,
            Glauben und wie es entgleitet
            und die Zerstörung dann?

Form nur ist Glaube und Tat,
die erst von Händen berührten,
doch dann den Händen entführten
Statuen bergen die Saat. (II, 134)

8. Klaus Mann, *Mephisto*, trans. Robin Smyth (New York: Penguin Books, 1983), 202, 203.

9. Unfair but perhaps not totally unexpected. The nadir of Benn's inebriation with nazism is surely his speech of 29 March 1934, in honor of Marinetti, in which he speaks of "the new Reich, to which *the Führer, whom all of us without exception admire*, has also given the writers a mission to lend a collaborating hand" (I, 478; italics mine).

10. For Benn's self-distancing from anti-Semitism, see particularly IV, 71–72.

11. Edgar Lohner, ed., *Dichter über ihre Dichtungen: Gottfried Benn* (Wiesbaden: Heimeran/Limes Verlag, 1969), 69. Translation by the author.

12. See also "Nach dem Nihilismus," IV, 151–61 (originally titled "Der Nihilismus und seine Überwindung").

13. The reference is to Nietzsche, quoted later (p. 477): "Jenseits des Eises, des Nordens, des Todes *unser* Leben, *unser* Glück" (Beyond the ice, the North, and death *our* life, *our* bliss).

14.   Künstlermoral
Nur in Worten darfst du dich zeigen,
die klar in Formen stehen
sein Menschliches muß verschweigen,
wer so mit Qualen versehn.

Du mußt dich selber verzehren—
gib acht, daß es niemand sieht,
und laß es keinen beschweren,
was dir so dunkel geschieht.

Du trägst deine eigenen Sünden,
du trägst dein eigenes Blut,
du darfst nur dir selber verkünden,
auf wem dein Sterbliches ruht. (II, 449)

15. Michael Hamburger, *Reason and Energy* (New York: Grove Press, 1957), 312.

16.   IV
Es ist ein Garten, den ich manchmal sehe
östlich der Oder, wo die Ebenen weit,
ein Graben, eine Brücke, und ich stehe
an Fliederbüschen, blau und rauschbereit.

Es ist ein Knabe, dem ich manchmal traure,
der sich am See in Schilf und Wogen ließ,
noch strömte nicht der Fluß, vor dem ich schauere,
der erst wie Glück und dann Vergessen hieß.

Es ist ein Spruch, dem oftmals ich gesonnen,
der alles sagt, da er dir nichts verheißt—
ich habe ihn auch in dies Buch versponnen,
er stand auf einem Grab: "tu sais"—du weißt.

V
Die vielen Dinge, die du tief versiegelt
durch deine Tage trägst in dir allein,
die du auch im Gespräche nie entriegelt,
in keinen Brief und Blick sie liessest ein,

die schweigenden, die guten und die bösen,
die so erlittenen, darin du gehst,
die kannst du erst in jener Sphäre lösen,
in der du stirbst und endend auferstehst. (II, 345)

17. Beda Allemann's essay "Statische Gedichte: Zu einem Gedicht von Gott-fried Benn" in *Interpretationen I: Deutsche Lyrik von Weckherlin bis Benn* (Frankfurt: Fischer Bücherei, 1965), 326–36, contains some valuable reflections on this theme in Benn's work.

Wyndham Lewis's Fascist Imagination and the Fiction of Paranoia (pp. 81–97)

1. In addition to other studies cited below, representative of the earlier, biographical-historical approach are Conor Cruise O'Brien's "Passion and Cunning: An Essay on the Politics of W. B. Yeats," in *In Excited Reverie: A Centenary Tribute to William Butler Yeats, 1865–1939*, ed. A. Norman Jeffares and K. G. W. Cross (London: Macmillan, 1965), 207–78; and Elizabeth Cullingford, *Yeats, Ireland and Fascism* (New York: New York University Press, 1981). Though these two studies disagree utterly in the conclusions they draw, they share common methodological presuppositions. See my review of Cullingford's book in *MLN* 97, no. 5 (1982): 1262–65.

2. Robert Casillo, *The Genealogy of Demons: Anti-Semitism, Fascism, and the Myths of Ezra Pound* (Evanston, Ill.: Northwestern University Press, 1988), viii. I should perhaps say that I don't find Casillo's attempt to discover a consistent ideology in Pound much more persuasive than Jameson's attempt to do the same with Lewis; see my review of Casillo in *American Literary History* 1 (Spring 1989):231–39.

3. Walter Benjamin, *Illuminations*, ed. Hannah Arendt, trans. Harry Zohn (New York: Harcourt, Brace & World, 1968), 243. It strikes me, however, that Benjamin's insight is even more disturbing and perceptive if reversed: perhaps the logical result of the introduction of aesthetics into politics is fascism.

4. One study that clearly exemplifies this ideal is Alice Yeager Kaplan's *Reproductions of Banality: Fascism, Literature and French Intellectual Life* (Minneapolis: University of Minnesota Press, 1986). I don't draw extensively on Kaplan's study here, however, because the aesthetic she is depicting in French fascism seems quite different from that of Anglo-American writers.

5. Jean-Paul Sartre, *What Is Literature and Other Essays* (Cambridge, Mass.: Harvard University Press, 1988), 68.

6. The most detailed study of the evolution and composition of the novel is Linda Sandler, "*The Revenge for Love* by Wyndham Lewis," unpublished thesis, University of Toronto, 1974. I have just completed a critical edition of *The Revenge for Love* (Santa Rosa, Calif.: Black Sparrow Press, 1991).

7. The editions of *The Revenge for Love* I am referring to are London: Pen-

guin, 1972, and South Bend, Ind.: Gateway Editions, 1978. Sandler cites numerous reviews of the novel (pp. 25–29) that refer to it as a civil war novel. Scholarly studies that discuss *The Revenge for Love* in the context of the Spanish civil war include Stanley Weintraub, *The Last Great Cause: The Intellectuals and the Spanish Civil War* (New York: Weybright and Talley, 1968), 175–78; Katharine Bail Hoskins, *Today the Struggle: Literature and Politics in England during the Spanish Civil War* (Austin: University of Texas Press, 1969), 167–77; and, most recently, Frank Kermode, *History and Value* (Oxford: Clarendon, 1988), 59–62. Hoskins's is the only one of these studies to recognize the prewar setting of the novel.

8. In his *Letter to Lord Byron*, quoted in Kermode, *History and Value*, 59.

9. Fredric Jameson, *Fables of Aggression: Wyndham Lewis, the Modernist as Fascist* (Berkeley: University of California Press, 1979), 180 (hereafter cited as *Fables*).

10. Wyndham Lewis, *The Art of Being Ruled*, ed. Reed Way Dasenbrock (Santa Rosa, Calif.: Black Sparrow Press, 1989), 320.

11. See John Harrison, *The Reactionaries: Yeats, Lewis, Pound, Eliot, Lawrence: A Study of the Anti-Democratic Intelligentsia* (New York: Schocken, 1967), 77–111, esp. 101–105; and Jeffrey Meyers, *The Enemy: A Biography of Wyndham Lewis* (Boston: Routledge & Kegan Paul, 1980), 132–35.

12. Another problem in Jameson's specification of anticommunism as the organizing center of Lewis's thought is to be found here, as Lewis's critique of ideology is, in fact, anticipatory in important respects of recent forms of Marxist thought—in this respect, of Althusser. This is, however, a resemblance with a difference: for Althusser, ideology produces false consciousness, but somehow Marxism (because it is scientific) escapes this and isn't a producer of the false consciousness produced by ideology. This means that, for Althusser, it is everyone else's consciousness that is false, and Lewis would have seen through this immediately.

13. For Derrida's defense of de Man, see his essay "Like the Sound of the Sea Deep within a Shell: Paul de Man's War," trans. Peggy Kamuf, *Critical Inquiry* 14 (1988): 590–652 reprinted in *Responses: On Paul de Man's Wartime Journalism*, ed. Werner Hamacher, Neil Hertz, and Thomas Kenan (Lincoln: University of Nebraska Press, 1989), 127–64. My essay on Paul de Man, "Paul de Man, the Modernist as Fascist," included here as the final chapter, offers one critique of Derrida's approach.

14. See George Orwell, *Homage to Catalonia* (1938; reprint, Harmondsworth, UK: Penguin, 1973), 153–72, 234–38.

15. It should probably be pointed out that Lewis's later work moves beyond this stance toward an ethical and finally religious critique of the political world. The key work here is the trilogy Lewis left unfinished at his death, *The Human Age*, though even his works of the 1930s—including *The Revenge for Love*— adumbrate this critique. For a discussion of this evolution on Lewis's part, see my *The Literary Vorticism of Ezra Pound and Wyndham Lewis: Towards the Condition of Painting* (Baltimore: Johns Hopkins University Press, 1985), 182–90.

16. This is not to say that Céline's politics have always been faced as forthrightly as they should have been. See George Steiner's essay, "Cry Havoc," in *Extraterritorial: Papers on Literature and the Language Revolution* (New York: Atheneum, 1971), 35–46, one of the best considerations of the politics of modernism.

17. The comparison I draw here to Pynchon and Mailer builds on the discussion in Timothy Materer, *Wyndham Lewis the Novelist* (Detroit: Wayne State University Press, 1976), 16–17, 164–66.

18. Norman Mailer, *The Naked and the Dead* (1948; reprinted, New York: Signet, n.d.), 140.

19. Thomas Pynchon, *Gravity's Rainbow* (New York: Viking, 1973), 188.

20. Quoted in D. G. Bridson, *The Filibuster: A Study of the Political Ideas of Wyndham Lewis* (London: Cassell, 1972), 97.

21. Wyndham Lewis, *Men without Art*, ed. Seamus Cooney (Santa Rosa, Calif.: Black Sparrow, 1987), 216.

22. Zeev Sternhell, *Neither Right nor Left: Fascist Ideology in France*, trans. David Maisel (Berkeley: University of California Press, 1986).

Fascists of the Final Hour (pp. 98–127)

1. For the details in this paragraph, see Charles A. Delzell, *Mussolini's Enemies: The Italian Anti-Fascist Resistance* Princeton, N.J.: Princeton University Press, 1967), 262; C. David Heyman, *Ezra Pound: The Last Rower* (New York: Viking, 1976), 143, 326, 333, 336; Humphrey Carpenter, *A Serious Character: The Life of Ezra Pound* (Boston: Houghton Mifflin, 1988), 619, 626–35.

2. For details of composition and publication, see Barbara Eastman, "The Gap in *The Cantos*: 72 and 73," *Paideuma* 8 (Winter 1979): 426; Massimo Bacigalupo, "The Poet at War: Ezra Pound's Suppressed Italian *Cantos*," *South Atlantic Quarterly* 83 (Winter 1984):71n; and Mary de Rachewiltz's notes to her Italian translation of Pound's *Cantos*, titled *I Cantos* (Milan: Mondadori, 1985), 1567. All references and English translations of Cantos 72 and 73 are based on this text, which is now included in the 1987 New Directions edition of *The Cantos*. All other quotations from *The Cantos* refer to *The Cantos of Ezra Pound* (New York: New Directions, 1972). Quotations from Ezra Pound's work are cited in the text using the following abbreviations; when the title of the work is sufficiently located, no citation appears:

J/M: *Jefferson and/or Mussolini* (New York: Liveright, 1935).
L: *The Letters of Ezra Pound, 1907–1941*, ed. D. D. Paige (New York: Harcourt Brace, 1950).
LE: *Literary Essays*, ed. T. S. Eliot (London: Faber and Faber, 1954).
C: *Confucius* (New York: New Directions, 1958).
SR: *The Spirit of Romance* (New York: New Directions, 1958).
GK: *Guide to Kulchur* (New York: New Directions, 1970).
SP: *Selected Prose, 1908–1965*, ed. William Cookson (New York: New Directions, 1972.
RB: *"Ezra Pound Speaking": Radio Speeches of World War II*, ed. Leonard W. Doob (Westport, Conn.: Greenwood Press, 1978).
PC: *Pound's Cavalcanti*, ed. David Anderson (Princeton, N.J.: Princeton University Press, 1983).

3. Delzell, *Mussolini's Enemies*, 472, 488, 489.

4. Hugh Kenner, *The Pound Era* (Berkeley: University of California Press, 1971), 469n.

5. Although the Italian *Cantos* have been readily available since 1987, at no point does Wendy Flory allude to them in her recent attempt not merely to mini-

mize but finally to deny Pound's fascism and anti-Semitism; see Flory, *The American Ezra Pound* (New Haven, Conn.: Yale University Press, 1989). Tim Redman, in a book that claims to treat Pound's fascism thoroughly, devotes no more than a page and a half to the Italian *Cantos*, mistakenly dismissing them as an uninteresting "anticlimax"; see Redman, *Ezra Pound and Italian Fascism* (Cambridge: Cambridge University Press, 1991), 269–70. Portraying the Italian *Cantos* as "exceptional" in Pound's corpus, Peter d'Epiro supports Barbara Eastman's contention that only in Canto 73 does Pound condone and glorify violence. Massimo Bacigalupo rightly finds this argument untenable. See d'Epiro, *A Touch of Rhetoric: Ezra Pound's Malatesta Cantos* (Ann Arbor, Mich.: UMI Research Press, 1983), 107, 148n; Eastman, "The Gap in *The Cantos*," 424; Bacigalupo, "The Poet at War," 78.

6. Bacigalupo, "The Poet at War," 73, 74.

7. T. S. Eliot, *After Strange Gods: A Primer of Modern Heresy* (New York: Harcourt, Brace, 1934), 47.

8. On vorticism and futurism, see Reed Way Dasenbrock, *The Literary Vorticism of Wyndham Lewis and Ezra Pound: Toward the Condition of Painting* (Baltimore: Johns Hopkins University Press, 1985), 23; Niccolo Zapponi, "Ezra Pound and Futurism," in *Italian Images of Ezra Pound*, ed. Angela Jung and Guido Palandri (Taipei, Taiwan: Mei Ya Publications, 1979), 129, 130, 131, 133–34; Archie Henderson, "Pound's Strelets Interview (1915)," *Paideuma* 11 (Winter 1982):476–77; Timothy Materer, *Vortex: Pound, Eliot, Lewis* (Ithaca, N.Y.: Cornell University Press, 1979), 16, 16–17n.

9. Bacigalupo, "The Poet at War," 8.

10. Quoted in Herman Finer, *Mussolini's Italy* (1935; reprinted, New York: Grosset and Dunlap, 1965), 109.

11. For Marinetti's and fascism's emphasis on youth, see Marinetti, *Selected Writings*, trans. F. W. Flint (New York: Farrar, Straus, Giroux, 1972), 156, 153; Michael Ledeen, *International Fascism: The Theory and Practice of the Fascist International* (New York: Howard Fertig, 1972), xv, xvii, 6, 31, 34, 37, 40, 41, 162.

12. Pound, *"Ezra Pound Speaking,"* 16.

13. Delzell, *Mussolini's Enemies*, 265–66, 378–79.

14. Eastman, "The Gap in *The Cantos*," 426.

15. Finer, *Mussolini's Italy*, 397, 402.

16. Ezra Pound, *Pound/Lewis: The Letters of Ezra Pound and Wyndham Lewis*, ed. Timothy Materer (New York: New Directions, 1985), 181.

17. Marinetti, *Writings*, 155; Pound, *Jefferson and/or Mussolini*, 17, 33–34, 85.

18. Marinetti, *Writings*, 153.

19. Pound, *Jefferson and/or Mussolini*, vii; Marinetti, *Writings*, 159.

20. Henderson, "Pound's Strelets Interview," 477.

21. Marinetti, *Writings*, 42, 45; Richard Webster, *The Cross and the Fasces: Christian Democracy and Fascism in Italy* (Stanford, Calif.: Stanford University Press, 1960), 197n.

22. Zapponi, "Ezra Pound and Futurism," 99–102.

23. Marinetti, *Writings*, 6, 42, 45, 72–73, 75, 91.

24. Dasenbrock, *Literary Vorticism*, 44–47; Materer, *Vortex*, 203.

25. Marinetti, *Writings*, 41, 42, 46, 59.

26. Zapponi, "Ezra Pound and Futurism," 130, 137n.

27. Marinetti, *Writings*, 76–79; Pound, *Confucius*, 65.

28. Marinetti, *Writings*, 154.

29. Marinetti, *Writings*, 154.

30. Pound, *Confucius*, 20, 177, 179.

31. For Pound's identification of Confucius with the *directio voluntatis*, see *Selected Prose*, 84, 88; *Confucius*, 22; for Cavalcanti on the will, see James J. Wilhelm, *Dante and Pound: The Epic of Judgement* (Orono: University of Maine Press, 1974), 143.

32. See *Confucius*, 97, 103, 105, 109, 112, 117, 153; *Cantos*, 464 (Canto 77); 540 (Canto 84).

33. Pound, *Confucius*, 127; *Cantos*, 468 (Canto 77).

34. Zapponi, "Ezra Pound and Futurism," 138n.

35. Finer, *Mussolini's Italy*, 14.

36. Heyman, *Ezra Pound*, 98.

37. Ernst Kantorowicz, *Frederick the Second*, trans. E. O. Lorimer (New York: Frederick Ungar, 1957), 611–12; see also pp. 615–16.

38. Bacigalupo, "The Poet at War," 77.

39. Dante Alighieri, *On World Government, or De Monarchia*, trans. Herbert W. Schneider (New York: Liberal Arts Press, 1957), 1:11, 14; 3:14, 16; Joan Ferrante, *The Political Vision of the Divine Comedy* (Princeton, N.J.: Princeton University Press, 1984), 76.

40. Dante Alighieri, *The Divine Comedy*, trans. John Sinclair (New York: Oxford University Press, 1948): *Inferno*, 10:119; 23:66; Kantorowicz, *Frederick the Second*, 142, 445.

41. See Pound, *Selected Prose*, 173, 177, 179, 180, 181, 320; *Guide to Kulchur*, 221, 294; *Literary Essays*, 149–83; *Pound's Cavalcanti*, 8–9; Luigi Valli, *Il linguaggio segreto di Dante e dei "Fideli d'Amore"* (1929; reprinted, Genoa: Dioscuri, 1988), 25, 26, 39, 40, 45, 46, 80, 116, 117, 147, 153, 154, 161, 208–9, 217, 419, 422, 423. Pound's view of the "Ghibelline spirit" is close to that of Kantorowicz, *Frederick the Second*, 67. Cino da Pistoia, a colleague of Dante and Cavalcanti, supported the Ghibelline cause; see Karl Vossler, *Medieval Culture: An Introduction to Dante and His Times*, trans. William Cranston Lawton (New York: Frederick Ungar, 1966) 1:339; Ferrante, *Political Vision*, 37n, 103; Valli, *Linguaggio segreto*, 205.

42. Valli, *Linguaggio segreto*, 46.

43. Alfredo Rocco, "The Political Doctrine of Fascism," in *International Conciliation*, no. 233 (Oct. 1926) (Washington, D.C.: Carnegie Endowment for International Peace, 1926), 411.

44. Pound, *Jefferson and/or Mussolini*, 16.

45. Pound, *"Ezra Pound Speaking,"* 209; Pound, quoted in Heyman, *Ezra Pound*, 97.

46. For neo-Guelfism, see William J. Halperin, *The Separation of Church and State in Italian Thought from Cavour to Mussolini* (Chicago: University of Chicago Press, 1937), 3; D. A. Binchy, *Church and State in Fascist Italy* (London: Oxford University Press, 1970), 17; Webster, *The Cross*, 116, 144, 146, 148, 150.

47. Webster, *The Cross*, 162–64, 165n.

48. For Cunizza, see Pound, *Cantos*, 141 (Canto 29), 619 (Canto 92).

49. Ezzelino's "La Ciprigna bella" [the beautiful Venus, the "Cyprian"], quotes the second line ["la bella Ciprigna"] of *Paradiso*, 8, in which Dante ascends to the sphere of Venus, where, in the next canto, he meets Cunizza.

50. Pound, *Cantos*, 41 (Canto 9), 34 (Canto 9), 47 (Canto 10).

51. D'Epiro, *Touch of Rhetoric*, 104–95, 108, 112. The terms "factive" and "volitionist" derive from *Guide to Kulchur*, 194.
52. D'Epiro, *Touch of Rhetoric*, xx, 133n.
53. Binchy, *Church and State*, 104.
54. Ferrante, *Political Vision*, 22.
55. Pound, *Cantos*, 602 (Canto 89).
56. Dante, *De Monarchia*, 3:10; *Divine Comedy, Paradiso*, 6:1–2; 20: 55–60.
57. Dante, *Inferno*, 19:115–17.
58. Dante, *De Monarchia*, 3:10; Vossler, *Medieval Culture*, 290–292.
59. Pound, "Letters to Elizabeth Winslow," *Paideuma* 9 (Fall 1980), 346, 348.
60. Webster, *The Cross*, 29, 109.
61. Pound, *"Ezra Pound Speaking,"* 189.
62. Niccolo Machiavelli, *The Chief Works and Others*, vol. 1, trans. Allan Gilbert (Durham, N.C.: Duke University Press, 1965), 228–29, 28–34, 93.
63. Jacob Burckhardt, *The Civilization of the Renaissance in Italy*, trans. S. G. C. Middlemore (Vienna: Phaidon, 1937), 61, 63.
64. Harry Fornari, *Mussolini's Gadfly: Roberto Farinacci* (Nashville, Tenn.: Vanderbilt University Press, 1971), xi, 3, 150–51.
65. Ibid., 94, 106, 112–13, 130, 132, 135, 161.
66. This paragraph is based on Fornari, *Mussolini's Gadfly*, 166–67, 169, 176, 181, 182, 185, 187, 193, 198; Binchy, *Church and State*, 607, 609–10, 613, 618; Webster, *The Cross*, 103, 164.
67. Pound, *Jefferson and/or Mussolini*, 53–54.
68. Pound, "Letters to Elizabeth Winslow," 347.
69. Fornari, *Mussolini's Gadfly*, 115, 146, 148.
70. Pound, *"Ezra Pound Speaking,"* 114, 115, 290, 296; *Selected Prose*, 341–42; Heyman, *Ezra Pound*, 326, 332.
71. See Halperin, *The Separation*, 86, 93, 100; Binchy, *Church and State*, 112, 345, 320, 322, 330, 694, 697; Webster, *The Cross*, 36–37; Pollard, *The Vatican and Italian Fascism, 1929–1932: A Study in Conflict* (Cambridge: Cambridge University Press, 1985), 192–93.
72. Binchy, *Church and State*, 108, 197, 205, 695; Pollard, *The Vatican*, 193.
73. Binchy, *Church and State*, 118, 684; Webster, *The Cross*, 111; Pollard, *The Vatican*, 193.
74. Pound, *Guide to Kulchur*, 38, 79; *Selected Prose*, 65, 90, 131–32.
75. Finer, *Mussolini's Italy*, 408.
76. Romano Bilenchi, "Rapallo, 1941," *Paideuma* 3 (Winter 1979):435.
77. See Pound, *Literary Essays*, 149, 158; *Guide to Kulchur*, 157; *Pound's Cavalcanti*, 7, 14.
78. Pound, *Pound's Cavalcanti*, 16.
79. Noted in Ferrante, *Political Vision*, 57.
80. Pound, *Literary Essays*, 149–200.
81. Pound, *Cantos*, 178 (Canto 36); Pound, *Literary Essays*, 159.
82. See Henderson, "Ezra Pound: Composer," *Paideuma* 9 (Fall and Winter 1980):499–509, esp. 502.
83. Pound, *Cantos*, 195 (Canto 39).
84. Pound, *Pound's Cavalcanti*, 12.
85. Pound, *Cantos*, 430, 431, 432 (Canto 74); 465 (Canto 77).

Notes   ■   263

86. Materer, *Vortex*, 198; Pound, *Cantos*, 449 (Canto 74); Pound, *Guide to Kulchur*, 152.

Fascist Models and Literary Subversion (pp. 128–42)

1. Considering the scope and duration of the Franco censorship, the list of relevant publications is very short. The most important publications by Spanish writers on the subject would include the following:

Manuel L. Abellán, *Censura y creación literaria en España (1939–1976)* (Barcelona: Ediciones Península, 1980). This is the first study based on archival documentation and official data.

Gabriel Arias-Salgado, *Textos de doctrina y política de la Información* (Madrid: Ministerio de Información, 1956), *Política española de la Información. Vol. 1: Textos* (Madrid: Ministerio de Información, 1957), and *Política Española de la Información. Vol. 2: Antología sistemática* (Madrid: Ministerio de Información, 1958). Although relatively early in dates of publication, these works by a former Spanish minister of information (whose purview included the officially nonexistent censorship) continue to be of prime importance.

Gonzalo Dueñas, *La ley de prensa de Manuel Fraga* (Paris: Ediciones Ruedo Ibérico, 1969), Manuel Fernández Areal, *La libertad de prensa en España (1938–1971)* (Madrid: Edicusa, 1971), and Cesar Molinero, *La intervención del estado en la prensa* (Barcelona: Dopesa, 1971) all appeared after approval of the 1966 law governing the press and publication, which legalized the censorship (i.e., established it as an acknowledged, official entity) and for the first time gave writers certain guidelines and suggestions as to what was and was not permissible. Even so, however, more than halfway through the eight-hundred-plus pages of the law's text was the escape valve: "except when in the national interest." Any work could still be banned by declaring it in the national interest not to publish it. Some lessening of repression did occur, at least on an individual and case-by-case basis; however, these three writers did not have access to the censorial archives, and their works are more ideological than factual in inspiration.

More specifically related to the effect of censorship on literature and literary matters is José M. Martínez Cachero, *La novela española entre 1939 y 1969* (Madrid: Castalia, 1973), of which two subsequent amplified editions have been printed, the second in 1986. Included are fascinating extracts of communications between the censors and writers.

Most recently, *Diálogos Hispánicos de Amsterdam*, No. 5 (Amsterdam: Rodopi, 1987), subtitled "Censura y literaturas peninsulares," reproduces a series of studies presented at a colloquium at the University of Amsterdam in 1985, all of them dealing in some way with fascist censorship of literature in the Peninsula (one concerns Portuguese literature). There are studies focused especially on the early years and the final years of book censorship, as well as several that concentrate on effects of the censorship on literature written in the vernacular languages (Catalan, Gallego, Basque, etc.).

2. The means for circumventing the censors adopted by the various writers may well be as varied as the writers themselves, and in this area, like that of the censorship per se, much remains to be investigated and understood. However, a few prior studies exist that explore and analyze a number of rhetorical techniques of dissent: Janet Pérez, "Functions of the Rhetoric of Silence in Contemporary

Spanish Literature," *South Central Review* 1, no. 1 (1984):108–30; "Techniques in the Rhetoric of Literary Dissent," *Selected Proceedings, 3rd Louisiana Conference on Hispanic Languages and Literatures* (Baton Rouge: Louisiana State University Press, 1984), 216–30; "The Game of the Possible: Francoist Censorship and Techniques of Dissent," *The Review of Contemporary Fiction* 4 (Fall 1984), 22–30; "La función desmitificadora de los mitos en la obra literaria de Gonzalo Torrente Ballester," *Actas del VIII Congreso de la Asociación Internacional de Hispanistas* (Providence: Brown University, 1986), 417–26; "Inversion, Evasion and Negation of the 'Madonna' Stereotype in Post-War Spanish Fiction," *Discurso literario* 4 (1986):185–200; "Silencios, alusiones, infantilismo: Dolores Medio y la retórica precavida de los cincuenta," *Letras femeninas* 14 (1988):1–2.

3. All citations from Rafael García Serrano, *La fiel infantería*, are from the second edition (Madrid: Eskúa, 1958). Translations are my own.

4. A detailed study of Torrente's treatment of mythic figures and materials may be found in Frieda H. Blackwell, "Demythification in Representative Novels of Gonzalo Torrente Ballester," Ph.D. diss. Vanderbilt University, 1981. Blackwell studies six of Torrente's novels (omitting *Javier Mariño*, which might well have been included but which utilizes a very different sort of myth). No stories or plays are mentioned, although Torrente used similar procedures in these genres as well.

5. Barthes indicates in his prologue to the 1957 edition that the series of essays in *Mythologies* was written over the period 1954 to 1956; Torrente states in the prologue to *Ifigenia y otros cuentos* (Barcelona: Destino, 1987) that the short story "Gerineldo" (initially published in 1944) was his "first attempt at demythification, not too clear yet, but real" (p. 8).

6. "Gerineldo" was originally published in a long-forgotten periodical of the 1940s, and for many years Torrente himself believed the story to be lost. I quote from the second edition of this tale, included in Torrente, *Ifigenia y otros cuentos*, pp. 155–73.

7. The novelist's working diaries from those years, portions of which are reprinted in the second volume of the paperback edition (Barcelona, 1982) of Torrente's theater, reveal that his original plan was to entitle this novel *Paris. Magdalena* (*Teatro*, 2:287).

8. I refer to the original edition of *El golpe de estado de Guadalupe Limón* (Madrid: Ediciones Nueva Epoca, 1946).

9. Torrente originally intended *Ifigenia* (Madrid: Afrodisio Aguado, 1949) to be the first in a series of "humorous tales for erudite readers." When it was ignored by critics and public alike, he renounced the rest of the project and withheld the second, an updating of "Sleeping Beauty," for more than three decades.

10. *La princesa durmiente va a la escuela* was eventually published by the Barcelona firm of Plaza y Janés in 1983. Torrente indicates that this is an unretouched version of his text from the early 1950s.

Henry de Montherlant (pp. 143–63)

1. Although Montherlant's reputation in France is not comparable to that of, for example, a Proust or a Sartre, his works continue to be published in the most prestigious series (there are four *Bibliothèque de la Pléiade* volumes of Monther-

lant's works), and the appearance of his *inédits* always stirs a good deal of critical interest.

2. In 1985, Terence Kilmartin's translation of the quartet of novels *Les jeunes filles* was reissued in paperback by Carroll and Graf. The cover blurb emphasized that the work was an international *succès de scandale* in the late 1930s when it was originally published.

3. De Man's review of *Le solstice de juin* is reproduced in de Man's *Wartime Journalism 1939–43*, ed. Werner Hamacher, Neil Hertz, and Thomas Keenan (Lincoln: University of Nebraska Press, 1988), 162–63.

4. For Derrida's comments on de Man's review of *Le solstice*, see "Like the Sound of the Sea Deep within a Shell" in *Responses: On Paul de Man's Wartime Journalism*, ed. Werner Hamacher, Neil Hertz, and Thomas Keenan (Lincoln: University of Nebraska Press, 1989), 137. For Hillis Miller's remarks, see "An Open Letter to Professor Jon Weiner" in *Responses*, 336, as well as his earlier remarks in the *Times Literary Supplement*, 17–23 June 1988.

5. See de Man's comments on Montherlant and *Le solstice* in the articles "Récits de guerre," dated 23 December 1941 (*Wartime Journalism*, 175) and "La littérature française devant les événements" dated 20 January 1942 (*Wartime Journalism*, 187).

6. Jeffrey Mehlman, *Legacies of Anti-Semitism in France* (Minneapolis: University of Minnesota Press, 1983), 15.

7. In subsequent references to works by Montherlant, the following abbreviations will be used.

M: "Mémoire," in *L'Equinoxe de septembre* suivi de *Le Solstice de juin* (Paris: Gallimard, 1976), 272–311.

E: *Essais* (Paris: Gallimard, Ed. de la Pléiade, 1963).

R *Romans et oeuvres de fiction non théâtrales* (Paris: Gallimard, Ed. de la Pléiade, 1959).

T: *Théâtre* (Paris: Gallimard, Ed. de la Pléiade, 1972).

8. See Montherlant's open letter to French youth, "Jeunesse 1938," dated 18 March 1938.

9. *Henry de Montherlant–Roger Peyrefitte Correspondance*, ed. Roger Peyrefitte and Pierre Sipriot (Paris: Laffont, 1983), 152.

10. The text in *Les lettres françaises* reads: "When Montherlant declines an invitation to Weimar after having solicited it, it is because of the announcement of the first Russian successes. Coward steeped in cowardice." All passages quoted from *Les lettres françaises* are quoted in Merrill A. Rosenberg, "Montherlant and the Critics of the French Resistance," *French Review* 44 (1971):839–51.

11. For the bombing of the Rive Gauche bookstore, see Herbert Lottman, *The Left Bank: Writers, Artists and Politics from the Popular Front to the Cold War* (Boston: Houghton Mifflin, 1982), 200; and Pascal Ory, *Les collaborateurs 1940–45* (Paris: Seuil, 1976), 231.

12. The tribute is contained in the *Essais* (1483–89) although it is not identified as having originally appeared in the *Deutschland Frankreich*.

13. See Pierre Assouline, *L'épuration des intellectuels* (Brussells: Editions Complexe, 1985), 39.

14. Louis-Ferdinand Céline, *Lettres à son avocat* (Paris: La Flute de Pan, 1984), 39.

15. For a brief discussion of *La Gerbe* and its founder, see David Pryce-Jones,

Paris in the Third Reich: A History of the German Occupation, 1940–1944 (New York: Holt, Rinehart and Winston, 1981), 51–52.

16. Robert O. Paxton, *Vichy France, Old Guard and New Order 1940–44* (New York: Columbia University Press, 1972), 256.

17. This article appeared on 17 April 1941.

18. Theweleit's massive two-volume study provides a great deal of evidence in support of the notion that hatred and fear of women are central to the fascist mindset and are, in fact, the source of its violent impulses. For an excellent summary of Theweleit's project and the relation of his theory of fascism to other such theories, see Jessica Benjamin and Anson Rabinach's "Foreword," in *Male Fantasies, Vol. 2: Male Bodies: Psychoanalyzing the White Terror* (Minneapolis: University of Minnesota Press 1989):ix–xxv.

19. This is the assessment of Richard Cobb, who lumps Montherlant together with the likes of Brasillach and Drieu la Rochelle in his book *French and Germans: Germans and French: A Personal Interpretation of France under Two Occupations* (Hanover, N.H.: University Press of New England, 1983), 161. As I shall argue here, Montherlant's case is more ambiguous than Cobb acknowledges.

20. Simone de Beauvoir, "Montherlant ou le pain du degoût," in *Les critiques de notre temps et Montherlant,* ed. André Blanc (Paris: Garnier, 1973), 57. All subsequent references to Beauvoir in the text are to this essay.

21. For Kaplan's discussion of the "fascist fantasy narrative" and *Mafarka* in particular, see her *Reproductions of Banality: Fascism, Literature and French Intellectual Life* (Minneapolis: University of Minnesota Press, 1986), 76–87.

22. For a discussion of Jünger's conversion to nationalism on the fields of battle of World War I, see Robert Wohl, *The Generation of 1914* (Cambridge, Mass.: Harvard University Press, 1986), 76–87.

23. Michel Raimond, *Les romans de Montherlant* (Paris: CEDES, 1982), 129.

24. It is important to note that *La rose de sable* and the essay "La sympathie" are not the only examples in Montherlant's prewar oeuvre of charity leading to leftist sympathies. During the late 1920s, Montherlant wrote a novel entitled *Moustique ou l'hôpital* sympathetic to the interests of the working class. The novel, however, was not published during the writer's lifetime.

25. Henry Perruchot, *Montherlant* (Paris: Gallimard, 1969), 153.

26. Simone de Beauvoir describes Montherlant's ideal women as "completely stupid and completely subjugated" (p. 62).

27. Similar oversimplifications characterize the reading of the play by the Resistance critics of *Les lettres françaises.* They condemn the play as profascist because it celebrates the victory of "reason of state" over "sentiment" and "happiness" (Rosenberg, "Montherlant and the Critics," 846).

28. In 1944, Montherlant published *L'éventail de fer* (Paris: Grasset, 1944), in which he praises the "true hero" as the individual who "pretends to believe, but doesn't believe" (p. 15). This theme of "futile service" is not a new one in Montherlant's work (see the 1936 book, *Service inutile*), but by 1944 it had assumed a rather pathetic quality, since Montherlant is trying to cast as "heroic" his own continuing acquiescence to a political cause in which he no longer really believes. In *Faux pas* (Paris: Gallimard, 1943), Maurice Blanchot remarks on the same phenomenon in Montherlant, but he attributes it to the writer's "insolence": "He throws himself into the current to show that, carried along by it, and

not possessing the means to struggle against it, he remains free in this current that subjugates him" (p. 349).

29. For example, the most infamous of de Man's wartime essays, "Les Juifs dans la littérature contemporaine," was published on 4 March 1941, and his pieces praising Montherlant's politics were published in November 1941 and June 1943, as already noted.

30. For Montherlant's postwar nihilism, see especially his notebooks *Va jouer avec cette poussière* (Paris: Gallimard, 1966) and *La marée du soir* (Paris: Gallimard, 1972) as well as the novel *Le chaos et la nuit* (Paris: Gallimard, 1963).

Fascists on Film (pp. 164–78)

1. Robert Brasillach and Maurice Bardèche, *Histoire du cinéma*, 1935. This work has been reedited several times (in 1943, 1948, 1954, 1963, and 1964), but the original 1935 edition, with which I am concerned here, is reprinted in *Oeuvres complètes de Robert Brasillach*, vol. 10, ed. Maurice Bardèche (Paris: Au Club de l'Honnête Homme, 1964). Page numbers referring to this edition appear in parentheses in my text.

2. Iris Barry, trans. and ed., *The History of Motion Pictures* (New York: W. W. Norton and The Museum of Modern Art, 1938). The translations appearing in my text are taken from the Barry version where indicated. When no reference to Barry is given, the translations are my own. The Barry translation omits certain passages of the original, apparently in the interests of condensation. In certain cases, however, Barry seems to have omitted remarks American readers might find offensive. I have indicated these in my text.

3. Introduction to *Histoire du cinéma*, in *Oeuvres complètes*, 10:3.

4. Peter J. Bukalsi, ed., *Film Research* (Boston: G. K. Hall, 1972). Cited in Alice Yaeger Kaplan, *Reproductions of Banality: Fascism, Literature, and French Intellectual Life* (Minneapolis: University of Minnesota Press, 1986), 143.

5. William R. Tucker, *The Fascist Ego: A Political Biography of Robert Brasillach* (Berkeley: University of California Press, 1975).

6. "The Movies: Brasillach and Bardèche," in Kaplan, *Reproductions of Banality*, 142–60.

7. Kaplan, *Reproductions of Banality*, 146.

8. Ibid., 148.

9. Tucker, *The Fascist Ego*, 3.

10. *Notre avant-guerre*, in *Oeuvres complètes*, 6:278–79.

11. "Lettre à un soldat de la classe 60," in *Oeuvres complètes*, 5:599.

12. *Notre avant-guerre*, *Oeuvres complètes*, 6:241.

13. Tucker, *The Fascist Ego*, 104.

14. The account, originally published in *La revue universelle*, 1 Oct. 1937, appears in both *Notre avant-guerre* and *Les sept couleurs*.

15. See "The Work of Art in the Age of Mechanical Reproduction," in *Illuminations* (New York: Schocken Books, 1969), 217–53.

16. Bukalsi, cited in Kaplan, *Reproductions of Banality*, 143.

17. In postwar editions, divided into two volumes, the entire second volume is devoted to talking films.

18. Kaplan, *Reproductions of Banality*, 148.

19. Barry, *History of Motion Pictures*, 384.

20. Ibid., 384.
21. Georges Sadoul, *French Film* (London: Falcon Press, 1953), 57.
22. Roy Armes, *French Cinema* (New York: Oxford University Press, 1985), 77.
23. Kaplan, *Reproduction of Banality*, 144.
24. "Mémorandum écrit par Robert Brasillach pour la préparation de son procès," in *Oeuvres complètes*, 5:639.
25. *Notre avant-guerre* in *Oeuvres complètes*, 6:147–48.
26. This omission is corrected in later editions.
27. *Notre avant-guerre* in *Oeuvres complètes* VI, pp. 88–90.
28. Although in 1935, Brasillach and Bardèche are not excessive in their praise of the German film industry—they are quite sensitive to its tradition of anti-French propaganda—they express no criticism of the Hitlerian domination and, in fact, even appear to be justifying it by pointing how little change it represents in the already centralized and propagandistically oriented German cinema. They, in fact, give what must be considered favorable reviews of two overt examples of Nazi propaganda, as well as Leni Riefenstahl's *Triumph of the Will*.
29. In an interview with Alice Kaplan, Bardèche admits he took his material on the history of American cinema from a book by Benjamin P. Hampton, although he claims he himself was not anti-Semitic. He adds, "I didn't invent the fact that Zukor and all those guys were Jews. It came from Hampton's book. I found it very amusing, this idea of Jewish furriers going into film" (Kaplan, *Reproduction of Banality*, 180).
30. This analogy is somewhat strange because order does not seem to have been one of Méliès's chief characteristics. However, Brasillach and Bardèche renew this metaphor in their later reference to Méliès's development of a "primitive alphabet."
31. For example, see Gerald Mast, *A Short History of the Movies* (Indianapolis: Bobbs-Merrill, 1977), 29.
32. In *Notre avant-guerre* and other texts, Brasillach explicitly stated his distaste for bourgeois values. He defined his fascism as "first of all, an anticonformist spirit, antibourgeois" (6:279).
33. For a discussion of this phenomenon, see my book, *Fiction in the Historical Present: French Writers and the Thirties* (Hanover, N.H.: University Press of New England, 1987), 92.
34. Ibid., 111.
35. See, for example, his statement about *A nous la liberté* in Cela McGerr, *René Clair* (Boston: Twayne, 1980), 101.
36. Ibid., 77.
37. *Notre avant-guerre*, in *Oeuvres complètes*, 6:90.
38. Ibid., 180.
39. Cited in Green, *Fiction in the Historical Present*, 112.
40. *Notre avant-guerre*, in *Oeuvres complètes*, 6:278.

Style, Subversion, Modernity (pp. 179–97)

1. "Les idées, rien n'est plus vulgaire. Les encyclopédies sont pleines d'idées, il y en a quarante volumes, énormes, remplis d'idées. Très bonnes, d'ailleurs. Excellentes. Qui ont fait leur temps. Mais ça n'est pas la question. Ce n'est pas

mon domaine, les idées, les messages. Je ne suis pas un homme à message. Je ne suis pas un homme à idées. Je suis un homme à style." Jean-Pierre Dauphin and Henri Godard, eds., *Cahiers Céline 2: Céline et l'actualité littéraire, 1957–61,* "Exposé enregistré: 'L.-F. Céline vous parle'" (Paris: Gallimard, 1976) 87. Unless otherwise indicated, translations are my own.

2. See Philippe Alméras, *Les idées de Céline* (Paris: Bibliothèque de la Littérature Française Contemporaine, 1987), esp. 229–63.

3. "... l'émotion ne se laisse capter que dans le "parlé" ... et reproduire à travers l'écrit, qu'au prix de peines, de mille patiences, qu'un con comme vous soupçonne même pas! ... [...] Je vous expliquerai le truc plus tard! déjà maintenant retenez au moins que l'émotion est chichiteuse, fuyeuse, qu'elle est d'essence: évanescente!" Louis-Ferdinand Céline, *Entretiens avec le Professeur Y* (Paris: Gallimard, 1955), 35.

4. The pseudonym for a brother–sister team that co-authored a prolific body of popular novels in France in the first half of the twentieth century.

5. "[M]ais les Delly! regardez un peu les Delly! ... qui gagnent cent millions par an, sans publicité, ni critiques ... est-ce qu'ils recherchent "l'émotion à travers le langage parlé"? eux? balivernes! ... et ils vont jamais en prison! eux! ils se tiennent très convenablement!" Céline, *Entretiens avec le Professeur Y*, 23.

6. See esp. Jean-Paul Louis, ed., *Cahiers Céline #6: Lettres à Albert Paraz,* (Paris: Gallimard, 1980).

7. See Jacqueline Morand, *Les idées politiques de Céline* (Paris: Librairie Générale de Droit et de Jurisprudence, 1972), and Eric Séebold, *Essai de situation des pamphlets de Louis-Ferdinand Céline,* (Tusson: du Lérot, 1985).

8. Julia Kristeva, *Powers of Horror: An Essay on Abjection,* trans. L. S. Roudiez (New York: Columbia University Press, 1982), 174.

9. Alice Y. Kaplan, *Reproductions of Banality: Fascism, Literature and French Intellectual Life* (Minneapolis: University of Minnesota Press, 1986), 107–40.

10. François Richard, *Les anarchistes de droite dans la littérature contemporaine* (Paris: Presse Universitaire de France, 1988). See also Pascal Ory's discussion of Céline's anarchism in *L'anarchisme de droite* (Paris: Bernard Grasset, 1985).

11. See Stanley Payne's discussion of the "fascist negations" (antiliberalism, anticommunism, and anticonservatism) in *Fascism: Comparison and Definition* (Madison: University of Wisconsin Press, 1980), 7.

12. As Hanns E. Kaminski's dizzying inventory of the individuals, organizations, political and artistic movements Céline labels Jewish in *Bagatelles* clearly illustrates, the author scatters the identity to such an extent that the signifier *juif* is divested of much of its signifying potential. See Kaminsky, *Céline en chemise brune* (1938; reprint, Paris: Editions Plasma, 1977), 31–35.

13. See Philippe Muray, "Le siècle de Céline," *Infini* 8 (Fall 1984): 31–40.

14. In her April 1988 response to Jon Wiener's discussion of the controversy surrounding Paul de Man's wartime journalism, literary critic Cynthia Chase strongly objects to Wiener's assessment of Julia Kristeva's analysis of Céline's work in *Powers of Horror,* writing: "Her five chapters on Céline are a study of the pathology of *this major Fascist writer,* for whom, she speculates, 'style' is made to fully occupy the place left vacant by the disappearance of God, Prophet, and Faith" (emphasis added). See *The Nation* 9 Apr. 1988, p. 482. Chase's characterization of Céline as a "major Fascist writer" conforms to the understanding that many nonspecialists have of Céline and of his place in literary history,

whereas Céline scholars have generally given greater nuance to the author's political portrait.

15. Michael Marrus and Robert Paxton note, for instance, that until late 1938 Jacques Doriot of the profascist PPF (Parti Populaire Français) was "relatively immune to anti-semitism," while Marcel Déat, another prominent authoritarian of the period, appears even to have taken steps to defend persecuted Jews. Similarly, Robert Soucy emphasizes French fascism's indifference to racialist concerns noting that both Pierre de Taittinger of the Jeunesse Patriote and Colonel de la Rocque of the Parti Social Français (formerly the Croix de Feu), two major political movements identified by contemporaries as fascist, welcomed Jews into their ranks. See Michael Marrus and Robert Paxton's *Vichy France and the Jews* (New York: Schocken Books, 1983), 45–54, and Robert Soucy's *French Fascism: The First Wave* (New Haven, Conn.: Yale University Press, 1986), 79–80.

16. See Jacqueline Morand, *Les idées politiques de Louis-Ferdinand Céline*. See also Patrick McCarthy "Céline during the Occupation," *The New Review* 14 (1975): 37–54, and "Occupation and Exile: 1940–1951," in *Critical Essays on Louis-Ferdinand Céline* (Boston: G. K. Hall, 1989), 204–26.

17. See Nicholas Hewitt's analysis of the relationship between Céline's anti-Semitism and Edouard Drumont's thought ("Anti-Semitism and the Ghost of Drumont") in *The Golden Age of Louis-Ferdinand Céline* (Leamington Spa, UK: Berg Publishers, 1987) and Philippe Alméras's treatment of the racialist foundations of Céline's political discourse in *Les Idées de Céline*, 119–228.

18. While a large percentage of immigrants to France in the late 1930s were Jews—again, many seeking refuge from fascist violence—the Jewish community was only a relatively small portion (15%) of total immigration to France between 1906 and 1939. See Paula Hyman, *From Dreyfus to Vichy: The Remaking of French Jewry, 1906–1939*, (New York, Columbia University Press, 1979), 68.

19. Paula Hyman notes that although French Jews were the first in Western Europe to secure full emancipation, the new civil status was predicated on the notion that total assimilation would eradicate all forms of cultural difference, making Jewish citizens of the nation entirely "indistinguishable from other Frenchmen." The many important civil liberties gained in the course of the French Revolution did not, she remarks, entitle Jews to retain an autonomous ethnic identity or to engage in forms of cultural expression distinct from that of established societal norms. See Hyman, *From Dreyfus to Vichy*, 1–62.

20. Hyman, *From Dreyfus to Vichy*, esp. 1–31.

21. The following excerpt from an April 1938 editorial by Robert Brasillach in *Je suis partout* both exhibits the antiforeign rather than racialist tenor of French fascist anti-Semitism and conveys a sense of the discord generated by the influx of displaced, stateless peoples in search of domicile in a nation rigorously ordered according to principles of cultural homogeneity: "What we want to say is that a giant step will have been taken toward justice and national security when the Jewish people are considered a foreign people. To consider Jews of foreign nationality as foreigners and oppose the most stringent obstacles to their naturalization-to consider all Jews established in France as a minority with special legal status that protects them at the same time that it protects us [. . .] These are the only ways to assure the absolute independence of French soil [. . .]." Cited in Marrus and Paxton, *Vichy France and the Jews*, 43–44.

22. See especially David H. Weinberg, *A Community on Trial: The Jews of Paris in the 1930s* (Chicago: University of Chicago Press, 1977), Marrus and

Paxton, "The Roots of Vichy Anti-Semitism," in *Vichy France and the Jews*, 25–71, and Hyman, *From Dreyfus to Vichy*, 63–152.

23. See Philippe Roussin, "Céline: Tirages d'un auteur à succès entre 1932 et 1944," in *Actes du Colloque International de Paris* (Tusson: du Lérot/Paris: Société des Etudes Céliniennes, 1987), 231–37. Roussin reports that at least 90,000 copies of *Bagatelles* were printed between 1937 and 1944, significantly outpacing prewar sales for his second novel *Mort à crédit*. Together, Céline's three anti-Semitic pamphlets (*Bagatelles pour un massacre, L'ecole des cadavres*, and *Les beaux draps*) sold nearly as well as his first novel *Voyage au bout de la nuit*, one of France's best-sellers between the two wars.

24. George Mosse, *Toward the Final Solution: A History of European Racism* (New York: Harper and Row, 1978), xi–xvi.

25. Enzo Traverso, "Auschwitz, l'histoire et les historiens," *Les temps modernes* 527 (June 1990): 3.

26. See Tzvetan Todorov's analysis of the distinction to be made between racism and racialism in *Nous et les autres: La réflexion française sur la diversité humaine* (Paris: Editions du Seuil, 1989), 123–28. For a more succinct treatment of this problematic in English translation, see Todorov's "'Race,' Writing, and Culture," trans. L. Mack, in *"Race," Writing and Difference*, ed. Henry Louis Gates, Jr. (Chicago: University of Chicago Press, 1985), 370–380.

27. Henry Louis Gates, Jr., "Writing "Race" and the Difference It Makes," in Henry Louis Gates, Jr., ed., *"Race," Writing and Difference*, 4.

28. See Mosse, *Toward the Final solution*, 128–49.

29. Reviewing *Batagelles pour un massacre* for the conservative right-wing newspaper *Action française* in January 1938, Brasillach wrote: "Certainly, he exaggerates. His portrait of literature is false, and very worthy of a man of letters, endowed with all the flaws of the species. [. . .] His Semitic obsession makes him see Jews everywhere. Critics? All Jews or jewified! Famous authors? All Jews! Cézanne? A Jew! Racine? Another Jew! The Pope, the Church, priests? Jews! The kings of France? 'Don't you find that they have a peculiar nose?'. It is quite evident that one would have difficulty discussing the Jewish question seriously with someone holding such opinions. [. . .] We are not in full agreement with him. Far from it." Cited in Séebold, *Essai de situation* 62–63.

30. See Jean-Pierre Dauphin and Pascal Fouché, eds., *Cahiers Céline 7: Céline et l'actualité, 1933–1961* (Paris: Gallimard, 1986).

31. Ibid., 137: "Raison de race doit surpasser raison d'Etat. Aucune explication à fournir. C'est bien simple. Racism fanatique total ou la mort! Et quelle mort! On nous attend! Que l'esprit mangouste nous anime, nous enfièvre!" The *Robert* dictionary defines the mongoose as a "small carnivorous mammal . . . used for the destruction of reptiles and snakes."

32. Ibid., 156:
Pendant que vous êtes aux Armées, il se passe de bien vilaines choses. Entre nous, en toute franchise, nous assistons en ce moment à un bien répugnant travail; le sabotage systématique du racisme en France par les antisémites eux-mêmes. Ils n'arrivent pas à s'entendre. Spectacle bien français. Combien sommes-nous d'antisémites en tout et pour tout, sur notre sol? Je ne parle pas des badauds. A peine une petite préfecture! . . . et, parmi ces émoustillés, combien de chefs? valables, armés, présentables? Une douzaine . . . En ce moment décisif, inspiré, mystique, à quelle tâche les voyons-nous passionnément s'a-donner? A se tirer dans les pattes!

33. For information concerning Céline's association with anti-Semitic extremists in the late 1930s, see Alice Y. Kaplan's *Relevé des sources et citations dans Bagatelles pour un massacre* (Tusson/Charente: du Lérot, 1987), 15–37. One of the more unsavory of these associates was Louis Darquier de Pellepoix, the racist crusader who succeeded Xavier Vallat in 1942 as Commissioner-General for Jewish Affairs and administratively orchestrated the deportion of French Jews to Poland from 1942 to early 1944.

34. Jean-Paul Aron, *Les modernes* (Paris: Gallimard, 1984), 94.

35. See Kaplan, *Reproductions of Banality*, 3–40, 142–60.

36. See François Gibault, *Céline: 1932–1944; délires et persécutions* (Paris: Mercure de France, 1985), 127–46.

37. Colin W. Nettelbeck, ed., *Cahiers Céline 5: Lettres à des amies* (Paris: Gallimard, 1979), 140: "Je suis revenu de Russie, quelle horreur! quel bluff ignoble! quelle salle stupide histoire! Comme tout cela est grotesque, théorique et criminel!"

38. Ibid., 238: "J'ai été à Leningrad pendant un mois. Tout cela est *abject, effroyable*, inconcevablement *infect*. Il faut voir pour croire. Une horreur. *Sale, pauvre-hideux*. Une prison de larves. Toute police, bureaucratie et infect chaos. Tout bluff et tyrannie."

39. Muray, "Le siècle de Céline," 31.

40. Jacques Donzelot defines the term *biopolitical* as "the proliferation of political technologies that invested the body, the health, modes of subsistence and lodging—the entire space of existence in European countries from the eighteenth century onward." See Donzelot, *The Policing of Families*, trans. Robert Hurley (New York: Pantheon, 1979), 7.

41. See Michel Foucault, *Surveiller et punir* (Paris: Gallimard, 1975).

42. Céline, *Mea culpa*, (1936; reprinted in *Cahier Céline 7*), p 36: "Tous les fords se ressemblent, Soviétique ou non!"

43. Céline, *Journey to the End of Night*, trans. Ralph Manheim (New York: New Directions, 1983), 194–95: "Les ouvriers penchés soucieux de faire tout le plaisir possible aux machines vous éoeurent, à leur passer les boulons au calibre et des boulons encore, au lieu d'en finir une fois pour toutes, avec cette odeur d'huile. . . . Il faut abolir la vie du dehors, en faire aussi d'elle de l'acier, quelque chose d'utile. On l'aimait pas assez tel qu'elle était, c'est pour ça. Faut en faire un objet donc, du solide, c'est la Règle. [. . .] Personne ne me parlait. On existait plus que par une sorte d'hésitation entre l'hébétude et le délire. Rien n'importait que la continuité fracassante des mille et mille instruments qui commandaient les hommes."

44. Céline, *Bagatelle pour un massacre* (Paris: Editions Denoël, 1937), 111: "La France matérialisée, rationalisée, parfaitement muflisée, parfaitement subjuguée, par la bassesse juive, alcoolisée jusqu'aux moelles, absolument stérilisée de tout lyrisme [. . .] est vouée à la destruction, au masscre enthousiaste par les Juifs." All further references to this text, abbreviated *BPM*, will be included in the text.

45. "Le Standard en toutes choses, c'est la panacée du Juif. Plus aucune révolte à redouter des individus pré-robotiques, que nous sommes, nos meubles, romans, films, voitures, langage, l'immense majorité des populations sont déjà standardisés. La civilisation moderne c'est la standardisation totale, âmes et corps sous le Juif."

46. . . . le Robot . . . [. . .] est lui l'aboutissement de tant d'efforts civilisateurs 'rationnels' . . . admirablement naturalistes et objectifs (toutefois Robot

frappé d'ivrognerie! seul trait humain du Robot à ce jour) . . . Depuis la Renaissance l'on tend à travailler de plus en plus passionnément pour l'avènement du Royaume des Sciences et du Robot social. Le plus dépouillé. . . . le plus objectif des langages c'est le parfait journalistique objectif langage Robot . . . Nous y sommes . . . Plus besoin d'avoir une âme en face des trous pour s'exprimer humainement . . . Que des volumes! [. . .] et de la publicité!. . . et n'importe quelle baliverne robotique triomphe! Nous y sommes. In his use of the word *trous* (holes), Céline is invoking a French slang term signifying orifices of the human body, in this context suggesting the actual physical presence of a human being.

47. Observez que tous les films français, anglais, américains, c'est-à-dire juifs, sont infiniment tendancieux, toujours, des plus bénins aux plus amoureux!. . . des plus historiques aux plus idéalistes . . . Il n'existent et ne se propagent que pour la plus grande gloire d'Israël . . . sous divers masques: démocratie, l'égalité des races, la haine des 'préjugés nationaux,' l'abolition des privilèges, la marche du progrès, etc. . . [. . .] leur but strict est d'abrutir le goye toujours davantage . . . de l'amener le plus tôt possible à renier toutes ses traditions, ses malheureux tabous, ses 'superstitions,' ses religions, à lui faire abjurer en somme tout son passé, sa race, son propre rythme au profit de l'idéal juif. De faire naître en lui, par le film, le goût irrésistible pour toutes les choses juives qui s'achètent, de la matière, du luxe, qu'il se fabrique ainsi lui-même, l'Aryen, les verges pour se battre et les chaînes pour s'enferrer, qu'il paye pour comble, chemin faisant, avec quel exorbitant 'surplus' tout l'appareil de son servage et de tout son abrutissement.

48. In *Les beaux draps*, Céline defines Labiche Communism as "du communisme petit bourgeois, avec le pavillon permis, héréditaire et bien de famille, insaisissable dans tous les cas, et le jardin de cinq cent mètres, et l'assurance contre tout. Tout le monde petit propriétaire" (petty bourgeois communism, with ownership and inheritance of a modest home allowed, and family estates, under no circumstances subject to confiscation and a five hundred meter garden, and insurance for everything. Everyone small proprietors). Céline, *Les beaux draps* (Paris: Editions Denoël, 1941), 137.

49. Hyman, *From Dreyfus to Vichy*, 15–16.

50. "L'Exposition 37 nous apporte à ce propos une magnifique démonstration, écrasante, de cette furie colonisatrice juive, de moins en moins soucieuse des ressentiments et des réactions des indigènes, plus avérée, plus clamoreuse chaque jour, à mesure que l'indigène, plus soumis, rampe plus gluant, plus lâche."

51. Céline, *Mea culpa*, 37: "La politique a pourri l'Homme encore plus profondément depuis ces trois derniers siècles que pendant toute la Préhistoire. Nous étions au Moyen Age plus près d'être unis qu'aujourd'hui . . . un esprit commun prenait forme. Le bobard était bien meilleur 'monté poésie,' plus intime. Il existe plus."

52. Ibid., 39: "Quand on mélange au hasard deux sangs, l'un pauvre, l'autre riche, on n'enrichit jamais le pauvre, on appauvrit toujours le riche. . ." The context in which Céline inserts this statement could easily lead one to conclude that he is actually ridiculing Communist pretentions of rationally perfecting human existence. In light of the very pronounced racist discourse in the three pamphlets that followed, however, this statement clearly has significance, conscious or un-

conscious, extending far beyond his mockery of Soviet communism and its revolutionary ideals.

53. See note 30.

54. See Kaplan, *Reproductions of Banality*, 25–35.

55. See Morand, *Les idées politiques* 136–44; Séebold, *Essai de situation* 34–40.

56. See Gibault, *Délires et persécutions* 254–55.

57. Kristeva, *Powers of Horror*, 4.

58. Ibid., 179.

59. Michel Foucault, "What Is an Author?" in *Textual Strategies: Perspectives in Post-Structural Criticism*, ed. Josué V. Harari (Ithaca, N.Y.: Cornell University Press, 1979), 158–59.

60. Céline was initially indicted in late 1945 on French charges of collaboration and high treason, Article 75 of the French criminal code, which carried the death penalty.

61. Céline, *Cahiers Céline 6: Lettres à Albert Paraz*, 202: "[D]ans cette démence se raccrocher à quoi? Bagatelles est sorti avant la guerre—expulsion voulait dire la *Palestine Rien de plus*—et aussi les empêcher de venir nous envahir de Pologne—Où est le crime? Je ne vois pas. Je vois surtout que mois je suis persécuté, volé, pillé, chassé de chez moi, de mon *lieu* de naissance—de mon gagne-pain. C'est tout. Je n'ai jamais demandé à ce qu'on les *traite* comme on me *traite*—jamais."

62. For an account of the circumstances surrounding Céline's imprisonment in Denmark, his extradition proceedings, and the trial that followed see François Gibault, *Céline: 1944–61; Cavalier de l'Apocalypse* (Paris: Mercure de France, 1981), 91–234.

If Looks Could Kill (pp. 198–211)

I would like to thank Professor Leah Hewitt and the Romance Languages Department of Amherst College for giving me the opportunity to present this material and for their helpful questions. I am also indebted to Dr. Stanley Rosenberg of the Dartmouth Medical School for several enlightening conversations.

1. Marguerite Duras, *The War: A Memoir*, trans. Barbara Bray (New York: Pantheon Books, 1986).

2. See Judith Miller, *One by One by One: Facing the Holocaust* (New York: Simon and Schuster, 1990), 112–57, for a vivid anecdotal account of the kinds of anxieties occasioned by the trial.

3. Herbert R. Lottman, *The People's Anger: Justice and Revenge in Post-Liberation France* (London: Hutchinson, 1986), 16 and passim.

4. Marguerite Duras, *L'Amant* (Paris: Editions de Minuit, 1984), and *La douleur* (Paris: P.O.L., 1985); Alain Robbe-Grillet, *Le Miroir qui revient* (Paris: Editions de Minuit, 1984) and *Angélique ou l'enchantement* (Paris: Editions de Minuit, 1987); Nathalie Sarraute, *Enfance* (Paris: Gallimard, 1983). All but Sarraute deal extensively with the period of the Occupation.

5. Robert Jay Lifton, *Death in Life: Survivors of Hiroshima* (New York: Basic Books, 1967), 48–51.

6. Louis Malle, *Au revoir les enfants*, trans. Anselm Hollo (New York: Grove Press, 1988), v. In the original screenplay, published in 1987 by Gallimard, the statement appears on the back cover. Further references will be to the translated edition, with pagination indicated in the text.

7. See Françoise Audé and Jean-Pierre Jeancolas, "Entretien avec Louis Malle sur "*Au revoir les enfants*," *Positif* 320 (October 1987): 32–39; "Ce matin de janvier 44; Malle parle de *Au revoir les enfants*," *Jeune cinéma* 183 (October–November 1987): 34–38; Jacques Gerstenkorn, "Malle pris aux mots," *Vertigo* 2 (April 1988): 121–35.

8. Jacques Mallecot, ed., *Louis Malle par Louis Malle* (Paris: Editions de l'A-thanor, 1979).

9. See, for example, Jean Delmas's review in *Jeune cinéma* 77 (March 1974): 33–35; "Lacombe Lucien et l'Occupation: Louis Malle s'explique; René Andrieu conteste," *Humanité dimanche* (3–7 Apr. 1974): 19–22; Michel Sineaux, "Le Hasard, le chagrin, la nécessité, la pitié (sur Lacombe Lucien)," *Positif* 157 (March 1974): 25–27; Pascal Bonitzer, "Histoire de sparadrap (Lacombe Lucien)," *Cahiers du cinéma* 250 (May 1974): 42–47. For a discussion of the debate itself from the perspective of the 1980s, see François Garçon, "La fin d'un mythe," *Vertigo* 2 (April 1988): 111–18.

10. Jean-Paul Sartre, *Le mur* (Paris: Gallimard, 1939); see also "Qu'est-ce qu'un collaborateur?" in *Situations III* (Paris: Gallimard, 1949), 43–61.

11. For evidence that the film's release in 1981 did indeed have the effect of a first shock, see Christian de la Mazière's description of the devastating effect of its belated release on his own life in "Nous, les français de la mauvaise chance: Le témoignage du volontaire de la division Charlemagne," *Paris match* (13 Nov. 1981); 128.

12. See, for example, "General de Gaulle's Speech to the French People, Broadcast from Algiers, April 4 1944," in *Two Speeches by General Charles de Gaulle, President of the French Committee of National Liberation* (New York: France Forever, 1944), French text, p. 30; English translation, p. 31:

A few traitors [*Quelques traitres*] were, are and will still be able to serve directly the enemy's interests. They are receiving or will receive the punishment they deserve. A few cowards and unreasoning persons [*Quelques lâches ou quelques aveugles*] associated voluntarily and willingly with the collaborating venture of these unworthy leaders: their weakness or blindness is being punished or will be punished. A few foolish men [*Quelques sots*] may try to play what is known as a 'parallel' game, which in fact ends up only in disunity; national determination will mete out justice to their absurd intrigues. But the great majority of Frenchmen, no matter what their opinions . . . are our unhappy brothers and must only be considered as fighting men gathered together to save the country which belongs to all of them.

13. André Bazin, *What Is Cinema?* trans. Hugh Gray (Berkeley: University of California Press, 1971), 148.

14. Sartre, *Réflexions sur la question juive* (Paris: Gallimard, 1946), 122, 131, 124–25, 173, and passim.

15. In addition, Malle may be alluding to the blindness of the Catholic church faced with the Holocaust.

16. Sigmund Freud, "From the History of an Infantile Neurosis (1918)," in *Three Case Histories* (New York: Collier Books, 1963), 187–316.

17. Geraldine Pederson-Krag, "Detective Stories and the Primal Scene," in *The Poetics of Murder, Detective Fiction and Literary Theory*, ed. Glenn W. Most and William W. Stowe (New York: Harcourt Brace Jovanovich, 1983), 13–20.

18. Geoffrey H. Hartman, "Literature High and Low: The Case of the Mys-

tery Story," in Most and Stowe, eds., *The Poetics of Murder*, 210–29.

19. Malle's preoccupation with racism is evident in the three films that immediately preceded *Au revoir les enfants: Alamo Bay* (1985), *God's Country* (1986), and *The Pursuit of Happiness* (1987).

20. Marie Balmary, *Psychoanalyzing Psychoanalysis: Freud and the Hidden Fault of the Father*, trans. Ned Lukacher (Baltimore: Johns Hopkins University Press, 1982); Ned Lukacher, *Primal Scenes: Literature, Philosophy, Psychoanalysis* (Ithaca, N.Y.: Cornell University Press, 1986).

21. Susan Sontag, "Fascinating Fascism," in *Under the Sign of Saturn* (New York: Farrar, Strauss & Giroux, 1980); Interview with Michel Foucault, *Cahiers du cinema* (July–August 1974): 251–52; Saul Friedländer, *Reflections of Nazism: An Essay on Kitsch and Death*, trans. Thomas Weyr (New York: Harper and Row, 1984).

22. Hayden White, *Metahistory: The Historical Imagination in Nineteenth Century Europe* (Baltimore: Johns Hopkins University Press, 1972).

Scandal and Aftereffect (pp. 212–28)

1. George Steiner, "Heidegger, Again," *Salmagundi*, no. 82–83 (1989): 36.

2. The set of mainstream objections to Heidegger are taken from Allan Megill, *Prophets of Extremity: Nietzsche, Heidegger, Foucault, Derrida* (Berkeley: University of California, 1985), 108–9; Gerald L. Bruns, *Heidegger's Estrangements: Language, Truth, and Poetry in the Later Writings* (New Haven, Conn.: Yale University Press, 1989), 2; and Anthony Gottlieb, "Heidegger for Fun and Profit," *New York Times Book Review*, 7 Jan. 1990, p. 22, respectively.

3. Christopher Fynsk, *Heidegger: Thought and Historicity* (Ithaca, N.Y.: Cornell University Press, 1986), 25.

4. Jürgen Habermas, "The Heidegger Controversy," *Critical Inquiry* 15 (1989): 443.

5. Pierre Bourdieu, *L'ontologie politique de Heidegger* (Paris: Minuit, 1988). The book is an expanded version of 1975 text published in *Actes de la recherche en sciences sociales*.

6. After André Malraux rejected Sartre's text at the Editions Gallimard, presumably for inclusion in the *Nouvelle revue française*, Paul Nizan helped to place it in *Bifur*, no. 8 (July 1931), where Sartre is identified as a "young philosopher . . . at work on a volume of destructive philosophy" (cited in John Gerassi, *Jean-Paul Sartre: Hated Conscience of His Century* [Chicago: University of Chicago Press, 1989], 1:97) See also Denis Hollier, "Plenty of Nothing: The Translation of Martin Heidegger's 'Wast ist Metaphysik?' Appears in the Final Issue of the Avant-Grade Journal *Bifur*," in Hollier, ed. *A New History of French Literature* (Cambridge, Mass.: Harvard University Press, 1989), 894–900.

7. Sartre was among the first in France to recognize the potential importance of Heidegger's extension of and departure from Husserlian phenomenology. But even before the *Bifur* translation appeared, Heidegger and Ernst Cassirer had participated in a 1929 meeting of French and German philosophers held at Davos, Switzerland. In February of the same year, Husserl came to the Sorbonne and gave the lectures on "Einleitung in die transzendentale Phänomenologie" (Introduction to Transcendental Phenomenology) that came to be known as *The Cartesian Meditations* and that Gabrielle Pfeiffer and Emmanuel Levinas soon translated into French (Paris: Armand Colin, 1931). Proceedings of the Davos talks have been published as Ernst Cassirer and Martin Heidegger, *Débat sur le*

kantisme et la philosophie, ed. Pierre Aubenque (Paris: Beauchesne, 1972). The "Letter on Humanism" first appears in a November 1945 response to a question by Jean Beaufret, who was Heidegger's strongest postwar advocate among the French. On the reception of German existentialism and phenomenology by the French, see the eye-witness accounts in Beaufret's *De l'existence à Heidegger* (Paris: Vrin, 1982) and Levinas's *En découvrant l'existence avec Husserl et Heidegger* (Paris: Vrin, 1967) as well as the more recent commentaries in Martin Jay's *Marxism and Totality: The Adventures of a Concept from Lukács to Habermas* (Berkeley: University of California Press, 1984) and Vincent Descombes's *Modern French Philosophy,* trans. L. Scott-Fox and J. M. Harding (New York: Cambridge University Press, 1980).

8. The Farías book, translated from Spanish and German by Myriam Benarroch and Jean-Baptiste Grasset, was first published in French (Paris: Verdier, 1987). A German edition appeared in 1988 with a foreword by Jürgen Habermas; an English translation was published in 1989 by Temple University Press. For an uneven but occasionally brilliant account of the 1955 Heidegger colloquium, see Jean-Paul Aron, "Auût 1955: Décade Heidegger à Cerisy," in *Les modernes* (Paris: Gallimard, 1984), 99–108.

9. Arnold I. Davidson, "Opening Debate," *Critical Inquiry* 15 (1989): 408.

10. Editorial preface to *Les temps modernes,* no. 4 (January 1946). Eric Weil refers to a Heidegger Affair in issue no. 22 (July 1947) of the same review.

11. In English, see, for example, the extensive references to secondary sources in German cited by Davidson, p. 408, n. 2. In English, see the concluding section of George Steiner's *Heidegger* (New York: Penguin, 1982) and Karsten Harries, "Heidegger as a Political Thinker," in *Heidegger and Modern Philosophy: Critical Essays* ed. Michael Murray (New Haven, Conn.: Yale University Press, 1978).

12. François Fédier, *Heidegger: Anatomie d'un scandale* (Paris: Robert Laffont, 1988), 30.

13. Herman Rapaport, "Literature and the Hermeneutics of Detection," *L'Esprit créateur,* 26, (Summer 1986): 48–59.

14. As Steiner remarks in a recent appraisal, "Owing to Farías's excavations, unscholarly and virulently selective as these often are, specific moments in Heidegger's abject treatment of endangered academic colleagues, in Heidegger's admiration for the Führer, and in Heidegger's cunning tactics of survival, can no longer be passed over" ("Heidegger, Again," *Salmagundi,* no. 82–83 [1989]: 45).

15. Sheehan's "Heidegger and the Nazis" and Paul Gottfried's "Heidegger on Trial," *Telos,* no. 78 (Spring 1988): 147–51, are convincing indictments of the tendentiousness with which Farías relies on existing sources and documentation. On the question of Heidegger's purported anti-Semitism, see also Fédier, esp. 211–28.

16. Rüdiger Bubner, *Modern German Philosophy,* trans. Eric Matthews (New York: Cambridge University Press, 1984), 6–7.

17. "Taking Heidegger Seriously," *New Republic,* 11 Apr. 1988, p. 32. Rorty's title echoes the following passage from a discussion of Heidegger's politics by Karsten Harries in which the notion of seriousness takes on a markedly different emphasis: "The more seriously we take Heidegger, the more weight we must give to the path he has cleared, the more carefully we must consider where he is leading us and by what authority" ("Heidegger's Politics," in *Heidegger and Modern Philosophy,* ed. Michael Murray [New Haven, Conn.: Yale University Press, 1978], 307).

18. Luc Ferry and Alain Renaut, *Heidegger and Modernity,* trans. Franklin

Philip (Chicago: University of Chicago Press, 1990), 53–54. I have changed some of Franklin Philip's phrasing.

19. Philippe Lacoue-Labarthe, *Heidegger, Art and Politics*, trans. Chris Turner (Cambridge: Blackwell, 1990), 15. There are two French versions of this text. Both are entitled *La fiction du politique: Heidegger, l'art et la nazisme*. The first appeared in February 1987 as a limited edition printed by the University of Strasbourg Press. A revised version (Paris: Christian Bourgois, 1988) included a postscript written after Lacoue-Labarthe read the Farías book while teaching at the University of California at Berkeley. References in the text will retain the French title; pages listed will be those of the translation by Chris Turner.

20. Hayden White, *The Content of the Form: Narrative Discourse and Historical Representation* (Baltimore: Johns Hopkins University Press, 1987), 4.

21. In the case of France, the most consistently stimulating discussions over the past decade are to be found in Zeev Sternhell, *La droite révolutionnaire*, rev. ed. (Paris: Seuil, 1984); *Neither Left nor Right: Fascist Ideology in France*, trans. David Maisel (Berkeley: University of California Press, 1986), and his chapter on the concept of fascism in Sternhell, Mario Sznajder, and Maia Asheri, *Naissance de l'idéologie fasciste* (Paris: Fayard, 1989). See also Robert J. Soucy, *French Fascism: The First Wave, 1924–1933* (New Haven, Conn.: Yale University Press, 1986); Alice Yaeger Kaplan, *Reproductions of Banality: Fascism, Literature, and French Intellectual Life* (Minneapolis: University of Minnesota Press, 1986); and Jeffrey Mehlman's *Legacies: Of Anti-Semitism in France* (Minneapolis: University of Minnesota Press, 1983).

Paul de Man (pp. 229–41)

1. This can be seen clearly enough in defenses of de Man such as Jacques Derrida, "Like the Sound of the Sea Deep within a Shell: Paul de Man's War," trans. Peggy Kamuf, *Critical Inquiry* 14 (1988): 590–652, reprinted in *Responses: On Paul de Man's Wartime Journalism*, ed. Werner Hamacher, Neil Hertz, & Thomas Keenan (Lincoln: University of Nebraska Press, 1989), 127–69; Christopher Norris, "Postscript: On de Man's Early Writings for 'Le Soir,'" in *Paul de Man: Deconstruction and the Critique of Aesthetic Ideology* (London: Methuen, 1989), 177–98; Jonathan Culler, "It's Time to Set the Record Straight about Paul de Man and His Wartime Articles for a Pro-Fascist Newspaper," *The Chronicle of Higher Education*, 13 July 1988, B1; as well as the various newspapers accounts that these apologists are responding to. It should be noted that Derrida, in his response to the comments on "Like the Sound of the Sea," denies vehemently that he is an apologist for de Man ("Biodegradables," trans. Peggy Kamuf [*Critical inquiry* 15 (1989): 840], despite his firm conclusion that de Man did not collaborate ("Sound," 638).

2. Norris provides a representative instance of the first claim:

All the same it must be said that the pieces in question—169 in all, contributed over a two-year period—are many of them wholly innocuous, apart from the fact of their having appeared alongside material of a much worse character.... Of those remaining, many are reviews of various cultural events—concert performances, chamber recitals, university seminars, poetry readings, and so forth—which occasionally touch on the question of national identity *vis-à-vis* the war and the current upheavals in European politics, but which cannot in all fairness be accused of exploiting those events for propaganda purposes. (Pp. 182–83)

Derrida alludes in a number of places to the probable influence of "the uncle" on de Man's actions ("Sound," 599, 604–6), as does Shoshana Felman in "Paul de Man's Silence" (*Critical Inquiry* 15 [1989]: 708–11) and, more briefly, Christopher Norris ("Postscript," 178). Norris, also, more usefully gives a brief account of Hendrik de Man's life and work (pp. 17–21).

3. Fredric Jameson, *Fables of Aggression: Wyndham Lewis, the Modernist as Fascist* (Berkeley: University of California Press, 1979).

4. All references to de Man's wartime writings are to Paul de Man, *Wartime Journalism, 1939–1943*, ed. Werner Hamacher, Neil Hertz, and Thomas Keenan (Lincoln: University of Nebraska Press, 1988), hereafter cited parenthetically by date and page number in this edition. (This article: January 1940, pp. 16–18). For the translations, I need to thank Richard J. Golsan.

5. Culler writes that de Man's articles "occasionally praise the energy of the German 'renewal' and the tradition of German culture, but not Hitler, not the Nazi party, not the German government or its policies. However dismaying their sentiments in the light of what later occurred, the articles are not pro-Nazi."

6. John Brenkman, in "Fascist Commitments," in *Responses*, ed. Werner Hamacher, Neil Hertz, and Thomas Keenan (Lincoln: University of Nebraska Press, 1989), describes the two articles on Pareti's lectures in a paragraph and makes the acute remark that de Man was "particularly attuned to the intellectual currents of Italian fascism" (p. 22) but doesn't develop these remarks.

7. Montale lost his job in 1938 for refusing to join the Fascist party; it is unlikely that de Man knew of this, equally unlikely that Donini did not.

8. See, for example, the "Symposium on Heidegger and Nazism," *Critical Inquiry* 15 (1989): 407–88, with pieces by Gadamer, Habermas, Derrida, Blanchot, Levinas, and others. The recent attention being paid to Heidegger's politics has been stimulated by Victor Farías's *Heidegger et le nazisme* (Paris: Verdier, 1987).

9. The literature on futurism is vast; for a good survey of the movement that does not slight its political interests, see Caroline Tisdall and Angelo Bozzolla, *Futurism* (New York: Oxford University Press, 1978).

Alice Yaeger Kaplan's *Reproductions of Banality: Fascism, Literature and French Intellectual Life* (Minneapolis: University of Minnesota Press, 1986), an illuminating study of French fascism that sheds light on the French context of de Man's fascism, discusses Marinetti's writings in the context of fascism.

10. Michael A. Ledeen, *The First Duce: D'Annunzio at Fiume* (Baltimore: Johns Hopkins University Press, 1977), vii. Ledeen's conclusion, however, is that D'Annunzio was not essentially fascist (p. 201), a conclusion rather at odds with the title of his study.

11. James Joll, *Antonio Gramsci* (New York: Viking, 1977), 129.

12. Denis Mack Smith, *Mussolini's Roman Empire* (New York: Viking, 1976), 12–14.

13. See particularly A. James Gregor, *Italian Fascism and Developmental Dictatorship* (Princeton, N.J.: Princeton University Press, 1979), and *Young Mussolini and the Intellectual Origins of Fascism* (Berkeley: University of California Press, 1979).

14. See Wyndham Lewis, *The Art of Being Ruled*, ed. Reed Way Dasenbrock (Santa Rosa, Calif.: Black Sparrow, 1989), 319–22 and passim; Peter Nicholls

has a good discussion of Pound's brief period of interest in Marxism in the 1920s in *Ezra Pound: Politics, Economics and Writing: A Study of* The Cantos (Atlantic Highlands, N.J.: Humanities, 1984), 47–59.

15. Walter Benjamin's famous phrase, "The logical result of Fascism is the introduction of aesthetics into political life" (*Iluminations*, trans. Harry Zohn [New York: Harcourt, Brace & World, 1968], 243), is, of course, the classic statement and critique of this view of aesthetics and politics. His conclusion: "All efforts to render politics aesthetic culminate in one thing: war."

16. The key sources I have drawn on concerning Hendrik de Man are Peter Dodge, *Beyond Marxism: The Faith and Works of Hendrik de Man* (The Hague: Martinus Nijhoof, 1966), a biography, and an anthology of de Man's writings compiled by Dodge, *A Documentary Study of Hendrik de Man: Socialist Critic of Marxism* (Princeton, N.J.: Princeton University Press, 1979), which has selections of a number of de Man's books and essays. Two of de Man's books were translated into English in the 1920s (see notes 17 and 18 below); his *The Remaking of a Mind: A Soldier's Thoughts on War and Reconstruction* (London: Allen & Unwin; New York: Scribner's, 1919) was written in English.

17. Henry de Man, *The Psychology of Socialism*, trans. Eden and Cedar Paul (London: Allen & Unwin, 1928).

18. The key work of de Man's in this regard is *Joy in Work*, trans. Eden and Cedar Paul (London: Allen & Unwin, 1929).

19. The key work here is *Massen und Führer* (Potsdam: Alfred Protte, 1932), translated into French under the title *Masses et chefs* (Brussels: l'Eglantine, 1937) but never translated into English.

20. A selection from the *Plan du travail* (1933) is available in Dodge's *Documentary Study*, 290–99. For some of Proudhon's ideas about credit, see "The Organization of Credit," in *Selected Writings of Pierre-Joseph Proudhon*, ed. Stewart Fraser, trans. Elizabeth Fraser (London: Macmillan, 1970), 71–80.

21. De Man's 1940 "Manifeste aux membres du Parti Ouvrier Belge," calling for collaboration with the Nazis, is translated in Dodge's *Documentary Study*, 326–28.

22. The date de Man stopped writing for the collaborationist newspapers has, like everything else, been subject to conflicting interpretations. According to Shoshana Felman,

> Thus 1942 marks a change in de Man's orientation, a change that, furthermore, *precedes* the turn of the fortunes of the war in the historical turning point that will take place only the following year, in February 1943, with the surrender of the German army in Stalingrad. Chronologically, this change of mind follows immediately, and thus seems to derive from, the tightening of Nazi censorship and the historical knowledge of the extermination of the Jews. (emphasis Felman's; p. 715)

Marjorie Perloff, noting the divergence between the dates when Hendrik and Paul ceased to collaborate, reads the dates rather differently: "[T]he question thus [is] not, 'Why did Paul leave in late 1942?' but on the contrary, 'why did he hang on for so long?' However we answer this question, it is hard to put the young de Man's actions in a favorable light. By late 1942, after the Battle of Stalingrad the tide was clearly turning against the Germans, and the victory of the Allies was in sight" (p. 772). Since the crucial question here is not when the Germans started losing the war but when it became apparent to de Man in Belgium that they were, I'm not sure a definitive answer will be forthcoming. But the evidence strikes me as supporting Perloff here, not Felman. Objectively, the Germans lost the war with the entry of the United States in December 1941, for it should have been clear to anyone (and was clear to many) that the combined populations of the United States, the Soviet Union, and the British Empire were going to defeat the vastly outnumbered Axis. But in any case, the tide of the war shifted fairly decisively in 1942, with the failure of the Germans to break through on the Russian front in 1942, the Battle of Midway in June, the British victory at El Alamein in October, the Anglo-American landings in North Africa in November, and finally the encirclement of the German army at Stalingrad in November and December. The surrender of the encircled German army in February 1943 highlighted by Felman was certainly not "the turning point of the war" as much as the last of a sequence of crucial Allied victories.

Moreover, Felman's and Perloff's assumption that 1942 was the crucial year for de Man can be challenged. De Man's writing and work for the *Bibliographie Dechenne* continued until March 1943, which is fully two-thirds of the way from the conquest to the liberation of Belgium, May 1940 to September 1944. It should also be noted that as late as September–October 1943 (by which time the Italians were out of the war and the Germans were in retreat in Italy and on the eastern front), Editions de la Toison d'Or published a book co-translated by de Man, A. E. Brinckmann's *Esprit des nations*, a book characterized by Derrida as "looked on more or less favorably by the Nazis" ("Sound," 616). This was the last of three books translated by de Man for Toison d'Or, and it was also reviewed by de Man in 1942 in *Het Vlaamsche Land* (29–30 Mar. 1942; pp. 300–3). Three contributors to *Responses*, Els de Bens ("Paul de Man and the Collaborationist Press," 90–91), Ortwin de Graef ("Aspects of the Context of Paul de Man's Earliest Publications," 103), and Thomas Fries ("Paul de Man's 1940–1942 Articles in Context," 198) present Toison d'Or as a publishing house under German control. Though de Man's work on this book may have ended well before the publication date, it is worth noting that de Man's visible collaborationist activity continued well into 1943, by which time it was clear to anyone that the Germans were losing the war.

23. These dates come from the chronology in *Responses*.

24. Norris, *Paul de Man*, 188–89. Quite a few defenders of de Man have seized on the reference to Péguy; in addition to Derrida ("Sound," 631), see in *Responses* references by Timothy Bahti ("Telephonic Crossroads: The Reversal and the Double Cross," 4), Ian Balfour ("Difficult Reading: Paul de Man's Itineraries," 8), J. Hillis-Miller ("An Open Letter to Professor Jon Weiner," 336), and Werner Hamacher ("Journals, Politics," 465). None of these critics betrays any awareness of the complexity of Péguy's politics or political influence.

25. Renzo De Felice, in *Mussolini il rivoluzionario: 1883–1920* (Turin: Giulio Einaudi, 1965), 41, quotes Mussolini's "Dottrina del fascismo": "in the great stream of Fascism, you find the currents that take off from Sorel, from Péguy." Péguy is also extensively quoted and discussed in Lewis's *The Art of Being Ruled*, as is Sorel.

26. Smith, *Mussolini's Roman Empire*, viii.

27. T. S. Eliot, "Ezra Pound," in *An Examination of Ezra Pound*, ed. Peter Russell (Norfolk, Conn. New Directions, 1950), 33.

28. A good deal of the discussion has focused on whether de Man would have known that Kafka was Jewish. His name is misspelled in the article, and since the list is offered as examples of writers not "poisoned" by Jewish intellectualism, it is at least possible that de Man was not aware of Kafka's Jewishness. This is a

point made in one of the responses to Derrida's *Critical Inquiry* article, W. Wolf-gang Holdheim's "Jacques Derrida's Apologia" (*Critical Inquiry* 15 [1989]: 790–91). Derrida claims that "de Man could not not know that Kafka was Jewish" ("Biodegradables," 821) without offering any evidence for this claim. Alice Kaplan ("Paul de Man, *Le Soir*, and the Francophone Collaboration [1940–1942]," 283) and Werner Hamacher also discuss this point. According to Kaplan, "Readers of the period would have recognized Kafka as a Jewish writer." According to Hamacher ("Journals, Politics," 460–61), it is probable but not certain that de Man knew Kafka was Jewish.

29. Stanley Corngold, "On Paul de Man's Collaborationist Writing," *Responses*, 85. Hamacher ("Journals, Politics," 461) also points this out.

30. Reed Way Dasenbrock, "Ezra Pound, the Last Ghibelline," *Journal of Modern Literature* 16 (1990): 511–33.

Selective Bibliography
(Recent Works in English)

Books

Casillo, Robert. *The Genealogy of Demons: Anti-Semitism, Fascism, and the Myths of Ezra Pound.* Evanston, Ill.: Northwestern University Press, 1988.

Chace, William. *The Political Indentities of Ezra Pound and Wyndham Lewis.* Stanford, Calif.: Stanford University Press, 1973.

Cobb, Richard. *French and Germans, Germans and French: A Personal Interpretation of France under Two Occupations, 1914–1918/1940–1944.* Hanover, N.H.: University Press of New England, 1983.

Cullingford, Elizabeth. *Yeats, Ireland and Fascism.* New York: New York University Press, 1981.

De Man, Paul. *Wartime Journalism 1939–43.* Edited by Werner Hamacher, Neil Hertz, and Thomas Keenan. Lincoln: University of Nebraska Press, 1988.

Farías, Victor. *Heidegger and Nazism.* Edited by Joseph Mangolis and Tom Rockmore. Philadelphia: Temple University Press, 1989.

Ferry, Luc, and Alain Renault. *Heidegger and Modernity.* Chicago: University of Chicago Press, 1990.

Hamacher, Werner, Neil Hertz, and Thomas Keenan, eds. *Responses: On Paul de Man's Wartime Journalism.* Lincoln: University of Nebraska Press, 1989.

Hamilton, Alistair. *The Appeal of Fascism: A Study of Intellectuals and Fascism, 1919–1945.* New York: Macmillan, 1971.

Jameson, Fredric. *Fables of Aggression: Wyndham Lewis, the Modernist as Fascist.* Berkeley: University of California Press, 1979.

Kaplan, Alice Yeager. *Reproductions of Banality: Fascism, Literature and French Intellectual Life.* Minneapolis: University of Minnesota Press, 1986.

Lewis, Wyndham. *The Art of Being Ruled.* Edited by Reed Way Dasenbrock. 1926. Reprint, Santa Rosa, Calif.: Black Sparrow Press, 1989.

Littlejohn, David. *The Patriotic Traitors: A History of Collaboration in German-Occupied Europe, 1940–43.* London: Heinemann, 1972.

Luce, Stanford L., ed. *Céline and His Critics: Scandals and Paradox.* Saratoga, Calif.: ANMA Libari, 1986.

Lyotard, Jean-François. *Heidegger and "the jews".* Minneapolis: University of Minnesota Press, 1990.

Mehlman, Jeffrey. *Legacies of Anti-Semitism in France.* Minneapolis: University of Minnesota Press, 1983.

O'Sullivan, Noël. *Fascism.* London: J. M. Dent and Sons, 1983.

Soucy, Robert. *Fascism in France: The Case of Maurice Barrès.* Berkeley: University of California Press, 1972.

————. *Fascist Intellectual: Drieu la Rochelle.* Berkeley: University of California Press, 1979.

————. *French Fascism: The First Wave, 1924–1933.* New Haven, Conn.: Yale University Press, 1986.

Sternhell, Zeev. *Neither Right nor Left: Fascist Ideology in France.* Translated by David Maisel. Berkeley: University of California Press, 1986.

Theweleit, Klaus. *Male Fantasies. Vol. 1, Women, Floods, Bodies, History.* Minneapolis: University of Minnesota, 1987.

————. *Male Fantasies. Vol. 2, Male Bodies: Psychoanalyzing the White Terror.* Minneapolis: University of Minnesota Press, 1989.

Special Issues and Sections of Scholarly Journals

"Fascism and Culture." *Stanford Italian Review* 8, nos. 1–2 (1990).

"Fascist Aesthetics." *South Central Review* 6 (Summer 1989).

"Heidegger: Art and Politics." *Diacritics* 19 (Fall–Winter 1989).

"Special Features on Heidegger and Nazism." *Critical Inquiry,* 15 (Winter 1989): 407–489.

"On Jacques Derrida's 'Paul de Man's War.'" *Critical Inquiry* 15 (Summer 1989): 765–873.

"On National Socialism: Robert Musil and Emmanual Levinas." *Critical Inquiry* 17 (Autumn 1990):35–71.

"On Paul de Man's *Wartime Journalism* and *Responses: On Paul de Man's Wartime Journalism.*" *Diacritics* 20 (Fall 1990).

Articles and Book Chapters

Bataille, Georges. "The Psychological Structure of Fascism." In *Visions of Excess: Selected 1927–1939,* edited by Allan Stoekl. Minneapolis: University of Minnesota Press, 1985.

Benjamin, Walter. "The Work of Art in the Age of Mechanical Reproduction." In *Illuminations,* edited by Hannah Arendt. New York: Schocken Books, 1969.

Berlin, Isiah. "Joseph de Maistre and the Origins of Fascism I–III." *New York Review of Books,* 27 Sept., 11 Oct., 25 Oct. 1990.

Berman, Russell. "Modernism, Fascism and the Institution of Literature." In *Modernism: Challenges and Perspectives,* edited by M. Chefdor, R. Quinones, and A. Nachtel. Champaign: University of Illinois Press, 1986.

Culler, Jonathan. "Paul de Man's Rhetoric." In *Framing the Sign: Criticism and Its Institutions.* Norman: University of Oklahoma Press, 1988.

Donoghue, Denis. "Solving Paul de Man's Case." *New York Review of Books,* 29 June 1989.

Golsan, Richard J. "Montherlant and Collaboration: The Politics of Disengagement." *Romance Quarterly* 35 (May 1988):139–49.

"Parlor Collaboration: The *Groupe Collaboration*." In Gordon, Bertram, *Collaboration in France during the Second World War*. Ithaca, N.Y.: Cornell University Press, 1980.

Green, Mary Jean. "Towards an Analysis of Fascist Fiction: The Contemptuous Narrator in the Works of Brasillach, Céline and Drieu la Rochelle." *Studies in Twentieth Century Literature* 10, no. 1 (1985): 81–97.

Kermode, Frank. "The Modern Apocalypse." In *The Sense of an Ending*. London: Oxford University Press, 1967.

————. "Paul de Man's Abyss." *London Review of Books*, 16 March 1989.

Mehlman, Jeffrey. "Deconstruction, Literature, History: The Case of *L'Arrêt de Mort*." Proceedings of the Northeastern University Center for Literary Studies, 2 (1984): 33–53.

————. "Literature and Collaboration: Benoist Méchin's Return to Proust." In *Lacan and Narration: The Psychoanalytic Difference in Narrative Theory*, edited by Robert Con Davis. Baltimore: Johns Hopkins University Press, 1983.

Norris, Christopher. "Postscript: On de Man's Early Writings in *Le Soir*." In *Paul de Man: Deconstruction and the Critique of Aesthetic Ideology*. New York and London: Routledge, 1988.

O'Brien, Conor Cruise. "Passion and Cunning: An Essay on the Politics of W. B. Yeats." In *Excited Reverie: A Centenary Tribute to William Butler Yeats. 1865–1939*, edited by A. Norman Jeffares and K. G. W. Cross. London: Macmillan, 1965.

Sheehan, Thomas. "Heidegger and the Nazis." *New York Review of Books*, 16 June 1988.

Sontag, Susan. "Fascinating Fascism." *New York Review of Books*, 6 February 1975.

Soucy, Robert. "Drieu la Rochelle and Modernist Anti-Modernism and Modernism in French Fascism." *MLN* 95 (1980): 922–37.

Steiner, George. "Cry Havoc." In *Extraterritorial: Papers on Literature and the Language Revolution*. New York: Atheneum, 1971), 35–46.

————. "Heidegger, Again." *Salmagundi*, no. 82–83 (1989): 31–55.

Contributors

RUSSELL BERMAN is Professor of German and Comparative Literature at Stanford University. His most recent books include *The Rise of the Modern German Novel: Crisis and Charisma* (Harvard, 1986) and *Modern Culture and Critical Theory: Art, Politics, and the Legacy of the Frankfurt School* (Wisconsin, 1989). He has published articles on Lukács, Adorno, Thomas Mann, and Benjamin, as well as essays on the relationship between fascism and modernity.

ROBERT CASILLO is Professor of English at the University of Miami, Florida. He is the author of *The Genealogy of Demons: Anti-Semitism, Fascism and the Myths of Ezra Pound* (Northwestern, 1988) as well as critical essays on Ruskin, Mumford, Stendhal, Hemingway, Stael, Solzhenitsyn, and other writers. He is currently co-writing with John Paul Russo a collection of essays entitled *After Columbus: Representations of Italian-Americans in Modernity*.

REED WAY DASENBROCK is Professor of English at New Mexico State University. His previous work on modernism and its politics includes *The Literary Vorticism of Ezra Pound and Wyndham Lewis* (Johns Hopkins, 1985) and a critical edition of Wyndham Lewis's *The Art of Being Ruled* (Black Sparrow, 1989); his work on literary theory includes editing a collection of essays, *Redrawing the Lines: Analytic Philosophy, Deconstruction and Literary Theory* (Minnesota, 1989).

RICHARD J. GOLSAN is Associate Professor of French at Texas A & M University. He has published *"Service inutile": A Study of the Tragic in the Theatre of Henry de Montherlant* (Romance Monographs, 1988), as well as articles on Camus, Montherlant, Ernest Psichari, Drieu la Rochelle, Patrick Modiano, Michel del Castillo, and René Girard in *Romance Quarterly, The French Review, Essays in French Literature, Helios,* and elsewhere. He is currently working on a book-length study of René Girard's theory of myth and co-editing an issue of *L'Esprit Créateur* devoted to the literature and film of the Occupation period in France during World War II.

MARY JEAN GREEN is Professor of French and Department Chair at Dartmouth College. She has written on French literature and politics in her book *Fiction in the Historical Present: French Writers and the Thirties* (UPNE, 1986), as well as in her earlier *Louis Guilloux: An Artisan of Language* (Summa, 1980). Pursuing her interest in the relationships between literature and ideology, she has written extensively on the francophone literature of Québec. She was the founding editor of the interdisciplinary journal *Québec Studies* and is currently working on a book on Québec women writers.

ANDREW HEWITT is Assistant Professor of Comparative Literature at SUNY Buffalo. His book *Fascist Modernism: The Aestheticization of Politics*, is forthcoming from Stanford University Press (1992). In May 1989 he co-organized SUNY Buffalo's International Colloquium entitled "Between Nationalism and Fascism."

LYNN A. HIGGINS, Professor of French at Dartmouth College, also teaches Film and Women's Studies. Her book *Parables of Theory: Jean Ricardou's Metafiction* was published in 1984 (Birmingham, Ala.: Summa Publications); a volume of essays co-edited with Brenda Silver, *Representing Rape*, has recently appeared (Columbia University Press, 1991). She is currently completing a book historicizing the New Novel and the New Wave. Her articles on Barthes, Duras, Wittig, Robbe-Grillet, Rochefort, and Simon have appeared in *Substance*, *The Romanic Review*, *L'Esprit Créateur*, *Studies in Twentieth Century Literature*, and elsewhere.

JANET PÉREZ is Paul Whitfield Horn Professor of Spanish and Associate Dean of the Graduate School at Texas Tech University. She has written six books since 1969, the most recent of which is *Women Writers of Contemporary Spain* (G. K. Hall, 1988), and has authored more than one hundred articles or chapters in books. She is presently researching a book on contemporary women poets of Spain, which will be the first comprehensive study of peninsular women poets (including those writing in Catalan and Gallego as well as Castilian), from romanticism to the present.

JOHN PAUL RUSSO, Professor of English at the University of Miami, is the author of *I. A. Richards: His Life and Work* (1989) as well as numerous essays in the history of criticism. He is currently co-writing with Robert Casillo a collection of essays entitled *After Columbus: Representations of Italians and Italian-Americans in Modernity*.

JEFFREY T. SCHNAPP is Associate Professor of Italian and Comparative Literature at Stanford University. He is the author of *The Transfiguration of History at the Center of Dante's Paradise* (Princeton, 1986) and *The Poetry of Allusion: Dante and Virgil in the 'Comedia'* (Stanford, forthcoming) and has co-edited a special issue of the *Stanford Italian Review* titled "Fascism and Culture." He has also published articles on Marinetti, D'Annunzio, and the cultural politics of the fascist period.

ROSEMARIE SCULLION is Assistant Professor of French at the University of Iowa. She is currently working on a book-length study of carceral space, disciplinary power, and modernity in Céline's novels.

WALTER A. STRAUSS is Treuhaft Professor of the Humanities at Case Western Reserve University. He is the author of *Proust and Literature: The Novelist as Critic* (Harvard, 1957), *Descent and Return: The Orphic Theme in Modern Literature* (Harvard, 1981), and *On the Threshold of a New Kabbalah: Kafka's Later Tales* (Peter Lang, 1988). He has also published articles on Dante, Rilke, Camus, Tournier, Böll, Trakl, Celan, Jabès, Beckett, and others.

STEVEN UNGAR, Professor of French and Comparative Literature at the University of Iowa, has published *Roland Barthes: The Professor of Desire* (University of Nebraska Press, 1983) and co-edited *Signs in Culture: Roland Barthes Today* (University of Iowa Press, 1989). His articles have appeared in *Diacritics, Yale French Studies*, and *Sub-Stance*. Forthcoming is his book-length project, *Aftereffects: Writing between Memory and History*.

Index